BIDDLE'S HAM RADIO STUDY GUIDE
TECHNICIAN CLASS 2022-2026

Rodney E Biddle, KX4HD
Amateur Extra, ARRL Instructor

http://www.BiddleBooks.com/

BIDDLE'S HAM RADIO STUDY GUIDE - TECHNICIAN LICENSE 2022-2026

ISBN - 978-0-9996491-5-2

The web addresses cited in this book were current as of MAY 2022, unless otherwise noted.

Disclaimer:
The information given in this book is solely for educational and entertainment purposes and in no way should be construed to be legal, medical or professional advice. The author and publisher assume no liability for any actions taken by any individual or group that is considered illegal, based on information in this book.

About the Author and About this Book – Forward

Rodney Biddle is a Ham Radio instructor and author located in Florida and has been working with Ham Radio since 2014. His original radio license though dated back into the 1980s after becoming licensed to operate and a commercial radio operator immediately out of college with a degree in Electronics. As fate had it his career took him directly into Computers where he worked a variety of areas from supporting computer networks and data centers, software and user training, and into software programming, website development and database development. Currently he is working as a technical writer developing software documentation and training documentation on custom developed web-based applications.

In 2014 on a trip with a friend in Georgia he attended a Prepper and Homesteading event during a home show. One of the speakers brought up the topics of power grid reliance that our society has and the sensitivity that we could have during a massive grid failure that could occur under a variety of events. From hurricanes to other natural disasters, an intentional man-made event such as an EMP or computer hacking, or from a solar event such as the 1859 Carrington event Rodney became interested in the risks that really existed – after all some of these risks sound like material for a science fiction movie, ad have been for many such movies.

Upon reading the risks that could have occurred if a Carrington-style solar flare were to affect the earth today and learning the fact that recently in July 2012 we almost were struck by a similarly sized solar flare, he became interested in taking up a certain level of readiness and preparedness I case such and event were to again occur. As a new single father of two after a unique situation, he took on the concern that many fathers and parents would have in the protection of family and children to ensure some levels of protection if such an occurrence were to happen again. As a computer software developer and network engineer, along with having past experience with commercial radio, he naturally gravitated towards Ham Radio.

With experience in training, he not only began learning about prepping and readiness, but also began doing writing about some of the topics including both ham radio and emergency power planning using generators and solar energy. In 2018 Rodney expanded his training on occasion to include Ham Radio classes where he still holds some training classes via Zoom classes on the topics, as well as trainings on emergency communications planning. Since 2017 Rodney has written over ten books, most of which are related to Ham Radio topics and Emergency Power planning for off-grid planning. He considers himself more of a "Hurricane Prepper" with focus on moderate term power planning and off-grid living for shorter periods of weeks to a few months as would be experienced most likely following this type of disaster. In 2018 Rodney also jumped in to begin working with his Florida ARES organization in an effort not just to help but to open new doors to learning both new aspects of Ham radio, but also emergency planning in a community and work with some of the many efforts that Ham radio clubs and organizations participate in.

In writing this new book, Rodney hopes to bring his experience as an instructor together with experience he has learned over recent years with working with students learning not just Ham radio but technologies in general. His goal is to expand upon the ham radio course by introducing supporting topics and helping the student learn more than just the basics – to have a strong grasp of the understanding of the topics they are learning as well as limitations, and necessary steps to move beyond the basics. This book, "Biddle's Ham Radio Tech Course 2022-2026" will be Rodney's eighth book on Ham Radio, and Tenth book including his two on Solar Power and Blackout power planning. With the completion of this course book for the Tech level examination he will soon be moving into Video tutorial planning as well as new topics related to Boondocking (Camping) and off-grid living.

Table of Contents

Chapter 1 – About this Book

You've thought about it, and you have decided to start preparing yourself for the Ham Radio Technician's License. Welcome!

Learning what you need to pass the exam is a process that will take time and studying using often many techniques, the first of which most often is picking up a book and stating to review the content for the test. The Ham Radio examination for 2022-2026 consists of 411 questions (Originally 412 with one removed) and will take anywhere from a couple of weeks to a couple of months depending upon your already existing knowledge level, and the amount of time you take to putting into studying.

What makes the examination unique is that you will be given the full pool of 411 questions along with one correct answer, and 3 incorrect answers. The question you find in the book and published by the NCVEC organization has the exact wording of the question that will appear on the exam. The answers that are provided for studying are in the exact wording of the answers that are on the examination, and the wording of the wrong answers are also the exact wording of the wrong answers on the exam. So, you are going to have a very good study pool to work with. What does change from the practice tests to the actual exam will be the order of the answers. So, though you may remember the wording of an answer, "A" on the practice questions in this book and in practice will not equate to "A" on the exam.

The Technician Examination test will come in the form of many variations of the test. There are 35 questions on the exam and the question pool of 411 is divided into ten separate pools of questions as shown with the corresponding question pool descriptions as shown below:

Section	Description of the Section	Question Groups	Total Questions	Questions on Exam
T1	COMMISSION'S RULES	6	67	6
T2	OPERATING PROCEDURES	3	36	3
T3	RADIO WAVE PROPAGATION	3	34	3
T4	AMATEUR RADIO PRACTICES	2	24	2
T5	ELECTRICAL PRINCIPLES	4	52	4
T6	ELECTRONIC AND ELECTRICAL COMPONENTS	4	47	4
T7	PRACTICAL CIRCUITS	4	44	4
T8	SIGNALS AND EMISSIONS	4	48	4
T9	ANTENNAS AND FEED LINES	2	24	2
T0	SAFETY	3	36	3

Total Questions on the Test: **35**

In the table shown on the previous page we see the ten question pools which are numbered from T1 thru T0 (T0 short for T10). Each question pool itself is then sub-divided in up to 6 groups containing from 11 to 13 questions each. Each group is generally based on the same type of topic, though it can easily be argued that many of these questions could fall into multiple groups or even multiple pools. In the third column in the table, we show how many questions from the pool will be included on the test. For example, in question pool T1 there are 6 groupings of questions, with a total of 67 questions in the pool. The last column of the table tells us that there are only 6 questions from the T1 pool on the test.

How this book is designed

In the design of this book, we have tried to consider multiple sections that facilitate different methods of studying since different students often benefit from different methods. In chapter two we will introduce you to a list of all the questions on the test along with the specific answers corresponding to the test questions. This section will work well for any student who leverages memorization of answers and as a focused review of the questions prior to going into your test session. Becoming familiar with the questions and answers using repetition works well for many students and is a method I use prior to exam day or exam time to solidify my knowledge of the answers.

In chapter three we present all the questions grouped in the same pool and groupings that the NCVEC released the questions with. In the presentation of these questions, we are providing a clean representation of the question and possible answers with no comments or explanations to allow you to not become distracted. In chapter four, in the Practice Test Answers key chapter and on page 4-5 you will find a page that you can photo copy or download from our website (https://www.BiddleBooks.com/HamTest/) that is formatted as an answer recording worksheet allowing you to work through the questions in chapter three without marking in the book. Then return to chapter four and review your answers, allowing you to have a written record of the questions you are needing to review and build your knowledge with.

Chapter five covers all 411 questions in the question pool and provides an explanation of the answer. For the math problems we work through step-by-step our recommended method of working through your answer.

In Chapter six we work through many of the problems in the test in more of a discussion format with related questions grouped and explained in more depth than what we cover with specific questions in chapter five. In this chapter we review roughly 2/3 of the questions broken down by topic – electricity, frequencies, math calculations, batteries, SWR, licensing topics, repeaters, and other grouped topics. By grouping the questions here mostly based on similar topics we cover and show how some of the questions and answers relate. In some cases, the questions are covered in multiple sections as they can easily fall under multiple topics.

For Chapter seven we decided to cover many topics that are not specifically on the test, but that do relate to our studying for our exam and that I believe may help you to understand the how and why in better detail for many of the questions to be found on the test. We discuss in this chapter topics such as locating of repeaters for VHF and UHF as well as distance limitations for these bands without repeaters, I discuss the construction of batter power boxes useful for powering a portable radio in the case of an emergency, utilizing better antennas, coax cable topics for feed lines, why Ham operators use Anderson power connectors, non-ham radio methods (FRS, GMRS, CB) and other topics. You can skip this chapter entirely by my hope is that providing topics that will be of interest to the Prepper and Emergency radio operator here, then you, the student, may grasp a better insight as to the importance and use of many of the concepts you will be learning.

Chapter eight is a review of only the 74 new question questions found in the 2022-2026 question pool – a section that will be of interest to students that have already prepared for the exam with older study materials for the 2018-2022 exam but have not been exposed to the new questions. Note – Besides the new questions there are over 100 questions which have been modified. In many cases though the modifications in the questions are minor and still have the same meaning with some modifications being limited to minor changes in how a question or answer is worded. Because so many of these are minor we have not broken them out for separate coverage.

Chapter nine touches on different organizations and sources for more information on emergency planning. We provide a general list of considerations to have in mind to get through an emergency such as a hurricane for communications planning or that you may consider if deciding to be part of a communications team.

Finally in chapter ten we touch briefly on considerations for preparing for the test looking at what you need to do planning for test day.

Following taking this book to print for publication we will be working on developing a series of YouTube videos to assist with preparing for the test based on the updated pool. These will be available by the time of the new testing starting in July 2022 on our website and can be found if you go to http://www.BiddleBooks.com/HamTest/.

Why are you getting licensed?

Many new ham operators are studying for their Tech level license as a method of emergency and backup communications. Many take to ham radio for the hobby, and some take to getting licensed as a part of working some form of emergency relevancy such as working with a government agency, fire department, emergency services, FEMA, or other such group. There are many types of radio services and systems available that do not require the level of study that the Ham Operators licenses provide, and there are multiple ham radio license that give you progressively more access to radio as your experience and license level increases.

All municipalities utilize some form of radio communications systems in their area. These are mostly UHF based radio that works from repeater towers allowing portable operation from dozens of miles from the main antenna tower systems. As a municipality these systems can operate on encrypted communications and in recent years most will most likely utilize some type of digital system such a P.25 digital for more efficient and better-quality communication. These digital systems add capabilities such as *Trunking* and

Encryption which are not available through ham radio allowing more conversations on the same frequencies and bandwidths. So why do we still need Ham radio and to be licensed for Ham operation?

Redundancy and planning for possible failures. During major hurricanes and major natural disasters, the municipality and local governments may often find the systems they rely on affected by the disaster and inoperable. I have spoken to multiple ham operators who have worked natural disasters and have had to improvise due to the failure of planned systems. During the 2010 earthquake in Haiti an operator I had a discussion with and worked that disaster told me of the satellite phones not working properly and the need to rely on short-range FRS handheld radios at the emergency center with the Hams relaying messages to offshore ships for supplies. After hurricane Michael in 2018, county communications were destroyed when the county communications tower toppled over cutting off communications to emergency shelters and outside resources. And after hurricane Maria in 2017, devastation was so widespread with not only communications failing across Puerto Rico, but power failures and the destruction of road systems left Ham radio as the ONLY method of communications in some areas for weeks.

As an emergency or county official having your Ham operator's license offers you both a better and stronger understanding of communications, but gives you access to alternative communications systems. In the December 2018 NIAC report by the President's National Infrastructure Advisory Council, **Surviving a Catastrophic Power Outage**, the report talks about potential problems with differing communications methods between various government agencies and private companies such as utilities that could cause problems during a large-scale power failure. The report touches on the possible use of Ham Radio to bring businesses and governments together on like systems during a large-scale emergency.

Ham operators that work in groups and teams are able to deploy quickly and establish communications within just a few hours if necessary. And who are these operators? In most cases these are amateur ham radio operators who can deploy with their own equipment, their own antennas, and their own communications tools.

Testing Levels

The Technician level license is the first level of a ham radio license. With this license, you will have full access to most UHF and VHF frequencies including the popular 70-cm UHF band, 2-Meter VHF Band, and 1.25-Meter VHF band. These bands work with handheld radios and mobile radios for short-range line-of-site radio frequencies (1-10 miles usually) and through repeater systems (10-50+ miles). In a local environment these frequencies and this license level will greatly assist you in your communications needs. Assuming repeaters are operational, and the Internet is up you can still communicate dozens to hundreds or even thousands of miles. If the Internet is affected but the repeaters are still operational you can expect communication ranges of dozens of miles assuming the internet is used for the repeater's backbone connection.

But – What if you need to communicate farther than a few dozen miles? In these cases, you need to look at HF Radio frequencies. These frequencies have **_Propagation_** qualities that allow you to communicate hundreds to thousands of miles through the reflection of radio signals in the atmosphere. As a technician you will actually have partial access to the 10-meter band (Which requires a radio capable of communicating on 10-Meters, AM/SSB) which can offer this range. But – for all other HF bands then by FCC regulation you need to have your "General" license to operate on those bands.

And before you think this – as many preppers do – sure during an emergency you could communicate without a license but becoming familiar with the equipment and communication methods puts you at a tremendous disadvantage when needing to do so and keeps you from being familiar with your equipment. Getting the proper level license gets you legal access to the frequencies you may need for long-distance use and allows you to properly use your equipment.

The General license will get you access to most of the frequencies in all of the bands – including all of the long-distance HF bands for long-distance emergency communications. This allows you to operate without a repeater simplex radio-to-radio. Operating in HF frequencies will require a more expensive radio, a better (and longer) antenna, and probably more equipment such as an Antenna tuner, dedicated 12-v power supply, more coaxial cable and better quality (More expensive) for feed lines, and more know-how on putting it all together. Don't be surprised to put out $2000 on radio equipment – but this will be what you need to get into the truly stand-alone long-distance radio capabilities. The good thing though – no, you do not need the radio equipment of expenses to get the license. Just invest in $20-$50 of new books ad study time, plus any testing fees and licensing fees which will cost you under $50 in total.

The next level license is the Amateur Extra (AE) license. I obtained this myself for two reasons which were:

1. I am a book author on Ham Radio and needed to move up to the highest level of license for my teaching and writing and…
2. I have a degree in electronics so most of the materials were simple for me.

The question though as to if the general operator for Emergency radio operation or prepping would need it? Most likely not. With the AE license you do gain more knowledge from the new topics you need to study, and the test is more difficult with 50 questions rather than the 35 on the Technician and General licenses, but the additional frequencies in the additional bands will only be needed if you are doing some types of specialty radio or experimenting. For general emergency or prepper communications, the General license will get you access to all of the radio bands you will need.

Beyond the Technician License

As mentioned above – after you get your "Technician" level license I recommend that the emergency and prepper operators start looking at moving up to a general license. Even without your own HF Radio, you will be legal to operate other operator's radios during an emergency event. In addition, due to the time it will take to prepare for the General level test (2 Weeks to 2-Months probably) this is a task best planned and performed ahead of time. But – besides the General license, what else should you do?

1. Start using your radio. Most new hams have what is called "Mic Fright". Get on the radio and start talking.
2. Find your local repeaters (See Chapter 7). You will need to program your radio for using these repeaters and understanding what the programming process is (See Chapter 7, section 7.3)
3. Find a club – Get involved with a Ham club.
4. If you want to do emergency radio operations, locate your local ARES or CERT group (See chapter 9).
5. If you only have a handheld radio – upgrade your antenna (Section 7.4) or even look into a more powerful mobile radio and antenna (Section 7.7).

And lastly – Find others with similar interests and learn from them. And – Carry your radio! I was once with a group of new Ham operators at a picnic, and we had a lost child in the park – a very large state park. We split up but didn't use our radios because 90% of the hams showed up without a radio on them or in their car. BE PREPARED.

1. Ham Radio in Emergency Operations
   https://www.domesticpreparedness.com/preparedness/ham-radio-in-emergency-operations/
2. Surviving a Catastrophic Power Outage – Dec 2018 – NIAC – The President's National Infrastructure Advisory Council
   https://www.cisa.gov/sites/default/files/publications/NIAC%20Catastrophic%20Power%20Outage%20Study_FINAL.pdf

Chapter 2 – Introducing Technician Level 2022-2026 Pool Questions

In section 2 we are going to provide the full list of the (411) 2022-2026 Technician License pool questions with only the correct answer. When you take the test, the verbiage of the answers will be exactly what is provided here in the questions which are produced every four years by the NCVEC.org (The National Conference of Volunteer Examiner Coordinators). In reviewing the questions covered on the next few pages, you will find the question, answer, and special status. The special status indicates if the question is NEW for this terms question pool, has been modified, or if no status is shown then the question remains from the past pool.

There are 74 new questions that were not in the last pool. These questions may be completely new or may be recycled from a prior pool. For the modified questions, these questions may range from minor wording modifications to more significant wording modifications in the question, answer, or both. In the table below you will see the ten sections listed for the ten areas that the questions over. The question groups column shows the number of sub-groups that the question pool is broken into with the total questions being the total number of questions in each pool. Each pool is limited to only a limited number of questions on the exam.

Section	Description of the Section	Question Groups	Total Questions	Questions on Exam	Page
T1	COMMISSION'S RULES	6	67	6	2-2
T2	OPERATING PROCEDURES	3	36	3	2-6
T3	RADIO WAVE PROPAGATION	3	34	3	2-8
T4	AMATEUR RADIO PRACTICES	2	24	2	2-11
T5	ELECTRICAL PRINCIPLES	4	52	4	2-12
T6	ELECTRONIC AND ELECTRICAL COMPONENTS	4	47	4	2-15
T7	PRACTICAL CIRCUITS	4	44	4	2-18
T8	SIGNALS AND EMISSIONS	4	48	4	2-21
T9	ANTENNAS AND FEED LINES	2	24	2	2-24
T0	SAFETY	3	36	3	2-25

Total Questions on the Test: **35**

T1: COMMISSION'S RULES - [6 Exam Questions - 6 Groups] 67 Questions

Section A. Purpose and permissible use of the Amateur Radio Service; Operator/primary station license grant; Meanings of basic terms used in FCC rules; Interference; RACES rules; Phonetics; Frequency Coordinator

T1	A	01	Which of the following is part of the Basis and Purpose of the Amateur Radio Service? *Advancing skills in the technical and communication phases of the radio art*	Modified Question
T1	A	02	Which agency regulates and enforces the rules for the Amateur Radio Service in the United States? *The FCC*	
T1	A	03	What do the FCC rules state regarding the use of a phonetic alphabet for station identification in the Amateur Radio Service? *It is encouraged*	
T1	A	04	How many operator/primary station license grants may be held by any one person? *One*	
T1	A	05	What proves that the FCC has issued an operator/primary license grant? *The license appears in the FCC ULS database*	Modified Question
T1	A	06	What is the FCC Part 97 definition of a beacon? *An amateur station transmitting communications for the purposes of observing propagation or related experimental activities*	
T1	A	07	What is the FCC Part 97 definition of a space station? An amateur station located more than 50 km above Earth's surface	
T1	A	08	Which of the following entities recommends transmit/receive channels and other parameters for auxiliary and repeater stations? *Volunteer Frequency Coordinator recognized by local amateurs*	
T1	A	09	Who selects a Frequency Coordinator? *Amateur operators in a local or regional area whose stations are eligible to be repeater or auxiliary stations*	
T1	A	10	What is the Radio Amateur Civil Emergency Service (RACES)? *All these choices are correct*	Modified Question
T1	A	11	When is willful interference to other amateur radio stations permitted? *At no time*	

Section B. Frequency allocations; Emission modes; Spectrum sharing; Transmissions near band edges; Contacting the International Space Station; Power output

T1	B	01	Which of the following frequency ranges are available for phone operation by Technician licensees? *28.300 MHz to 28.500 MHz*	NEW Question
T1	B	02	Which amateurs may contact the International Space Station (ISS) on VHF bands? *Any amateur holding a Technician class or higher license*	Modified Question
T1	B	03	Which frequency is in the 6 meter amateur band? *52.525 MHz*	Modified Question
T1	B	04	Which amateur band includes 146.52 MHz? *2 meters*	Modified Question

T1	B	05	How may amateurs use the 219 to 220 MHz segment of 1.25-meter band? **_Fixed digital message forwarding systems only_**	Modified Question
T1	B	06	On which HF bands does a "Technician" class operator have phone privileges? **_10-meter band only_**	
T1	B	07	Which of the following VHF/UHF band segments are limited to CW only? **_50.0 MHz to 50.1 MHz and 144.0 MHz to 144.1 MHz_**	Modified Question
T1	B	08	How are US amateurs restricted in segments of bands where the Amateur Radio Service is secondary? **_U.S. amateurs may find non-amateur stations in those segments, and must avoid interfering with them_**	Modified Question
T1	B	09	Why should you not set your transmit frequency to be exactly at the edge of an amateur band or sub-band? **_All these choices are correct_**	
T1	B	10	Where may SSB phone be used in amateur bands above 50 MHz? **_In at least some segment of all these bands_**	NEW Question
T1	B	11	What is the maximum peak envelope power output for Technician class operators in their HF band segments? **_200 watts_**	Modified Question
T1	B	12	Except for some specific restrictions, what is the maximum peak envelope power output for Technician class operators using frequencies above 30 MHz? **_1500 watts_**	

Section C. Licensing: classes, sequential and vanity call sign systems, places where the Amateur Radio Service is regulated by the FCC, name and address on FCC license database, term, renewal, grace period, maintaining mailing address; International communications

T1	C	01	For which license classes are new licenses currently available from the FCC? **_Technician, General, Amateur Extra_**	
T1	C	02	Who may select a desired call sign under the vanity call sign rules? **_Any licensed amateur_**	
T1	C	03	What types of international communications are an FCC-licensed amateur radio station permitted to make? **_Communications incidental to the purposes of the Amateur Radio Service and remarks of a personal character_**	
T1	C	04	What may happen if the FCC is unable to reach you by email? **_Revocation of the station license or suspension of the operator license_**	NEW Question
T1	C	05	Which of the following is a valid Technician class call sign format? **_KF1XXX_**	Modified Question
T1	C	06	From which of the following locations may an FCC-licensed amateur station transmit? **_From any vessel or craft located in international waters and documented or registered in the United States_**	
T1	C	07	Which of the following can result in revocation of the station license or suspension of the operator license? **_Failure to provide and maintain a correct email address with the FCC_**	NEW Question

T1	C	08	What is the normal term for an FCC-issued amateur radio license? ***Ten years***	Modified Question
T1	C	09	What is the grace period for renewal if an amateur license expires? ***Two years***	Modified Question
T1	C	10	How soon after passing the examination for your first amateur radio license may you transmit on the amateur radio bands? ***As soon as your operator/station license grant appears in the FCC's license database***	Modified Question
T1	C	11	If your license has expired and is still within the allowable grace period, may you continue to transmit on the amateur radio bands? ***No, you must wait until the license has been renewed***	Modified Question

Section D. Authorized and prohibited transmissions: communications with other countries, music, exchange of information with other services, indecent language, compensation for operating, retransmission of other amateur signals, encryption, sale of equipment, unidentified transmissions, one-way transmission.

T1	D	01	With which countries are FCC-licensed amateur radio stations prohibited from exchanging communications? ***Any country whose administration has notified the International Telecommunication Union (ITU) that it objects to such communications***	
T1	D	02	Under which of the following circumstances are one-way transmissions by an amateur station prohibited? ***Broadcasting***	NEW Question
T1	D	03	When is it permissible to transmit messages encoded to obscure their meaning? ***Only when transmitting control commands to space stations or radio control craft***	
T1	D	04	Under what conditions is an amateur station authorized to transmit music using a phone emission? ***When incidental to an authorized retransmission of manned spacecraft communications***	
T1	D	05	When may amateur radio operators use their stations to notify other amateurs of the availability of equipment for sale or trade? ***When selling amateur radio equipment and not on a regular basis***	Modified Question
T1	D	06	What, if any, are the restrictions concerning transmission of language that may be considered indecent or obscene? ***Any such language is prohibited***	
T1	D	07	What types of amateur stations can automatically retransmit the signals of other amateur stations? ***Repeater, auxiliary, or space stations***	
T1	D	08	In which of the following circumstances may the control operator of an amateur station receive compensation for operating that station? ***When the communication is incidental to classroom instruction at an educational institution***	
T1	D	09	When may amateur stations transmit information in support of broadcasting, program production, or news gathering, assuming no other means is available? ***When such communications are directly related to the immediate safety of human life or protection of property***	Modified Question

T1	D	10	How does the FCC define broadcasting for the Amateur Radio Service? ***Transmissions intended for reception by the general public***	Modified Question
T1	D	11	When may an amateur station transmit without identifying on the air? ***When transmitting signals to control model craft***	Modified Question

Section E: Control operator: eligibility, designating, privileges, duties, location, required; Control point; Control types: automatic, remote

T1	E	01	When may an amateur station transmit without a control operator? ***Never***	
T1	E	02	Who may be the control operator of a station communicating through an amateur satellite or space station? ***Any amateur allowed to transmit on the satellite uplink frequency***	Modified Question
T1	E	03	Who must designate the station control operator? ***The station licensee***	
T1	E	04	What determines the transmitting frequency privileges of an amateur station? ***The class of operator license held by the control operator***	
T1	E	05	What is an amateur station's control point? ***The location at which the control operator function is performed***	
T1	E	06	When, under normal circumstances, may a Technician class licensee be the control operator of a station operating in an Amateur Extra Class band segment? ***At no time***	Modified Question
T1	E	07	When the control operator is not the station licensee, who is responsible for the proper operation of the station? ***The control operator and the station licensee***	Modified Question
T1	E	08	Which of the following is an example of automatic control? ***Repeater operation***	
T1	E	09	Which of the following are required for remote control operation? ***All these choices are correct***	
T1	E	10	Which of the following is an example of remote control as defined in Part 97? ***Operating the station over the internet***	
T1	E	11	Who does the FCC presume to be the control operator of an amateur station, unless documentation to the contrary is in the station records? ***The station licensee***	

Section F: Station identification; Repeaters; Third party communications; Club stations; FCC inspection

T1	F	01	When must the station and its records be available for FCC inspection? ***At any time upon request by an FCC representative***	
T1	F	02	How often must you identify with your FCC-assigned call sign when using tactical call signs such as "Race Headquarters"? ***At the end of each communication and every ten minutes during a communication***	Modified Question
T1	F	03	When are you required to transmit your assigned call sign? ***At least every 10 minutes during and at the end of a communication***	Modified Question

T1	F	04	What language may you use for identification when operating in a phone sub-band? **English**	Modified Question
T1	F	05	What method of call sign identification is required for a station transmitting phone signals? **Send the call sign using a CW or phone emission**	
T1	F	06	Which of the following self-assigned indicators are acceptable when using a phone transmission? **All these choices are correct**	
T1	F	07	Which of the following restrictions apply when a non-licensed person is allowed to speak to a foreign station using a station under the control of a licensed amateur operator? **The foreign station must be in a country with which the U.S. has a third-party agreement**	Modified Question
T1	F	08	What is the definition of third-party communications? **A message from a control operator to another amateur station control operator on behalf of another person**	
T1	F	09	What type of amateur station simultaneously retransmits the signal of another amateur station on a different channel or channels? **Repeater station**	
T1	F	10	Who is accountable if a repeater inadvertently retransmits communications that violate the FCC rules? **The control operator of the originating station**	
T1	F	11	Which of the following is a requirement for the issuance of a club station license grant? **The club must have at least four members**	

T2: OPERATING PROCEDURES - [3 Exam Questions - 3 Groups] - 36 Questions

Section A. Station operation: choosing an operating frequency, calling another station, test transmissions; Band plans: calling frequencies, repeater offsets

T2	A	01	What is a common repeater frequency offset in the 2-meter band? **Plus or minus 600 kHz**
T2	A	02	What is the national calling frequency for FM simplex operations in the 2-meter band? **146.520 MHz**
T2	A	03	What is a common repeater frequency offset in the 70 cm band? **Plus or minus 5 MHz**
T2	A	04	What is an appropriate way to call another station on a repeater if you know the other station's call sign? **Say the station's call sign, then identify with your call sign**
T2	A	05	How should you respond to a station calling CQ? **Transmit the other station's call sign followed by your call sign**
T2	A	06	Which of the following is required when making on-the-air test transmissions? **Identify the transmitting station**
T2	A	07	What is meant by "repeater offset"? **The difference between a repeater's transmit and receive frequencies**

T2	A	08	What is the meaning of the procedural signal "CQ"? **_Calling any station_**	
T2	A	09	Which of the following indicates that a station is listening on a repeater and looking for a contact? **_The station's call sign followed by the word "monitoring"_**	NEW Question
T2	A	10	What is a band plan, beyond the privileges established by the FCC? **_A voluntary guideline for using different modes or activities within an amateur band_**	
T2	A	11	What term describes an amateur station that is transmitting and receiving on the same frequency? **_Simplex_**	
T2	A	12	What should you do before calling CQ? **_All these choices are correct_**	Modified Question

Section B. VHF/UHF operating practices: FM repeater, simplex, reverse splits; Access tones: CTCSS, DTMF; DMR operation; Resolving operational problems; Q signals

T2	B	01	How is a VHF/UHF transceiver's "reverse" function used? **_To listen on a repeater's input frequency_**	Modified Question
T2	B	02	What term describes the use of a sub-audible tone transmitted along with normal voice audio to open the squelch of a receiver? **_CTCSS_**	
T2	B	03	Which of the following describes a linked repeater network? **_A network of repeaters in which signals received by one repeater are transmitted by all the repeaters in the network_**	NEW Question
T2	B	04	Which of the following could be the reason you are unable to access a repeater whose output you can hear? **_All these choices are correct_**	
T2	B	05	What would cause your FM transmission audio to be distorted on voice peaks? **_You are talking too loudly_**	Modified Question
T2	B	06	What type of signaling uses pairs of audio tones? **_DTMF_**	Modified Question
T2	B	07	How can you join a digital repeater's "talkgroup"? **_Program your radio with the group's ID or code_**	
T2	B	08	Which of the following applies when two stations transmitting on the same frequency interfere with each other? **_The stations should negotiate continued use of the frequency_**	Modified Question
T2	B	09	Why are simplex channels designated in the VHF/UHF band plans? **_So stations within range of each other can communicate without tying up a repeater_**	NEW Question
T2	B	10	Which Q signal indicates that you are receiving interference from other stations? **_QRM_**	
T2	B	11	Which Q signal indicates that you are changing frequency? **_QSY_**	
T2	B	12	What is the purpose of the color code used on DMR repeater systems? **_Must match the repeater color code for access_**	NEW Question

T2	B	13	What is the purpose of a squelch function? ***Mute the receiver audio when a signal is not present***	NEW Question

Section T2C. Public service: emergency operations, applicability of FCC rules, RACES and ARES, net and traffic procedures, operating restrictions during emergencies, use of phonetics in message handling

T2	C	01	When do FCC rules NOT apply to the operation of an amateur station? ***FCC rules always apply***	
T2	C	02	Which of the following are typical duties of a Net Control Station? **Call the net to order and direct communications between stations checking in**	NEW Question
T2	C	03	What technique is used to ensure that voice messages containing unusual words are received correctly? ***Spell the words using a standard phonetic alphabet***	NEW Question
T2	C	04	What is RACES? ***An FCC part 97 amateur radio service for civil defense communications during national emergencies***	NEW Question
T2	C	05	What does the term "traffic" refer to in net operation? ***Messages exchanged by net stations***	
T2	C	06	What is the Amateur Radio Emergency Service (ARES)? ***A group of licensed amateurs who have voluntarily registered their qualifications and equipment for communications duty in the public service***	NEW Question
T2	C	07	Which of the following is standard practice when you participate in a net? ***Unless you are reporting an emergency, transmit only when directed by the net control station***	NEW Question
T2	C	08	Which of the following is a characteristic of good traffic handling? ***Passing messages exactly as received***	
T2	C	09	Are amateur station control operators ever permitted to operate outside the frequency privileges of their license class? ***Yes, but only in situations involving the immediate safety of human life or protection of property***	
T2	C	10	What information is contained in the preamble of a formal traffic message? ***Information needed to track the message***	
T2	C	11	What is meant by "check" in a radiogram header? ***The number of words or word equivalents in the text portion of the message***	Modified Question

T3: RADIO WAVE PROPAGATION – [3 Exam Questions - 3 Groups] - 34 Questions
Section T3-A. Radio wave characteristics: how a radio signal travels, fading, multipath, polarization, wavelength vs absorption; Antenna orientation

T3	A	01	Why do VHF signal strengths sometimes vary greatly when the antenna is moved only a few feet? ***Multipath propagation cancels or reinforces signals***	NEW Question
T3	A	02	What is the effect of vegetation on UHF and microwave signals? ***Absorption***	NEW Question

T3	A	03	What antenna polarization is normally used for long-distance CW and SSB contacts on the VHF and UHF bands? ***Horizontal***	
T3	A	04	What happens when antennas at opposite ends of a VHF or UHF line of sight radio link are not using the same polarization? ***Received signal strength is reduced***	Modified Question
T3	A	05	When using a directional antenna, how might your station be able to communicate with a distant repeater if buildings or obstructions are blocking the direct line of sight path? ***Try to find a path that reflects signals to the repeater***	
T3	A	06	What is the meaning of the term "picket fencing"? ***Rapid flutter on mobile signals due to multipath propagation***	NEW Question
T3	A	07	What weather condition might decrease range at microwave frequencies? ***Precipitation***	NEW Question
T3	A	08	What is a likely cause of irregular fading of signals propagated by the ionosphere? ***Random combining of signals arriving via different paths***	
T3	A	09	Which of the following results from the fact that signals propagated by the ionosphere are elliptically polarized? ***Either vertically or horizontally polarized antennas may be used for transmission or reception***	
T3	A	10	What effect does multi-path propagation have on data transmissions? ***Error rates are likely to increase***	Modified Question
T3	A	11	Which region of the atmosphere can refract or bend HF and VHF radio waves? ***The ionosphere***	Modified Question
T3	A	12	What is the effect of fog and rain on signals in the 10 meter and 6-meter bands? ***There is little effect***	Modified Question

Section T3-B. Electromagnetic wave properties: wavelength vs frequency, nature and velocity of electromagnetic waves, relationship of wavelength and frequency; Electromagnetic spectrum definitions: UHF, VHF, HF

T3	B	01	What is the relationship between the electric and magnetic fields of an electromagnetic wave? ***They are at right angles***	NEW Question
T3	B	02	What property of a radio wave defines its polarization? ***The orientation of the electric field***	
T3	B	03	What are the two components of a radio wave? ***Electric and magnetic fields***	
T3	B	04	What is the velocity of a radio wave traveling through free space? ***Speed of light***	Modified Question
T3	B	05	What is the relationship between wavelength and frequency? ***Wavelength gets shorter as frequency increases***	
T3	B	06	What is the formula for converting frequency to approximate wavelength in meters? ***Wavelength in meters equals 300 divided by frequency in megahertz***	

T3	B	07	In addition to frequency, which of the following is used to identify amateur radio bands? ***The approximate wavelength in meters***	Modified Question
T3	B	08	What frequency range is referred to as VHF? ***30 MHz to 300 MHz***	
T3	B	09	What frequency range is referred to as UHF? ***300 to 3000 MHz***	
T3	B	10	What frequency range is referred to as HF? ***3 to 30 MHz***	
T3	B	11	What is the approximate velocity of a radio wave in free space? ***300,000,000 meters per second***	

Section T3-C. Propagation modes: sporadic E, meteor scatter, auroral propagation, tropospheric ducting; F region skip; Line of sight and radio horizon

T3	C	01	Why are simplex UHF signals rarely heard beyond their radio horizon? ***UHF signals are usually not propagated by the ionosphere***	Modified Question
T3	C	02	What is a characteristic of HF communication compared with communications on VHF and higher frequencies? ***Long-distance ionospheric propagation is far more common on HF***	Modified Question
T3	C	03	What is a characteristic of VHF signals received via auroral backscatter? ***They are distorted, and signal strength varies considerably***	Modified Question
T3	C	04	Which of the following types of propagation is most commonly associated with occasional strong signals on the 10, 6, and 2 meter bands from beyond the radio horizon? ***Sporadic E***	
T3	C	05	Which of the following effects may allow radio signals to travel beyond obstructions between the transmitting and receiving stations? ***Knife-edge diffraction***	
T3	C	06	What type of propagation is responsible for allowing over-the-horizon VHF and UHF communications to ranges of approximately 300 miles on a regular basis? ***Tropospheric ducting***	Modified Question
T3	C	07	What band is best suited for communicating via meteor scatter? ***6 meters***	
T3	C	08	What causes tropospheric ducting? ***Temperature inversions in the atmosphere***	
T3	C	09	What is generally the best time for long-distance 10-meter band propagation via the F region? ***From dawn to shortly after sunset during periods of high sunspot activity***	
T3	C	10	Which of the following bands may provide long-distance communications via the ionosphere's F region during the peak of the sunspot cycle? ***6 and 10 meters***	
T3	C	11	Why is the radio horizon for VHF and UHF signals more distant than the visual horizon? ***The atmosphere refracts radio waves slightly***	NEW Question

T4: AMATEUR RADIO PRACTICES – [2 Exam Questions - 2 Groups] - 24 Questions

Section T4-A. Station setup: connecting a microphone, a power source, a computer, digital equipment, an SWR meter; bonding; Mobile radio installation

T4	A	01	Which of the following is an appropriate power supply rating for a typical 50-watt output mobile FM transceiver? ***13.8 volts at 12 amperes***	NEW Question
T4	A	02	Which of the following should be considered when selecting an accessory SWR meter? ***The frequency and power level at which the measurements will be made***	NEW Question
T4	A	03	Why are short, heavy-gauge wires used for a transceiver's DC power connection? ***To minimize voltage drop when transmitting***	NEW Question
T4	A	04	How are the transceiver audio input and output connected in a station configured to operate using FT8? ***To the audio input and output of a computer running WSJT-X software***	NEW Question
T4	A	05	Where should an RF power meter be installed? ***In the feed line, between the transmitter and antenna***	NEW Question
T4	A	06	What signals are used in a computer-radio interface for digital mode operation? ***Receive audio, transmit audio, and transmitter keying***	NEW Question
T4	A	07	Which of the following connections is made between a computer and a transceiver to use computer software when operating digital modes? ***Computer "line in" to transceiver speaker connector***	NEW Question
T4	A	08	Which of the following conductors is preferred for bonding at RF? ***Flat copper strap***	
T4	A	09	How can you determine the length of time that equipment can be powered from a battery? ***Divide the battery ampere-hour rating by the average current draw of the equipment***	NEW Question
T4	A	10	What function is performed with a transceiver and a digital mode hot spot? ***Communication using digital voice or data systems via the internet***	NEW Question
T4	A	11	Where should the negative power return of a mobile transceiver be connected in a vehicle? ***At the 12-volt battery chassis ground***	Modified Question
T4	A	12	What is an electronic keyer? ***A device that assists in manual sending of Morse code***	NEW Question

Section T4-B. Operating controls: frequency tuning, use of filters, squelch function, AGC, memory channels, noise blanker, microphone gain, receiver incremental tuning (RIT), bandwidth selection, digital transceiver configuration

T4	B	01	What is the effect of excessive microphone gain on SSB transmissions? ***Distorted transmitted audio***	Modified Question
T4	B	02	Which of the following can be used to enter a transceiver's operating frequency? ***The keypad or VFO knob***	
T4	B	03	How is squelch adjusted so that a weak FM signal can be heard? ***Set the squelch threshold so that receiver output audio is on all the time***	NEW Question

T4	B	04	What is a way to enable quick access to a favorite frequency or channel on your transceiver? *Store it in a memory channel*	
T4	B	05	What does the scanning function of an FM transceiver do? *Tunes through a range of frequencies to check for activity*	NEW Question
T4	B	06	Which of the following controls could be used if the voice pitch of a single-sideband signal returning to your CQ call seems too high or low? *The RIT or Clarifier*	
T4	B	07	What does a DMR "code plug" contain? *Access information for repeaters and talkgroups*	NEW Question
T4	B	08	What is the advantage of having multiple receive bandwidth choices on a multimode transceiver? *Permits noise or interference reduction by selecting a bandwidth matching the mode*	
T4	B	09	How is a specific group of stations selected on a digital voice transceiver? *By entering the group's identification code*	NEW Question
T4	B	10	Which of the following receiver filter bandwidths provides the best signal-to-noise ratio for SSB reception? *2400 Hz*	
T4	B	11	Which of the following must be programmed into a D-STAR digital transceiver before transmitting? *Your call sign in CW for automatic identification*	NEW Question
T4	B	12	What is the result of tuning an FM receiver above or below a signal's frequency? *Distortion of the signal's audio*	NEW Question

T5: ELECTRICAL PRINCIPLES – [4 Exam Questions - 4 Groups] - 52 Questions

Section T5-A. Current and voltage: terminology and units, conductors and insulators, alternating and direct current

T5	A	01	Electrical current is measured in which of the following units? *Amperes*	
T5	A	02	Electrical power is measured in which of the following units? *Watts*	
T5	A	03	What is the name for the flow of electrons in an electric circuit? *Current*	
T5	A	04	What are the units of electrical resistance? *Ohms*	NEW Question
T5	A	05	What is the electrical term for the force that causes electron flow? *Voltage*	Modified Question
T5	A	06	What is the unit of frequency? *Hertz*	NEW Question
T5	A	07	Why are metals generally good conductors of electricity? *They have many free electrons*	NEW Question
T5	A	08	Which of the following is a good electrical insulator? *Glass*	

T5	A	09	Which of the following describes alternating current? *Current that alternates between positive and negative directions*	NEW Question
T5	A	10	Which term describes the rate at which electrical energy is used? *Power*	
T5	A	11	What type of current flow is opposed by resistance? *All of these choices are correct*	NEW Question
T5	A	12	What describes the number of times per second that an alternating current makes a complete cycle? *Frequency*	

Section T5-B. Math for electronics: conversion of electrical units, decibels

T5	B	01	How many milliamperes is 1.5 amperes? *1500 milliamperes*	
T5	B	02	Which is equal to 1,500,000 hertz? *1500 kHz*	Modified Question
T5	B	03	Which is equal to one kilovolt? *One thousand volts*	
T5	B	04	Which is equal to one microvolt? *One one-millionth of a volt*	
T5	B	05	Which is equal to 500 milliwatts? *0.5 watts*	
T5	B	06	Which is equal to 3000 milliamperes? *3 amperes*	Modified Question
T5	B	07	Which is equal to 3.525 MHz? *3525 kHz*	Modified Question
T5	B	08	Which is equal to 1,000,000 picofarads? *1 microfarad*	Modified Question
T5	B	09	Which decibel value most closely represents a power increase from 5 watts to 10 watts? *3 dB*	
T5	B	10	Which decibel value most closely represents a power decrease from 12 watts to 3 watts? *-6 dB*	
T5	B	11	Which decibel value represents a power increase from 20 watts to 200 watts? *10 dB*	
T5	B	12	Which is equal to 28400 kHz? *28.400 MHz*	
T5	B	13	Which is equal to 2425 MHz? *2.425 GHz*	Modified Question

Section T5-C. Capacitance and inductance terminology and units; Radio frequency definition and units; Impedance definition and units; Calculating power

T5	C	01	What describes the ability to store energy in an electric field? **_Capacitance_**	
T5	C	02	What is the unit of capacitance? **_The farad_**	
T5	C	03	What describes the ability to store energy in a magnetic field? **_Inductance_**	
T5	C	04	What is the unit of inductance? **_The henry_**	
T5	C	05	What is the unit of impedance? **_The ohm_**	
T5	C	06	What does the abbreviation "RF" mean? **_Radio frequency signals of all types_**	
T5	C	07	What is the abbreviation for megahertz? **_MHz_**	NEW Question
T5	C	08	What is the formula used to calculate electrical power (P) in a DC circuit? **_P = E x I_**	Modified Question
T5	C	09	How much power is delivered by a voltage of 13.8 volts DC and a current of 10 amperes? **_138 watts_**	
T5	C	10	How much power is delivered by a voltage of 12 volts DC and a current of 2.5 amperes? **_30 watts_**	
T5	C	11	How much current is required to deliver 120 watts at a voltage of 12 volts DC? **_10 amperes_**	Modified Question
T5	C	12	What is impedance? **_The opposition to AC current flow_**	Modified Question
T5	C	13	What is the abbreviation for kilohertz? **_kHz_**	Modified Question

Section T5-D. Ohm's Law; Series and parallel circuits

T5	D	01	What formula is used to calculate current in a circuit? **_I = E / R_**	Modified Question
T5	D	02	What formula is used to calculate voltage in a circuit? **_E = I x R_**	Modified Question
T5	D	03	What formula is used to calculate resistance in a circuit? **_R = E / I_**	Modified Question
T5	D	04	What is the resistance of a circuit in which a current of 3 amperes flows when connected to 90 volts? **_30 ohms_**	

T5	D	05	What is the resistance of a circuit for which the applied voltage is 12 volts and the current flow is 1.5 amperes? ***8 ohms***	
T5	D	06	What is the resistance of a circuit that draws 4 amperes from a 12-volt source? ***3 ohms***	
T5	D	07	What is the current in a circuit with an applied voltage of 120 volts and a resistance of 80 ohms? ***1.5 amperes***	
T5	D	08	What is the current through a 100-ohm resistor connected across 200 volts? ***2 amperes***	
T5	D	09	What is the current through a 24-ohm resistor connected across 240 volts? ***10 amperes***	
T5	D	10	What is the voltage across a 2-ohm resistor if a current of 0.5 amperes flows through it? ***1 volt***	
T5	D	11	What is the voltage across a 10-ohm resistor if a current of 1 ampere flows through it? ***10 volts***	
T5	D	12	What is the voltage across a 10-ohm resistor if a current of 2 amperes flows through it? ***20 volts***	
T5	D	13	In which type of circuit is DC current the same through all components? ***Series***	NEW Question
T5	D	14	In which type of circuit is voltage the same across all components? ***Parallel***	NEW Question

T6: ELECTRONIC AND ELECTRICAL COMPONENTS – [4 Exam Questions - 4 Groups] - 47 Questions
Section T6-A. Fixed and variable resistors; Capacitors; Inductors; Fuses; Switches; Batteries

T6	A	01	What electrical component opposes the flow of current in a DC circuit? ***Resistor***
T6	A	02	What type of component is often used as an adjustable volume control? ***Potentiometer***
T6	A	03	What electrical parameter is controlled by a potentiometer? ***Resistance***
T6	A	04	What electrical component stores energy in an electric field? ***Capacitor***
T6	A	05	What type of electrical component consists of conductive surfaces separated by an insulator? ***Capacitor***
T6	A	06	What type of electrical component stores energy in a magnetic field? ***Inductor***
T6	A	07	What electrical component is typically constructed as a coil of wire? ***Inductor***

T6	A	08	What is the function of an SPDT switch? ***A single circuit is switched between one of two other circuits***	NEW Question
T6	A	09	What electrical component is used to protect other circuit components from current overloads? ***Fuse***	
T6	A	10	Which of the following battery chemistries is rechargeable? ***All these choices are correct***	
T6	A	11	Which of the following battery chemistries is not rechargeable? ***Carbon-zinc***	
T6	A	12	What type of switch is represented by component 3 in figure T-2? ***Single-pole single-throw***	NEW Question

Section T6-B. Semiconductors: basic principles and applications of solid-state devices, diodes and transistors

T6	B	01	Which is true about forward voltage drop in a diode? ***It is lower in some diode types than in others***	NEW Question
T6	B	02	What electronic component allows current to flow in only one direction? ***Diode***	
T6	B	03	Which of these components can be used as an electronic switch? ***Transistor***	Modified Question
T6	B	04	Which of the following components can consist of three regions of semiconductor material? ***Transistor***	
T6	B	05	What type of transistor has a gate, drain, and source? ***Field-effect***	NEW Question
T6	B	06	How is the cathode lead of a semiconductor diode often marked on the package? ***With a stripe***	
T6	B	07	What causes a light-emitting diode (LED) to emit light? ***Forward current***	NEW Question
T6	B	08	What does the abbreviation FET stand for? ***Field Effect Transistor***	
T6	B	09	What are the names for the electrodes of a diode? ***Anode and cathode***	
T6	B	10	Which of the following can provide power gain? ***Transistor***	Modified Question
T6	B	11	What is the term that describes a device's ability to amplify a signal? ***Gain***	
T6	B	12	What are the names of the electrodes of a bipolar junction transistor? ***Emitter, base, collector***	NEW Question

Section T6-C. Circuit diagrams: use of schematics, basic structure; Schematic symbols of basic components

T6	C	01	What is the name of an electrical wiring diagram that uses standard component symbols? ***Schematic***	

T6	C	02	What is component 1 in figure T-1? **Resistor**	
T6	C	03	What is component 2 in figure T-1? **Transistor**	
T6	C	04	What is component 3 in figure T-1? **Lamp**	
T6	C	05	What is component 4 in figure T-1? **Battery**	
T6	C	06	What is component 6 in figure T-2? **Capacitor**	
T6	C	07	What is component 8 in figure T-2? **Light emitting diode**	
T6	C	08	What is component 9 in figure T-2? **Variable resistor**	
T6	C	09	What is component 4 in figure T-2? **Transformer**	
T6	C	10	What is component 3 in figure T-3? **Variable inductor**	
T6	C	11	What is component 4 in figure T-3? **Antenna**	
T6	C	12	Which of the following is accurately represented in electrical schematics? **Component connections**	NEW Question

Section T6-D. Component functions: rectifiers, relays, voltage regulators, meters, indicators, integrated circuits, transformers; Resonant circuit; Shielding

T6	D	01	Which of the following devices or circuits changes an alternating current into a varying direct current signal? **Rectifier**	
T6	D	02	What is a relay? **An electrically controlled switch**	
T6	D	03	Which of the following is a reason to use shielded wire? **To prevent coupling of unwanted signals to or from the wire**	NEW Question
T6	D	04	Which of the following displays an electrical quantity as a numeric value? **Meter**	
T6	D	05	What type of circuit controls the amount of voltage from a power supply? **Regulator**	
T6	D	06	What component changes 120 V AC power to a lower AC voltage for other uses? **Transformer**	Modified Question
T6	D	07	Which of the following is commonly used as a visual indicator? **LED**	
T6	D	08	Which of the following is combined with an inductor to make a resonant circuit? **Capacitor**	

T6	D	09	What is the name of a device that combines several semiconductors and other components into one package? **Integrated circuit**	
T6	D	10	What is the function of component 2 in figure T-1? **Control the flow of current**	
T6	D	11	Which of the following is a resonant or tuned circuit? **An inductor and a capacitor in series or parallel**	Modified Question

T7 - PRACTICAL CIRCUITS – [4 Exam Questions - 4 Groups] - 44 Questions

Section T7-A. Station equipment: receivers, transceivers, transmitter amplifiers, receive amplifiers, transverters; Basic radio circuit concepts and terminology: sensitivity, selectivity, mixers, oscillators, PTT, modulation

T7	A	01	Which term describes the ability of a receiver to detect the presence of a signal? **Sensitivity**	
T7	A	02	What is a transceiver? **A device that combines a receiver and transmitter**	Modified Question
T7	A	03	Which of the following is used to convert a signal from one frequency to another? **Mixer**	
T7	A	04	Which term describes the ability of a receiver to discriminate between multiple signals? **Selectivity**	
T7	A	05	What is the name of a circuit that generates a signal at a specific frequency? **Oscillator**	
T7	A	06	What device converts the RF input and output of a transceiver to another band? **Transverter**	
T7	A	07	What is the function of a transceiver's PTT input? **Switches transceiver from receive to transmit when grounded**	Modified Question
T7	A	08	Which of the following describes combining speech with an RF carrier signal? **Modulation**	
T7	A	09	What is the function of the SSB/CW-FM switch on a VHF power amplifier? **Set the amplifier for proper operation in the selected mode**	
T7	A	10	What device increases the transmitted output power from a transceiver? **An RF power amplifier**	Modified Question
T7	A	11	Where is an RF preamplifier installed? **Between the antenna and receiver**	

Section T7-B. Symptoms, causes, and cures of common transmitter and receiver problems: overload and overdrive, distortion, interference and consumer electronics, RF feedback

T7	B	01	What can you do if you are told your FM handheld or mobile transceiver is over-deviating? **Talk farther away from the microphone**	

T7	B	02	What would cause a broadcast AM or FM radio to receive an amateur radio transmission unintentionally? ***The receiver is unable to reject strong signals outside the AM or FM band***	
T7	B	03	Which of the following can cause radio frequency interference? ***All these choices are correct***	
T7	B	04	Which of the following could you use to cure distorted audio caused by RF current on the shield of a microphone cable? ***Ferrite choke***	NEW Question
T7	B	05	How can fundamental overload of a non-amateur radio or TV receiver by an amateur signal be reduced or eliminated? ***Block the amateur signal with a filter at the antenna input of the affected receiver***	
T7	B	06	Which of the following actions should you take if a neighbor tells you that your station's transmissions are interfering with their radio or TV reception? ***Make sure that your station is functioning properly and that it does not cause interference to your own radio or television when it is tuned to the same channel***	
T7	B	07	Which of the following can reduce overload of a VHF transceiver by a nearby commercial FM station? ***Installing a band-reject filter***	
T7	B	08	What should you do if something in a neighbor's home is causing harmful interference to your amateur station? ***All these choices are correct***	
T7	B	09	What should be the first step to resolve non-fiber optic cable TV interference caused by your amateur radio transmission? ***Be sure all TV feed line coaxial connectors are installed properly***	NEW Question
T7	B	19	What might be a problem if you receive a report that your audio signal through an FM repeater is distorted or unintelligible? ***All these choices are correct***	
T7	B	11	What is a symptom of RF feedback in a transmitter or transceiver? ***Reports of garbled, distorted, or unintelligible voice transmissions***	

Section T7-C. Antenna and transmission line measurements and troubleshooting: measuring SWR, effects of high SWR, causes of feed line failures; Basic coaxial cable characteristics; Use of dummy loads when testing

T7	C	01	What is the primary purpose of a dummy load? ***To prevent transmitting signals over the air when making tests***	
T7	C	02	Which of the following is used to determine if an antenna is resonant at the desired operating frequency? ***An antenna analyzer***	
T7	C	03	What does a dummy load consist of? ***A non-inductive resistor mounted on a heat sink***	NEW Question
T7	C	04	What reading on an SWR meter indicates a perfect impedance match between the antenna and the feed line? ***1:1***	
T7	C	05	Why do most solid-state transmitters reduce output power as SWR increases beyond a certain level? ***To protect the output amplifier transistor***	

T7	C	06	What does an SWR reading of 4:1 indicate? ***Impedance mismatch***	
T7	C	07	What happens to power lost in a feed line? ***It is converted into heat***	
T7	C	08	Which instrument can be used to determine SWR? ***Directional wattmeter***	Modified Question
T7	C	09	Which of the following causes failure of coaxial cables? ***Moisture contamination***	Modified Question
T7	C	10	Why should the outer jacket of coaxial cable be resistant to ultraviolet light? ***Ultraviolet light can damage the jacket and allow water to enter the cable***	
T7	C	11	What is a disadvantage of air core coaxial cable when compared to foam or solid dielectric types? ***It requires special techniques to prevent moisture in the cable***	

Section T7-D. Using basic test instruments: voltmeter, ammeter, and ohmmeter; Soldering

T7	D	01	Which instrument would you use to measure electric potential? ***A voltmeter***	
T7	D	02	How is a voltmeter connected to a component to measure applied voltage? ***In parallel***	
T7	D	03	When configured to measure current, how is a multimeter connected to a component? ***In series***	Modified Question
T7	D	04	Which instrument is used to measure electric current? ***An ammeter***	
T7	D	05	How is an ohmmeter connected to a component to measure its resistance? - **QUESTION REMOVED FROM TEST** ***In parallel***	DELETED
T7	D	06	Which of the following can damage a multimeter? ***Attempting to measure voltage when using the resistance setting***	
T7	D	07	Which of the following measurements are made using a multimeter? ***Voltage and resistance***	
T7	D	08	Which of the following types of solder should not be used for radio and electronic applications? ***Acid-core solder***	NEW Question
T7	D	09	What is the characteristic appearance of a cold tin-lead solder joint? ***A rough or lumpy surface***	Modified Question
T7	D	10	What reading indicates that an ohmmeter is connected across a large, discharged capacitor? ***Increasing resistance with time***	NEW Question
T7	D	11	Which of the following precautions should be taken when measuring in-circuit resistance with an ohmmeter? ***Ensure that the circuit is not powered***	

T8: SIGNALS AND EMISSIONS – [4 Exam Questions - 4 Groups] - 48 Questions

Section T8-A. Basic characteristics of FM and SSB; Bandwidth of various modulation modes: CW, SSB, FM, fast-scan TV; Choice of emission type: selection of USB vs LSB, use of SSB for weak signal work, use of FM for VHF packet and repeaters

T8	A	01	Which of the following is a form of amplitude modulation? ***Single sideband***	
T8	A	02	What type of modulation is commonly used for VHF packet radio transmissions? ***FM or PM***	Modified Question
T8	A	03	Which type of voice mode is often used for long-distance (weak signal) contacts on the VHF and UHF bands? ***SSB***	
T8	A	04	Which type of modulation is commonly used for VHF and UHF voice repeaters? ***FM or PM***	Modified Question
T8	A	05	Which of the following types of signal has the narrowest bandwidth? ***CW***	
T8	A	06	Which sideband is normally used for 10 meter HF, VHF, and UHF single-sideband communications? ***Upper sideband***	
T8	A	07	What is a characteristic of single sideband (SSB) compared to FM? ***SSB signals have narrower bandwidth***	Modified Question
T8	A	08	What is the approximate bandwidth of a typical single sideband (SSB) voice signal? ***3 kHz***	
T8	A	09	What is the approximate bandwidth of a VHF repeater FM voice signal? ***Between 10 and 15 kHz***	
T8	A	10	What is the approximate bandwidth of AM fast-scan TV transmissions? ***About 6 MHz***	Modified Question
T8	A	11	What is the approximate bandwidth required to transmit a CW signal? ***150 Hz***	
T8	A	12	Which of the following is a disadvantage of FM compared with single sideband? ***Only one signal can be received at a time***	NEW Question

Section T8-B. Amateur satellite operation: Doppler shift, basic orbits, operating protocols, modulation mode selection, transmitter power considerations, telemetry and telecommand, satellite tracking programs, beacons, uplink and downlink mode definitions, spin fading, definition of "LEO", setting uplink power

T8	B	01	What telemetry information is typically transmitted by satellite beacons? ***Health and status of the satellite***
T8	B	02	What is the impact of using excessive effective radiated power on a satellite uplink? ***Blocking access by other users***
T8	B	03	Which of the following are provided by satellite tracking programs? ***All these choices are correct***
T8	B	04	What mode of transmission is commonly used by amateur radio satellites? ***All these choices are correct***

T8	B	05	What is a satellite beacon?	
			A transmission from a satellite that contains status information	
T8	B	06	Which of the following are inputs to a satellite tracking program?	
			The Keplerian elements	
T8	B	07	What is Doppler shift in reference to satellite communications?	
			An observed change in signal frequency caused by relative motion between the satellite and Earth station	
T8	B	08	What is meant by the statement that a satellite is operating in U/V mode?	
			The satellite uplink is in the 70-centimeter band and the downlink is in the 2-meter band	
T8	B	09	What causes spin fading of satellite signals?	
			Rotation of the satellite and its antennas	
T8	B	10	What is a LEO satellite?	Modified Question
			A satellite in low earth orbit	
T8	B	11	Who may receive telemetry from a space station?	Modified Question
			Anyone	
T8	B	12	Which of the following is a way to determine whether your satellite uplink power is neither too low nor too high?	
			Your signal strength on the downlink should be about the same as the beacon	

Section T8-C. Operating activities: radio direction finding, contests, linking over the internet, exchanging grid locators

T8	C	01	Which of the following methods is used to locate sources of noise interference or jamming?
			Radio direction finding
T8	C	02	Which of these items would be useful for a hidden transmitter hunt?
			A directional antenna
T8	C	03	What operating activity involves contacting as many stations as possible during a specified period?
			Contesting
T8	C	04	Which of the following is good procedure when contacting another station in a contest?
			Send only the minimum information needed for proper identification and the contest exchange
T8	C	05	What is a grid locator?
			A letter-number designator assigned to a geographic location
T8	C	06	How is over the air access to IRLP nodes accomplished?
			By using DTMF signals
T8	C	07	What is Voice Over Internet Protocol (VoIP)?
			A method of delivering voice communications over the internet using digital techniques
T8	C	08	What is the Internet Radio Linking Project (IRLP)?
			A technique to connect amateur radio systems, such as repeaters, via the internet using Voice Over Internet Protocol (VoIP)

T8	C	09	Which of the following protocols enables an amateur station to transmit through a repeater without using a radio to initiate the transmission?	NEW
			EchoLink	Question
T8	C	10	What is required before using the EchoLink system?	NEW
			Register your call sign and provide proof of license	Question
T8	C	11	What is an amateur radio station that connects other amateur stations to the internet?	
			A gateway	

Section T8-D. Non-voice and digital communications: image signals and definition of NTSC, CW, packet radio, PSK, APRS, error detection and correction, amateur radio networking, Digital Mobile Radio, WSJT modes, Broadband-Hamnet

T8	D	01	Which of the following is a digital communications mode?	
			All these choices are correct	
T8	D	02	What is a "talkgroup" on a DMR repeater?	NEW
			A way for groups of users to share a channel at different times without hearing other users on the channel	Question
T8	D	03	What kind of data can be transmitted by APRS?	NEW
			All these choices are correct	Question
T8	D	04	What type of transmission is indicated by the term "NTSC?"	
			An analog fast-scan color TV signal	
T8	D	05	Which of the following is an application of APRS?	
			Providing real-time tactical digital communications in conjunction with a map showing the locations of stations	
T8	D	06	What does the abbreviation "PSK" mean?	
			Phase Shift Keying	
T8	D	07	Which of the following describes DMR?	Modified
			A technique for time-multiplexing two digital voice signals on a single 12.5 kHz repeater channel	Question
T8	D	08	Which of the following is included in packet radio transmissions?	
			All these choices are correct	
T8	D	09	What is CW?	Modified
			Another name for a Morse code transmission	Question
T8	D	10	Which of the following operating activities is supported by digital mode software in the WSJT-X software suite?	
			All these choices are correct	
T8	D	11	What is an ARQ transmission system?	Modified
			An error correction method in which the receiving station detects errors and sends a request for retransmission	Question
T8	D	12	Which of the following best describes an amateur radio mesh network?	Modified
			An amateur radio-based data network using commercial Wi-Fi equipment with modified firmware	Question
T8	D	13	What is FT8?	Modified
			A digital mode capable of low signal-to-noise operation	Question

T9: ANTENNAS AND FEED LINES - [2 Exam Questions - 2 Groups] - 24 Questions

Section T9-A. Antennas: vertical and horizontal polarization, concept of antenna gain, definition and types of beam antennas, antenna loading, common portable and mobile antennas, relationships between resonant length and frequency, dipole pattern

T9	A	01	What is a beam antenna? *An antenna that concentrates signals in one direction*	
T9	A	02	Which of the following describes a type of antenna loading? *Electrically lengthening by inserting inductors in radiating elements*	Modified Question
T9	A	03	Which of the following describes a simple dipole oriented parallel to Earth's surface? *A horizontally polarized antenna*	
T9	A	04	What is a disadvantage of the short, flexible antenna supplied with most handheld radio transceivers, compared to a full-sized quarter-wave antenna? *It has low efficiency*	Modified Question
T9	A	05	Which of the following increases the resonant frequency of a dipole antenna? *Shortening it*	Modified Question
T9	A	06	Which of the following types of antenna offers the greatest gain? *Yagi*	NEW Question
T9	A	07	What is a disadvantage of using a handheld VHF transceiver with a flexible antenna inside a vehicle? *Signal strength is reduced due to the shielding effect of the vehicle*	Modified Question
T9	A	08	What is the approximate length, in inches, of a quarter-wavelength vertical antenna for 146 MHz? *19*	
T9	A	09	What is the approximate length, in inches, of a half-wavelength 6 meter dipole antenna? *112*	
T9	A	10	In which direction does a half-wave dipole antenna radiate the strongest signal? *Broadside to the antenna*	
T9	A	11	What is antenna gain? *The increase in signal strength in a specified direction compared to a reference antenna*	
T9	A	12	What is an advantage of a 5/8 wavelength whip antenna for VHF or UHF mobile service? *It has more gain than a 1/4-wavelength antenna*	Modified Question

Section T9-B. Feed lines: types, attenuation vs frequency, selecting; SWR concepts; Antenna tuners (couplers); RF Connectors: selecting, weather protection

T9	B	01	What is a benefit of low SWR? *Reduced signal loss*	Modified Question
T9	B	02	What is the most common impedance of coaxial cables used in amateur radio? *50 ohms*	Modified Question
T9	B	03	Why is coaxial cable the most common feed line for amateur radio antenna systems? *It is easy to use and requires few special installation considerations*	

T9	B	04	What is the major function of an antenna tuner (antenna coupler)? *It matches the antenna system impedance to the transceiver's output impedance*	
T9	B	05	What happens as the frequency of a signal in coaxial cable is increased? *The loss increases*	Modified Question
T9	B	06	Which of the following RF connector types is most suitable for frequencies above 400 MHz? *Type N*	
T9	B	07	Which of the following is true of PL-259 type coax connectors? *They are commonly used at HF and VHF frequencies*	Modified Question
T9	B	08	Which of the following is a source of loss in coaxial feed line? *All these choices are correct*	NEW Question
T9	B	09	What can cause erratic changes in SWR? *Loose connection in the antenna or feed line*	
T9	B	10	What is the electrical difference between RG-58 and RG-213 coaxial cable? *RG-213 cable has less loss at a given frequency*	NEW Question
T9	B	11	Which of the following types of feed line has the lowest loss at VHF and UHF? *Air-insulated hardline*	
T9	B	12	What is standing wave ratio (SWR)? *A measure of how well a load is matched to a transmission line*	NEW Question

T0: SAFETY – [3 Exam Questions - 3 Groups] - 36 Questions

Section T0-A. Power circuits and hazards: hazardous voltages, fuses and circuit breakers, grounding, electrical code compliance; Lightning protection; Battery safety

T0	A	01	Which of the following is a safety hazard of a 12-volt storage battery? *Shorting the terminals can cause burns, fire, or an explosion*	
T0	A	02	What health hazard is presented by electrical current flowing through the body? *All these choices are correct*	
T0	A	03	In the United States, what circuit does black wire insulation indicate in a three-wire 120 V cable? *Hot*	NEW Question
T0	A	04	What is the purpose of a fuse in an electrical circuit? *To remove power in case of overload*	Modified Question
T0	A	05	Why should a 5-ampere fuse never be replaced with a 20-ampere fuse? *Excessive current could cause a fire*	
T0	A	06	What is a good way to guard against electrical shock at your station? *All these choices are correct*	
T0	A	07	Where should a lightning arrester be installed in a coaxial feed line? *On a grounded panel near where feed lines enter the building*	Modified Question
T0	A	08	Where should a fuse or circuit breaker be installed in a 120V AC power circuit? *In series with the hot conductor only*	Modified Question
T0	A	09	What should be done to all external ground rods or earth connections? *Bond them together with heavy wire or conductive strap*	

T0	A	10	What hazard is caused by charging or discharging a battery too quickly? **Overheating or out-gassing**	Modified Question
T0	A	11	What hazard exists in a power supply immediately after turning it off? **Charge stored in filter capacitors**	Modified Question
T0	A	12	Which of the following precautions should be taken when measuring high voltages with a voltmeter? **Ensure that the voltmeter and leads are rated for use at the voltages to be measured**	NEW Question

Section T0-B. Antenna safety: tower safety and grounding, installing antennas, antenna supports

T0	B	01	Which of the following is good practice when installing ground wires on a tower for lightning protection? **Ensure that connections are short and direct**	NEW Question
T0	B	02	What is required when climbing an antenna tower? **All these choices are correct**	NEW Question
T0	B	03	Under what circumstances is it safe to climb a tower without a helper or observer? **Never**	
T0	B	04	Which of the following is an important safety precaution to observe when putting up an antenna tower? **Look for and stay clear of any overhead electrical wires**	
T0	B	05	What is the purpose of a safety wire through a turnbuckle used to tension guy lines? **Prevent loosening of the turnbuckle from vibration**	NEW Question
T0	B	06	What is the minimum safe distance from a power line to allow when installing an antenna? **Enough so that if the antenna falls, no part of it can come closer than 10 feet to the power wires**	
T0	B	07	Which of the following is an important safety rule to remember when using a crank-up tower? **This type of tower must not be climbed unless it is retracted, or mechanical safety locking devices have been installed**	
T0	B	08	Which is a proper grounding method for a tower? **Separate eight-foot ground rods for each tower leg, bonded to the tower and each other**	
T0	B	09	Why should you avoid attaching an antenna to a utility pole? **The antenna could contact high-voltage power lines**	
T0	B	10	Which of the following is true when installing grounding conductors used for lightning protection? **Sharp bends must be avoided**	
T0	B	11	Which of the following establishes grounding requirements for an amateur radio tower or antenna? **Local electrical codes**	

Section T0-C. RF hazards: radiation exposure, proximity to antennas, recognized safe power levels, radiation types, duty cycle

T0	C	01	What type of radiation are radio signals? **Non-ionizing radiation**	
T0	C	02	At which of the following frequencies does maximum permissible exposure have the lowest value? **50 MHz**	
T0	C	03	How does the allowable power density for RF safety change if duty cycle changes from 100 percent to 50 percent? **It increases by a factor of 2**	NEW Question
T0	C	04	What factors affect the RF exposure of people near an amateur station antenna? **All these choices are correct**	
T0	C	05	Why do exposure limits vary with frequency? **The human body absorbs more RF energy at some frequencies than at others**	
T0	C	06	Which of the following is an acceptable method to determine whether your station complies with FCC RF exposure regulations? **All these choices are correct**	
T0	C	07	What hazard is created by touching an antenna during a transmission? **RF burn to skin**	Modified Question
T0	C	08	Which of the following actions can reduce exposure to RF radiation? **Relocate antennas**	Modified Question
T0	C	09	How can you make sure your station stays in compliance with RF safety regulations? **By re-evaluating the station whenever an item in the transmitter or antenna system is changed**	
T0	C	10	Why is duty cycle one of the factors used to determine safe RF radiation exposure levels? **It affects the average exposure to radiation**	
T0	C	11	What is the definition of duty cycle during the averaging time for RF exposure? **The percentage of time that a transmitter is transmitting**	
T0	C	12	How does RF radiation differ from ionizing radiation (radioactivity)? **RF radiation does not have sufficient energy to cause chemical changes in cells and damage DNA**	Modified Question
T0	C	13	Who is responsible for ensuring that no person is exposed to RF energy above the FCC exposure limits? **The station licensee**	NEW Question

Chapter 3 – Practice Test Questions

Section 3 will introduce you to all 411 questions that are in the 2022-2026 question pool. When testing, only 35 of these questions will appear on your test, and there are several versions of the test meaning if you fail and choose to immediately retake the test you will not receive the same test that you previously failed.

We are limiting diagrams in this section to only those that you will be seeing on the actual tests. The order the questions are provided here are in the same order as provided by the NCVEC broken into 10 main categories, each of which the categories are broken into between two and six sub-groups. When running through the practice tests it is recommended that you use either a separate sheet to record your answers or create a copy of the worksheet provided on page 4-5 which will allow you to work through a number of sections to record your answers.

Using the practice test worksheet, record the Section you are testing in, and then which answer (A-B-C-D) you believe to be correct. Then use the Practice Test Answers located in section 4 to check yourself. Pay attention to the questions you missed, and you can review those questions in sections 5 and 6 to help understand why you were wrong with your answers.

Following are the pages for each of the ten groups covered on the test.

Section	Page Number
T1	3-2
T2	3-15
T3	3-22
T4	3-29
T5	3-34
T6	3-44
T7	3-55
T8	3-64
T9	3-73
T0	3-78

Heads Up!

All questions and answers use the exact verbiage as will be used on the test. The order of the answers will change on the actual tests, so an answer in position "A" in practice may be in positions "B", "C", or "D" on the actual test.

Practice Test Worksheet (Photocopy)

Section	Question #	Answer (Mark One)	Section	Question #	Answer (Mark one)
T_____	01	A B C D	T_____	01	A B C D
	02	A B C D		02	A B C D
	03	A B C D		03	A B C D
	04	A B C D		04	A B C D
	05	A B C D		05	A B C D
	06	A B C D		06	A B C D
	07	A B C D		07	A B C D
	08	A B C D		08	A B C D
	09	A B C D		09	A B C D
	10	A B C D		10	A B C D
	11	A B C D		11	A B C D
	12	A B C D		12	A B C D
	13	A B C D		13	A B C D
T_____	01	A B C D		01	A B C D
	02	A B C D		02	A B C D
	03	A B C D		03	A B C D
	04	A B C D		04	A B C D
	05	A B C D		05	A B C D
	06	A B C D		06	A B C D
	07	A B C D		07	A B C D
	08	A B C D		08	A B C D
	09	A B C D		09	A B C D
	10	A B C D		10	A B C D
	11	A B C D		11	A B C D
	12	A B C D		12	A B C D
	13	A B C D		13	A B C D
	01	A B C D		01	A B C D
	02	A B C D		02	A B C D
	03	A B C D		03	A B C D
	04	A B C D		04	A B C D
	05	A B C D		05	A B C D
	06	A B C D		06	A B C D
	07	A B C D		07	A B C D
	08	A B C D		08	A B C D
	09	A B C D		09	A B C D
	10	A B C D		10	A B C D
	11	A B C D		11	A B C D
	12	A B C D		12	A B C D
	13	A B C D		13	A B C D

T1A01 (Modified Question from the 2018-2022 Pool)
Which of the following is part of the Basis and Purpose of the Amateur Radio Service?

A. Providing personal radio communications for as many citizens as possible
B. Providing communications for international non-profit organizations
C. Advancing skills in the technical and communication phases of the radio art
D. All these choices are correct

T1A02
Which agency regulates and enforces the rules for the Amateur Radio Service in the United States?

A. FEMA
B. Homeland Security
C. The FCC
D. All of these choices are correct

T1A03
What do the FCC rules state regarding the use of a phonetic alphabet for station identification in the Amateur Radio Service?

A. It is required when transmitting emergency messages
B. It is encouraged
C. It is required when in contact with foreign stations
D. All these choices are correct

T1A04
How many operator/primary station license grants may be held by any one person?

A. One
B. No more than Two
C. One for each band on which the person plans to operate
D. One for each permanent station location from which the person plans to operate

T1A05 (Modified Question from the 2018-2022 Pool)
What proves that the FCC has issued an operator/primary license grant?

A. A printed copy of the certificate of successful completion of examination
B. An email notification from the NCVEC granting the license
C. The license appears in the FCC ULS database
D. All these choices are correct

T1A06
What is the FCC Part 97 definition of a beacon?

A. A government transmitter marking the amateur radio band edges
B. A bulletin sent by the FCC to announce a national emergency
C. A continuous transmission of weather information authorized in the amateur bands by the National Weather
   Service
D. An amateur station transmitting communications for the purposes of observing propagation or related
   experimental activities

T1A07
What is the FCC Part 97 definition of a space station?

A. Any satellite orbiting Earth
B. A manned satellite orbiting Earth
C. An amateur station located more than 50 km above Earth's surface
D. An amateur station using amateur radio satellites for relay of signals

T1A08
Which of the following entities recommends transmit/receive channels and other parameters for auxiliary and repeater stations?

A. Frequency Spectrum Manager appointed by the FCC
B. Volunteer Frequency Coordinator recognized by local amateurs
C. FCC Regional Field Office
D. International Telecommunication Union

T1A09
Who selects a Frequency Coordinator?

A. The FCC Office of Spectrum Management and Coordination Policy
B. The local chapter of the Office of National Council of Independent Frequency Coordinators
C. Amateur operators in a local or regional area whose stations are eligible to be repeater or auxiliary stations
D. FCC Regional Field Office

T1A10 (Modified Question from the 2018-2022 Pool)
What is the Radio Amateur Civil Emergency Service (RACES)?

A. A radio service using amateur frequencies for emergency management or civil defense communications
B. A radio service using amateur stations for emergency management or civil defense communications
C. An emergency service using amateur operators certified by a civil defense organization as being enrolled in
   that organization
D. All these choices are correct

T1A11
When is willful interference to other amateur radio stations permitted?

A. To stop another amateur station that is breaking the FCC rules
B. At no time
C. When making short test transmissions
D. At any time, stations in the Amateur Radio Service are not protected from willful interference

T1B01 (New Question for the 2022-2026 Pool)
Which of the following frequency ranges are available for phone operation by Technician licensees?

A. 28.050 MHz to 28.150 MHz
B. 28.100 MHz to 28.300 MHz
C. 28.300 MHz to 28.500 MHz
D. 28.500 MHz to 28.600 MHz

T1B02 (Modified Question from the 2018-2022 Pool)
Which amateurs may contact the International Space Station (ISS) on VHF bands?

A. Any amateur holding a General class or higher license
B. Any amateur holding a Technician class or higher license
C. Any amateur holding a General class or higher license who has applied for and received approval from NASA
D. Any amateur holding a Technician class or higher license who has applied for and received approval from NASA

T1B03 (Modified Question from the 2018-2022 Pool)
Which frequency is in the 6-meter amateur band?

A. 49.00 MHz
B. 52.525 MHz
C. 28.50 MHz
D. 222.15 MHz

T1B04 (Modified Question from the 2018-2022 Pool)
Which amateur band includes 146.52 MHz?

A. 6 meters
B. 20 meters
C. 70 centimeters
D. 2 meters

T1B05 (Modified Question from the 2018-2022 Pool)
How may amateurs use the 219 to 220 MHz segment of 1.25 meter band?

A. Spread spectrum only
B. Fast-scan television only
C. Emergency traffic only
D. Fixed digital message forwarding systems only

T1B06
On which HF bands does a Technician class operator have phone privileges?

A. None
B. 10 meter band only
C. 80 meter, 40 meter, 15 meter, and 10 meter bands
D. 30 meter band only

T1B07 (Modified Question from the 2018-2022 Pool)
Which of the following VHF/UHF band segments are limited to CW only?

A. 50.0 MHz to 50.1 MHz and 144.0 MHz to 144.1 MHz
B. 219 MHz to 220 MHz and 420.0 MHz to 420.1 MHz
C. 902.0 MHz to 902.1 MHz
D. All these choices are correct

T1B08 (Modified Question from the 2018-2022 Pool)
How are US amateurs restricted in segments of bands where the Amateur Radio Service is secondary?

A. U.S. amateurs may find non-amateur stations in those segments, and must avoid interfering with them
B. U.S. amateurs must give foreign amateur stations priority in those segments
C. International communications are not permitted in those segments
D. Digital transmissions are not permitted in those segments

T1B09
Why should you not set your transmit frequency to be exactly at the edge of an amateur band or sub-band?

A. To allow for calibration error in the transmitter frequency display
B. So that modulation sidebands do not extend beyond the band edge
C. To allow for transmitter frequency drift
D. All these choices are correct

T1B10 (New Question for the 2022-2026 Pool)
Where may SSB phone be used in amateur bands above 50 MHz?

A. Only in sub-bands allocated to General class or higher licensees
B. Only on repeaters
C. In at least some segment of all these bands
D. On any band if the power is limited to 25 watts

T1B11 (Modified Question from the 2018-2022 Pool)
What is the maximum peak envelope power output for Technician class operators in their HF band segments?

A. 200 watts
B. 100 watts
C. 50 watts
D. 10 watts

T1B12
Except for some specific restrictions, what is the maximum peak envelope power output for Technician class operators using frequencies above 30 MHz?

A. 50 watts
B. 100 watts
C. 500 watts
D. 1500 watts

T1C01
For which license classes are new licenses currently available from the FCC?

A. Novice, Technician, General, Amateur Extra
B. Technician, Technician Plus, General, Amateur Extra
C. Novice, Technician Plus, General, Advanced
D. Technician, General, Amateur Extra

T1C02
Who may select a desired call sign under the vanity call sign rules?

A. Only a licensed amateur with a General or Amateur Extra Class license
B. Only a licensed amateur with an Amateur Extra Class license
C. Only a licensed amateur who has been licensed continuously for more than 10 years
D. Any licensed amateur

T1C03
What types of international communications are an FCC-licensed amateur radio station permitted to make?

A. Communications incidental to the purposes of the Amateur Radio Service and remarks of a personal character
B. Communications incidental to conducting business or remarks of a personal nature
C. Only communications incidental to contest exchanges; all other communications are prohibited
D. Any communications that would be permitted by an international broadcast station

T1C04 (New Question for the 2022-2026 Pool)
What may happen if the FCC is unable to reach you by email?

A. Fine and suspension of operator license
B. Revocation of the station license or suspension of the operator license
C. Revocation of access to the license record in the FCC system
D. Nothing; there is no such requirement

T1C05 (Modified Question from the 2018-2022 Pool)
Which of the following is a valid Technician class call sign format?

A. KF1XXX
B. KA1X
C. W1XX
D. All these choices are correct

T1C06
From which of the following locations may an FCC-licensed amateur station transmit?

A. From within any country that belongs to the International Telecommunication Union
B. From within any country that is a member of the United Nations
C. From anywhere within International Telecommunication Union (ITU) Regions 2 and 3
D. From any vessel or craft located in international waters and documented or registered in the United States

T1C07 (New Question for the 2022-2026 Pool)
Which of the following can result in revocation of the station license or suspension of the operator license?

A. Failure to inform the FCC of any changes in the amateur station following performance of an RF safety environmental evaluation
B. Failure to provide and maintain a correct email address with the FCC
C. Failure to obtain FCC type acceptance prior to using a home-built transmitter
D. Failure to have a copy of your license available at your station

T1C08 (Modified Question from the 2018-2022 Pool)
What is the normal term for an FCC-issued amateur radio license?

A. Five Years
B. Life
C. Ten years
D. Eight years

T1C09 (Modified Question from the 2018-2022 Pool)
What is the grace period for renewal if an amateur license expires?

A. Two years
B. Three years
C. Five years
D. Ten years

T1C10 (Modified Question from the 2018-2022 Pool)
How soon after passing the examination for your first amateur radio license may you transmit on the amateur radio bands?

A. Immediately on receiving your Certificate of Successful Completion of Examination (CSCE)
B. As soon as your operator/station license grant appears on the ARRL website
C. As soon as your operator/station license grant appears in the FCC's license database
D. As soon as you receive your license in the mail from the FCC

T1C11 (Modified Question from the 2018-2022 Pool)
If your license has expired and is still within the allowable grace period, may you continue to transmit on the amateur radio bands?

A. Yes, for up to two years
B. Yes, as soon as you apply for renewal
C. Yes, for up to one year
D. No, you must wait until the license has been renewed

T1D01
With which countries are FCC-licensed amateur radio stations prohibited from exchanging communications?

A. Any country whose administration has notified the International Telecommunication Union (ITU) that it objects to such communications
B. Any country whose administration has notified the American Radio Relay League (ARRL) that it objects to such communications
C. Any country banned from such communications by the International Amateur Radio Union (IARU)
D. Any country banned from making such communications by the American Radio Relay League (ARRL)

T1D02 (New Question for the 2022-2026 Pool)
Under which of the following circumstances are one-way transmissions by an amateur station prohibited?

A. In all circumstances
B. Broadcasting
C. International Morse Code Practice
D. Telecommand or transmissions of telemetry

T1D03

When is it permissible to transmit messages encoded to obscure their meaning?

A. Only during contests
B. Only when transmitting certain approved digital codes
C. Only when transmitting control commands to space stations or radio control craft
D. Never

T1D04

Under what conditions is an amateur station authorized to transmit music using a phone emission?

A. When incidental to an authorized retransmission of manned spacecraft communications
B. When the music produces no spurious emissions
C. When transmissions are limited to less than three minutes per hour
D. When the music is transmitted above 1280 MHz

T1D05 (Modified Question from the 2018-2022 Pool)
When may amateur radio operators use their stations to notify other amateurs of the availability of equipment for sale or trade?

A. Never
B. When the equipment is not the personal property of either the station licensee, or the control operator, or their close relatives
C. When no profit is made on the sale
D. When selling amateur radio equipment and not on a regular basis

T1D06

What, if any, are the restrictions concerning transmission of language that may be considered indecent or obscene?

A. The FCC maintains a list of words that are not permitted to be used on amateur frequencies
B. Any such language is prohibited
C. The ITU maintains a list of words that are not permitted to be used on amateur frequencies
D. There is no such prohibition

T1D07
What types of amateur stations can automatically retransmit the signals of other amateur stations?

A. Auxiliary, beacon, or Earth stations
B. Earth, repeater, or space stations
C. Beacon, repeater, or space stations
D. Repeater, auxiliary, or space stations

T1D08
In which of the following circumstances may the control operator of an amateur station receive compensation for operating that station?

A. When the communication is related to the sale of amateur equipment by the control operator's employer
B. When the communication is incidental to classroom instruction at an educational institution
C. When the communication is made to obtain emergency information for a local broadcast station
D. All these choices are correct

T1D09 (Modified Question from the 2018-2022 Pool)
When may amateur stations transmit information in support of broadcasting, program production, or news gathering, assuming no other means is available?

A. When such communications are directly related to the immediate safety of human life or protection of property
B. When broadcasting communications to or from the space shuttle
C. Where noncommercial programming is gathered and supplied exclusively to the National Public Radio network
D. Never

T1D10 (Modified Question from the 2018-2022 Pool)
How does the FCC define broadcasting for the Amateur Radio Service?

A. Two-way transmissions by amateur stations
B. Any transmission made by the licensed station
C. Transmission of messages directed only to amateur operators
D. Transmissions intended for reception by the general public

T1D11 (Modified Question from the 2018-2022 Pool)
When may an amateur station transmit without identifying on the air?

A. When the transmissions are of a brief nature to make station adjustments
B. When the transmissions are unmodulated
C. When the transmitted power level is below 1 watt
D. When transmitting signals to control model craft

T1E01
When may an amateur station transmit without a control operator?

A. When using automatic control, such as in the case of a repeater
B. When the station licensee is away and another licensed amateur is using the station
C. When the transmitting station is an auxiliary station
D. Never

T1E02 (Modified Question from the 2018-2022 Pool)
Who may be the control operator of a station communicating through an amateur satellite or space station?

A. Only an Amateur Extra Class operator
B. A General class or higher licensee with a satellite operator certification
C. Only an Amateur Extra Class operator who is also an AMSAT member
D. Any amateur allowed to transmit on the satellite uplink frequency

T1E03
Who must designate the station control operator?

A. The station licensee
B. The FCC
C. The frequency coordinator
D. Any licensed operator

T1E04
What determines the transmitting frequency privileges of an amateur station?

A. The frequency authorized by the frequency coordinator
B. The frequencies printed on the license grant
C. The highest class of operator license held by anyone on the premises
D. The class of operator license held by the control operator

T1E05
What is an amateur station's control point?

A. The location of the station's transmitting antenna
B. The location of the station's transmitting apparatus
C. The location at which the control operator function is performed
D. The mailing address of the station licensee

T1E06 (Modified Question from the 2018-2022 Pool)
When, under normal circumstances, may a Technician class licensee be the control operator of a station operating in an Amateur Extra Class band segment?

A. At no time
B. When designated as the control operator by an Amateur Extra Class licensee
C. As part of a multi-operator contest team
D. When using a club station whose trustee holds an Amateur Extra Class license

T1E07 (Modified Question from the 2018-2022 Pool)
When the control operator is not the station licensee, who is responsible for the proper operation of the station?

A. All licensed amateurs who are present at the operation
B. Only the station licensee
C. Only the control operator
D. The control operator and the station licensee

T1E08
Which of the following is an example of automatic control?

A. Repeater operation
B. Controlling a station over the internet
C. Using a computer or other device to send CW automatically
D. Using a computer or other device to identify automatically

T1E09
Which of the following are required for remote control operation?

A. The control operator must be at the control point
B. A control operator is required at all times
C. The control operator must indirectly manipulate the controls
D. All these choices are correct

T1E10
Which of the following is an example of remote control as defined in Part 97?

A. Repeater operation
B. Operating the station over the internet
C. Controlling a model aircraft, boat, or car by amateur radio
D. All these choices are correct

T1E11
Who does the FCC presume to be the control operator of an amateur station, unless documentation to the contrary is in the station records?

A. The station custodian
B. The third party participant
C. The person operating the station equipment
D. The station licensee

T1F01
When must the station and its records be available for FCC inspection?

A. At any time ten days after notification by the FCC of such an inspection
B. At any time upon request by an FCC representative
C. At any time after written notification by the FCC of such inspection
D. Only when presented with a valid warrant by an FCC official or government agent

T1F02 (Modified Question from the 2018-2022 Pool)
How often must you identify with your FCC-assigned call sign when using tactical call signs such as "Race Headquarters"?

A. Never, the tactical call is sufficient
B. Once during every hour
C. At the end of each communication and every ten minutes during a communication
D. At the end of every transmission

T1F03 (Modified Question from the 2018-2022 Pool)
When are you required to transmit your assigned call sign?

A. At the beginning of each contact, and every 10 minutes thereafter
B. At least once during each transmission
C. At least every 15 minutes during and at the end of a communication
D. At least every 10 minutes during and at the end of a communication

T1F04 (Modified Question from the 2018-2022 Pool)
What language may you use for identification when operating in a phone sub-band?

A. Any language recognized by the United Nations
B. Any language recognized by the ITU
C. English
D. English, French, or Spanish

T1F05
What method of call sign identification is required for a station transmitting phone signals?

A. Send the call sign followed by the indicator RPT
B. Send the call sign using a CW or phone emission
C. Send the call sign followed by the indicator R
D. Send the call sign using only a phone emission

T1F06
Which of the following self-assigned indicators are acceptable when using a phone transmission?

A. KL7CC stroke W3
B. KL7CC slant W3
C. KL7CC slash W3
D. All these choices are correct

T1F07 (Modified Question from the 2018-2022 Pool)
Which of the following restrictions apply when a non-licensed person is allowed to speak to a foreign station using a station under the control of a licensed amateur operator?

A. The person must be a U.S. citizen
B. The foreign station must be in a country with which the U.S. has a third party agreement
C. The licensed control operator must do the station identification
D. All these choices are correct

T1F08
What is the definition of third party communications?

A. A message from a control operator to another amateur station control operator on behalf of another person
B. Amateur radio communications where three stations are in communications with one another
C. Operation when the transmitting equipment is licensed to a person other than the control operator
D. Temporary authorization for an unlicensed person to transmit on the amateur bands for technical experiments

T1F09
What type of amateur station simultaneously retransmits the signal of another amateur station on a different channel or channels?

A. Beacon station
B. Earth station
C. Repeater station
D. Message forwarding station

T1F10
Who is accountable if a repeater inadvertently retransmits communications that violate the FCC rules?

A. The control operator of the originating station
B. The control operator of the repeater
C. The owner of the repeater
D. Both the originating station and the repeater owner

T1F11
Which of the following is a requirement for the issuance of a club station license grant?

A. The trustee must have an Amateur Extra Class operator license grant
B. The club must have at least four members
C. The club must be registered with the American Radio Relay League
D. All these choices are correct

T2A01
What is a common repeater frequency offset in the 2 meter band?

A. Plus or minus 5 MHz
B. Plus or minus 600 kHz
C. Plus or minus 500 kHz
D. Plus or minus 1 MHz

T2A02
What is the national calling frequency for FM simplex operations in the 2 meter band?

A. 146.520 MHz
B. 145.000 MHz
C. 432.100 MHz
D. 446.000 MHz

T2A03
What is a common repeater frequency offset in the 70 cm band?

A. Plus or minus 5 MHz
B. Plus or minus 600 kHz
C. Plus or minus 500 kHz
D. Plus or minus 1 MHz

T2A04
What is an appropriate way to call another station on a repeater if you know the other station's call sign?

A. Say "break, break," then say the station's call sign
B. Say the station's call sign, then identify with your call sign
C. Say "CQ" three times, then the other station's call sign
D. Wait for the station to call CQ, then answer

T2A05
How should you respond to a station calling CQ?

A. Transmit "CQ" followed by the other station's call sign
B. Transmit your call sign followed by the other station's call sign
C. Transmit the other station's call sign followed by your call sign
D. Transmit a signal report followed by your call sign

T2A06
Which of the following is required when making on-the-air test transmissions?

A. Identify the transmitting station
B. Conduct tests only between 10 p.m. and 6 a.m. local time
C. Notify the FCC of the transmissions
D. All these choices are correct

T2A07
What is meant by "repeater offset"?

A. The difference between a repeater's transmit and receive frequencies
B. The repeater has a time delay to prevent interference
C. The repeater station identification is done on a separate frequency
D. The number of simultaneous transmit frequencies used by a repeater

T2A08
What is the meaning of the procedural signal "CQ"?

A. Call on the quarter hour
B. Test transmission, no reply expected
C. Only the called station should transmit
D. Calling any station

T2A09 (New Question for the 2022-2026 Pool)
Which of the following indicates that a station is listening on a repeater and looking for a contact?

A. "CQ CQ" followed by the repeater's call sign
B. The station's call sign followed by the word "monitoring"
C. The repeater call sign followed by the station's call sign
D. "QSY" followed by your call sign

T2A10
What is a band plan, beyond the privileges established by the FCC?

A. A voluntary guideline for using different modes or activities within an amateur band
B. A list of operating schedules
C. A list of available net frequencies
D. A plan devised by a club to indicate frequency band usage

T2A11
What term describes an amateur station that is transmitting and receiving on the same frequency?

A. Full duplex
B. Diplex
C. Simplex
D. Multiplex

T2A12 (Modified Question from the 2018-2022 Pool)
What should you do before calling CQ?

A. Listen first to be sure that no one else is using the frequency
B. Ask if the frequency is in use
C. Make sure you are authorized to use that frequency
D. All these choices are correct

T2B01 (Modified Question from the 2018-2022 Pool)
How is a VHF/UHF transceiver's "reverse" function used?

A. To reduce power output
B. To increase power output
C. To listen on a repeater's input frequency
D. To listen on a repeater's output frequency

T2B02
What term describes the use of a sub-audible tone transmitted along with normal voice audio to open the squelch of a receiver?

A. Carrier squelch
B. Tone burst
C. DTMF
D. CTCSS

T2B03 (New Question for the 2022-2026 Pool)
Which of the following describes a linked repeater network?

A. A network of repeaters in which signals received by one repeater are transmitted by all the repeaters in the network
B. A single repeater with more than one receiver
C. Multiple repeaters with the same control operator
D. A system of repeaters linked by APRS

T2B04
Which of the following could be the reason you are unable to access a repeater whose output you can hear?

A. Improper transceiver offset
B. You are using the wrong CTCSS tone
C. You are using the wrong DCS code
D. All these choices are correct

T2B05 (Modified Question from the 2018-2022 Pool)
What would cause your FM transmission audio to be distorted on voice peaks?

A. Your repeater offset is inverted
B. You need to talk louder
C. You are talking too loudly
D. Your transmit power is too high

T2B06 (Modified Question from the 2018-2022 Pool)
What type of signaling uses pairs of audio tones?

A. DTMF
B. CTCSS
C. GPRS
D. D-STAR

T2B07
How can you join a digital repeater's "talkgroup"?

A. Register your radio with the local FCC office
B. Join the repeater owner's club
C. Program your radio with the group's ID or code
D. Sign your call after the courtesy tone

T2B08 (Modified Question from the 2018-2022 Pool)
Which of the following applies when two stations transmitting on the same frequency interfere with each other?

A. The stations should negotiate continued use of the frequency
B. Both stations should choose another frequency to avoid conflict
C. Interference is inevitable, so no action is required
D. Use subaudible tones so both stations can share the frequency

T2B09 (New Question for the 2022-2026 Pool)
Why are simplex channels designated in the VHF/UHF band plans?

A. So stations within range of each other can communicate without tying up a repeater
B. For contest operation
C. For working DX only
D. So stations with simple transmitters can access the repeater without automated

T2B10
Which Q signal indicates that you are receiving interference from other stations?

A. QRM
B. QRN
C. QTH
D. QSB

T2B11
Which Q signal indicates that you are changing frequency?

A. QRU
B. QSY
C. QSL
D. QRZ

T2B12 (New Question for the 2022-2026 Pool)
What is the purpose of the color code used on DMR repeater systems?

A. Must match the repeater color code for access
B. Defines the frequency pair to use
C. Identifies the codec used
D. Defines the minimum signal level required for access

T2B13 (New Question for the 2022-2026 Pool)
What is the purpose of a squelch function?

A. Reduce a CW transmitter's key clicks
B. Mute the receiver audio when a signal is not present
C. Eliminate parasitic oscillations in an RF amplifier
D. Reduce interference from impulse noise

T2C01
When do FCC rules NOT apply to the operation of an amateur station?

A. When operating a RACES station
B. When operating under special FEMA rules
C. When operating under special ARES rules
D. FCC rules always apply

T2C02 (New Question for the 2022-2026 Pool)
Which of the following are typical duties of a Net Control Station?

A. Choose the regular net meeting time and frequency
B. Ensure that all stations checking into the net are properly licensed for operation on the net frequency
C. Call the net to order and direct communications between stations checking in
D. All these choices are correct

T2C03 (New Question for the 2022-2026 Pool)
What technique is used to ensure that voice messages containing unusual words are received correctly?

A. Send the words by voice and Morse code
B. Speak very loudly into the microphone
C. Spell the words using a standard phonetic alphabet
D. All these choices are correct

T2C04 (New Question for the 2022-2026 Pool)
What is RACES?

A. An emergency organization combining amateur radio and citizens band operators and frequencies
B. An international radio experimentation society
C. A radio contest held in a short period, sometimes called a "sprint"
D. An FCC part 97 amateur radio service for civil defense communications during national emergencies

T2C05
What does the term "traffic" refer to in net operation?

A. Messages exchanged by net stations
B. The number of stations checking in and out of a net
C. Operation by mobile or portable stations
D. Requests to activate the net by a served agency

T2C06 (New Question for the 2022-2026 Pool)
What is the Amateur Radio Emergency Service (ARES)?

A. A group of licensed amateurs who have voluntarily registered their qualifications and equipment for communications duty in the public service
B. A group of licensed amateurs who are members of the military and who voluntarily agreed to provide message handling services in the case of an emergency
C. A training program that provides licensing courses for those interested in obtaining an amateur license to use during emergencies
D. A training program that certifies amateur operators for membership in the Radio Amateur Civil Emergency Service

T2C07 (New Question for the 2022-2026 Pool)
Which of the following is standard practice when you participate in a net?

A. When first responding to the net control station, transmit your call sign, name, and address as in the FCC database
B. Record the time of each of your transmissions
C. Unless you are reporting an emergency, transmit only when directed by the net control station
D. All these choices are correct

T2C08
Which of the following is a characteristic of good traffic handling?

A. Passing messages exactly as received
B. Making decisions as to whether messages are worthy of relay or delivery
C. Ensuring that any newsworthy messages are relayed to the news media
D. All these choices are correct

T2C09
Are amateur station control operators ever permitted to operate outside the frequency privileges of their license class?

A. No
B. Yes, but only when part of a FEMA emergency plan
C. Yes, but only when part of a RACES emergency plan
D. Yes, but only in situations involving the immediate safety of human life or protection of property

T2C10
What information is contained in the preamble of a formal traffic message?

A. The email address of the originating station
B. The address of the intended recipient
C. The telephone number of the addressee
D. Information needed to track the message

T2C11 (Modified Question from the 2018-2022 Pool)
What is meant by "check" in a radiogram header?

A. The number of words or word equivalents in the text portion of the message
B. The call sign of the originating station
C. A list of stations that have relayed the message
D. A box on the message form that indicates that the message was received and/or relayed

T3A01 (New Question for the 2022-2026 Pool)
Why do VHF signal strengths sometimes vary greatly when the antenna is moved only a few feet?

A. The signal path encounters different concentrations of water vapor
B. VHF ionospheric propagation is very sensitive to path length
C. Multipath propagation cancels or reinforces signals
D. All these choices are correct

T3A02 (New Question for the 2022-2026 Pool)
What is the effect of vegetation on UHF and microwave signals?

A. Knife-edge diffraction
B. Absorption
C. Amplification
D. Polarization rotation

T3A03
What antenna polarization is normally used for long-distance CW and SSB contacts on the VHF and UHF bands?

A. Right-hand circular
B. Left-hand circular
C. Horizontal
D. Horizontal

T3A04 (Modified Question from the 2018-2022 Pool)
What happens when antennas at opposite ends of a VHF or UHF line of sight radio link are not using the same polarization?

A. The modulation sidebands might become inverted
B. Received signal strength is reduced
C. Signals have an echo effect
D. Nothing significant will happen

T3A05
When using a directional antenna, how might your station be able to communicate with a distant repeater if buildings or obstructions are blocking the direct line of sight path?

A. Change from vertical to horizontal polarization
B. Try to find a path that reflects signals to the repeater
C. Try the long path
D. Increase the antenna SW

T3A06 (New Question for the 2022-2026 Pool)
What is the meaning of the term "picket fencing"?

A. Alternating transmissions during a net operation
B. Rapid flutter on mobile signals due to multipath propagation
C. A type of ground system used with vertical antennas
D. Local vs long-distance communications

T3A07 (New Question for the 2022-2026 Pool)
What weather condition might decrease range at microwave frequencies?

A. High winds
B. Low barometric pressure
C. Precipitation
D. Colder temperatures

T3A08
What is a likely cause of irregular fading of signals propagated by the ionosphere?

A. Frequency shift due to Faraday rotation
B. Interference from thunderstorms
C. Intermodulation distortion
D. Random combining of signals arriving via different paths

T3A09
Which of the following results from the fact that signals propagated by the ionosphere are elliptically polarized?

A. Digital modes are unusable
B. Either vertically or horizontally polarized antennas may be used for transmission or reception
C. FM voice is unusable
D. Both the transmitting and receiving antennas must be of the same polarization

T3A10 (Modified Question from the 2018-2022 Pool)
What effect does multi-path propagation have on data transmissions?

A. Transmission rates must be increased by a factor equal to the number of separate paths observed
B. Transmission rates must be decreased by a factor equal to the number of separate paths observed
C. No significant changes will occur if the signals are transmitted using FM
D. Error rates are likely to increase

T3A11 (Modified Question from the 2018-2022 Pool)
Which region of the atmosphere can refract or bend HF and VHF radio waves?

A. The stratosphere
B. The troposphere
C. The ionosphere
D. The mesosphere

T3A12 (Modified Question from the 2018-2022 Pool)
What is the effect of fog and rain on signals in the 10 meter and 6 meter bands?

A. Absorption
B. There is little effect
C. Deflection
D. Range increase

T3B01 (New Question for the 2022-2026 Pool)
What is the relationship between the electric and magnetic fields of an electromagnetic wave?

A. They travel at different speeds
B. They are in parallel
C. They revolve in opposite directions
D. They are at right angles

T3B02
What property of a radio wave defines its polarization?

A. The orientation of the electric field
B. The orientation of the magnetic field
C. The ratio of the energy in the magnetic field to the energy in the electric field
D. The ratio of the velocity to the wavelength

T3B03
What are the two components of a radio wave?

A. Impedance and reactance
B. Voltage and current
C. Electric and magnetic fields
D. Ionizing and non-ionizing radiation

T3B04 (Modified Question from the 2018-2022 Pool)
What is the velocity of a radio wave traveling through free space?

A. Speed of light
B. Speed of sound
C. Speed inversely proportional to its wavelength
D. Speed that increases as the frequency increases

T3B05
What is the relationship between wavelength and frequency?

A. Wavelength gets longer as frequency increases
B. Wavelength gets shorter as frequency increases
C. Wavelength and frequency are unrelated
D. Wavelength and frequency increase as path length increases

T3B06
What is the formula for converting frequency to approximate wavelength in meters?

A. Wavelength in meters equals frequency in hertz multiplied by 300
B. Wavelength in meters equals frequency in hertz divided by 300
C. Wavelength in meters equals frequency in megahertz divided by 300
D. Wavelength in meters equals 300 divided by frequency in megahertz

T3B07 (Modified Question from the 2018-2022 Pool)
In addition to frequency, which of the following is used to identify amateur radio bands?

A. The approximate wavelength in meters
B. Traditional letter/number designators
C. Channel numbers
D. All these choices are correct

T3B08
What frequency range is referred to as VHF?

A. 30 kHz to 300 kHz
B. 30 MHz to 300 MHz
C. 300 kHz to 3000 kHz
D. 300 MHz to 3000 MHz

T3B09
What frequency range is referred to as UHF?

A. 30 to 300 kHz
B. 30 to 300 MHz
C. 300 to 3000 kHz
D. 300 to 3000 MHz

T3B10
What frequency range is referred to as HF?

A. 300 to 3000 MHz
B. 30 to 300 MHz
C. 3 to 30 MHz
D. 300 to 3000 kHz

T3B11
What is the approximate velocity of a radio wave in free space?

A. 150,000 meters per second
B. 300,000,000 meters per second
C. 300,000,000 miles per hour
D. 150,000 miles per hour

T3C01 (Modified Question from the 2018-2022 Pool)
Why are simplex UHF signals rarely heard beyond their radio horizon?

A. They are too weak to go very far
B. FCC regulations prohibit them from going more than 50 miles
C. UHF signals are usually not propagated by the ionosphere
D. UHF signals are absorbed by the ionospheric D region

T3C02 (Modified Question from the 2018-2022 Pool)
What is a characteristic of HF communication compared with communications on VHF and higher frequencies?

A. HF antennas are generally smaller
B. HF accommodates wider bandwidth signals
C. Long-distance ionospheric propagation is far more common on HF
D. There is less atmospheric interference (static) on HF

T3C03 (Modified Question from the 2018-2022 Pool)
What is a characteristic of VHF signals received via auroral backscatter?

A. They are often received from 10,000 miles or more
B. They are distorted and signal strength varies considerably
C. They occur only during winter nighttime hours
D. They are generally strongest when your antenna is aimed west

T3C04
Which of the following types of propagation is most commonly associated with occasional strong signals on the 10, 6, and 2 meter bands from beyond the radio horizon?

A. Backscatter
B. Sporadic E
C. D region absorption
D. Gray-line propagation

T3C05
Which of the following effects may allow radio signals to travel beyond obstructions between the transmitting and receiving stations?

A. Knife-edge diffraction
B. Faraday rotation
C. Quantum tunneling
D. Doppler shift

T3C06 (Modified Question from the 2018-2022 Pool)
What type of propagation is responsible for allowing over-the-horizon VHF and UHF communications to ranges of approximately 300 miles on a regular basis?

A. Tropospheric ducting
B. D region refraction
C. F2 region refraction
D. Faraday rotation

T3C07
What band is best suited for communicating via meteor scatter?

A. 33 centimeters
B. 6 meters
C. 2 meters
D. 70 centimeters

T3C08
What causes tropospheric ducting?

A. Discharges of lightning during electrical storms
B. Sunspots and solar flares
C. Updrafts from hurricanes and tornadoes
D. Temperature inversions in the atmosphere

T3C09
What is generally the best time for long-distance 10 meter band propagation via the F region?

A. From dawn to shortly after sunset during periods of high sunspot activity
B. From shortly after sunset to dawn during periods of high sunspot activity
C. From dawn to shortly after sunset during periods of low sunspot activity
D. From shortly after sunset to dawn during periods of low sunspot activity

T3C10
Which of the following bands may provide long-distance communications via the ionosphere's F region during the peak of the sunspot cycle?

A. 6 and 10 meters
B. 23 centimeters
C. 70 centimeters and 1.25 meters
D. All these choices are correct

T3C11 (New Question for the 2022-2026 Pool)
Why is the radio horizon for VHF and UHF signals more distant than the visual horizon?

A. Radio signals move somewhat faster than the speed of light
B. Radio waves are not blocked by dust particles
C. The atmosphere refracts radio waves slightly
D. Radio waves are blocked by dust particles

T4A01 (New Question for the 2022-2026 Pool)
Which of the following is an appropriate power supply rating for a typical 50 watt output mobile FM transceiver?

A. 24.0 volts at 4 amperes
B. 13.8 volts at 4 amperes
C. 24.0 volts at 12 amperes
D. 13.8 volts at 12 amperes

T4A02 (New Question for the 2022-2026 Pool)
Which of the following should be considered when selecting an accessory SWR meter?

A. The frequency and power level at which the measurements will be made
B. The distance that the meter will be located from the antenna
C. The types of modulation being used at the station
D. All these choices are correct

T4A03 (New Question for the 2022-2026 Pool)
Why are short, heavy-gauge wires used for a transceiver's DC power connection?

A. To minimize voltage drop when transmitting
B. To provide a good counterpoise for the antenna
C. To avoid RF interference
D. All these choices are correct

T4A04 (New Question for the 2022-2026 Pool)
How are the transceiver audio input and output connected in a station configured to operate using FT8?

A. To a computer running a terminal program and connected to a terminal node controller unit
B. To the audio input and output of a computer running WSJT-X software
C. To an FT8 conversion unit, a keyboard, and a computer monitor
D. To a computer connected to the FT8converter.com website

T4A05 (New Question for the 2022-2026 Pool)
Where should an RF power meter be installed?

A. In the feed line, between the transmitter and antenna
B. At the power supply output
C. In parallel with the push-to-talk line and the antenna
D. In the power supply cable, as close as possible to the radio

T4A06 (New Question for the 2022-2026 Pool)
What signals are used in a computer-radio interface for digital mode operation?

A. Receive and transmit mode, status, and location
B. Antenna and RF power
C. Receive audio, transmit audio, and transmitter keying
D. NMEA GPS location and DC power

T4A07 (New Question for the 2022-2026 Pool)
Which of the following connections is made between a computer and a transceiver to use computer software when operating digital modes?

A. Computer "line out" to transceiver push-to-talk
B. Computer "line in" to transceiver push-to-talk
C. Computer "line in" to transceiver speaker connector
D. Computer "line out" to transceiver speaker connector

T4A08
Which of the following conductors is preferred for bonding at RF?

A. Copper braid removed from coaxial cable
B. Steel wire
C. Twisted-pair cable
D. Flat copper strap

T4A09 (New Question for the 2022-2026 Pool)
How can you determine the length of time that equipment can be powered from a battery?

A. Divide the watt-hour rating of the battery by the peak power consumption of the equipment
B. Divide the battery ampere-hour rating by the average current draw of the equipment
C. Multiply the watts per hour consumed by the equipment by the battery power rating
D. Multiply the square of the current rating of the battery by the input resistance of the equipment

T4A10 (New Question for the 2022-2026 Pool)
What function is performed with a transceiver and a digital mode hot spot?

A. Communication using digital voice or data systems via the internet
B. FT8 digital communications via AFSK
C. RTTY encoding and decoding without a computer
D. High-speed digital communications for meteor scatter

T4A11 (Modified Question from the 2018-2022 Pool)
Where should the negative power return of a mobile transceiver be connected in a vehicle?

A. At the 12 volt battery chassis ground
B. At the antenna mount
C. To any metal part of the vehicle
D. Through the transceiver's mounting bracket

T4A12 (New Question for the 2022-2026 Pool)
What is an electronic keyer?

A. A device for switching antennas from transmit to receive
B. A device for voice activated switching from receive to transmit
C. A device that assists in manual sending of Morse code
D. An interlock to prevent unauthorized use of a radio

T4B01 (Modified Question from the 2018-2022 Pool)
What is the effect of excessive microphone gain on SSB transmissions?

A. Frequency instability
B. Distorted transmitted audio
C. Increased SWR
D. All these choices are correct

T4B02
Which of the following can be used to enter a transceiver's operating frequency?

A. The keypad or VFO knob
B. The CTCSS or DTMF encoder
C. The Automatic Frequency Control
D. All these choices are correct

T4B03 (New Question for the 2022-2026 Pool)
How is squelch adjusted so that a weak FM signal can be heard?

A. Set the squelch threshold so that receiver output audio is on all the time
B. Turn up the audio level until it overcomes the squelch threshold
C. Turn on the anti-squelch function
D. Enable squelch enhancement

T4B04
What is a way to enable quick access to a favorite frequency or channel on your transceiver?

A. Enable the frequency offset
B. Store it in a memory channel
C. Enable the VOX
D. Use the scan mode to select the desired frequency

T4B05 (New Question for the 2022-2026 Pool)
What does the scanning function of an FM transceiver do?

A. Checks incoming signal deviation
B. Prevents interference to nearby repeaters
C. Tunes through a range of frequencies to check for activity
D. Checks for messages left on a digital bulletin board

T4B06
Which of the following controls could be used if the voice pitch of a single-sideband signal returning to your CQ call seems too high or low?

A. The AGC or limiter
B. The bandwidth selection
C. The tone squelch
D. The RIT or Clarifier

T4B07 (New Question for the 2022-2026 Pool)
What does a DMR "code plug" contain?

A. Your call sign in CW for automatic identification
B. Access information for repeaters and talkgroups
C. The codec for digitizing audio
D. The DMR software version

T4B08
What is the advantage of having multiple receive bandwidth choices on a multimode transceiver?

A. Permits monitoring several modes at once by selecting a separate filter for each mode
B. Permits noise or interference reduction by selecting a bandwidth matching the mode
C. Increases the number of frequencies that can be stored in memory
D. Increases the amount of offset between receive and transmit frequencies

T4B09 (New Question for the 2022-2026 Pool)
How is a specific group of stations selected on a digital voice transceiver?

A. By retrieving the frequencies from transceiver memory
B. By enabling the group's CTCSS tone
C. By entering the group's identification code
D. By activating automatic identification

T4B10
Which of the following receiver filter bandwidths provides the best signal-to-noise ratio for SSB reception?

A. 500 Hz
B. 1000 Hz
C. 2400 Hz
D. 5000 Hz

T4B11 (New Question for the 2022-2026 Pool)
Which of the following must be programmed into a D-STAR digital transceiver before transmitting?

A. Your call sign in CW for automatic identification
B. Your output power
C. The codec type being used
D. All these choices are correct

T4B12 (New Question for the 2022-2026 Pool)
What is the result of tuning an FM receiver above or below a signal's frequency?

A. Change in audio pitch
B. Sideband inversion
C. Generation of a heterodyne tone
D. Distortion of the signal's audio

T5A01
Electrical current is measured in which of the following units?

A. Volts
B. Watts
C. Ohms
D. Amperes

T5A02
Electrical power is measured in which of the following units?

A. Volts
B. Watts
C. Watt-hours
D. Amperes

T5A03
What is the name for the flow of electrons in an electric circuit?

A. Voltage
B. Resistance
C. Capacitance
D. Current

T5A04 (New Question for the 2022-2026 Pool)
What are the units of electrical resistance?

A. Siemens
B. Mhos
C. Ohms
D. Coulombs

T5A05 (Modified Question from the 2018-2022 Pool)
What is the electrical term for the force that causes electron flow?

A. Voltage
B. Ampere-hours
C. Capacitance
D. Inductance

T5A06 (New Question for the 2022-2026 Pool)
What is the unit of frequency?

A. Hertz
B. Henry
C. Farad
D. Tesla

T5A07 (New Question for the 2022-2026 Pool)
Why are metals generally good conductors of electricity?

A. They have relatively high density
B. They have many free electrons
C. They have many free protons
D. All these choices are correct

T5A08
Which of the following is a good electrical insulator?

A. Copper
B. Glass
C. Aluminum
D. Mercury

T5A09 (New Question for the 2022-2026 Pool)
Which of the following describes alternating current?

A. Current that alternates between a positive direction and zero
B. Current that alternates between a negative direction and zero
C. Current that alternates between positive and negative directions
D. All these answers are correct

T5A10
Which term describes the rate at which electrical energy is used?

A. Resistance
B. Current
C. Power
D. Voltage

T5A11 (New Question for the 2022-2026 Pool)
What type of current flow is opposed by resistance?

A. Direct current
B. Alternating current
C. RF Current
D. All of these choices are correct

T5A12
What describes the number of times per second that an alternating current makes a complete cycle?

A. Pulse rate
B. Speed
C. Wavelength
D. Frequency

T5B01
How many milliamperes is 1.5 amperes?

A. 15 milliamperes
B. 150 milliamperes
C. 1500 milliamperes
D. 15,000 milliamperes

T5B02 (Modified Question from the 2018-2022 Pool)
Which is equal to 1,500,000 hertz?

A. 1500 kHz
B. 1500 MHz
C. 15 GHz
D. 150 kHz

T5B03
Which is equal to one kilovolt?

A. One one-thousandth of a volt
B. One hundred volts
C. One thousand volts
D. One million volts

T5B04
Which is equal to one microvolt?

A. One one-millionth of a volt
B. One million volts
C. One thousand kilovolts
D. One one-thousandth of a volt

T5B05
Which is equal to 500 milliwatts?

A. 0.02 watts
B. 0.5 watts
C. 5 watts
D. 50 watts

T5B06 (Modified Question from the 2018-2022 Pool)
Which is equal to 3000 milliamperes?

A. 0.003 amperes
B. 0.3 amperes
C. 3,000,000 amperes
D. 3 amperes

T5B07 (Modified Question from the 2018-2022 Pool)
Which is equal to 3.525 MHz?

A. 0.003525 kHz
B. 35.25 kHz
C. 3525 kHz
D. 3,525,000 kHz

T5B08 (Modified Question from the 2018-2022 Pool)
Which is equal to 1,000,000 picofarads?

A. 0.001 microfarads
B. 1 microfarad
C. 1000 microfarads
D. 1,000,000,000 microfarads

T5B09
Which decibel value most closely represents a power increase from 5 watts to 10 watts?

A. 2 dB
B. 3 dB
C. 5 dB
D. 10 dB

T5B10
Which decibel value most closely represents a power decrease from 12 watts to 3 watts?

A. -1 dB
B. -3 dB
C. -6 dB
D. -9 dB

T5B11
Which decibel value represents a power increase from 20 watts to 200 watts?

A. 10 dB
B. 12 dB
C. 18 dB
D. 28 dB

T5B12
Which is equal to 28400 kHz?

A. 28.400 kHz
B. 2.800 MHz
C. 284.00 MHz
D. 28.400 MHz

T5B13 (Modified Question from the 2018-2022 Pool)
Which is equal to 2425 MHz?

A. 0.002425 GHz
B. 24.25 GHz
C. 2.425 GHz
D. 2425 GHz

T5C01

What describes the ability to store energy in an electric field?

A. Inductance
B. Resistance
C. Tolerance
D. Capacitance

T5C02

What is the unit of capacitance?

A. The farad
B. The ohm
C. The volt
D. The henry

T5C03

What describes the ability to store energy in a magnetic field?

A. Admittance
B. Capacitance
C. Resistance
D. Inductance

T5C04

What is the unit of inductance?

A. The coulomb
B. The farad
C. The henry
D. The ohm

T5C05
What is the unit of impedance?

A. The volt
B. The ampere
C. The coulomb
D. The ohm

T5C06
What does the abbreviation "RF" mean?

A. Radio frequency signals of all types
B. The resonant frequency of a tuned circuit
C. The real frequency transmitted as opposed to the apparent frequency
D. Reflective force in antenna transmission lines

T5C07 (New Question for the 2022-2026 Pool)
What is the abbreviation for megahertz?

A. MH
B. mh
C. Mhz
D. MHz

T5C08 (Modified Question from the 2018-2022 Pool)
What is the formula used to calculate electrical power (P) in a DC circuit?

A. $P = E \times I$
B. $P = E / I$
C. $P = E - I$
D. $P = E + I$

T5C09
How much power is delivered by a voltage of 13.8 volts DC and a current of 10 amperes?

A. 138 watts
B. 0.7 watts
C. 23.8 watts
D. 3.8 watts

T5C10
How much power is delivered by a voltage of 12 volts DC and a current of 2.5 amperes?

A. 4.8 watts
B. 30 watts
C. 14.5 watts
D. 0.208 watts

T5C11 (Modified Question from the 2018-2022 Pool)
How much current is required to deliver 120 watts at a voltage of 12 volts DC?

A. 0.1 amperes
B. 10 amperes
C. 12 amperes
D. 132 amperes

T5C12 (Modified Question from the 2018-2022 Pool)
What is impedance?

A. The opposition to AC current flow
B. The inverse of resistance
C. The Q or Quality Factor of a component
D. The power handling capability of a component

T5C13 (Modified Question from the 2018-2022 Pool)
What is the abbreviation for kilohertz?

A. KHZ
B. khz
C. khZ
D. kHz

T5D01 (Modified Question from the 2018-2022 Pool)
What formula is used to calculate current in a circuit?

A. I = E x R
B. I = E / R
C. I = E + R
D. I = E − R

T5D02 (Modified Question from the 2018-2022 Pool)
What formula is used to calculate voltage in a circuit?

A. E= I x R
B. E= I / R
C. E= I + R
D. E = I − R

T5D03 (Modified Question from the 2018-2022 Pool)
What formula is used to calculate resistance in a circuit?

A. R = E x I
B. R = E / I
C. R = E + I
D. R = E − I

T5D04
What is the resistance of a circuit in which a current of 3 amperes flows when connected to 90 volts?

A. 3 ohms
B. 30 ohms
C. 93 ohms
D. 270 ohms

T5D05
What is the resistance of a circuit for which the applied voltage is 12 volts and the current flow is 1.5 amperes?

A. 18 ohms
B. 0.125 ohms
C. 8 ohms
D. 13.5 ohms

T5D06
What is the resistance of a circuit that draws 4 amperes from a 12-volt source?

A. 3 ohms
B. 16 ohms
C. 48 ohms
D. 8 ohms

T5D07
What is the current in a circuit with an applied voltage of 120 volts and a resistance of 80 ohms?

A. 9600 amperes
B. 200 amperes
C. 0.667 amperes
D. 1.5 amperes

T5D08
What is the current through a 100-ohm resistor connected across 200 volts?

A. 20,000 amperes
B. 0.5 amperes
C. 2 amperes
D. 100 amperes

T5D09
What is the current through a 24-ohm resistor connected across 240 volts?

A. 24,000 amperes
B. 0.1 amperes
C. 10 amperes
D. 216 amperes

T5D10
What is the voltage across a 2-ohm resistor if a current of 0.5 amperes flows through it?

A. 1 volt
B. 0.25 volts
C. 2.5 volts
D. 1.5 volts

T5D11
What is the voltage across a 10-ohm resistor if a current of 1 ampere flows through it?

A. 1 volt
B. 10 volts
C. 11 volts
D. 9 volts

T5D12
What is the voltage across a 10-ohm resistor if a current of 2 amperes flows through it?

A. 8 volts
B. 0.2 volts
C. 12 volts
D. 20 volts

T5D13 (New Question for the 2022-2026 Pool)
In which type of circuit is DC current the same through all components?

A. Series
B. Parallel
C. Resonant
D. Branch

T5D14 (New Question for the 2022-2026 Pool)
In which type of circuit is voltage the same across all components?

A. Series
B. Parallel
C. Resonant
D. Branch

T6A01
What electrical component opposes the flow of current in a DC circuit?

A. Inductor
B. Resistor
C. Inverter
D. Transformer

T6A02
What type of component is often used as an adjustable volume control?

A. Fixed resistor
B. Power resistor
C. Potentiometer
D. Transformer

T6A03
What electrical parameter is controlled by a potentiometer?

A. Inductance
B. Resistance
C. Capacitance
D. Field strength

T6A04
What electrical component stores energy in an electric field?

A. Varistor
B. Capacitor
C. Inductor
D. Diode

T6A05
What type of electrical component consists of conductive surfaces separated by an insulator?

A. Resistor
B. Potentiometer
C. Oscillator
D. Capacitor

T6A06
What type of electrical component stores energy in a magnetic field?

A. Varistor
B. Capacitor
C. Inductor
D. Diode

T6A07
What electrical component is typically constructed as a coil of wire?

A. Switch
B. Capacitor
C. Diode
D. Inductor

T6A08 (New Question for the 2022-2026 Pool)
What is the function of an SPDT switch?

A. A single circuit is opened or closed
B. Two circuits are opened or closed
C. A single circuit is switched between one of two other circuits
D. Two circuits are each switched between one of two other circuits

T6A09
What electrical component is used to protect other circuit components from current overloads?

A. Fuse
B. Thyratron
C. Varactor
D. All these choices are correct

T6A10
Which of the following battery chemistries is rechargeable?

A. Nickel-metal hydride
B. Lithium-ion
C. Lead-acid
D. All these choices are correct

T6A11
Which of the following battery chemistries is not rechargeable?

A. Nickel-cadmium
B. Carbon-zinc
C. Lead-acid
D. Lithium-ion

T6A12 (New Question for the 2022-2026 Pool)
What type of switch is represented by component 3 in figure T-2?

A. Single-pole single-throw
B. Single-pole double-throw
C. Double-pole single-throw
D. Double-pole double-throw

T6B01 (New Question for the 2022-2026 Pool)
Which is true about forward voltage drop in a diode?

A. It is lower in some diode types than in others
B. It is proportional to peak inverse voltage
C. It indicates that the diode is defective
D. It has no impact on the voltage delivered to the load

T6B02
What electronic component allows current to flow in only one direction?

A. Resistor
B. Fuse
C. Diode
D. Driven element

T6B03 (Modified Question from the 2018-2022 Pool)
Which of these components can be used as an electronic switch?

A. Varistor
B. Potentiometer
C. Transistor
D. Thermistor

T6B04
Which of the following components can consist of three regions of semiconductor material?

A. Alternator
B. Transistor
C. Triode
D. Pentagrid converter

T6B05 (New Question for the 2022-2026 Pool)
What type of transistor has a gate, drain, and source?

A. Varistor
B. Field-effect
C. Tesla-effect
D. Bipolar junction

T6B06
How is the cathode lead of a semiconductor diode often marked on the package?

A. With the word "cathode"
B. With a stripe
C. With the letter C
D. With the letter K

T6B07 (New Question for the 2022-2026 Pool)
What causes a light-emitting diode (LED) to emit light?

A. Forward current
B. Reverse current
C. Capacitively-coupled RF signal
D. Inductively-coupled RF signal

T6B08
What does the abbreviation FET stand for?

A. Frequency Emission Transmitter
B. Fast Electron Transistor
C. Free Electron Transmitter
D. Field Effect Transistor

T6B09
What are the names for the electrodes of a diode?

A. Plus and minus
B. Source and drain
C. Anode and cathode
D. Gate and base

T6B10 (Modified Question from the 2018-2022 Pool)
Which of the following can provide power gain?

A. Transformer
B. Transistor
C. Reactor
D. Resistor

T6B11
What is the term that describes a device's ability to amplify a signal?

A. Gain
B. Forward resistance
C. Forward voltage drop
D. On resistance

T6B12 (New Question for the 2022-2026 Pool)
What are the names of the electrodes of a bipolar junction transistor?

A. Signal, bias, power
B. Emitter, base, collector
C. Input, output, supply
D. Pole one, pole two, output

T6C01
What is the name of an electrical wiring diagram that uses standard component symbols?

A. Bill of materials
B. Connector pinout
C. Schematic
D. Flow chart

DIAGRAM QUESTIONS – FIGURE T-1
Use the following diagram for questions T6C02 thru T6C05 on the upcoming page.

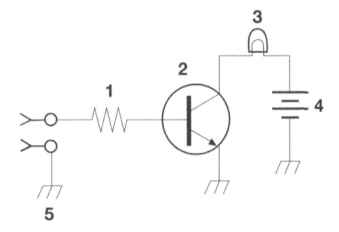

Figure T-1

T6C02
What is component 1 in figure T-1?

A. Resistor
B. Transistor
C. Battery
D. Connector

T6C03
What is component 2 in figure T-1?

A. Resistor
B. Transistor
C. Indicator lamp
D. Connector

T6C04
What is component 3 in figure T-1?

A. Resistor
B. Transistor
C. Lamp
D. Ground Symbol

T6C05
What is component 4 in figure T-1?

A. Resistor
B. Transistor
C. Ground Symbol
D. Battery

DIAGRAM QUESTIONS – FIGURE T-2
Use the following diagram for questions T6C06 thru T6C09 below.

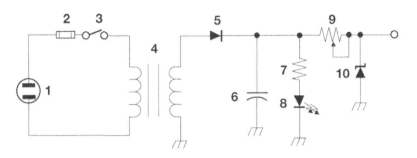

Figure T-2

T6C06
What is component 6 in figure T-2?

A. Resistor
B. Capacitor
C. Regulator IC
D. Transistor

T6C07
What is component 8 in figure T-2?

A. Resistor
B. Inductor
C. Regulator IC
D. Light emitting diode

T6C08
What is component 9 in figure T-2?

A. Variable capacitor
B. Variable inductor
C. Variable resistor
D. Variable transformer

T6C09
What is component 4 in figure T-2?

A. Variable inductor
B. Double-pole switch
C. Potentiometer
D. Transformer

DIAGRAM QUESTIONS – FIGURE T-3
Use the following diagram for questions T6C10 thru T6C11 below.

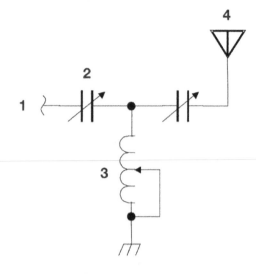

Figure T-3

T6C10
What is component 3 in figure T-3?

A. Connector
B. Meter
C. Variable capacitor
D. Variable inductor

T6C11
What is component 4 in figure T-3?

A. Antenna
B. Transmitter
C. Dummy load
D. Ground

T6C12 (New Question for the 2022-2026 Pool)
Which of the following is accurately represented in electrical schematics?

A. Wire lengths
B. Physical appearance of components
C. Component connections
D. All these choices are correct

T6D01
Which of the following devices or circuits changes an alternating current into a varying direct current signal?

A. Transformer
B. Rectifier
C. Amplifier
D. Reflector

T6D02
What is a relay?

A. An electrically-controlled switch
B. A current controlled amplifier
C. An inverting amplifier
D. A pass transistor

T6D03 (New Question for the 2022-2026 Pool)
Which of the following is a reason to use shielded wire?

A. To decrease the resistance of DC power connections
B. To increase the current carrying capability of the wire
C. To prevent coupling of unwanted signals to or from the wire
D. To couple the wire to other signals

T6D04
Which of the following displays an electrical quantity as a numeric value?

A. Potentiometer
B. Transistor
C. Meter
D. Relay

T6D05
What type of circuit controls the amount of voltage from a power supply?

A. Regulator
B. Oscillator
C. Filter
D. Phase inverter

T6D06 (Modified Question from the 2018-2022 Pool)
What component changes 120 V AC power to a lower AC voltage for other uses?

A. Variable capacitor
B. Transformer
C. Transistor
D. Diode

T6D07
Which of the following is commonly used as a visual indicator?

A. LED
B. FET
C. Zener diode
D. Bipolar transistor

T6D08
Which of the following is combined with an inductor to make a resonant circuit?

A. Resistor
B. Zener diode
C. Potentiometer
D. Capacitor

T6D09
What is the name of a device that combines several semiconductors and other components into one package?

A. Transducer
B. Multi-pole relay
C. Integrated circuit
D. Transformer

T6D10
What is the function of component 2 in figure T-1?

A. Give off light when current flows through it
B. Supply electrical energy
C. Control the flow of current
D. Convert electrical energy into radio waves

T6D11 (Modified Question from the 2018-2022 Pool)
Which of the following is a resonant or tuned circuit?

A. An inductor and a capacitor in series or parallel
B. A linear voltage regulator
C. A resistor circuit used for reducing standing wave ratio
D. A circuit designed to provide high-fidelity audio

T7A01
Which term describes the ability of a receiver to detect the presence of a signal?

A. Linearity
B. Sensitivity
C. Selectivity
D. Total Harmonic Distortion

T7A02 (Modified Question from the 2018-2022 Pool)
What is a transceiver?

A. A device that combines a receiver and transmitter
B. A device for matching feed line impedance to 50 ohms
C. A device for automatically sending and decoding Morse code
D. A device for converting receiver and transmitter frequencies to another band

T7A03
Which of the following is used to convert a signal from one frequency to another?

A. Phase splitter
B. Mixer
C. Inverter
D. Amplifier

T7A04
Which term describes the ability of a receiver to discriminate between multiple signals?

A. Discrimination ratio
B. Sensitivity
C. Selectivity
D. Harmonic distortion

T7A05
What is the name of a circuit that generates a signal at a specific frequency?

A. Reactance modulator
B. Phase modulator
C. Low-pass filter
D. Oscillator

T7A06
What device converts the RF input and output of a transceiver to another band?

A. High-pass filter
B. Low-pass filter
C. Transverter
D. Phase converter

T7A07 (Modified Question from the 2018-2022 Pool)
What is the function of a transceiver's PTT input?

A. Input for a key used to send CW
B. Switches transceiver from receive to transmit when grounded
C. Provides a transmit tuning tone when grounded
D. Input for a preamplifier tuning tone

T7A08
Which of the following describes combining speech with an RF carrier signal?

A. Impedance matching
B. Oscillation
C. Modulation
D. Low-pass filtering

T7A09
What is the function of the SSB/CW-FM switch on a VHF power amplifier?

A. Change the mode of the transmitted signal
B. Set the amplifier for proper operation in the selected mode
C. Change the frequency range of the amplifier to operate in the proper segment of the band
D. Reduce the received signal noise

T7A10 (Modified Question from the 2018-2022 Pool)
What device increases the transmitted output power from a transceiver?

A. A voltage divider
B. An RF power amplifier
C. An impedance network
D. All these choices are correct

T7A11

Where is an RF preamplifier installed?

A. Between the antenna and receiver
B. At the output of the transmitter power amplifier
C. Between the transmitter and the antenna tuner
D. At the output of the receiver audio amplifier

T7B01

What can you do if you are told your FM handheld or mobile transceiver is over-deviating?

A. Talk louder into the microphone
B. Let the transceiver cool off
C. Change to a higher power level
D. Talk farther away from the microphone

T7B02
What would cause a broadcast AM or FM radio to receive an amateur radio transmission unintentionally?

A. The receiver is unable to reject strong signals outside the AM or FM band
B. The microphone gain of the transmitter is turned up too high
C. The audio amplifier of the transmitter is overloaded
D. The deviation of an FM transmitter is set too low

T7B03
Which of the following can cause radio frequency interference?

A. Fundamental overload
B. Harmonics
C. Spurious emissions
D. All these choices are correct

T7B04 (New Question for the 2022-2026 Pool)
Which of the following could you use to cure distorted audio caused by RF current on the shield of a microphone cable?

A. Band-pass filter
B. Low-pass filter
C. Preamplifier
D. Ferrite choke

T7B05
How can fundamental overload of a non-amateur radio or TV receiver by an amateur signal be reduced or eliminated?

A. Block the amateur signal with a filter at the antenna input of the affected receiver
B. Block the interfering signal with a filter on the amateur transmitter
C. Switch the transmitter from FM to SSB
D. Switch the transmitter to a narrow-band mode

T7B06
Which of the following actions should you take if a neighbor tells you that your station's transmissions are interfering with their radio or TV reception?

A. Make sure that your station is functioning properly and that it does not cause interference to your own radio or television when it is tuned to the same channel
B. Immediately turn off your transmitter and contact the nearest FCC office for assistance
C. Install a harmonic doubler on the output of your transmitter and tune it until the interference is eliminated
D. All these choices are correct

T7B07
Which of the following can reduce overload of a VHF transceiver by a nearby commercial FM station?

A. Installing an RF preamplifier
B. Using double-shielded coaxial cable
C. Installing bypass capacitors on the microphone cable
D. Installing a band-reject filter

T7B08
What should you do if something in a neighbor's home is causing harmful interference to your amateur station?

A. Work with your neighbor to identify the offending device
B. Politely inform your neighbor that FCC rules prohibit the use of devices that cause interference
C. Make sure your station meets the standards of good amateur practice
D. All these choices are correct

T7B09 (New Question for the 2022-2026 Pool)
What should be the first step to resolve non-fiber optic cable TV interference caused by your amateur radio transmission?

A. Add a low-pass filter to the TV antenna input
B. Add a high-pass filter to the TV antenna input
C. Add a preamplifier to the TV antenna input
D. Be sure all TV feed line coaxial connectors are installed properly

T7B10
What might be a problem if you receive a report that your audio signal through an FM repeater is distorted or unintelligible?

A. Your transmitter is slightly off frequency
B. Your batteries are running low
C. You are in a bad location
D. All these choices are correct

T7B11
What is a symptom of RF feedback in a transmitter or transceiver?

A. Excessive SWR at the antenna connection
B. The transmitter will not stay on the desired frequency
C. Reports of garbled, distorted, or unintelligible voice transmissions
D. Frequent blowing of power supply fuses

T7C01
What is the primary purpose of a dummy load?

A. To prevent transmitting signals over the air when making tests
B. To prevent over-modulation of a transmitter
C. To improve the efficiency of an antenna
D. To improve the signal-to-noise ratio of a receiver

T7C02
Which of the following is used to determine if an antenna is resonant at the desired operating frequency?

A. A VTVM
B. An antenna analyzer
C. A Q meter
D. A frequency counter

T7C03 (New Question for the 2022-2026 Pool)
What does a dummy load consist of?

A. A high-gain amplifier and a TR switch
B. A non-inductive resistor mounted on a heat sink
C. A low-voltage power supply and a DC relay
D. A 50-ohm reactance used to terminate a transmission line

T7C04
What reading on an SWR meter indicates a perfect impedance match between the antenna and the feed line?

A. 50:50
B. Zero
C. 1:1
D. Full Scale

T7C05
Why do most solid-state transmitters reduce output power as SWR increases beyond a certain level?

A. To protect the output amplifier transistors
B. To comply with FCC rules on spectral purity
C. Because power supplies cannot supply enough current at high SWR
D. To lower the SWR on the transmission line

T7C06
What does an SWR reading of 4:1 indicate?

A. Loss of -4 dB
B. Good impedance match
C. Gain of +4 dB
D. Impedance mismatch

T7C07
What happens to power lost in a feed line?

A. It increases the SWR
B. It is radiated as harmonics
C. It is converted into heat
D. It distorts the signal

T7C08 (Modified Question from the 2018-2022 Pool)
Which instrument can be used to determine SWR?

A. Voltmeter
B. Ohmmeter
C. Iambic pentameter
D. Directional wattmeter

T7C09 (Modified Question from the 2018-2022 Pool)
Which of the following causes failure of coaxial cables?

A. Moisture contamination
B. Solder flux contamination
C. Rapid fluctuation in transmitter output power
D. Operation at 100% duty cycle for an extended period

T7C10

Why should the outer jacket of coaxial cable be resistant to ultraviolet light?

A. Ultraviolet resistant jackets prevent harmonic radiation
B. Ultraviolet light can increase losses in the cable's jacket
C. Ultraviolet and RF signals can mix, causing interference
D. Ultraviolet light can damage the jacket and allow water to enter the cable

T7C11

What is a disadvantage of air core coaxial cable when compared to foam or solid dielectric types?

A. It has more loss per foot
B. It cannot be used for VHF or UHF antennas
C. It requires special techniques to prevent moisture in the cable
D. It cannot be used at below freezing temperatures

T7D01

Which instrument would you use to measure electric potential?

A. An ammeter
B. A voltmeter
C. A wavemeter
D. An ohmmeter

T7D02
How is a voltmeter connected to a component to measure applied voltage?

A. In series
B. In parallel
C. In quadrature
D. In phase

T7D03 (Modified Question from the 2018-2022 Pool)
When configured to measure current, how is a multimeter connected to a component?

A. In series
B. In parallel
C. In quadrature
D. In phase

T7D04
Which instrument is used to measure electric current?

A. An ohmmeter
B. An electrometer
C. A voltmeter
D. An ammeter

T7D05 (D)
How is an ohmmeter connected to a component to measure its resistance? - QUESTION REMOVED FROM TEST

A. In parallel
B. In series
C. In cascade
D. All these choices are correct

T7D06
Which of the following can damage a multimeter?

A. Attempting to measure resistance using the voltage setting
B. Failing to connect one of the probes to ground
C. Attempting to measure voltage when using the resistance setting
D. Not allowing it to warm up properly

T7D07
Which of the following measurements are made using a multimeter?

A. Signal strength and noise
B. Impedance and reactance
C. Voltage and resistance
D. All these choices are correct

T7D08 (New Question for the 2022-2026 Pool)
Which of the following types of solder should not be used for radio and electronic applications?

A. Acid-core solder
B. Lead-tin solder
C. Rosin-core solder
D. Tin-copper solder

T7D09 (Modified Question from the 2018-2022 Pool)
What is the characteristic appearance of a cold tin-lead solder joint?

A. Dark black spots
B. A bright or shiny surface
C. A rough or lumpy surface
D. Excessive solder

T7D10 (New Question for the 2022-2026 Pool)
What reading indicates that an ohmmeter is connected across a large, discharged capacitor?

A. Increasing resistance with time
B. Decreasing resistance with time
C. Steady full-scale reading
D. Alternating between open and short circuit

T7D11
Which of the following precautions should be taken when measuring in-circuit resistance with an ohmmeter?

A. Ensure that the applied voltages are correct
B. Ensure that the circuit is not powered
C. Ensure that the circuit is grounded
D. Ensure that the circuit is operating at the correct frequency

T8A01
Which of the following is a form of amplitude modulation?

A. Spread spectrum
B. Packet radio
C. Single sideband
D. Phase shift keying (PSK)

T8A02 (Modified Question from the 2018-2022 Pool)
What type of modulation is commonly used for VHF packet radio transmissions?

A. FM or PM
B. SSB
C. AM
D. PSK

T8A03
Which type of voice mode is often used for long-distance (weak signal) contacts on the VHF and UHF bands?

A. FM
B. DRM
C. SSB
D. PM

T8A04 (Modified Question from the 2018-2022 Pool)
Which type of modulation is commonly used for VHF and UHF voice repeaters?

A. AM
B. SSB
C. PSK
D. FM or PM

T8A05
Which of the following types of signal has the narrowest bandwidth?

A. FM voice
B. SSB voice
C. CW
D. Slow-scan TV

T8A06
Which sideband is normally used for 10 meter HF, VHF, and UHF single-sideband communications?

A. Upper sideband
B. Lower sideband
C. Suppressed sideband
D. Inverted sideband

T8A07 (Modified Question from the 2018-2022 Pool)
What is a characteristic of single sideband (SSB) compared to FM?

A. SSB signals are easier to tune in correctly
B. SSB signals are less susceptible to interference
C. SSB signals have narrower bandwidth
D. All these choices are correct

T8A08
What is the approximate bandwidth of a typical single sideband (SSB) voice signal?

A. 1 kHz
B. 3 kHz
C. 6 kHz
D. 15 kHz

T8A09
What is the approximate bandwidth of a VHF repeater FM voice signal?

A. Less than 500 Hz
B. About 150 kHz
C. Between 10 and 15 kHz
D. Between 50 and 125 kHz

T8A10 (Modified Question from the 2018-2022 Pool)
What is the approximate bandwidth of AM fast-scan TV transmissions?

A. More than 10 MHz
B. About 6 MHz
C. About 3 MHz
D. About 1 MHz

T8A11
What is the approximate bandwidth required to transmit a CW signal?

A. 2.4 kHz
B. 150 Hz
C. 1000 Hz
D. 15 kHz

T8A12 (New Question for the 2022-2026 Pool)
Which of the following is a disadvantage of FM compared with single sideband?

A. Voice quality is poorer
B. Only one signal can be received at a time
C. FM signals are harder to tune
D. All these choices are correct

T8B01
What telemetry information is typically transmitted by satellite beacons?

A. The signal strength of received signals
B. Time of day accurate to plus or minus 1/10 second
C. Health and status of the satellite
D. All these choices are correct

T8B02
What is the impact of using excessive effective radiated power on a satellite uplink?

A. Possibility of commanding the satellite to an improper mode
B. Blocking access by other users
C. Overloading the satellite batteries
D. Possibility of rebooting the satellite control computer

T8B03
Which of the following are provided by satellite tracking programs?

A. Maps showing the real-time position of the satellite track over Earth
B. The time, azimuth, and elevation of the start, maximum altitude, and end of a pass
C. The apparent frequency of the satellite transmission, including effects of Doppler shift
D. All these choices are correct

T8B04
What mode of transmission is commonly used by amateur radio satellites?

A. SSB
B. FM
C. CW/data
D. All these choices are correct

T8B05
What is a satellite beacon?

A. The primary transmit antenna on the satellite
B. An indicator light that shows where to point your antenna
C. A reflective surface on the satellite
D. A transmission from a satellite that contains status information

T8B06
Which of the following are inputs to a satellite tracking program?

A. The satellite transmitted power
B. The Keplerian elements
C. The last observed time of zero Doppler shift
D. All these choices are correct

T8B07
What is Doppler shift in reference to satellite communications?

A. A change in the satellite orbit
B. A mode where the satellite receives signals on one band and transmits on another
C. An observed change in signal frequency caused by relative motion between the satellite and Earth station
D. A special digital communications mode for some satellites

T8B08
What is meant by the statement that a satellite is operating in U/V mode?

A. The satellite uplink is in the 15 meter band and the downlink is in the 10 meter band
B. The satellite uplink is in the 70 centimeter band and the downlink is in the 2 meter band
C. The satellite operates using ultraviolet frequencies
D. The satellite frequencies are usually variable

T8B09
What causes spin fading of satellite signals?

A. Circular polarized noise interference radiated from the sun
B. Rotation of the satellite and its antennas
C. Doppler shift of the received signal
D. Interfering signals within the satellite uplink band

T8B10 (Modified Question from the 2018-2022 Pool)
What is a LEO satellite?

A. A sun synchronous satellite
B. A highly elliptical orbit satellite
C. A satellite in low energy operation mode
D. A satellite in low earth orbit

T8B11 (Modified Question from the 2018-2022 Pool)
Who may receive telemetry from a space station?

A. Anyone
B. A licensed radio amateur with a transmitter equipped for interrogating the satellite
C. A licensed radio amateur who has been certified by the protocol developer
D. A licensed radio amateur who has registered for an access code from AMSAT

T8B12
Which of the following is a way to determine whether your satellite uplink power is neither too low nor too high?

A. Check your signal strength report in the telemetry data
B. Listen for distortion on your downlink signal
C. Your signal strength on the downlink should be about the same as the beacon
D. All these choices are correct

T8C01
Which of the following methods is used to locate sources of noise interference or jamming?

A. Echolocation
B. Doppler radar
C. Radio direction finding
D. Phase locking

T8C02
Which of these items would be useful for a hidden transmitter hunt?

A. Calibrated SWR meter
B. A directional antenna
C. A calibrated noise bridge
D. All these choices are correct

T8C03
What operating activity involves contacting as many stations as possible during a specified period?

A. Simulated emergency exercises
B. Net operations
C. Public service events
D. Contesting

T8C04
Which of the following is good procedure when contacting another station in a contest?

A. Sign only the last two letters of your call if there are many other stations calling
B. Contact the station twice to be sure that you are in his log
C. Send only the minimum information needed for proper identification and the contest exchange
D. All these choices are correct

T8C05
What is a grid locator?

A. A letter-number designator assigned to a geographic location
B. A letter-number designator assigned to an azimuth and elevation
C. An instrument for neutralizing a final amplifier
D. An instrument for radio direction finding

T8C06
How is over the air access to IRLP nodes accomplished?

A. By obtaining a password that is sent via voice to the node
B. By using DTMF signals
C. By entering the proper internet password
D. By using CTCSS tone codes

T8C07
What is Voice Over Internet Protocol (VoIP)?

A. A set of rules specifying how to identify your station when linked over the internet to another station
B. A technique employed to "spot" DX stations via the internet
C. A technique for measuring the modulation quality of a transmitter using remote sites monitored via the internet
D. A method of delivering voice communications over the internet using digital techniques

T8C08
What is the Internet Radio Linking Project (IRLP)?

A. A technique to connect amateur radio systems, such as repeaters, via the internet using Voice Over Internet Protocol (VoIP)
B. A system for providing access to websites via amateur radio
C. A system for informing amateurs in real time of the frequency of active DX stations
D. A technique for measuring signal strength of an amateur transmitter via the internet

T8C09 (New Question for the 2022-2026 Pool)
Which of the following protocols enables an amateur station to transmit through a repeater without using a radio to initiate the transmission?

A. IRLP
B. D-STAR
C. DMR
D. EchoLink

T8C10 (New Question for the 2022-2026 Pool)
What is required before using the EchoLink system?

A. Complete the required EchoLink training
B. Purchase a license to use the EchoLink software
C. Register your call sign and provide proof of license
D. All these choices are correct

T8C11
What is an amateur radio station that connects other amateur stations to the internet?

A. A gateway
B. A repeater
C. A digipeater
D. A beacon

T8D01
Which of the following is a digital communications mode?

A. Packet radio
B. IEEE 802.11
C. FT8
D. All these choices are correct

T8D02 (New Question for the 2022-2026 Pool)
What is a "talkgroup" on a DMR repeater?

A. A group of operators sharing common interests
B. A way for groups of users to share a channel at different times without hearing other users on the channel
C. A protocol that increases the signal-to-noise ratio when multiple repeaters are linked together
D. A net that meets at a specified time

T8D03 (New Question for the 2022-2026 Pool)
What kind of data can be transmitted by APRS?

A. GPS position data
B. Text messages
C. Weather data
D. All these choices are correct

T8D04
What type of transmission is indicated by the term "NTSC?"

A. A Normal Transmission mode in Static Circuit
B. A special mode for satellite uplink
C. An analog fast-scan color TV signal
D. A frame compression scheme for TV signals

T8D05
Which of the following is an application of APRS?

A. Providing real-time tactical digital communications in conjunction with a map showing the locations of stations
B. Showing automatically the number of packets transmitted via PACTOR during a specific time interval
C. Providing voice over internet connection between repeaters
D. Providing information on the number of stations signed into a repeater

T8D06
What does the abbreviation "PSK" mean?

A. Pulse Shift Keying
B. Phase Shift Keying
C. Packet Short Keying
D. Phased Slide Keying

T8D07 (Modified Question from the 2018-2022 Pool)
Which of the following describes DMR?

A. A technique for time-multiplexing two digital voice signals on a single 12.5 kHz repeater channel
B. An automatic position tracking mode for FM mobiles communicating through repeaters
C. An automatic computer logging technique for hands-off logging when communicating while operating a vehicle
D. A digital technique for transmitting on two repeater inputs simultaneously for automatic error correction

T8D08
Which of the following is included in packet radio transmissions?

A. A check sum that permits error detection
B. A header that contains the call sign of the station to which the information is being sent
C. Automatic repeat request in case of error
D. All these choices are correct

T8D09 (Modified Question from the 2018-2022 Pool)
What is CW?

A. A type of electromagnetic propagation
B. A digital mode used primarily on 2 meter FM
C. A technique for coil winding
D. Another name for a Morse code transmission

T8D10
Which of the following operating activities is supported by digital mode software in the WSJT-X software suite?

A. Earth-Moon-Earth
B. Weak signal propagation beacons
C. Meteor scatter
D. All these choices are correct

T8D11 (Modified Question from the 2018-2022 Pool)
What is an ARQ transmission system?

A. A special transmission format limited to video signals
B. A system used to encrypt command signals to an amateur radio satellite
C. An error correction method in which the receiving station detects errors and sends a request for retransmission
D. A method of compressing data using autonomous reiterative Q codes prior to final encoding

T8D12 (Modified Question from the 2018-2022 Pool)
Which of the following best describes an amateur radio mesh network?

A. An amateur-radio based data network using commercial Wi-Fi equipment with modified firmware
B. A wide-bandwidth digital voice mode employing DMR protocols
C. A satellite communications network using modified commercial satellite TV hardware
D. An internet linking protocol used to network repeaters

T8D13 (Modified Question from the 2018-2022 Pool)
What is FT8?

A. A wideband FM voice mode
B. A digital mode capable of low signal-to-noise operation
C. An eight-channel multiplex mode for FM repeaters
D. A digital slow-scan TV mode with forward error correction and automatic color compensation

T9A01
What is a beam antenna?

A. An antenna built from aluminum I-beams
B. An omnidirectional antenna invented by Clarence Beam
C. An antenna that concentrates signals in one direction
D. An antenna that reverses the phase of received signals

T9A02 (Modified Question from the 2018-2022 Pool)
Which of the following describes a type of antenna loading?

A. Electrically lengthening by inserting inductors in radiating elements
B. Inserting a resistor in the radiating portion of the antenna to make it resonant
C. Installing a spring in the base of a mobile vertical antenna to make it more flexible
D. Strengthening the radiating elements of a beam antenna to better resist wind damage

T9A03
Which of the following describes a simple dipole oriented parallel to Earth's surface?

A. A ground-wave antenna
B. A horizontally polarized antenna
C. A travelling-wave antenna
D. A vertically polarized antenna

T9A04 (Modified Question from the 2018-2022 Pool)
What is a disadvantage of the short, flexible antenna supplied with most handheld radio transceivers, compared to a full-sized quarter-wave antenna?

A. It has low efficiency
B. It transmits only circularly polarized signals
C. It is mechanically fragile
D. All these choices are correct

T9A05 (Modified Question from the 2018-2022 Pool)
Which of the following increases the resonant frequency of a dipole antenna?

A. Lengthening it
B. Inserting coils in series with radiating wires
C. Shortening it
D. Adding capacitive loading to the ends of the radiating wires

T9A06 (New Question for the 2022-2026 Pool)
Which of the following types of antenna offers the greatest gain?

A. 5/8 wave vertical
B. Isotropic
C. J pole
D. Yagi

T9A07 (Modified Question from the 2018-2022 Pool)
What is a disadvantage of using a handheld VHF transceiver with a flexible antenna inside a vehicle?

A. Signal strength is reduced due to the shielding effect of the vehicle
B. The bandwidth of the antenna will decrease, increasing SWR
C. The SWR might decrease, decreasing the signal strength
D. All these choices are correct

T9A08
What is the approximate length, in inches, of a quarter-wavelength vertical antenna for 146 MHz?

A. 112
B. 50
C. 19
D. 12

T9A09
What is the approximate length, in inches, of a half-wavelength 6 meter dipole antenna?

A. 6
B. 50
C. 112
D. 236

T9A10
In which direction does a half-wave dipole antenna radiate the strongest signal?

A. Equally in all directions
B. Off the ends of the antenna
C. In the direction of the feed line
D. Broadside to the antenna

T9A11
What is antenna gain?

A. The additional power that is added to the transmitter power
B. The additional power that is required in the antenna when transmitting on a higher frequency
C. The increase in signal strength in a specified direction compared to a reference antenna
D. The increase in impedance on receive or transmit compared to a reference antenna

T9A12 (Modified Question from the 2018-2022 Pool)
What is an advantage of a 5/8 wavelength whip antenna for VHF or UHF mobile service?

A. It has more gain than a 1/4-wavelength antenna
B. It radiates at a very high angle
C. It eliminates distortion caused by reflected signals
D. It has 10 times the power gain of a 1/4 wavelength whip

T9B01 (Modified Question from the 2018-2022 Pool)
What is a benefit of low SWR?

A. Reduced television interference
B. Reduced signal loss
C. Less antenna wear
D. All these choices are correct

T9B02 (Modified Question from the 2018-2022 Pool)
What is the most common impedance of coaxial cables used in amateur radio?

A. 8 ohms
B. 50 ohms
C. 600 ohms
D. 12 ohms

T9B03
Why is coaxial cable the most common feed line for amateur radio antenna systems?

A. It is easy to use and requires few special installation considerations
B. It has less loss than any other type of feed line
C. It can handle more power than any other type of feed line
D. It is less expensive than any other type of feed line

T9B04
What is the major function of an antenna tuner (antenna coupler)?

A. It matches the antenna system impedance to the transceiver's output impedance
B. It helps a receiver automatically tune in weak stations
C. It allows an antenna to be used on both transmit and receive
D. It automatically selects the proper antenna for the frequency band being used

T9B05 (Modified Question from the 2018-2022 Pool)
What happens as the frequency of a signal in coaxial cable is increased?

A. The characteristic impedance decreases
B. The loss decreases
C. The characteristic impedance increases
D. The loss increases

T9B06
Which of the following RF connector types is most suitable for frequencies above 400 MHz?

A. UHF (PL-259/SO-239)
B. Type N
C. RS-213
D. DB-25

T9B07 (Modified Question from the 2018-2022 Pool)
Which of the following is true of PL-259 type coax connectors?

A. They are preferred for microwave operation
B. They are watertight
C. They are commonly used at HF and VHF frequencies
D. They are a bayonet-type connector

T9B08 (New Question for the 2022-2026 Pool)
Which of the following is a source of loss in coaxial feed line?

A. Water intrusion into coaxial connectors
B. High SWR
C. Multiple connectors in the line
D. All these choices are correct

T9B09
What can cause erratic changes in SWR?

A. Local thunderstorm
B. Loose connection in the antenna or feed line
C. Over-modulation
D. Overload from a strong local station

T9B10 (New Question for the 2022-2026 Pool)
What is the electrical difference between RG-58 and RG-213 coaxial cable?

A. There is no significant difference between the two types
B. RG-58 cable has two shields
C. RG-213 cable has less loss at a given frequency
D. RG-58 cable can handle higher power levels

T9B11
Which of the following types of feed line has the lowest loss at VHF and UHF?

A. 50-ohm flexible coax
B. Multi-conductor unbalanced cable
C. Air-insulated hardline
D. 75-ohm flexible coax

T9B12 (New Question for the 2022-2026 Pool)
What is standing wave ratio (SWR)?

A. A measure of how well a load is matched to a transmission line
B. The ratio of amplifier power output to input
C. The transmitter efficiency ratio
D. An indication of the quality of your station's ground connection

T0A01
Which of the following is a safety hazard of a 12-volt storage battery?

A. Touching both terminals with the hands can cause electrical shock
B. Shorting the terminals can cause burns, fire, or an explosion
C. RF emissions from a nearby transmitter can cause the electrolyte to emit poison gas
D. All these choices are correct

T0A02
What health hazard is presented by electrical current flowing through the body?

A. It may cause injury by heating tissue
B. It may disrupt the electrical functions of cells
C. It may cause involuntary muscle contractions
D. All these choices are correct

T0A03 (New Question for the 2022-2026 Pool)
In the United States, what circuit does black wire insulation indicate in a three-wire 120 V cable?

A. Neutral
B. Hot
C. Equipment ground
D. Black insulation is never used

T0A04 (Modified Question from the 2018-2022 Pool)
What is the purpose of a fuse in an electrical circuit?

A. To prevent power supply ripple from damaging a component
B. To remove power in case of overload
C. To limit current to prevent shocks
D. All these choices are correct

T0A05

Why should a 5-ampere fuse never be replaced with a 20-ampere fuse?

A. The larger fuse would be likely to blow because it is rated for higher current
B. The power supply ripple would greatly increase
C. Excessive current could cause a fire
D. All these choices are correct

T0A06

What is a good way to guard against electrical shock at your station?

A. Use three-wire cords and plugs for all AC powered equipment
B. Connect all AC powered station equipment to a common safety ground
C. Install mechanical interlocks in high-voltage circuits
D. All these choices are correct

T0A07 (Modified Question from the 2018-2022 Pool)
Where should a lightning arrester be installed in a coaxial feed line?

A. At the output connector of a transceiver
B. At the antenna feed point
C. At the ac power service panel
D. On a grounded panel near where feed lines enter the building

T0A08 (Modified Question from the 2018-2022 Pool)
Where should a fuse or circuit breaker be installed in a 120V AC power circuit?

A. In series with the hot conductor only
B. In series with the hot and neutral conductors
C. In parallel with the hot conductor only
D. In parallel with the hot and neutral conductors

T0A09
What should be done to all external ground rods or earth connections?

A. Waterproof them with silicone caulk or electrical tape
B. Keep them as far apart as possible
C. Bond them together with heavy wire or conductive strap
D. Tune them for resonance on the lowest frequency of operation

T0A10 (Modified Question from the 2018-2022 Pool)
What hazard is caused by charging or discharging a battery too quickly?

A. Overheating or out-gassing
B. Excess output ripple
C. Half-wave rectification
D. Inverse memory effect

T0A11 (Modified Question from the 2018-2022 Pool)
What hazard exists in a power supply immediately after turning it off?

A. Circulating currents in the dc filter
B. Leakage flux in the power transformer
C. Voltage transients from kickback diodes
D. Charge stored in filter capacitors

T0A12 (New Question for the 2022-2026 Pool)
Which of the following precautions should be taken when measuring high voltages with a voltmeter?

A. Ensure that the voltmeter has very low impedance
B. Ensure that the voltmeter and leads are rated for use at the voltages to be measured
C. Ensure that the circuit is grounded through the voltmeter
D. Ensure that the voltmeter is set to the correct frequency

T0B01 (New Question for the 2022-2026 Pool)
Which of the following is good practice when installing ground wires on a tower for lightning protection?

A. Put a drip loop in the ground connection to prevent water damage to the ground system
B. Make sure all ground wire bends are right angles
C. Ensure that connections are short and direct
D. All these choices are correct

T0B02 (New Question for the 2022-2026 Pool)
What is required when climbing an antenna tower?

A. Have sufficient training on safe tower climbing techniques
B. Use appropriate tie-off to the tower at all times
C. Always wear an approved climbing harness
D. All these choices are correct

T0B03
Under what circumstances is it safe to climb a tower without a helper or observer?

A. When no electrical work is being performed
B. When no mechanical work is being performed
C. When the work being done is not more than 20 feet above the ground
D. Never

T0B04
Which of the following is an important safety precaution to observe when putting up an antenna tower?

A. Wear a ground strap connected to your wrist at all times
B. Insulate the base of the tower to avoid lightning strikes
C. Look for and stay clear of any overhead electrical wires
D. All these choices are correct

T0B05 (New Question for the 2022-2026 Pool)
What is the purpose of a safety wire through a turnbuckle used to tension guy lines?

A. Secure the guy line if the turnbuckle breaks
B. Prevent loosening of the turnbuckle from vibration
C. Provide a ground path for lightning strikes
D. Provide an ability to measure for proper tensioning

T0B06
What is the minimum safe distance from a power line to allow when installing an antenna?

A. Add the height of the antenna to the height of the power line and multiply by a factor of 1.5
B. The height of the power line above ground
C. 1/2 wavelength at the operating frequency
D. Enough so that if the antenna falls, no part of it can come closer than 10 feet to the power wires

T0B07
Which of the following is an important safety rule to remember when using a crank-up tower?

A. This type of tower must never be painted
B. This type of tower must never be grounded
C. This type of tower must not be climbed unless it is retracted, or mechanical safety locking devices have been installed
D. All these choices are correct

T0B08
Which is a proper grounding method for a tower?

A. A single four-foot ground rod, driven into the ground no more than 12 inches from the base
B. A ferrite-core RF choke connected between the tower and ground
C. A connection between the tower base and a cold water pipe
D. Separate eight-foot ground rods for each tower leg, bonded to the tower and each other

T0B09
Why should you avoid attaching an antenna to a utility pole?

A. The antenna will not work properly because of induced voltages
B. The 60 Hz radiations from the feed line may increase the SWR
C. The antenna could contact high-voltage power lines
D. All these choices are correct

T0B10
Which of the following is true when installing grounding conductors used for lightning protection?

A. Use only non-insulated wire
B. Wires must be carefully routed with precise right-angle bends
C. Sharp bends must be avoided
D. Common grounds must be avoided

T0B11
Which of the following establishes grounding requirements for an amateur radio tower or antenna?

A. FCC Part 97 rules
B. Local electrical codes
C. FAA tower lighting regulations
D. UL recommended practices

T0C01
What type of radiation are radio signals?

A. Gamma radiation
B. Ionizing radiation
C. Alpha radiation
D. Non-ionizing radiation

T0C02
At which of the following frequencies does maximum permissible exposure have the lowest value?

A. 3.5 MHz
B. 50 MHz
C. 440 MHz
D. 1296 MHz

T0C03 (New Question for the 2022-2026 Pool)
How does the allowable power density for RF safety change if duty cycle changes from 100 percent to 50 percent?

A. It increases by a factor of 3
B. It decreases by 50 percent
C. It increases by a factor of 2
D. There is no adjustment allowed for lower duty cycle

T0C04
What factors affect the RF exposure of people near an amateur station antenna?

A. Frequency and power level of the RF field
B. Distance from the antenna to a person
C. Radiation pattern of the antenna
D. All these choices are correct

T0C05
Why do exposure limits vary with frequency?

A. Lower frequency RF fields have more energy than higher frequency fields
B. Lower frequency RF fields do not penetrate the human body
C. Higher frequency RF fields are transient in nature
D. The human body absorbs more RF energy at some frequencies than at others

T0C06
Which of the following is an acceptable method to determine whether your station complies with FCC RF exposure regulations?

A. By calculation based on FCC OET Bulletin 65
B. By calculation based on computer modeling
C. By measurement of field strength using calibrated equipment
D. All these choices are correct

T0C07 (Modified Question from the 2018-2022 Pool)
What hazard is created by touching an antenna during a transmission?

A. Electrocution
B. RF burn to skin
C. Radiation poisoning
D. All these choices are correct

T0C08 (Modified Question from the 2018-2022 Pool)
Which of the following actions can reduce exposure to RF radiation?

A. Relocate antennas
B. Relocate the transmitter
C. Increase the duty cycle
D. Increase the duty cycle

T0C09
How can you make sure your station stays in compliance with RF safety regulations?

A. By informing the FCC of any changes made in your station
B. By re-evaluating the station whenever an item in the transmitter or antenna system is changed
C. By making sure your antennas have low SWR
D. All these choices are correct

T0C10
Why is duty cycle one of the factors used to determine safe RF radiation exposure levels?

A. It affects the average exposure to radiation
B. It affects the peak exposure to radiation
C. It takes into account the antenna feed line loss
D. It takes into account the thermal effects of the final amplifier

T0C11
What is the definition of duty cycle during the averaging time for RF exposure?

A. The difference between the lowest power output and the highest power output of a transmitter
B. The difference between the PEP and average power output of a transmitter
C. The percentage of time that a transmitter is transmitting
D. The percentage of time that a transmitter is not transmitting

T0C12 (Modified Question from the 2018-2022 Pool)
How does RF radiation differ from ionizing radiation (radioactivity)?

A. RF radiation does not have sufficient energy to cause chemical changes in cells and damage DNA
B. RF radiation can only be detected with an RF dosimeter
C. RF radiation is limited in range to a few feet
D. RF radiation is perfectly safe

T0C13 (New Question for the 2022-2026 Pool)
Who is responsible for ensuring that no person is exposed to RF energy above the FCC exposure limits?

A. The FCC
B. The station licensee
C. Anyone who is near an antenna
D. The local zoning board

Chapter 4 – Practice Test Answers Key

On the next four pages you will find the answer keys to the questions in the proceeding practice questions. You can use the sample test form on page 4-5 and make copies for using when running through the practice questions.

When you take the actual test, remember:

- The test will consist of 35 multiple choice questions.
- You will NOT be able to carry a cell phone in for the calculator – you CAN carry a calculator with the memory cleared.
- Effective April 19th 2022 the application fee for a Ham Radio License has risen to $35. This fee applies to new, renewal, rule waiver, and modification applications for new call signs (Including Vanity signs). This fee is per application. *Upgrades of your license are exempt from this fee.*
- The $35 application fee is NOT paid at the exam time – it will be paid directly to the FCC via their CORES system.
- At the time of testing there is a $15 examination fee that is paid directly to the VEC team providing the testing. The VEC Teams are local clubs and organizations that volunteer to provide testing. ***Bring cash, a check, or money order. If bringing a check you should make it out on site. If cash, bring exact amount.***
- Bring your Driver's License or form of state identification such as:
  - State Driver's License
  - Government issued Passport
  - Military or Law Enforcement Officer Photo ID card
  - Student School Photo ID card
  - State Photo ID card
  - If none of these are available, you can still get your license by bringing identification items as listed here: http://www.arrl.org/what-to-bring-to-an-exam-session
- If upgrading your license, bring a COPY of your current license or be able to show proof of your license.
- Bring your FRN Number – This is a number you will need to register for ahead of time. It is your FCC Registration Number (FRN) and can be obtained for free by logging into the FCC CORES system at this website: https://apps.fcc.gov/cores/userLogin.do (A valid email address is now mandatory)
- Two number two pencils with erasers

For a more exact list of testing day requirements visit the ARRL Website at the following URL:

http://www.arrl.org/what-to-bring-to-an-exam-session

T1-A:

T1A01	C
T1A02	C
T1A03	B
T1A04	A
T1A05	C
T1A06	D
T1A07	C
T1A08	B
T1A09	C
T1A10	D
T1A11	B

T1-B:

T1B01	C
T1B02	B
T1B03	B
T1B04	D
T1B05	D
T1B06	B
T1B07	A
T1B08	A
T1B09	D
T1B10	C
T1B11	A
T1B12	D

T1-C:

T1C01	D
T1C02	D
T1C03	A
T1C04	B
T1C05	A
T1C06	D
T1C07	B
T1C08	C
T1C09	A
T1C10	C
T1C11	D

T1-D:

T1D01	A
T1D02	B
T1D03	C
T1D04	A
T1D05	D
T1D06	B
T1D07	D
T1D08	B
T1D09	A
T1D10	D
T1D11	D

T1-E:

T1E01	D
T1E02	D
T1E03	A
T1E04	D
T1E05	C
T1E06	A
T1E07	D
T1E08	A
T1E09	D
T1E10	B
T1E11	D

T1-F:

T1F01	B
T1F02	C
T1F03	D
T1F04	C
T1F05	B
T1F06	D
T1F07	B
T1F08	A
T1F09	C
T1F10	A
T1F11	B

T2-A:

T2A01	B
T2A02	A
T2A03	A
T2A04	B
T2A05	C
T2A06	A
T2A07	A
T2A08	D
T2A09	B
T2A10	A
T2A11	C
T2A12	D

T2-B:

T2B01	C
T2B02	D
T2B03	A
T2B04	D
T2B05	C
T2B06	A
T2B07	C
T2B08	A
T2B09	A
T2B10	A
T2B11	B
T2B12	A
T2B13	B

T2-C:

T2C01	D
T2C02	C
T2C03	C
T2C04	D
T2C05	A
T2C06	A
T2C07	C
T2C08	A
T2C09	D
T2C10	D
T2C11	A

T3-A:

T3A01	C
T3A02	B
T3A03	C
T3A04	B
T3A05	B
T3A06	B
T3A07	C
T3A08	D
T3A09	B
T3A10	D
T3A11	C
T3A12	B

T3-B:

T3B01	D
T3B02	A
T3B03	C
T3B04	A
T3B05	B
T3B06	D
T3B07	A
T3B08	B
T3B09	D
T3B10	C
T3B11	B

T3-C:

T3C01	C
T3C02	C
T3C03	B
T3C04	B
T3C05	A
T3C06	A
T3C07	B
T3C08	D
T3C09	A
T3C10	A
T3C11	C

T4-A:

T5-B:

T6-A:

T6-D:

T4A01	D
T4A02	A
T4A03	A
T4A04	B
T4A05	A
T4A06	C
T4A07	C
T4A08	D
T4A09	B
T4A10	A
T4A11	A
T4A12	C

T4-B:

T4B01	B
T4B02	A
T4B03	A
T4B04	B
T4B05	C
T4B06	D
T4B07	B
T4B08	B
T4B09	C
T4B10	C
T4B11	A
T4B12	D

T5-A:

T5A01	D
T5A02	B
T5A03	D
T5A04	C
T5A05	A
T5A06	A
T5A07	B
T5A08	B
T5A09	C
T5A10	C
T5A11	D
T5A12	D

T5B01	C
T5B02	A
T5B03	C
T5B04	A
T5B05	B
T5B06	D
T5B07	C
T5B08	B
T5B09	B
T5B10	C
T5B11	A
T5B12	D
T5B13	C

T5-C:

T5C01	D
T5C02	A
T5C03	D
T5C04	C
T5C05	D
T5C06	A
T5C07	D
T5C08	A
T5C09	A
T5C10	B
T5C11	B
T5C12	A
T5C13	D

T5-D:

T5D01	B
T5D02	A
T5D03	B
T5D04	B
T5D05	C
T5D06	A
T5D07	D
T5D08	C
T5D09	C
T5D10	A
T5D11	B
T5D12	D
T5D13	A
T5D14	B

T6A01	B
T6A02	C
T6A03	B
T6A04	B
T6A05	D
T6A06	C
T6A07	D
T6A08	C
T6A09	A
T6A10	D
T6A11	B
T6A12	A

T6-B:

T6B01	A
T6B02	C
T6B03	C
T6B04	B
T6B05	B
T6B06	B
T6B07	A
T6B08	D
T6B09	C
T6B10	B
T6B11	A
T6B12	B

T6-C:

T6C01	C
T6C02	A
T6C03	B
T6C04	C
T6C05	D
T6C06	B
T6C07	D
T6C08	C
T6C09	D
T6C10	D
T6C11	A
T6C12	C

T6D01	B
T6D02	A
T6D03	C
T6D04	C
T6D05	A
T6D06	B
T6D07	A
T6D08	D
T6D09	C
T6D10	C
T6D11	A

T7-A:

T7A01	B
T7A02	A
T7A03	B
T7A04	C
T7A05	D
T7A06	C
T7A07	B
T7A08	C
T7A09	B
T7A10	B
T7A11	A

T7-B:

T7B01	D
T7B02	A
T7B03	D
T7B04	D
T7B05	A
T7B06	A
T7B07	D
T7B08	D
T7B09	D
T7B10	D
T7B11	C

T7-C:

T8-B:

T9-A:

T0-B:

T7C01	A	T8B01	C	T9A01	C	T0B01	C
T7C02	B	T8B02	B	T9A02	A	T0B02	D
T7C03	B	T8B03	D	T9A03	B	T0B03	D
T7C04	C	T8B04	D	T9A04	A	T0B04	C
T7C05	A	T8B05	D	T9A05	C	T0B05	B
T7C06	D	T8B06	B	T9A06	D	T0B06	D
T7C07	C	T8B07	C	T9A07	A	T0B07	C
T7C08	D	T8B08	B	T9A08	C	T0B08	D
T7C09	A	T8B09	B	T9A09	C	T0B09	C
T7C10	D	T8B10	D	T9A10	D	T0B10	C
T7C11	C	T8B11	A	T9A11	C	T0B11	B
		T8B12	C	T9A12	A		

T7-D:

T7D01	B	**T8-C:**		**T9-B:**		**T0-C:**	
T7D02	B	T8C01	C	T9B01	B	T0C01	D
T7D03	A	T8C02	B	T9B02	B	T0C02	B
T7D04	D	T8C03	D	T9B03	A	T0C03	C
T7D05	A	T8C04	C	T9B04	A	T0C04	D
T7D06	C	T8C05	A	T9B05	D	T0C05	D
T7D07	C	T8C06	B	T9B06	B	T0C06	D
T7D08	A	T8C07	D	T9B07	C	T0C07	B
T7D09	C	T8C08	A	T9B08	D	T0C08	A
T7D10	A	T8C09	D	T9B09	B	T0C09	B
T7D11	B	T8C10	C	T9B10	C	T0C10	A
		T8C11	A	T9B11	C	T0C11	C
				T9B12	A	T0C12	A
T8-A:		**T8-D:**				T0C13	B
T8A01	C	T8D01	D	**T0-A:**			
T8A02	A	T8D02	B	T0A01	B		
T8A03	C	T8D03	D	T0A02	D		
T8A04	D	T8D04	C	T0A03	B		
T8A05	C	T8D05	A	T0A04	B		
T8A06	A	T8D06	B	T0A05	C		
T8A07	C	T8D07	A	T0A06	D		
T8A08	B	T8D08	D	T0A07	D		
T8A09	C	T8D09	D	T0A08	A		
T8A10	B	T8D10	D	T0A09	C		
T8A11	B	T8D11	C	T0A10	A		
T8A12	B	T8D12	A	T0A11	D		
		T8D13	B	T0A12	B		

Practice Test Worksheet

Section	Question #	Answer (Mark One)		Section	Question #	Answer (Mark one)
T_____	01	A B C D		T_____	01	A B C D
	02	A B C D			02	A B C D
	03	A B C D			03	A B C D
	04	A B C D			04	A B C D
	05	A B C D			05	A B C D
	06	A B C D			06	A B C D
	07	A B C D			07	A B C D
	08	A B C D			08	A B C D
	09	A B C D			09	A B C D
	10	A B C D			10	A B C D
	11	A B C D			11	A B C D
	12	A B C D			12	A B C D
	13	A B C D			13	A B C D
T_____	01	A B C D			01	A B C D
	02	A B C D			02	A B C D
	03	A B C D			03	A B C D
	04	A B C D			04	A B C D
	05	A B C D			05	A B C D
	06	A B C D			06	A B C D
	07	A B C D			07	A B C D
	08	A B C D			08	A B C D
	09	A B C D			09	A B C D
	10	A B C D			10	A B C D
	11	A B C D			11	A B C D
	12	A B C D			12	A B C D
	13	A B C D			13	A B C D
	01	A B C D			01	A B C D
	02	A B C D			02	A B C D
	03	A B C D			03	A B C D
	04	A B C D			04	A B C D
	05	A B C D			05	A B C D
	06	A B C D			06	A B C D
	07	A B C D			07	A B C D
	08	A B C D			08	A B C D
	09	A B C D			09	A B C D
	10	A B C D			10	A B C D
	11	A B C D			11	A B C D
	12	A B C D			12	A B C D
	13	A B C D			13	A B C D

Chapter 5 – Pool Questions – Explained

In Chapter 5 we will review each of the 411 questions that are on the question pool in the same order as provided by the NCVEC organization (https://www.ncvec.org/). We will provide a brief or a more detailed answer based on the complexity of the question. Some of the questions will include additional visuals. In addition to the explanations covered, chapter 6 after this chapter covers several discussions on related topics. Though that chapter does not delve into each question, we do cover about 2/3 of the questions in discussions based on the general topic category.

For any questions that are covered in this chapter, if there is an additional area in chapter 6 where the question is also covered then that page or pages will be shown at the bottom of the explanation.

T1A04

How many operator/primary station license grants may be held by any one person?

Correct Answer is "A" - **One**

A Ham operator receives only one HAM license. As you progress up to a General License or an Amateur Extra license, your license will be "Upgraded" to the next level.

This does NOT apply to other types of licenses such as a GMRS Radio license or a Commercial Operator's license which IS considered as a separate license.

Read more on this question on the following page(s): 6-68

Following are where you can find the beginning of each section for this chapter:

T1-A	5-2	T4-A	5-41	T7-C	5-85
T1-B	5-5	T4-B	5-45	T7-D	5-87
T1-C	5-9	T5-A	5-48	T8-A	5-90
T1-D	5-12	T5-B	5-52	T8-B	5-92
T1-E	5-15	T5-C	5-56	T8-C	5-95
T1-F	5-18	T5-D	5-60	T8-D	5-98
T2-A	5-22	T6-A	5-64	T9-A	5-102
T2-B	5-25	T6-B	5-67	T9-B	5-106
T2-C	5-28	T6-C	5-72	T0-A	5-109
T3-A	5-31	T6-D	5-76	T0-B	5-112
T3-B	5-35	T7-A	5-79	T0-C	5-115
T3-C	5-38	T7-B	5-82		

T1A01 - (M)
Which of the following is part of the Basis and Purpose of the Amateur Radio Service?
Correct Answer is "C" - **Advancing skills in the technical and communication phases of the radio art**

The point with this question is to stress the emphasis of the consideration of Ham radio as not only a technical hobby but that it is also considered an "Art". There is a heavy technical aspect to ham radio - Formulas, science and engineering. But in many ways Ham radio is an art as the best operators grow to understand all of the many factors that participate in the success of good radio communication using a wide variety of frequencies and different operating conditions.

T1A02
Which agency regulates and enforces the rules for the Amateur Radio Service in the United States?

Correct Answer is "C" - **The FCC**

The Federal Communications Commission is the agency in the United States that oversees all rules and enforcement for all forms of radio operation in the United States.

T1A03
What do the FCC rules state regarding the use of a phonetic alphabet for station identification in the Amateur Radio Service?

Correct Answer is "B" - **It is encouraged**

Here we are referring to the Phonetic alphabet, used in Military radio operations and encouraged to learn for Ham radio to enhance the ability to understand the spelling of letters and words during communication. In the Phonetic alphabet each of the 26 alphabet letters has a word assigned to it that is easiy rememberable. For instance, "Alpha" for "A", "Bravo" for "B", and "Charlie" for "C".

If you have difficulty in remembering what are considered "Normal" words, use of other words is acceptable such as "Apple" for "A", "Baseball" for "B", or "Christmas" for "C".

A - Alpha	H - Hotel	O - Oscar	V - Victor
B - Bravo	I - India	P - Papa	W - Whiskey
C - Charlie	J - Juliet	Q - Quebec	X - X-Ray
D - Delta	K - Kilo	R - Romeo	Y - Yankee
E - Echo	L - Lima	S - Siera	Z - Zulu
F - Foxtrot	M - Mike	T - Tango	
G - Gulf	N - November	U - Uniform	

T1A04

How many operator/primary station license grants may be held by any one person?

Correct Answer is "A" - **One**

A Ham operator receives only one HAM license. As you progress up to a General License or an Amateur Extra license, your license will be "Upgraded" to the next level.

This does NOT apply to other types of licenses such as a GMRS Radio license or a Commercial Operator's license which IS considered as a separate license.

Read more on this question on the following page(s): 6-68

T1A05 - (M)

What proves that the FCC has issued an operator/primary license grant?

Correct Answer is "C" - **The license appears in the FCC ULS database**

Once your name makes it into the database you are legal to start using your Ham Radio and start talking through repeaters. Just make sure you follow the basic rules announcing yourself as you start your communication.

The link to the database can be found at https://wireless2.fcc.gov/UlsApp/UlsSearch/searchLicense.jsp

At some point after your name is in the database you should receive and email message with a link that you can use to download and print your actual FCC License. You should keep this with you when you are operating your radio as physical proof of your license status.

Read more on this question on the following page(s): 6-67

T1A06

What is the FCC Part 97 definition of a beacon?

Correct Answer is "D" - **An amateur station transmitting communications for the purposes of observing propagation or related experimental activities**

A Beacon station is a station that transmits a signal on a set frequency from a set location allowing amateur operators to confirm their ability to receive the signal. Beacons exist in locations of the 28, 50, 144, 222 and 432-MHz amateur bands, and all amateur bands above 450-MHz. Transmitter power of a beacon must not exceed 100 W (watts).

T1A07

What is the FCC Part 97 definition of a space station?

Correct Answer is "C" - **An amateur station located more than 50 km above Earth's surface**

Some hams experiment with use of satellites for communication which do exist orbiting the earth. In addition to satellites ham operators can also communicate with the International Space Station (ISS) on UHF/VHF frequencies. The ISS provides a unique communication opportunity for hams n VHF/UHF frequencies at distances that you will not normally be able to reach due to obstructions found on the ground.

Read more on this question on the following page(s): 6-79

T1A08
Which of the following entities recommends transmit/receive channels and other parameters for auxiliary and repeater stations?

Correct Answer is "B" - **Volunteer Frequency Coordinator recognized by local amateurs**

The Volunteer Frequency Coordinator is an individual or individuals local to a particular area that manage frequencies & frequency assignments for purposes such as repeater operation to avoid conflicts.

Read more on this question on the following page(s): 6-79

T1A09
Who selects a Frequency Coordinator?

Correct Answer is "C" - **Amateur operators in a local or regional area whose stations are eligible to be repeater or auxiliary stations**

The selection of frequency coordinators in an area are selected by the local community of operators in an area.

Read more on this question on the following page(s): 6-79

T1A10 - (M)
What is the Radio Amateur Civil Emergency Service (RACES)?

Correct Answer is "D" - **All these choices are correct**

Two popular emergency radio groups are RACES and ARES. RACES is specifically associated with Civil Defense communications. RACES organizations work more closely with local government agencies. RACES is different from ARES in that it is more closely tied to county and government agencies where ARES is associated with the ARRL (Amateur Radio Relay League). RACES is activated before, during and after an emergency and is active only during the emergency and following if government offices need their assistance.

T1A11
When is willful interference to other amateur radio stations permitted?

Correct Answer is "B" - **At no time**

Willful interference is the act of purposefully transmitting or causing interference with other radio operators. At no time is this considered to be allowed or acceptable. Interference that is NOT purposeful or willful but should be avoided at all times.

T1B01 - (N)
Which of the following frequency ranges are available for phone operation by Technician licensees?

Correct Answer is "C" - **28.300 MHz to 28.500 MHz**

This is an important question to remember - As a licensed Tech Ham operator you do have privileges on the 10-meter band which is the only HF band that you will have access to. You will not have full access to 10-meters. But you will have limited access within this frequency range. In the US a Tech will have access to frequencies from 28.000 MHz to 28.300 MHz for CW, RTTY and data, while having access from 28.300 MHz to 28.500 MHz for voice/phone operation. General license holders have full access to the band which runs up to 29.700 MHz.

The frequency range in the 10-Meter band that you will have permissions for use of are for AM modulation. With a proper AM 10-Meter radio using SSB you will get radio ranges often up to 50 miles without the use of a repeater - far greater than you will normally get with 6-Meter, 2-Meter or even 70-cm bands. Some operators using SSB and at proper propagation times can make long-distance contacts far greater than 50-miles.

Read more on this question on the following page(s): 6-19

T1B02 - (M)
Which amateurs may contact the International Space Station (ISS) on VHF bands?

Correct Answer is "B" - **Any amateur holding a Technician class or higher license**

As a Technician license holder you will have the ability to communicate with the ISS on VHF and UHF frequencies. In the US, VHF is primarily used using the frequencies of 145.800 for downlink and the uplink frequency of 144.490. The ISS also has a simplex UHF Frequency of 437.550 MHz though this is not frequently used.

Reaching the ISS on VHF or UHF bands may require use of a special directional antenna such as a Yagi or Dish antenna.

Read more on this question on the following page(s): 6-79

T1B03 - (M)
Which frequency is in the 6 meter amateur band?

Correct Answer is "B" - **52.525 MHz**

The 6-Meter band is a VHF Frequency which sits between 30-MHz and 300-MHz. If you remember what the range is for VHF, then this rues out one of the options immediately (28.5 MHz). Others can be ruled out if you can remember that the 6-Meter band starts at 50-MHz. That rules out 49.0 MHz as being too low and out of the band, and 222.15 MHz as being too high.

The 6-Meter band runs from 50.0 MHz to 54.0 MHz.

Read more on this question on the following page(s): 6-23

T1B04 - (M)

Which amateur band includes 146.52 MHz?

Correct Answer is "D" - **2 meters**

146.52 MHz is the simplex "Calling Frequency" for the 2-Meter band. The calling frequency is the frequency you should set your radio to if looking for someone to reach in an area and know of no other frequencies. This is the "Universal" frequency to call out on for 2-Meter simplex.

Other frequency bands have calling frequencies as well. These are:

70-cm is 446.000 MHz   6-Meter is 50.300 MHz
1.25-Meter is 223.500 MHz   10-Meter is 28.385 MHz
2-Meter is146.520 MHz

Read more on this question on the following page(s): 6-24

T1B05 - (M)

How may amateurs use the 219 to 220 MHz segment of 1.25 meter band?

Correct Answer is "D" - **Fixed digital message forwarding systems only**

A "Fixed Digital Message Forwarding system" is also known as a "Digipeter" which is a device that stores and forwards digital messages. Amateur operators including those with Tech licenses have approval to use these frequencies as "Secondary Users" provided they are not interfering with someone considered a "Primary User".

Read more on this question on the following page(s): 6-20

T1B06

On which HF bands does a Technician class operator have phone privileges?

Correct Answer is "B" - **10 meter band only**

Hams with a Tech license have access to a portion of the 10-Meter band. The 10-Meter band for General and Advanced Extra license holders is between 28 MHz and 29.7 MHz. As a technician your privileges are limited between 28.0 MHz and 28.5 Mhz with that being split for CW, RTTY and data from 28 MHz to 28.3 MHz, and voice operation from 28.3 MHz and 28.5 MHz.

As an HF band, the frequencies available will operate at longer distances and have propagation characteristics not available in the VHF/UHF bands. Technician operators will require an AM radio, not an FM based modulated radio, for operation. Using these frequencies with the proper type of radio will allow communication ranges from 50 miles to much greater.

Read more on this question on the following page(s): 6-23

T1B07 - (M)
Which of the following VHF/UHF band segments are limited to CW only?

Correct Answer is "A" - **50.0 MHz to 50.1 MHz and 144.0 MHz to 144.1 MHz**

All frequency bands have some levels of CW/Morse Code permissions. In some cases some ranges are limited to CW/Morse code use only and cannot be used for voice/phone communication. In the 2-Meter band, 144.0 MHz to 144.1 MHz is limited to CW use while in the 6-Meter band 50.0 to 50.1 MHz is limited to CW.

Read more on this question on the following page(s): 6-19

T1B08 - (M)
How are US amateurs restricted in segments of bands where the Amateur Radio Service is secondary?

Correct Answer is "A" - **U.S. amateurs may find non-amateur stations in those segments, and must avoid interfering with them**

Some frequencies and even some bands that are available to ham operators to use may have other uses which could take priority over the use of Ham radio operators. For instance - The 60 meter band has frequencies which the government has priority use over. If a Ham radio operator trying to use a frequency in the 60-meter band but hears official communication from government officials, they must relinquish use of that frequency and not cause interference.

Other radio types have these restrictions as well - MURS for instance uses frequencies that some businesses have priority use over due to past licensing history.

T1B09
Why should you not set your transmit frequency to be exactly at the edge of an amateur band or sub-band?

Correct Answer is "D" - **All these choices are correct**

For this question, the issue boils down to the bandwidth of the frequency when you transmit. See - The frequency you key in is the dead-on center and specific frequency you will be transmitting in. But - Your transmission takes up frequencies on either side of the transmit frequency. One side is the UPPER Sideband, the other side is the LOWER sideband.

I wideband transmission uses a 25kHz wide channel with 5kHz deviation while a narrow band transmission uses just 12.5kHz with 2.5kHz deviation. (Note - Digital modes such as DMR use 12.5-kHz wide channels allowing (2) channels to ride on the same transmission as a single Ham 25-kHz signal. This is part of the push to digital - more use of the same frequencies).

So - If you are communicating on a wide-band channel on 148-MHz (Top edge of the VHF 2-Meter band) then your communication actually extends 12.5-kHz ABOVE the 148.000 center of the frequency, so you are transmitting into 148.125-MHz which is outside of the band and you are now illegal. This explains why our "B" answer is correct. As for "A" and "C" - these are correct also because even if you transmit at 147.875-MHz which would put you at 148.000 at the upper edge, if your radio has a calibration error or your radio has a transmitter frequency drift, then you could cross the edge of the legal band.

Read more on this question on the following page(s): 6-22

T1B10 - (N)
Where may SSB phone be used in amateur bands above 50 MHz?

Correct Answer is "C" - **In at least some segment of all these bands**

SSB Phone use refers to Single-Site-Band Voice transmissions in frequencies above 50 MHz. When you get your license, your most common radios being used will be FM Modulated (Frequency Modulated) radios which do not perform SSB or Single-Side-Band communications. SSB is a function of AM Radio which is used with higher end radios and performs very differently from the handheld FM Radios you may be using or more familiar with starting out.

All of the bands offer some frequencies where you are allowed to use SSB modes. SSB does have some advantages over FM in that it allows better use of the power in the radio and more opportunities for greater distance.

https://hamradioschool.com/single-sideband-2-meters-vhf-mode/

T1B11 - (M)
What is the maximum peak envelope power output for Technician class operators in their HF band segments?

Correct Answer is "A" - **200 watts**

As a technician, you do have limits that do not exist as a General license holder. A Tech can transmit at 200-watts on HF bands, and 10-Meters is the only band open to Techs. As a General license holder you will have permission to all of the HF Bands, and you will have a maximum power transmission limit of 1500-watts.

You must remember - As a Tech, the 200-watt limit is for HF bands only. On VHF/UHF bands, maximum power levels of 1500 watts is allowed. You need to keep this difference in mind - 200-watts on HF, 1500-watts on VHF/UHF.

Read more on this question on the following page(s): 6-69

T1B12
Except for some specific restrictions, what is the maximum peak envelope power output for Technician class operators using frequencies above 30 MHz?

Correct Answer is "D" - **1500 watts**

The limitation for 10-Meters for a technician is 200-watts which is in the 28-MHz frequency range (Below this 30-MHz). This is something that you need to remember - 200-watts for HF, otherwise 1500-watts.

Read more on this question on the following page(s): 6-69

T1C01

For which license classes are new licenses currently available from the FCC?

Correct Answer is "D" - **Technician, General, Amateur Extra**

All of these answers have 1 thing in common EXCEPT for the correct answer - A, B, and C all have 4 license levels listed. Currently there are only 3 license levels: Technician, General, and Amateur Extra. In the past there were 2 additional levels which were Novice and Advanced. The Novice used to be the entry-level license. The Advanced license came after the General and before the Amateur Extra license level.

Remember - 3 License levels.

Read more on this question on the following page(s): 6-68

T1C02

Who may select a desired call sign under the vanity call sign rules?

Correct Answer is "D" - **Any licensed amateur**

A Vanity call sign is a custom call sign that you MIGHT be able to request provided the call sign is available. This allows you to personalize your call sign. But - Be aware - Sometimes you could have a call sign that does not "Roll" off the tongue during conversations. I discovered this after getting a vanity call sign when I got my general - The characters just conflicted and did not roll off the tongue together very well. When I later received my AE call sign, I actually got a good call sign so I did not try to get another vanity call sign.

When you receive your Tech call sign, that call sign stays with you when you get your General license but a new one will be assigned to you when you get an Amateur Extra license. At any time you can apply for a vanity call sign.

T1C03

What types of international communications are an FCC-licensed amateur radio station permitted to make?

Correct Answer is "A" - **Communications incidental to the purposes of the Amateur Radio Service and remarks of a personal character**

Ham radio is intended for amateur use for general conversation, but not for any form of business. This is for international and local communications. Under extreme situations such as disasters and emergencies, ham radio is used for communication emergency information, calls for assistance and aid, and information needed for emergency organization and planning.

Broadcasting - the act of transmitting communications for wide or public use is not legal with ham radio. However - communications that you may be providing during emergencies is also never considered private and cannot be coded or encrypted, so is available to any ham operators with the ability to receive and monitor frequencies you may be using.

T1C04 - (N)
What may happen if the FCC is unable to reach you by email?

Correct Answer is "B" - **Revocation of the station license or suspension of the operator license**

You are required to keep your current address up to date in the FCC database for any communication that they may send to you. If your address information is not up to date after you are reached out to, your station license may be revoked or suspended.

Read more on this question on the following page(s): 6-69

T1C05 - (M)
Which of the following is a valid Technician class call sign format?

Correct Answer is "A" - **KF1XXX**

Call sign formats have "Adjusted" over the years. Currently the valid call sign structure for a Tech is:

- First 2 letters based on region of the ham operator's home location
- Single number more specific based on region of the ham operator's home location
- Last 3-letters also varying based on region, but ALWAYS ending with 3-letters. This means - 2-Letters, 1-Number, 3-Letters. Also referred to as a 2x3 call sign. In the past, hams would have a 1-character prefix, or a 1x3 call sign, but all of the 1x3 have been assigned.

When you move to an AE license, you will to a 2x2 call sign. As such, you can tell that an operator is an AE licensed operator because they only have 2 characters at the end of the call sign following the number.
This structure is for the US. Other countries may follow other call sign structures.

https://www.fcc.gov/wireless/bureau-divisions/mobility-division/amateur-radio-service/amateur-call-sign-systems

Read more on this question on the following page(s): 6-67

T1C06
From which of the following locations may an FCC-licensed amateur station transmit?

Correct Answer is "D" - **From any vessel or craft located in international waters and documented or registered in the United States**

Of the choices, and it is important to stress that the answer is from the choices given, a radio operator that has an FCC License is legally able to transmit from any vessel, boat or ship that is in international waters AND REGISTERED in the United States. If the vessel is NOT licensed in the United States then the ability to transmit is not allowed.

T1C07 - (N)
Which of the following can result in revocation of the station license or suspension of the operator license?

Correct Answer is "B" - **Failure to provide and maintain a correct email address with the FCC**

In is a requirement that your contact information remain current with the FCC. They may try to reach out to you via Mail or Email. If they are unable to reach you because your contact information is not up to date, they may suspend your license.

T1C08 - (M)
What is the normal term for an FCC-issued amateur radio license?

Correct Answer is "C" - **Ten years**

The FCC License term runs ten years from the date you receive your first license. The term clock does NOT reset when you jump to General license or Amateur Extra license. Renewal for your license is simple and does not require retesting unless you let your license lapse, at which point you may need to retest.

Read more on this question on the following page(s): 6-67

T1C09 - (M)
What is the grace period for renewal if an amateur license expires?

Correct Answer is "A" - **Two years**

If you fail to renew your license when it expires you will have two years in which to renew the license. During this time, you are not supposed to talk on the radio - you can always listen but not transmit. During the two years renewal is simple. After two years you will be required to retest and may lose your call sign.

Read more on this question on the following page(s): 6-67

T1C10 - (M)
How soon after passing the examination for your first amateur radio license may you transmit on the amateur radio bands?

Correct Answer is "C" - **As soon as your operator/station license grant appears in the FCC's license database**

Before you receive an email with a link to download and print your license, you will appear in the Radio License lookup database. As soon as you do, you are good to go and start transmitting. If someone hears you and decides to look you up, the license database is where they will validate your license level and information.

Read more on this question on the following page(s): 6-67

T1C11 - (M)

If your license has expired and is still within the allowable grace period, may you continue to transmit on the amateur radio bands?

Correct Answer is "D" - **No, you must wait until the license has been renewed**

During the renewal grace period you are NOT allowed to transmit. You may listen, but not talk and participate in ham communications. Remember also that after your two-year grace period expires, if you have not renewed you must re-test.

Read more on this question on the following page(s): 6-67

T1D01

With which countries are FCC-licensed amateur radio stations prohibited from exchanging communications?

Correct Answer is "A" - **Any country whose administration has notified the International Telecommunication Union (ITU) that it objects to such communications**

If a country identifies themselves as objecting to Ham operators communicating with their citizens, then those countries will be listed and you should not attempt to reach anyone in those countries. If you do unwittingly establish communications with an operator from a banned country you should politely end the conversation. According to the FCC, as of January 2022 there are NO banned countries. For up to date information from the FCC check out this URL:

https://www.fcc.gov/wireless/bureau-divisions/mobility-division/amateur-radio-service/international-arrangements

Read more on this question on the following page(s): 6-69

T1D02 - (N)

Under which of the following circumstances are one-way transmissions by an amateur station prohibited?

Correct Answer is "B" - **Broadcasting**

"Broadcasting" is the act of going on a frequency and talking to the general public with no other party responding. As a Ham operator, you are not a news broadcaster, traffic reporter, or weather person. You should not be broadcasting.

If you are on a net that is coordinating the passing of information, such an emergency net, or a storm net that is actively collecting reports, that is not broadcasting. In that case you are communicating with a control operator who may be collecting information. Also during a storm updates a control operator may give weather updates out with the expectation of other hams participating in the conversation. Sometimes there may be a fine line between "Broadcasting" and normal operation - but that generally is separated with the formation of an active net and multiple individuals participating in the information such as a storm net. We have these often in Florida with hurricane nets or Skywarn nets.

T1D03
When is it permissible to transmit messages encoded to obscure their meaning?

Correct Answer is "C" - **Only when transmitting control commands to space stations or radio control craft**

During normal communications including voice communications you should never try to encode your messages. The exception is in the control of remote aircraft or space stations (Satellites) where there needs to be a level of security over the devices you are controlling. The purpose is not for sending hidden messages but rather for the safe operation of remote craft.

T1D04
Under what conditions is an amateur station authorized to transmit music using a phone emission?

Correct Answer is "A" - **When incidental to an authorized retransmission of manned spacecraft communications**

The only exception to the "No Music" rule is when you are in communication through Ham Radio to a manned spacecraft such as the ISS. Sending a wakeup ring in music for instance - but only when you are authorized to do so. This includes music playing in the background during a regular voice communication. If talking, turn down (or off) the radio. Also - be aware that a bad microphone where the PTT can cause broadcasting of music if you are unaware the radio PTT button is pressed.

T1D05 - (M)
When may amateur radio operators use their stations to notify other amateurs of the availability of equipment for sale or trade?

Correct Answer is "D" - **When selling amateur radio equipment and not on a regular basis**

What this means is you cannot hold a sale or auction or any type of marketing/sales events on the radio. That would be profiting and falls under one of the areas not legal. If however, you are having a discussion or net and the topic of looking for equipment or having something you want to sell comes up and it is not the purpose of the net, then it is acceptable to discuss selling of equipment.

T1D06
What, if any, are the restrictions concerning transmission of language that may be considered indecent or obscene?

Correct Answer is "B" - **Any such language is prohibited**

Ham radio is considered a mature, polite and clean hobby. Ham Operators enjoy being helpful to others getting into the hobby and enjoy expanding the number of folks who participate in the hobby. As such we expect others to be considerate and polite on the radio. Use of foul and obscene language does not fall within the expectations and is prohibited - Not that it doesn't happen.

T1D07

What types of amateur stations can automatically retransmit the signals of other amateur stations?

Correct Answer is "D" - **Repeater, auxiliary, or space stations**

A Repeater is an "OPEN" station which will rebroadcast an inbound communication back out. When we say they are "Open" - they are available for any ham operator to transmit through using the proper frequency and tone signals.

An "Auxiliary" station is very similar, but these are "CLOSED" systems that require special codes to activate and operate. An auxiliary station also operates on very specific frequencies in the bands. They can also not only be used for repeating voice communications, but they could be used for controlling remote devices.

A Space station is any space satellite that can be used to repeat communications. A Ham can communicate to a satellite for instance and his message recorded for playback later to other hams elsewhere. A good place to start for more information on Satellite commutations is the website https://heavens-above.com/.

Read more on this question on the following page(s): 6-75

T1D08

In which of the following circumstances may the control operator of an amateur station receive compensation for operating that station?

Correct Answer is "B" - **When the communication is incidental to classroom instruction at an educational institution**

Ham Radio is not considered a hobby that someone can specifically make money in. Use of the Ham radio is for amateur radio use ONLY. Not for commercial operation, not for dispatching, and not for any form of business. The only way that income can be earned in operating a Ham Radio is when it is in part of the teaching ham radio. Students who pay a fee for a ham radio course, and where Ham radio is used live in the class by the instructor, is allowed. Students who are not licensed ham operators cannot operate a ham radio in a way that involves transmitting but can operate a radio in receiving/listening mode.

This does not apply to individuals working in respects to setting up equipment, installation of antennas, or performing any services that do not involve transmitting on ham radio or acting as control operator. If you are hired to install an antenna to be used in ham radio this is perfectly allowable as long as you are not being hired to operate the radio outside of educational instruction.

T1D09 - (M)

When may amateur stations transmit information in support of broadcasting, program production, or news gathering, assuming no other means is available?

Correct Answer is "A" - **When such communications are directly related to the immediate safety of human life or protection of property**

We have learned and know that "Broadcasting" is not permissible in ham radio. There is an exception however in that during an emergency when other means of communications are not available, using the radio to disseminate information through broadcasting or requesting of participation from other licensed radio operators is allowed.

T1D10 - (M)
How does the FCC define broadcasting for the Amateur Radio Service?

Correct Answer is "D" - **Transmissions intended for reception by the general public**

Broadcasting is the act of transmitting communications out to the general public and not necessarily for the purpose of requesting information from others. This is not an allowable action under normal circumstances, however, may be allowable during an emergency event when normal communications has failed. If working during an emergency event, the local Emergency Operation Centers or local government may call up teams of ham operators to perform these functions.

T1D11 - (M)
When may an amateur station transmit without identifying on the air?

Correct Answer is "D" - **When transmitting signals to control model craft**

Ham operators are ALWAYS required to identify themselves by their call sign or by a tactical call sign as a member of a team, and identify every ten minutes during radio operation.

The ONLY exception to this is when transmitting to control a remote craft such as a radio controlled plane or boat where you are controlling a remote device and not holding a two-way communication.

T1E01
When may an amateur station transmit without a control operator?

Correct Answer is "D" - **Never**

An Amateur station can NEVER transmit without a control operator. Even with a repeater - there needs to be a control operator. The control operator may not necessarily be present, however must have a method of remote controlling and being able to shut down the repeater if necessary. Though not present, this level of control does meet the requirements of a control station.

T1E02 - (M)
Who may be the control operator of a station communicating through an amateur satellite or space station?

Correct Answer is "D" - **Any amateur allowed to transmit on the satellite uplink frequency**

In this question we are looking at the person who is transmitting through the remote satellite or space station, not the person in charge of the remote satellite or space station. In this case, we are not concerned with the rules around the satellite or space station, only the rules around the station communicating. As such, the amateur operator themselves must be in control of their own transmitting station - not the space station or satellite.

T1E03

Who must designate the station control operator?

Correct Answer is "A" - **The station licensee**

The licensee is the person holding the license. Basically - if you have a license and you loan your radio out to someone, you are taking responsibility to make sure that that person you are loaning the radio to has the proper license level to operate that station within the frequencies that they will be operating the radio under. If you are a "General" license holder and you loan a radio capable of HF/VHF/UHF frequencies, you must make sure the operator you loan the station to only operates in the proper frequency ranges. So, a Tech can only operate under VHF/UHF frequencies plus the very limited frequencies available in the 10-Meter band.

The Control Operator must be licensed, but the owner of the station may hold some responsibility as well for laws broken by loaning of equipment to unlicensed or not properly licensed operators.

Read more on this question on the following page(s): 6-68

T1E04

What determines the transmitting frequency privileges of an amateur station?

Correct Answer is "D" - **The class of operator license held by the control operator**

If as an operator you only have a TECH level license, but you are operating a radio capable of other frequencies such as an ICOM-7100 radio (My portable HF/VHF/UHF Radio) - You can ONLY transmit on frequencies based on your license. The radio capabilities do not add to what you can do.

Read more on this question on the following page(s): 6-68

T1E05

What is an amateur station's control point?

Correct Answer is "C" - **The location at which the control operator function is performed**

The control point is where the radio station is being controlled. For a handheld radio that is literally your hand. For a radio that may have a 200' antenna attached, the control point is not the point where the transmissions are emanating from (The antenna) but where the transceiver is being used - where you are at holding the microphone.

If remotely controlling a device such as a repeater, the control point is still the location where the remote control is being performed. Since repeaters can be controlled from locations many miles away, that control point therefore is that location where control is being rendered - not the repeater location.

T1E06 - (M)

When, under normal circumstances, may a Technician class licensee be the control operator of a station operating in an Amateur Extra Class band segment?

Correct Answer is "A" - **At no time**

A Technical class operator can ONLY transmit on the frequencies covered by their license. Once you obtain your General License you will have access to ALL of the bands, but not all of the frequencies.

In may frequency bands there are still a limited number of frequencies only allowed to AE operators which include as shown here :

80 Meters
3.500-3.600 MHz: CW, RTTY/Data
3.600-4.000 MHz: CW, Phone, Image

40 Meters
7.000-7.125 MHz : CW, RTTY/Data
7.125-7.300 MHz:: CW, Phone, Image

20 Meters
14.000 – 14.150 MHz CW, RTTY/Data
14.150 -14.350 MHz: CW, Phone, Image

15 Meters
21.000-21.200 MHz: CW, RTTY/Data
21.200-21.450 MHz: CW, Phone, Image

AT NO TIME can a Tech Class operator use frequencies outside of those covered by their Tech license.

Read more on this question on the following page(s): 6-68

T1E07 - (M)
When the control operator is not the station licensee, who is responsible for the proper operation of the station?

Correct Answer is "D" - **The control operator and the station licensee**

What this refers to - When a radio is loaned out, both the operator of the radio and the owner of the radio are responsible for proper operation of the radio station. ALWAYS LOAN YOUR EQUIPMENT TO KNOWN RESPONSIBLE RADIO OPERATORS. You may be found responsible for improper use as well as the person improperly using the radio!

Read more on this question on the following page(s): 6-68

T1E08
Which of the following is an example of automatic control?

Correct Answer is "A" - **Repeater operation**

A repeater is considered under "Automatic" control because it normally operates without an actual hand-on operator. This does not mean that it has no control operator - There must be a control operator capable of shutting it off or resetting it if a problem occurs. But the control operator may perform this function remotely and not necessarily onsite. During regular operation, the repeater will be under "Automatic Control" as well as remote control by a control operator.

Read more on this question on the following page(s): 6-75

T1E09

Which of the following are required for remote control operation?

Correct Answer is "D" - **All these choices are correct**

For remote control operation an operator must be at the control point. This could be as simple as a handheld radio using DTMF codes for remote operation. The control operator must be available at all times. This may be as simple as the remote operator being able to be called by telephone to perform remote operation or receiving a Text or call out message to perform the operational task. The control must be able to indirectly manipulate the controls - This may be having the ability to reset or shut off a remote system if necessary which could be performed through a remote radio connection, Smart phone control, or via an Internet connection,

T1E10

Which of the following is an example of remote control as defined in Part 97?

Correct Answer is "B" - **Operating the station over the internet**

Stations can be controlled easily through Internet communications using a desktop, laptop, tablet or even a smart phone. In the age of Zoom calls and classes, remote control via the Internet is easy.

A repeater falls under "Automatic Control" as it normally is operating automatically.

A model aircraft, boat or car is being operated DIRECTLY by the control operator of the device.

T1E11

Who does the FCC presume to be the control operator of an amateur station, unless documentation to the contrary is in the station records?

Correct Answer is "D" - **The station licensee**

If someone from the FCC walks up to you regarding an issue with a particular amateur radio station (Such as a station broadcasting outside of allowable frequencies), it will be presumed that the operator of the station is the control operator and owner of the station unless you have station documentation that states otherwise. So if borrowing a radio from someone, it could be a good idea to get some form of ownership documentation on the station that states who owns the station. This could be of particular interest if the station is a non-manufactured custom build radio station.

T1F01

When must the station and its records be available for FCC inspection?

Correct Answer is "B" - **At any time upon request by an FCC representative**

If a FCC representative makes a request for station records then those records MUST be made available when requested. This question is more applicable for custom built radio systems though it applies to ALL radios.

As a Tech you are much less likely to keep these types of records - particularly for inexpensive handheld radios or mass manufactured radios where no customizations are being made. If the radio is home-built where there is more chance for problems this could be more important of an issue.

T1F02 - (M)

How often must you identify with your FCC-assigned call sign when using tactical call signs such as "Race Headquarters"?

Correct Answer is "C" - **At the end of each communication and every ten minutes during a communication**

TACTICAL CALL SIGNS: During an event you may be using a Tactical call sign - This makes it easier to identify the NET CONTROL of the radio net when radio net operators switch out. In an emergency a radio net could go on for days, but across multiple operators the NET CONTROL call sign with a Tactical call sign would ALWAYS remain the same.

During a conversation it is normal to identify yourself at the beginning of a conversation. In addition, per FCC rules, you always identify yourself at the end of your communication and every ten minutes during a communication. This does not mean at the end of every message - But when you end your total conversation identify yourself at that point, and if the conversation extends longer than ten minutes then identify yourself every ten minutes.

Remember this - This rule DOES NOT STATE IDENTIFYING YOURSELF AT THE BEGINNING OF A CONVERSATION THOUGH NORMALLY WE DO. THIS RULE STATES EVERY TEN MINUTES AND AT THE END.

T1F03 - (M)
When are you required to transmit your assigned call sign?

Correct Answer is "D" - **At least every 10 minutes during and at the end of a communication**

NOTE: This is similar to T1F02 - but that question relates to TACTICAL signs where this one refers to your Personal call sign.

During a conversation it is normal to identify yourself at the beginning of a conversation. In addition, per FCC rules, you always identify yourself at the end of your communication and every ten minutes during a communication. This does not mean at the end of every message - But when you end your total conversation identify yourself at that point, and if the conversation extends longer than ten minutes then identify yourself every ten minutes.

Remember this - This rule DOES NOT STATE IDENTIFYING YOURSELF AT THE BEGINNING OF A CONVERSATION THOUGH NORMALLY WE DO. THIS RULE STATES EVERY TEN MINUTES AND AT THE END.

Read more on this question on the following page(s): 6-67

T1F04 - (M)
What language may you use for identification when operating in a phone sub-band?

Correct Answer is "C" - **English**

During a conversation you may use another language other than English - But ALL IDENTIFICATION IN THE US MUST BE PERFORMED USING ENGLISH.

T1F05
What method of call sign identification is required for a station transmitting phone signals?

Correct Answer is "B" - **Send the call sign using a CW or phone emission**

Call sign identification can be performed using either Voice signaling (Verbal speaking) or optionally can use CW/Morse code. If you ever key up a repeater and hear tones, that is the identification of the repeater station via Morse code (CW). This is perfectly legal under FCC Rules and is normal for repeaters though often repeaters may use robotic verbal identification.

T1F06
Which of the following self-assigned indicators are acceptable when using a phone transmission?

Correct Answer is "D" - **All these choices are correct**

A Self-assigned indicator is an addition you make to your call sign when you are using your call sign in a region other than your home region. In this example the call sign KL7CC starts with "KL7" which indicates a location of Alaska. By adding the "stroke", "Slant" or "Slash" W3 at the end, you are telling listeners that you are working in region "W3" temporarily, in this case "W" indicates the lower 48 states, and "3" indicates Pennsylvania, Maryland or Delaware.

The use of "Stroke", "Slant" or "Slash" does not matter - Po-"TA"-to or Po-"Tah"-to so to say.

T1F07 - (M)
Which of the following restrictions apply when a non-licensed person is allowed to speak to a foreign station using a station under the control of a licensed amateur operator?

Correct Answer is "B" - **The foreign station must be in a country with which the U.S. has a third party agreement**

In Ham Radio, a "3rd Party" is an individual that is communicating that is not a licensed operator. Some countries do not allow non-licensed operators to communicate to their citizens. For a country to allow a third party to communicate to one of their citizens, then a third party agreement must exist. A list of countries that the United States has a third party agreement with can be found at the following website:

https://www.fcc.gov/wireless/bureau-divisions/mobility-division/amateur-radio-service/international-arrangements

T1F08
What is the definition of third party communications?

Correct Answer is "A" - **A message from a control operator to another amateur station control operator on behalf of another person**

A third party communication can be either a message that a control operator from one station passes to the control operator of a second station on behalf of a third party, or could be an actual non-licensed person speaking over a radio under the control of a licensed operator. So a third party is an operator OTHER than the licensed operator. It has nothing to do with a third radio station and has nothing to do with who has the license of the transmitting equipment. It also has nothing to do with temporary authorization to transmit.

T1F09

What type of amateur station simultaneously retransmits the signal of another amateur station on a different channel or channels?

Correct Answer is "C" - **Repeater station**

A repeater works by immediately retransmitting an incoming signal back out on a slightly different frequency set off enough so that is does not conflict with the incoming signal. Separation on better repeaters is performed using high quality signals. The key - The repeater receives AND transmits back out.

A beacon station refers to a station that simply sends out a broadcast for some type of identification purpose - if does not receive.

An earth station simply a station that is located within 50km of the earth's surface.

And a Message Forwarding station would receive a message and then retransmit it after being received - not retransmit simultaneously. (A Simplex repeater will fall into this category whereas the repeater this question is referring to is a "Duplex Repeater" retransmitting simultaneously as it is receiving.

Read more on this question on the following page(s): 6-75

T1F10

Who is accountable if a repeater inadvertently retransmits communications that violate the FCC rules?

Correct Answer is "A" - **The control operator of the originating station**

It is important to understand the exact meaning of this question. We are not referring to a repeater that is tuned properly and retransmitting back out on a legal ham frequency. So we are not talking about the proper or improper frequencies - we are talking about the content of the message. Let's say someone is talking through a repeater using foul language. The content of the message is what is in violation. So - if a repeater is repeating a message that breaks the FCC rules, who is responsible?

The repeater in this case is not at fault, so the second and third answers are NOT correct. Since both of those are incorrect, then the fourth answer is incorrect.

The correct answer is "A" - The control operator of the originating station is the person responsible.

Read more on this question on the following page(s): 6-75

T1F11

Which of the following is a requirement for the issuance of a club station license grant?

Correct Answer is "B" - **The club must have at least four members**

Would you like to form your own club and get a club license? You need FOUR participating members to make a club.

Read more on this question on the following page(s): 6-68

T2A01

What is a common repeater frequency offset in the 2 meter band?

Correct Answer is "B" - **Plus or minus 600 kHz**

This is a question best memorized - 600 kHz is the frequency shift between receive and transmit on a 2-Meter repeater. With the lower frequency, the lower value applies, though not the lowest. You have to memorize two valid possibilities - 600-kHz as used for 2-Meters, and 5.0-MHz as used for 70-cm.

2-Meters band ranges from 144-MHz to 148-MHz using 600-kHz offset. 70-cm band ranges from 420-MHz to 450-MHz. using 5.0-MHz offset.

Read more on this question on the following page(s): 6-77

T2A02

What is the national calling frequency for FM simplex operations in the 2-meter band?

Correct Answer is "A" - **146.520 MHz**

A Calling frequency is like CB Radio Channel "19". It is a frequency to use when you have no set frequency in mind that you want to reach out to. In a remote area this would be the frequency that you would first use in calling ut in an emergency or calling out when trying to reach another ham operator with no other known frequency in mind. It is also a "SIMPLEX" frequency - Not a repeater-based frequency. So your range is going to be more limited.

On 2-Meters the simplex calling frequency is 146.520 MHz, no tone needed and no off shift frequency. (Off shift frequencies and tones would be used to communicate with a repeater.)

On the 70-cm band, the simplex calling frequency is 446.000-MHz

Most bands will have a Simplex calling frequency. A list of all band simplex calling frequencies can be found at the following URL:
  https://www.hamuniverse.com/simplexoperating.html

Read more on this question on the following page(s): 6-24

T2A03

What is a common repeater frequency offset in the 70 cm band?

Correct Answer is "A" - **Plus or minus 5 MHz**

The standard off-shift amount is the difference that a repeater uses between the transmit frequency and the receive frequency. For the 2-Meter band, the offset is 600-kHz. For the 70-cm band, the proper offset is 5.0-MHz. The offset for 70-cm is larger due to the higher frequency levels.

If a repeater is transmitting at 442.500 MHz, then it will have a receiving frequency that is 5.0-Mhz above that which is 447.500-MHz.

Note that the offset direction, or whether the the difference if the 5.0-MHz difference is above (+) or below (-) the repeaters transmit frequency is determined by what the repeaters trasnmit frequency is.

Read more on this question on the following page(s): 6-77

T2A04

What is an appropriate way to call another station on a repeater if you know the other station's call sign?

Correct Answer is "B" - **Say the station's call sign, then identify with your call sign**

Calling out to another known operator is easy - Simply give their call sign over the radio followed by your own call sign. "Calling XK123, this is YK567". You may do this multiple times. Often if you do not get a response, meaning the station you are calling is not on the air, you can end the communication with "YK567 Standing By".

Read more on this question on the following page(s): 6-79

T2A05

How should you respond to a station calling CQ?

Correct Answer is "C" - **Transmit the other station's call sign followed by your call sign**

Your response can be as simple as "XK123 this is YK566". Then hold your conversation in simple english, no coding or lingo needed. Just remember to identify yourself every ten minutes and at the end of your conversation.

T2A06

Which of the following is required when making on-the-air test transmissions?

Correct Answer is "A" - **Identify the transmitting station**

When testing your radio, antenna, or installation you should always identify yourself with your call sign when you transmit.

T2A07

What is meant by "repeater offset"?

Correct Answer is "A" - **The difference between a repeater's transmit and receive frequencies**

The repeater offset is the amount of frequency difference that exists between a repeater's transmit frequency and it's receive-frequency. This is important to remember and will be on your test. The offset for 2-Meters is 600-kHz (+ or -). The offset for 70-cm is 5.0 MHz (+ or -). The (+) of (-) indicates that the receive frequency is above or below the transmit frequency.

Read more on this question on the following page(s): 6-77

T2A08

What is the meaning of the procedural signal "CQ"?

Correct Answer is "D" - **Calling any station**

"CQ" is an abbreviation commonly used for "Calling any station" and is more often used on HF frequencies in calling out over longer distances.

T2A09 - (N)

Which of the following indicates that a station is listening on a repeater and looking for a contact?

Correct Answer is "B" - **The station's call sign followed by the word "monitoring"**

When calling out on a repeater frequency, or often calling out in general, a Ham operator will call out with the language "YK567 Monitoring". This lets monitoring stations know who you are and that you are standing by for a response. You may choose to respond, or not.

Optionally if you are talking on a repeater network which has multiple repeaters in multiple areas communicating, you could use "YK567 on the TAMPA repeater, Monitoring." This let's listening stations know that you are online listening and where you are generally located.

Read more on this question on the following page(s): 6-79

T2A10

What is a band plan, beyond the privileges established by the FCC?

Correct Answer is "A" - **A voluntary guideline for using different modes or activities within an amateur band**

In a region or area, ham operators form groups called "Frequency Coordinators" made up of volunteers to coordinate the use of ham radio frequencies within their area. These areas may be state-wide or greater areas. The frequency coordinator organizations will develop "Band Plans" to set aside certain frequencies or frequency ranges to be used for different purposes - Simplex, Repeater use, SSB, CW, Beacons, Radio remote control, and other purposes.

More about Frequency Coordination can be found here:
https://www.hamuniverse.com/hamrepeatercoordination.html

T2A11

What term describes an amateur station that is transmitting and receiving on the same frequency?

Correct Answer is "C" - **Simplex**

For the answers, just think of "SIMPLE" related to "SIMPLEX". Simplex is the act of transmitting and receiving on the same frequency. There is no second frequency, no tone coding, and no offset settings.
Full Duplex refers to the use of two frequencies for transmit and receiving simultaneously.
Duplex refers to the transmitting of two independent signals simultaneously on the same carrier frequency.
Multiplex refers to transmitting multiple signals or messages on the same channel. Simplex is the correct answer.

T2A12 - (M)

What should you do before calling CQ?

Correct Answer is "D" - **All these choices are correct**

Before calling CQ or initiating communication on a frequency, the operator should:

1. Listen first to be sure there is no one using the frequency.
2. Ask if the frequency is in use.

3. Lastly make sure that you have authorization to use that frequency. This revolves around making sure that the frequency falls within the allowance of your radio license use.

All of the choices in this question are correct.

T2B01 - (M)
How is a VHF/UHF transceiver's "reverse" function used?

Correct Answer is "C" - **To listen on a repeater's input frequency**

When listening to a repeater, ham radios - including the popular Baofeng radio used by many new Ham operators, preppers and experienced ham operators as backup radios. The "Reverse" function is a button or button combination you can press on your radio that allows the radio to receive on a repeater's receiving frequency instead of its transmitting frequency, and to transmit on the repeater's transmit frequency. Reversing the transmit/receive frequencies.

Why would you need to do this? This is handy for troubleshooting a repeater or listening for a weak signal close by trying to hit a repeater. If an operator is transmitting to a repeater with a weak signal, a NET CONTROL operator can ask if anyone can hear the weak signal and relay the message using their radio's Reverse function. Other radio operators close to the operator with the weak signal may be able to hear the weak transmitter and relay the message.

So the Reverse function allows a radio operator to listen on a repeaters input/receive frequency instead of the repeaters output/transmit frequency.

Read more on this question on the following page(s): 6-78

T2B02
What term describes the use of a sub-audible tone transmitted along with normal voice audio to open the squelch of a receiver?

Correct Answer is "D" - **CTCSS**

CTCSS stands for "Continuous-Tone-Coded-Squelch-System" and is a sub-audible tone that is transmitted when you are transmitting on a frequency. This sub-audible tone can be one of many frequencies and is used as a sort of "Hand-shake" with the repeaters. When the repeater hears the correct CTCSS tone, it knows that the incoming communication is intended specifically for itself, and it then proceeds to rebroadcast the communication out on its transmitting frequency. If the correct CTCSS Tone frequency is not heard, then the communication is ignored and is not repeated.

Read more on this question on the following page(s): 6-77

T2B03 - (N)
Which of the following describes a linked repeater network?

Correct Answer is "A" - **A network of repeaters in which signals received by one repeater are transmitted by all the repeaters in the network**

Linked repeaters are "The Bomb" so to say - A set of repeaters that are linked together act over a much greater geographical area than a single individual repeater would. In my state of Florida, our SARNET repeater network allows Tech level operators to communicate with other ham radio operators all across the state, from the panhandle of Pensacola and Panama City, east to Jacksonville, South to Miami and into the Florida Keys, and up along the west coast of Florida including Ft. Myers and Tampa.

Read more on this question on the following page(s): 6-76

T2B04
Which of the following could be the reason you are unable to access a repeater whose output you can hear?

Correct Answer is "D" - **All these choices are correct**

There are many reasons why you may not be able to access a repeater. In our choices we have improper

transceiver offset - If you set your radio to an offset value different from what the repeater is expecting, then it will not be listening for you on the frequency you are transmitting on. You are using the wrong CTCSS tone - A repeater uses either an audible CTCSS tone or a Digital Code Squelch (DCS) to activate the repeater. If you are not transmitting the proper CTCSS Audible tone, then the repeater will not repeat your message. You are likely using the wrong DCS tone - A repeater uses either an audible CTCSS tone or a Digital Code Squelch (DCS) to activate the repeater. If you are not transmitting the proper DCS Digital code, then the repeater will not repeat your communication.

Read more on this question on the following page(s): 6-78

T2B05 - (M)
What would cause your FM transmission audio to be distorted on voice peaks?

Correct Answer is "C" - **You are talking too loudly**

Distortion is often caused by one of two causes - You are talking too loudly into the microphone, or you are talking too closely into the microphone. In this question you have four possible answers.

If the repeater offset is inverted then you will not be heard at all.

If you need to talk louder as in our second option, your voice will come across weak.

If the transmit power is too high, then the entire transmission would be distorted. According to the question here, the FM transmission audio is distorted ONLY on voice peaks.

The thing to remember with this question is that they are talking about VOICE PEAKS which will be tied directly to your speaking into the microphone.

T2B06 - (M)
What type of signaling uses pairs of audio tones?

Correct Answer is "A" - **DTMF**

DTMF (Dual-Tone-Multi-Frequency) is a method of dual-tones generated through the keypad of a radio sent during a transmission and are used to control remote equipment or used as access tones. This is the same as used in a push-button telephone.

T2B07

How can you join a digital repeater's "talkgroup"?

Correct Answer is "C" - **Program your radio with the group's ID or code**

Talkgroups are used in Digital radio modes to allow your radio to participate in specific group talks on the radio. This is a function available using DMR radio and other digital modes. You can program your radio with a specific talk group ID or code. Talkgroup criteria can be based on topic that has been established or a regional criteria such as country, states, counties, cities, etc.

T2B08 - (M)

Which of the following applies when two stations transmitting on the same frequency interfere with each other?

Correct Answer is "A" - **The stations should negotiate continued use of the frequency**

No ham owns a frequency. An operator may own a repeater but use of a particular frequency must be shared and users that are on the same frequency must negotiate the use of the frequency. Ultimately the stations may choose another frequency to avoid conflict, however that is NOT the primary action. It is true that interference MAY be inevitable but taking no action does not resolve the conflict. Subaudible tones can help in filtering communications but two stations transmitting at the same time may still have problems that filtering will not help with. The proper answer is that the stations should negotiate the continued use of the frequency

T2B09 - (N)

Why are simplex channels designated in the VHF/UHF band plans?

Correct Answer is "A" - **So stations within range of each other can communicate without tying up a repeater**

As a general rule Repeaters are used to establish contact with other operators. However - If you are close enough to another ham operator that you have made contact with, you should move to a simplex channel. This frees up the repeater for others to use, and it also gives you some level of privacy. Though others can still hear you, you are limiting the others listening to you to the range of your simplex communication which is much less than your range to the repeater. Often Simplex range will be 1 to 3 miles whereas repeater range is often 25 miles or more. (Depending upon location, geography, and equipment you could get 100 miles or more using simplex on 70-cm/2-m)

T2B10

Which Q signal indicates that you are receiving interference from other stations?

Correct Answer is "A" - **QRM**

"Q" codes are short-hand codes that ham operators use to convey a message in a brief manner. The abbreviated Q code for "Interference from other stations" is QRM.

QRN is short for Natural or Atmospheric Interference. QTH is short for Location. QSB is short for "Fading Signal".

T2B11
Which Q signal indicates that you are changing frequency?

Correct Answer is "B" - **QSY**

"Q" codes are short-hand codes that ham operators use to convey a message in a brief manner. The abbreviated Q code for "Changing Frequency" is QSY. I remembered this one by thinking of QSY as moving to the SYDE (Purposeful misspelling of "Side").

QRU is short for "Have you anything for me". QSL is short for "Can you acknowledge Receipt?". QRZ is short for "Who is calling me?".

T2B12 - (N)
What is the purpose of the color code used on DMR repeater systems?

Correct Answer is "A" - **Must match the repeater color code for access**

Color codes are used by DMR repeaters much the same was as analog repeaters may use CTCSS or DCS codes. There are 16 different possible color codes. To access a DMR repeater you must use the appropriate color code. The color code will establish the group of users on the repeater.

Read more on this question on the following page(s): 6-73

T2B13 - (N)
What is the purpose of a squelch function?

Correct Answer is "B" - **Mute the receiver audio when a signal is not present**

Ham radios will have either an analog squelch controlled with a dial, or a digital squelch set through a menu setting. The squelch will mute weaker signals only allowing stronger signals to be heard, cutting out noise and weak signals from being heard on the radio. While many radios have an analog squelch dial on them, many handheld radios such as the Baofeng radio has a digital squelch that is adjusted through the radio's Menu setting;

T2C01
When do FCC rules NOT apply to the operation of an amateur station?

Correct Answer is "D" - **FCC rules always apply**

The rules established by the FCC will ALWAYS apply to the operation of amateur radio stations in the United States and in US controlled areas such as international waters or US territories.

Read more on this question on the following page(s): 6-69

T2C02 - (N)
Which of the following are typical duties of a Net Control Station?

Correct Answer is "C" - **Call the net to order and direct communications between stations checking in**
The Net Control Station or Net Control Operator is the person who operates a radio net and acts as a "Traffic Cop" to control the flow of information and tracks the users checking into the radio net. The NCS/NCO actually runs the net but he is not top dog in net planning. The Net Manager is actually the one who works out

details on Net meeting time, schedule and frequency to use.

Since A & B are not correct, we can rule out answer D leaving only answer C as the correct answer - Calling the net to order and direct communications between stations checking in.

T2C03 - (N)
What technique is used to ensure that voice messages containing unusual words are received correctly?

Correct Answer is "C" - **Spell the words using a standard phonetic alphabet**

The phonetic alphabet is a word representation for all letters in the alphabet that are easy to recognize when spoken. Using the phonetic alphabet for spelling out words or call signs makes it much easier to understand over the radio - especially when signals may be weak.

For instance:

"Alpha" for "A"
"Bravo" for "B"
"Charlie" for "C"...

T2C04 - (N)
What is RACES?

Correct Answer is "D" - **An FCC part 97 amateur radio service for civil defense communications during national emergencies**

RACES is a volunteer radio organization that works under Civil Defense to provide communications under emergencies. The RACES organization is called up by a government agency to assist with radio communications and remains operational during an emergency only as long as necessary by government offices. Another organization not to be confused with RACES is ARES which is organized by the ARRL and works with Government Emergency Agencies as needed.

T2C05
What does the term "traffic" refer to in net operation?

Correct Answer is "A" - **Messages exchanged by net stations**

The term "Traffic" in radio net operations refers to messages that are being passed by calling radio operators. Traffic can range from messages being passed from area to area such as welfare messages sent during a disaster when normal communications are down, or it could mean announcements or information reports.

T2C06 - (N)
What is the Amateur Radio Emergency Service (ARES)?

Correct Answer is "A" - **A group of licensed amateurs who have voluntarily registered their qualifications and equipment for communications duty in the public service**

ARES is a group organized by the ARRL that works together to provide emergency communications during emergency events. ARES works with emergency operation groups such as state and county Sheriff agencies or EOC centers. ARES members are licensed ham operators who participate working at shelters, hospitals, or remote locations as needed.

T2C07 - (N)
Which of the following is standard practice when you participate in a net?

Correct Answer is "C" - **Unless you are reporting an emergency, transmit only when directed by the net control station**

When participating in an emergency net, participating operators are expected to remain on the frequency but not transmit unless necessary to reduce unneccsary traffic and communications that takes up air time. Unnecessary communications could make it difficult for others active on the net to talk.

T2C08
Which of the following is a characteristic of good traffic handling?

Correct Answer is "A" - **Passing messages exactly as received**

It is important as a Net Control operator to pass messages exactly as they are received clearly. It is not the responsibility of the operator to make any decisions on the traffic being passed or to make any corrections to the messages. It is also NOT the responsibility of the operator to pass messages to the media or act as a liason with the media.

T2C09
Are amateur station control operators ever permitted to operate outside the frequency privileges of their license class?

Correct Answer is "D" - **Yes, but only in situations involving the immediate safety of human life or protection of property**

With Ham radio there is a rule - Anyone can communicate over any radio method available including AE Privileged frequencies without a license but ONLY when necessary for the immediate safety of human life and the protection of property. Under normal operating conditions, amateur operators are still restricted to operate ONLY in the frequencies for which their operator's license covers.

Even if operating as a team during an emergency event, a Tech license holder can only operate on those frequencies as covered by his or her license.

Read more on this question on the following page(s): 6-68

T2C10
What information is contained in the preamble of a formal traffic message?

Correct Answer is "D" - **Information needed to track the message**

The preamble of a message contains several fields that are used to track the message. These fields include:

- Message Number - A Serialized number used during the particular event.
- Message Precedence - Determines the priority of the message as Emergency, Priority, Welfare, Routine or other categories.
- Handling Instructions - Optional and only if needed.
- Station of Origin - The call sign for the station that originated the message.
- Check - The number of word groups in the text of all messages and is required.
- Place of Origin - City and State the message originated from.
- Time filed - optional, containing the time when the message was created by the originating station.
- Month filed - The month number when the message was created.
- Day filed - The day of the month when the message was created.

More on this can be found at: http://www.arrl.org/files/file/Public%20Service/MPG104A.pdf

T2C11 - (M)
What is meant by "check" in a radiogram header?

Correct Answer is "A" - **The number of words or word equivalents in the text portion of the message**

The check is an error checking number used to confirm the number of words passed in a message. The number can be verified between sending station and receiving station as a way to confirm the message that was being passed.

T3A01 - (N)
Why do VHF signal strengths sometimes vary greatly when the antenna is moved only a few feet?

Correct Answer is "C" - **Multipath propagation cancels or reinforces signals**

VHF is a line-of-sight frequency range and the movement of only a few feet can affect the quality of signal because of obstacles that can potentially block the signal, Multipath Propagation is another problem - radio signals may at times reflect off buildings or other obstacles and arrive at the destination station at clightly different times causing distortion or signal strength differences.

Read more on this question on the following page(s): *6-54*

T3A02 - (N)
What is the effect of vegetation on UHF and microwave signals?

Correct Answer is "B" - **Absorption**

Vegetation can affect greatly the range and performance of radio signals - particularly in higher frequency ranges of UHF and Microwave. During winter months when vegetation is sparse, and leaves are fallen from trees UHF and microwave frequencies do travel farther and are less inhibited.

https://www.co.new-kent.va.us/DocumentCenter/View/5217/Measurement-of-Propagation-Loss-in-Trees-at-SHF-Frequencies-PDF?bidId= https://cdn.intechopen.com/pdfs/42732/InTech-Radio_wave_propagation_through_vegetation.pdf

Read more on this question on the following page(s): 6-54

T3A03
What antenna polarization is normally used for long-distance CW and SSB contacts on the VHF and UHF bands?

Correct Answer is "C" - **Horizontal**

Normally under regular operation antennas will be mounted horizontally such as from handheld radios or from antennas mounted on a vehicle. If however the radio operator is looking to work long-distance CW and SSB on VHF or UHF frequency bands, then horizontal polarization is a better mounting position. This allows a better chance of reception from frequencies that may skip in the atmosphere, even though atmospheric propagation is not as common with these bands.

Read more on this question on the following page(s): 6-49

T3A04 - (M)
What happens when antennas at opposite ends of a VHF or UHF line of sight radio link are not using the same polarization?

Correct Answer is "B" - **Received signal strength is reduced**

When two antennas attempting to communicate are using different polarization angles - One using horizontal and another using vertical, then the angle of the radio waves to antenna will cross as a 90 degree angle instead of straight on.

Read more on this question on the following page(s): 6-49

T3A05
When using a directional antenna, how might your station be able to communicate with a distant repeater if buildings or obstructions are blocking the direct line of sight path?

Correct Answer is "B" - **Try to find a path that reflects signals to the repeater**

A directional antenna is capable of picking up weaker signals. Under some frequency bands, some bands, such as VHF and UHF, have characteristics of being easily reflected. If you are having a problem with receiving a signal from a remote location, you may find that by angling a directional antenna away from the direction of the inbound transmitting antenna you may be able to receive the wanted radio signal with better reception quality.

Read more on this question (T3A05) on the following page(s): 6-54

T3A06 - (N)

What is the meaning of the term "picket fencing"?

Correct Answer is "B" - **Rapid flutter on mobile signals due to multipath propagation**

Picket fencing can occur either in a mobile radio while driving, or from a stationary radio station receiving a signal from a moving remote station. The result of picket fencing is the fluttering of signals heard in the quality f the radio signal.

Read more on this question on the following page(s): 6-54

T3A07 - (N)

What weather condition might decrease range at microwave frequencies?

Correct Answer is "C" - **Precipitation**

Water moisture in the air will decrease radio range in higher frequencies in the form of rain, snow, or fog.

Read more on this question on the following page(s): 6-54

T3A08

What is a likely cause of irregular fading of signals propagated by the ionosphere?

Correct Answer is "D" - **Random combining of signals arriving via different paths**

When we talk about signal paths through the ionosphere, we are usually talking about HF radio

communications since VHF/UHF signals do not propagate well through the atmosphere. So we are also talking about greater distances that can go for hundreds or thousands of miles. With these greater distances the chances that your signals going out, or the signals you are receiving, have found multiple paths in their transmission. As such, you may hear differences in the quality of the signals as stronger signals combine and drop that you are receiving.

T3A09

Which of the following results from the fact that signals propagated by the ionosphere are elliptically polarized?

Correct Answer is "B" - **Either vertically or horizontally polarized antennas may be used for transmission or reception**

This is a problem more common with HF frequencies below 10-MHz. As signals pass through the atmosphere can be turned and come back down differently so the normal polarization issue of trying to have the same polarization for receiving and transmitting stations may not apply. As the transmission moves through the atmosphere and becomes distorted in polarization, these changes will result in received signals of mixed polarization allowing either type of polarized types of antennas to be used.

T3A10 - (M)
What effect does multi-path propagation have on data transmissions?

Correct Answer is "D" - **Error rates are likely to increase**

Due to data being received in from multiple paths when multi-path propagation is occurring, it can easily be read incorrectly creating an increased number of error rates. Increasing the transmission rate would increase the number of errors while decreasing may also have no effect on the quality of your data coming through. FM will also have problems with multipath propagation and there is no guarantee that communicating via FM would have any affect, plus FM is only available on VHF/UHF Frequencies and above in Ham radio.

The better solution would be to try to adjust your antenna if possible to reduce path reflection, though this would not necessarily be practical or helpful with HF Transmissions.

Read more on this question on the following page(s): 6-54

T3A11 - (M)
Which region of the atmosphere can refract or bend HF and VHF radio waves?

Correct Answer is "C" - **The ionosphere**

The ionosphere is a layer of ionized atoms and molecules stretching from about 30 miles above the surface to about 600 miles and overlaps into the mesosphere and thermosphere and is responsible for the refraction of radio waves back to earth. Though VHF radio waves can be refracted, this action of refraction is much more effective with HF radio waves - longer radio waves - and is of less use to Tech level ham operators relating those only with a Tech license to more range-limiting line-of-sight frequencies.

The layers of the atmosphere in order from surface to space are: Troposphere, Stratosphere, Mesosphere, Thermosphere, Exosphere and Ionosphere.

Read more on this question on the following page(s): 6-54

T3A12 - (M)
What is the effect of fog and rain on signals in the 10 meter and 6 meter bands?

Correct Answer is "B" - **There is little effect**

While fog and rain may have a larger effect on some frequencies more than others. For 10-meter and 6-meter band there is little effect. For frequencies in the VHF and UHF bands however, the effect is much greater. Think of watching television in bad weather. Your lower frequencies in the lower channels are less impacted than your higher UHF frequency channels. Channels 2 thru 13 operate in the VHF bands between 54-MHz and 216-MHz while UHF channels 14 thru channel 69 operate from 470-MHz to 806-MHz.

Read more on this question on the following page(s): 6-54

T3B01 - (N)
What is the relationship between the electric and magnetic fields of an electromagnetic wave?

Correct Answer is "D" - **They are at right angles**

Electric fields and Magnetic fields that are emanating in an Electromagnetic wave at right angles to each other. They both travel at the same speed - The speed of light. They are not parallel, and do not revolve.

T3B02
What property of a radio wave defines its polarization?

Correct Answer is "A" - **The orientation of the electric field**

The radio wave has an orientation that matches the antenna that the waves are being broadcast from. Most VHF and UHF antennas which are in line-of-sight bands are held in a vertical orientation - therefore the polarization of the radio waves is also vertical. Therefore, when using a handheld radio, it is best to hold the radio upright vertically. Most HF radio communication is performed using longer horizontal antennas. The horizontally polarized antenna broadcasts signal broad side to the horizontal orientation of the antenna, into the atmosphere for reflection in the atmosphere.

T3B03
What are the two components of a radio wave?

Correct Answer is "C" - **Electric and magnetic fields**

Radio waves are made up of two components - Electric and Magnetic. Electric is easy to remember because power is used to generate the radio wave and remember the magnetic field which can have an effect on our radio signals.

The key here is to remember that a radio wave is an Electromagnetic wave.

T3B04 - (M)
What is the velocity of a radio wave traveling through free space?

Correct Answer is "A" - **Speed of light**

Radio waves are like light - They travel at the speed of light. Light moves in waves as well but at a much higher frequency measured in nano meters instead of meters. Formulas used in calculating antenna lengths are based on radio waves moving at light speed at 300,000,000 meters per second.

T3B05
What is the relationship between wavelength and frequency?

Correct Answer is "B" - **Wavelength gets shorter as frequency increases**

There is a very direct relationship between wavelength and frequency - One that you need to understand. The relationship is used in formulas and helps us to understand why certain wavelengths have certain types of characteristics.

As the frequency of the wavelength rises, aka the number of times per second the radio wave completes a full up-down-up cycle, then you have more completed cycles for a given measured distance. As such, your wavelength is shorter - you are squeezing more cycles into a given distance, so each cycle needs to be compressed and shorter. Higher frequency, shorter wavelength.

Likewise as you slow down and reduce the number of completed cycles per given distance. So each wavelength becomes longer and the frequency lowers. So - The wavelength gets shorter as the frequency increases.

Read more on this question on the following page(s): 6-14

T3B06

What is the formula for converting frequency to approximate wavelength in meters?

Correct Answer is "D" - **Wavelength in meters equals 300 divided by frequency in megahertz**

There is a formula for this - Memorize the formulas and you will be able to apply them to several possible answers.

Wavelength (Meters) = 300 / Frequency (MHZ)

For instance, for the 2-Meter calling frequency:

Wavelength (Meters) = 300 / 146.52;　　　　　Wavelength (Meters) = 2.0475 Meters.

To convert this to inches, we need to know the following:

- 1 Meter = 3.28 Feet, so 2.0475 x 3.28 = 6.7158 Feet, or 80.5896 inches.
- To make a 1/2 wavelength antenna, make it 40.2948 inches
- To make a 1/2 wavelength dipole antenna make each of the 2 segments 20.1474 inches, connected in the middle.
- A 5/8 antenna would be 80.5896 inches x 0.625 = 50.3685 inches long connected at the bottom.

Read more on this question on the following page(s): 6-17

T3B07 - (M)

In addition to frequency, which of the following is used to identify amateur radio bands?

Correct Answer is "A" - **The approximate wavelength in meters**

Since frequencies are directly correlated to wavelengths, knowing the wavelength in meters also identifies the radio bands. Be aware however that the "Bands" and Ham frequencies are related, though not exactly the same. For instance - The "2-Meter Band" for ham radio includes the frequencies of 144-MHz to 148-MHz, which is roughly 2-Meter wavelengths (2.027-Meters to 2.083-Meters to be more precise).

The wavelength range for MURS, which is not in the ham frequency range, is 1.940-Meters to 1.976-Meters. This makes MURS the close neighbor to the Ham 2-Meter band, but with different rules under the FCC limiting power output of MURS to 2-Meters with no license needed. This power limit makes MURS excellent for close-by communications but a poor choice for any emergency or distance communications. .

T3B08

What frequency range is referred to as VHF?

Correct Answer is "B" - **30 MHz to 300 MHz**

It will be important to memorize the frequency ranges for HF Radio, VHF, and UHF.

- HF is 3-MHz to 30-MHz (High Frequency - Better for very long-distance non-repeater communications)
- VHF is 30-MHz to 300-MHz (Very High Frequency - Short Distance, Repeater Communications, Outdoor use line-of-sight)
- UHF is 300-MHz to 3,000-MHz (3-GHz - Ultra High Frequency - Short Distance, Outdoor & Indoor radio use, Line of Sight)

Read more on this question on the following page(s): 6-21, 6-22

T3B09

What frequency range is referred to as UHF?

Correct Answer is "D" - **300 to 3000 MHz**

It will be important to memorize the frequency ranges for HF Radio, VHF, and UHF.

- HF is 3-MHz to 30-MHz (High Frequency - Better for very long-distance non-repeater communications)
- VHF is 30-MHz to 300-MHz (Very High Frequency - Short Distance, Repeater Communications, Outdoor use line-of-sight)
- UHF is 300-MHz to 3,000-MHz (3-GHz - Ultra High Frequency - Short Distance, Repeaters, Outdoor & Indoor radio use, Line of Sight)

Read more on this question on the following page(s): 6-21, 6-22

T3B10

What frequency range is referred to as HF?

Correct Answer is "C" - **3 to 30 MHz**

It will be important to memorize the frequency ranges for HF Radio, VHF, and UHF.

- HF is 3-MHz to 30-MHz (High Frequency - Better for very long-distance non-repeater communications)
- VHF is 30-MHz to 300-MHz (Very High Frequency - Short Distance, Repeater Communications, Outdoor use line-of-sight)
- UHF is 300-MHz to 3,000-MHz (3-GHz - Ultra High Frequency - Short Distance, Repeaters, Outdoor & Indoor radio use, Line of Sight)

Read more on this question on the following page(s): 6-20, 6-21

T3B11
What is the approximate velocity of a radio wave in free space?

Correct Answer is "B" - **300,000,000 meters per second**

This is a very important number to memorize, as it will be used in many of your formulas through the test. The velocity of radio waves in free space is the same as the velocity of light - 300,000,000 meters per second.

Memorize this answer. This is also the speed of light in meters per second.

Read more on this question on the following page(s): 6-20, 6-22

T3C01 - (M)
Why are simplex UHF signals rarely heard beyond their radio horizon?

Correct Answer is "C" - **UHF signals are usually not propagated by the ionosphere**

UHF Signals are higher frequency and shorter wavelength radio waves which rarely reflect in the ionosphere and instead penetrate and continue into space. The higher the frequency, the shorter the wavelength and the less likely any propagation will occur. I always consider short wavelength/high frequencies to be "Sharper" and cut through the ionosphere where the HF longer wavelength/lower frequencies are duller and will reflect.

Read more on this question on the following page(s): 6-52

T3C02 - (M)
What is a characteristic of HF communication compared with communications on VHF and higher frequencies?

Correct Answer is "C" - **Long-distance ionospheric propagation is far more common on HF**

The far biggest characteristic of HF Radio communication over higher frequency communication in VHF and UHF frequencies is the ability for HF frequencies to bounce through the atmosphere for far, far, greater ranges. You might not be guaranteed of hitting the same operator at the other end due to variances in signal propagation, but you have a greater opportunity for longer distance communication without the use of repeaters (Operator-to-Operator) using HF frequencies.

Read more on this question on the following page(s): 6-55

T3C03 - (M)
What is a characteristic of VHF signals received via auroral backscatter?

Correct Answer is "B" - **They are distorted and signal strength varies considerably**

Auroral backscatter is the dispersal of electrons in the upper atmosphere during auroral events in the atmosphere caused by solar winds from the sun. During stronger solar winds, caused by CMEs (Coronal Mass Ejections) the auroras become more active and backscatter increases. When these occur the effects on HF radio which propagates through the Ionosphere can be negatively impacted, but at the same time there is a new opportunity for VHF radio operator. In the HF radio frequencies, absorption increases reducing propagation. For VHF radio operators, there will be some levels of VHF Radio propagation that don't normally exist though they will be distorted, and the signal strength will vary.

https://www.electronics-notes.com/articles/antennas-propagation/auroral-backscatter-propagation/basics.php https://www.electronics-notes.com/articles/ham_radio/amateur-propagation/auroral-propagation.php

Read more on this question on the following page(s): 6-56

T3C04

Which of the following types of propagation is most commonly associated with occasional strong signals on the 10, 6, and 2-meter bands from beyond the radio horizon?

Correct Answer is "B" - **Sporadic E**

Propagation is the reflection of radio signals through the Ionosphere - mostly around HF Radio. Sporadic E propagation occurs when ionized regions or "Clouds" occur in the atmosphere's "E" region which is located between 80 and 150 kilometers above the surface. This most commonly affects frequencies in the 25-MHz to 150-MHz ranges which include the 10-Meter, 6-Meter and 2-Meter bands. The strongest effect will be in the 50-MHz/6-Meter range. These ionized clouds may be small or large and the effect from this type of propagation my last only for short periods.

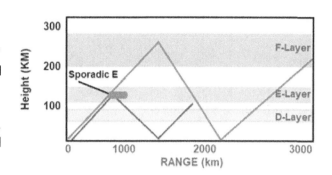

https://3fs.net.au/sporadic-e-propagation/

T3C05

Which of the following effects may allow radio signals to travel beyond obstructions between the transmitting and receiving stations?

Correct Answer is "A" - **Knife-edge diffraction**

Knife-edge diffraction can cause the "Bending" of radio waves around objects such as buildings or even mountains when the signal strikes a well-defined object. "Knife" is used in the name of this effect because it occurs when the object that the radio waves are passing over have a sharp edge to them. If the edge of the object is rounded then more diffraction loss will occur.

For zero diffraction to occur, the path of the radio wave from transmission point to reception point must clear the obstruction by several wavelengths in distance.

https://www.smeter.net/propagation/diffrac1.php

Read more on this question on the following page(s): 6-55

T3C06 - (M)

What type of propagation is responsible for allowing over-the-horizon VHF and UHF communications to ranges of approximately 300 miles on a regular basis?

Correct Answer is "A" - **Tropospheric ducting**

Tropospheric ducting is the propagation of radio signals through the lower layer of the atmosphere under certain conditions that can extend the range of frequencies in the VHF and UHF ranges far beyond normal line of sight distances. In some cases, radio contacts of 1000 miles or more. The effect is caused when periods of temperature inversion when there is a rise in the temperatures of the upper atmosphere instead of the normal lower temperatures. This is most likely to occur during summer and autumn months.

Read more on this question on the following page(s): 6-55

T3C07

What band is best suited for communicating via meteor scatter?

Correct Answer is "B" - **6 meters**

Meteor scatter is the reflection of radio signals from meteors during a a meteor shower. The frequency band where this best occurs is 6-meters. As you might expecting - bouncing a radio signal from a meteor would be a very short duration event - Talk fast...

This is a Memorization question.

Read more on this question on the following page(s): 6-23

T3C08

What causes tropospheric ducting?

Correct Answer is "D" - **Temperature inversions in the atmosphere**

Tropospheric ducting which can result in the propagation of VHF and UHF frequencies for 500 miles or more is caused by conditions such as weather frontal boundaries when warmer temperatures occur higher in the atmosphere than the temperatures at lower levels creating layers of air stacked allowing for the propagation extensions to occur.

Read more on this question on the following page(s): 6-55

T3C09

What is generally the best time for long-distance 10-meter band propagation via the F region?

Correct Answer is "A" - **From dawn to shortly after sunset during periods of high sunspot activity**

The 10-Meter wavelength propagates best during daylight hours, but also during times in which there is a high level of sunspot activity. The best propagation is said to follow the sunlight - During the morning hours in the US you will be more likely to hear European stations than other times of the day. During the middle of the day will be the best times to hear stations across the US, and in the evenings will be the best times to hear stations to the west including the Pacific and east Asia.

Read more on this question on the following page(s): 6-55

T3C10

Which of the following bands may provide long-distance communications via the ionosphere's F region during the peak of the sunspot cycle?

Correct Answer is "A" - **6 and 10 meters**

Key to remember with this question is that the higher frequencies - including 70cm and 23cm - are UHF frequencies - shorter wavelengths which cut through the ionosphere into space without reflection. The 1.25-meter frequency is a longer wavelength in the VHF band, but still does not reflect through the atmosphere. The 6 and 10-meter bands in our selections have the longer wavelength and do have a reflection characteristic in the atmosphere. In fact - remember that the 10-meter band is HF which reflects very good propagation characteristics. In our answers, remember the higher / sharper frequencies cut through the atmosphere ruling out B and C from our options, and thus ruling out D.

Read more on this question on the following page(s): 6-23, 6-55

T3C11 - (N)

Why is the radio horizon for VHF and UHF signals more distant than the visual horizon?

Correct Answer is "C" - **The atmosphere refracts radio waves slightly**

Assuming that we have nothing in our way blocking our signal, such as buildings, trees, leaves, mountains, and hills, and we are on a totally flat surface, the atmospheric conditions can have an effect on our radio waves that allow the radio waves to travel farther than our line of sight and bend around the curvature of the earth. Now this bending does not allow for a great deal of additional distance, but it does allow our radio signals under perfect conditions to travel farther than line of sight. Due to this, our "Radio Horizon" is farther than our line of sight, but again not by a great distance.

Read more on this question on the following page(s): 6-52

T4A01 - (N)

Which of the following is an appropriate power supply rating for a typical 50 watt output mobile FM transceiver?

Correct Answer is "D" - **13.8 volts at 12 amperes**

50-watt radios are designed to work using the standard voltage from our cars. Though we call our car power system a "12-volt" system, the operational voltage is higher at 13.8 volts (And a battery can still power your radio at 12-volts).

Knowing this, we can narrow down our options to B or C, both 13.8-volt options. As for the amps required, be careful here. If you divide 50-watts by 13.8 volts you get 3.62-Amps - so you might think that "B" would be correct - "13.8-volts at 4 amperes". But this is wrong. The 50-watt radio actually needs 12-amps of power. As most cigarette lighter outlets are limited to 10-amps, attempting to plug in a 50-watt radio into a 10-amp outlet will blow a fuse. For that reason, we always need to wire up our mobile radios that are 50-watts to a power source providing at least the 12-amps needed.

Read more on this question on the following page(s): 6-29

T4A02 - (N)

Which of the following should be considered when selecting an accessory SWR meter?

Correct Answer is "A" - **The frequency and power level at which the measurements will be made**

When selecting a SWR meter to measure your radio with - pay attention to the frequencies covered by the meter. Many SWR meters work only for a limited frequency range. They may also only work measuring certain power levels. I have many SWR meters. Some are for my CB Radio (HF) which also work with HF Frequencies. Some are designed for VHF/UHF only. My favorite and handiest fits atop my handheld radios but has a low power rating and is limited to VHF/UHF only.

Read more on this question on the following page(s): 6-71

T4A03 - (N)

Why are short, heavy-gauge wires used for a transceiver's DC power connection?

Correct Answer is "A" - **To minimize voltage drop when transmitting**

All wire has a resistance factor to it. The longer and thinner a wire, the higher the resistance and the more power that will be burned up as heat. Keep your power wires as short and thick as possible (Realistically). Remember the thicker the wire, the more expensive - so don't get crazy. No need to use a wire thicker than necessary - sized based on the power going through the wire.

T4A04 - (N)

How are the transceiver audio input and output connected in a station configured to operate using FT8?

Correct Answer is "B" - **To the audio input and output of a computer running WSJT-X software**

FT8 is a digital mode of radio that is designed to work with extremely weak signals. It uses the sound card of your computer, thus the references to the audio input and output ports of your computer. FT8 is a computer-based software program that communicates through its sound card and through your ham radio. It is popular in HF bands but is also popular on the 6-meter band making it a digital mode available to new Tech license holders.

The key to remembering the answer to this question is to remember that FT8 works with the audio sound card of your computer. Only one answer mentions both the word "Audio" and "Computer".

Read more on this question on the following page(s): 6-73

T4A05 - (N)

Where should an RF power meter be installed?

Correct Answer is "A" - **In the feed line, between the transmitter and antenna**

An RF power meter is used to measure the power output of a radio through the antenna. As such, the placement of the power meter will be on the radio transmitter output and with the antenna connected on the other side of the meter. The RF power meter measures the radio wave output from the radio.

Answer B is not correct because To measure the power supply output you would use a VOLTMETER or an AMP METER.

Answer C is not correct because there is no relationship with the "Push to talk Line" (Assuming the

microphone wire to the radio) and power supply output.
Answer D is not correct as you would use a volt meter to measure any power out of the power supply.

Read more on this question on the following page(s): 6-29

T4A06 - (N)
What signals are used in a computer-radio interface for digital mode operation?

Correct Answer is "C" - **Receive audio, transmit audio, and transmitter keying**

You have to understand that a computer will connect to a radio through it's sound card. As such, the connectivity is based on audio signals. Audio signals are made throguh receive audio and transmit audio. Transmitter keying is a third signal allowing the control of the transmitter.

T4A07 - (N)
Which of the following connections is made between a computer and a transceiver to use computer software when operating digital modes?

Correct Answer is "C" - **Computer "line in" to transceiver speaker connector**

In this question we are looking at the physical connections between the computer and the radio transceiver.

- Transceiver Audio-out/Speaker --> Computer "Line In"
- Transceiver Microphone <-- Computer "Line Out"

Read more on this question on the following page(s): 6-71

T4A08
Which of the following conductors is preferred for bonding at RF?

Correct Answer is "D" - **Flat copper strap**

Copper is one of the best conductors for electrons and electricity. Of the answers given, only two refer to copper. When electrons travel along a conductor, they actually travel along the outside of the conductor, so a flat strap will give more area for electricity to travel along vs braided copper. Copper straps are using for bonding at RF and are better for running grounding.

4A09 - (N)
How can you determine the length of time that equipment can be powered from a battery?

Correct Answer is "B" - **Divide the battery ampere-hour rating by the average current draw of the equipment**

The Amp-Hour rating of a battery tells the number of amps that the battery can output at a constant rate over an hour's time. An example of this would be in the use of a 100-amp/hour rated battery to power a radio which consistently consumes 10-amps of power each hour. By dividing the amp/hour rating of the battery, 100 in this case, but the number of amps our radio consumes each hour, 10 in this case, then we find that we can power our radio for 10 hours. (100 / 10 = 10).

Read more on this question on the following page(s): 6-47

T4A10 - (N)
What function is performed with a transceiver and a digital mode hot spot?

Correct Answer is "A" - **Communication using digital voice or data systems via the internet**

Whenever you hear about a "Hot Spot" you can think of some sort of operation over the Internet, and in turn we are going to be doing some type of digital communications instead of traditional analog communications. A Hotspot acts as a miniature ham radio repeater. It allows your ham radio, often a handheld such as a DMR radio, to connect to the hotspot. Then the hotspot connects to the internet either via a direct wired connection or a wireless connection. Once on the Internet, you can communicate with digital repeaters also on the internet anywhere around the world allowing your small digital handheld access throughout the globe. The Internet connection that your radio hotspot connects to could be a connection at home, at a business, or even a mobile hotspot allowing you communications while on the road.

Remember though - Connectivity will only be as good as your internet connection. (Meaning during a communications, grid, or internet failure your hot spot will not work).

Read more on this question on the following page(s): 6-72

T4A11 - (M)
Where should the negative power return of a mobile transceiver be connected in a vehicle?

Correct Answer is "A" - **At the 12 volt battery chassis ground**

The 12-volt chassis ground should have the same ground point as the negative point on the 12-volt battery or power source. Note that just connecting to metal in the vehicle does not necessarily equate to 12-volt ground. But - If in your vehicle it does, then this will be an acceptable point to attach your negative power return to.

The Antenna mount will have nothing to do with the power connections.

Any metal part of the vehicle is NOT right because other metal points may not share the same ground point as the power source.

And never through the transceiver's mounting bracket.

Read more on this question on the following page(s): 6-48

T4A12 - (N)
What is an electronic "Keyer"?

Correct Answer is "C" - **A device that assists in manual sending of Morse code**

An electronic keyer is a type of paddle device or keying device that the operator uses to create morse code tones for transmitting over ham radio.

It is NOT any form of switching device, and it is not a security device for securing your radio. It is used for transmitting of morse code tones.

T4B01 - (M)

What is the effect of excessive microphone gain on SSB transmissions?

Correct Answer is "B" - **Distorted transmitted audio**

On many sophisticated radios - and we are not referring to the popular Baofeng handheld radio, but rather sophisticated base radio systems you have much more control over a wide variety of settings for your radio communications. On many of these you can control and increase the gain on your microphone to better your transmitting quality. However - excessive gain or boost on your microphone can create distortions in your transmissions. This can also be caused by talking too closely or loudly into your microphone. The later - talking too closely or loudly, can occur with both simple handhelds and mobile radios.

T4B02

Which of the following can be used to enter a transceiver's operating frequency?

Correct Answer is "A" - **The keypad or VFO knob**

On handheld radios the common method of entering a transceiver's frequency will be the keypad, though many radios also have a VFO knob that also allows the dialing of frequencies. On mobile radios, there also is often both a VFO dial and a keypad on the microphone to allow you to enter a frequency. Think of the radio dial on your car radio (If your car radio even still has one).

The CTCSS or DTMF encoder is NOT the correct answer - These are used for sending CTCSS or DTMF tones or codes with your transmission which allow communications through a repeater or an remote radio listening for the appropriate tones or codes.

The Automatic Frequency Control which is a circuit on many radios to help keep the radio on frequency - not for adjusting frequency.

T4B03 - (N)

How is squelch adjusted so that a weak FM signal can be heard?

Correct Answer is "A" - **Set the squelch threshold so that receiver output audio is on all the time**

The squelch control on a radio is used to filter out weak signals and noise received by the radio. Turning the squelch to 0 on a digital squelch or tuning it down to 0 on a dial squelch will allow everything received to be heard - again usually static. Under normal operation, only strong radio transmissions will be heard when the squelch is tuned "Up" to silence the unnecessary noise. This however will also silence weak signals coming from remote operators that are just out of range of transmitting a strong signal. Turn the squelch down for a period of time to be able to hear potentially weak signals.

T4B04

What is a way to enable quick access to a favorite frequency or channel on your transceiver?

Correct Answer is "B" - **Store it in a memory channel**

Radios have memory channels allowing you to quickly key in a particular channel. Some radios, such as the popular Baofeng are limited to just 128 channels whereas others can have thousands of channels. Radios such as digital DMR radios can also have "Groups" of channels so that you may tune to a specific group and then tune to a limited number of channels within that group.

T4B05 - (N)
What does the scanning function of an FM transceiver do?

Correct Answer is "C" - **Tunes through a range of frequencies to check for activity**

The scanning function allows your radio to quickly move through pre-set frequencies or channels listening for activities. When scanning through frequencies the radio will take "Baby steps" going through a large range of frequencies. It will quickly listen for a transmission and move on if nothing heard. If scanning channels, it will quickly scan through only the channels that you have programmed, so if you program with just a small number of scannable channels the radio will continuously scan through those channels until it hears a transmission. Note that some radios scan faster than others. Frequency scanning is a much longer process than channel scanning. When channel scanning you can use software such as CHIRP to identify if a channel should be included in the scan or skipped.

T4B06
Which of the following controls could be used if the voice pitch of a single-sideband signal returning to your CQ call seems too high or low?

Correct Answer is "D" - **The RIT or Clarifier**

The RIT (Receiver Incrementing Tuner) allows for slight adjustments in the receiver frequency without changing the transmitting frequency to allow fine tuning of an incoming signal. This is an advanced feature on more sophisticated radios and not likely to be found on any handheld or mobile radios.

T4B07 - (N)
What does a DMR "code plug" contain?

Correct Answer is "B" - **Access information for repeaters and talkgroups**

The "Code Plug" is a term used with DMR Radios. It is a configuration stored in the radio, and that can be shared with other DMR radio operators, that contains information needed for accessing repeaters and talk groups.

Read more on this question on the following page(s): 6-72

T4B08
What is the advantage of having multiple receive bandwidth choices on a multimode transceiver?

Correct Answer is "B" - **Permits noise or interference reduction by selecting a bandwidth matching the mode**

Sometimes when communicating in a particular bandwidth setting you may pick up noise that will not exist when you change your bandwidth setting. This could be because of another station transmitting at another bandwidth level and you are picking up additional noise - for instance if they are transmitting in a narrow bandwidth and you are receiving in a wider bandwidth - you may be hearing their transmission plus additional noise outside of their bandwidth. Likewise, you may be transmitting in an alternate mode, such as CW which requires a very narrow bandwidth to transmit in, Mode examples can include FM-Wide which uses 25-kHz or FM-Narrow using only 12.5-kHz. CW which is a "Continuous Wave" - Either on or off, takes only 150Hz.

T4B09 - (N)
How is a specific group of stations selected on a digital voice transceiver?

Correct Answer is "C" - **By entering the group's identification code**
On a digital voice transceiver you can key in a groups Identification code to select a specific group of stations. One of the many advantages of Digital communications is how you can identify stations and receivers using digital codes.

Read more on this question on the following page(s): 6-72

T4B10
Which of the following receiver filter bandwidths provides the best signal-to-noise ratio for SSB reception?

Correct Answer is "C" - **2400 Hz**

For SSB, remember you are only sending or receiving based on half of the signal - which is a more power efficient mode and can help with distance. A normal SSB signal - have of a full carrier wave signal - is about 3-kHz in width. However - when operating in SSB mode, there is no signal directly on the dead-set frequency, so our required width is a little narrower. Also - It is quite possible that other frequencies are transmitting adjacent or even overlapping our signal coming in. So, by tuning our bandwidth to just under the 3000 Hz level, but not too much, we are going to be able to receive most of our signal while avoiding some of the noise likely to be coming in.

Of our answers, A and B will be simply too narrow forcing the cutoff of most of the signal. 5000 Hz is too much, so 2400 is our answer. Just below our 3000 bandwidth but not too small.

T4B11 - (N)
Which of the following must be programmed into a D-STAR digital transceiver before transmitting?

Correct Answer is "A" - **Your call sign in CW for automatic identification**

Many types of digital radios require your call sign to be programmed into the radio. In this case, D-STAR is a digital mode developed in Japan and has a high popularity from Japan. This digital radio system is heavily supported by ICOM, Kenwood and FlexRadio systems.

T4B12 - (N)
What is the result of tuning an FM receiver above or below a signal's frequency?

Correct Answer is "D" - **Distortion of the signal's audio**

If you have an FM Receiver that is out of tune with a signal's frequency then you will hear distortion of the audio signal on the radio. This is because naturally you are not properly tuned. Think of a car radio - if you have a frequency tuned into the radio very close to an actual frequency but not right on, you may hear a part of the signal along its a lot of popping and static.

The pitch will not be changed. FM receivers do not operate in Sideband mode (AM Radio only). And your radio will not generate any type of tone. You will simply hear distortion.

T5A01
Electrical current is measured in which of the following units?

Correct Answer is "D" - **Amperes**

The actual measure of the electrical current is called an "AMPERE" or "AMP" for short. There are three items that are in play with tracking and measuring power.
"AMPERES" represent the unit for the current that flows in an electrical circuit. Think of AMPS as the water that is running through a pipe.

"Volts" represents the difference in power between two points - Think of "VOLTS" as the pressure that is applied to the water that is running through a pipe and how fast that water is moving.

The third component of power is "Watts" which is a combined measure of the Volts and Amps (Volts x Amps = Watts). Think of this as the combination of water moving down a pipe at a specified rate.

The last option in this question is Ohms which is a measure of the resistance of the electricity moving through a wire.

Read more on this question on the following page(s): 6-37

T5A02
Electrical power is measured in which of the following units?

Correct Answer is "B" - **Watts**

"Watts" is the total measurement of power a device uses and is a multiplied combination of Voltage x Amperes running through a device. Any electrical device that consumes power consumes it in a total measurement of "Watts", though similar devices may use different voltages and different amperes.

For instance - A device that uses 500 watts at a voltage of 120 volts is using 4.16 Amps
(Voltage x Amperes = Wattage).

A device that uses 500 watts at a voltage of 240 volts is using 2.08 Amps (Voltage x Amperes = Wattage).

We can use variances of the power formula to determine our voltage, wattage, or amperes. For instance - In a situation where we have a 1000-watt power amplifier for an Antenna signal we can use these formulas:

  Watts = Voltage x Amperes (120-volts x 8.3333-amps = 999.996 Watts) which is 1000 watts rounded off

  Voltage = Watts / Amps (1000-watts / 8.3333-amps = 120 volts)

  Amps = Watts / Voltage (1000-watts / 120-volts = 8.3333-amps)

In our possible answers:

- Voltage is wrong because it is the measure of electrical difference between two points. "Volts" represents the difference in power between two points - Think of "VOLTS" as the pressure that is applied to the water that is running through a pipe and how fast that water is moving.

- Watt-Hours is wrong because it is the measure of the amount of power consumed in one hour.

- Amperes is wrong because it is the measure of current moving in a circuit, device or wire. "AMPERES" represent the unit for the current that flows in an electrical circuit. Think of AMPS as the water that is running through a pipe.

- "Watts" is an overall power measure which is a combination my multiplication of the Volts and Amps (Volts x Amps = Watts). Think of this as the combination of water moving down a pipe at a specified rate.

- The last option in this question is Ohms which is a measure of the resistance of the electricity moving through a wire.

Read more on this question on the following page(s): 6-37

T5A03

What is the name for the flow of electrons in an electric circuit?

Correct Answer is "D" - **Current**

If you can remember our analogy of Electrical and electrical terms being like water flowing through a pipe or in a stream, this one would be easy. Electricity flows through a wire much the same way as water flows through a pipe or a stream. In this case, we think of water flowing through a stream and we refer to the flow of water as a Current. With electricity, we call the flow of electrons in an electric circuit or a wire also Current.

Voltage is the difference in charge between two points similar to how water pressure works in a pipe.

Resistance is just that - the resistance to the flow of electricity.

Capacitance is the ability of a device to store electricity much the same as a battery - Capacitance as in Capacity.

Read more on this question on the following page(s): 6-38

T5A04 - (N)
What are the units of electrical resistance?

Correct Answer is "C" - **Ohms**

Electrical resistance is the opposition to the flow of electricity. We can have a little resistance, or a lot of resistance. Think of this as a water valve that your water hose is attached to. High resistance only lets a little electricity flow through - like if you are rinsing off something delicate. Low resistance allows a high flow of electricity through to power a big device - just like opening the valve all the way for a strong amount of water needed to hose off your car or a fireman's hose.

The measure of resistance is an Ohm.

Read more on this question (T5A04) on the following page(s): 6-40

T5A05 - (M)
What is the electrical term for the force that causes electron flow?

Correct Answer is "A" - **Voltage**

Voltage is a force that causes electrons to flow between two points. Think of it like the pressure of water flowing through a pipe. The higher the pressure in the pipe the more water that flows through the pipe. You can increase the amount of water you are pumping by either increasing the size of the pipe under the same pressure - go from a 1" pipe to a 2" pipe and more water can get through the pipe. Same with electricity - A thicker wire can conduct more electricity than a small wire can. (A small wire will heat up and burn up if too much electricity flows through it.

Another way of increasing electricity is to increase voltage much the same as increasing water pressure. Push twice as much water through the same 1" pipe and you get twice the water. With electricity - if you increase voltage, you are increasing the force behind the flow of electricity through the same wire and therefore getting more power through.

This is an important concept to remember.

Read more on this question on the following page(s): 6-6

T5A06 - (N)
What is the unit of frequency?

Correct Answer is "A" - **Hertz**

Frequency is the measure of how often a wave cycle occurs each cycle. Hertz is the unit of measure we refer to related to this. Home AC Electric power occurs at a frequency of hertz, or 60 cycles per second. Radio waves are similar but at much higher frequencies. The calling frequency on the 2-Meter band is 144.56 MHz (Mega-Hertz), or 144,560,000 Hertz. The calling frequency on the 70-cm band is 446.000 MHz, or 446,000,000 Hertz.

T5A07 - (N)
Why are metals generally good conductors of electricity?

Correct Answer is "B" - **They have many free electrons**

Materials that electricity can flow through are called Conductors while materials that block electricity are called Insulators. Conductors are used to pass electricity while conductors protect us from electrical flow. One of the best conductors that is common is copper. Conductors work well because the material they are made up from have many free electrons that can be used for conducting electrical flow. Remember that this is the only answer which has Electrons in it which is similar to the word electricity.

Read more on this question on the following page(s): 6-39

T5A08
Which of the following is a good electrical insulator?

Correct Answer is "B" - **Glass**

An insulator is something that does not conduct electricity. It blocks the flow of electricity. Like rubber or plastic based insulators running through a power wire, and insulator will protect you from the electricity. Of our answers, only glass is an insulator. Copper, Aluminum, and mercury all are CONDUCTORS which will allow the flow of electrical current through them.

Read more on this question on the following page(s): 6-39

T5A09 - (N)
Which of the following describes alternating current?

Correct Answer is "C" - **Current that alternates between positive and negative directions**

Alternating current is current which changes up and down in voltage values - It literally alternates between positive and negative values and direction. Home electricity for instance runs from 120-volts positive to 120-volts negative - a swing of 240 volts.

Answers A & B are both wrong because they indicate that current alternates between something (Positive or Negative) and zero. Absolutely wrong - it alternates between positive and negative directions.

Read more on this question on the following page(s): 6-42

T5A10
Which term describes the rate at which electrical energy is used?

Correct Answer is "C" - **Power**

Power is a total measurement of how much electricity is being used. Electricity can be measured in Voltage and Amperage - The voltage is the level of force that the electricity is under (How fast it is moving) and amperage refers to the quantity of electricity that is flowing through the circuit or device. By multiplying these two together, where "A" is an abbreviation for Amperage and "E" or "V" is an abbreviation for Volts (Or Electric Potential). So, the formula to measure Power (P) is P = E x A.

Note that you will see either "E" or "V" as an abbreviation for Voltage, or Electrical Potential. With all of the formulas we use for Ham Radio tests, the letter "E" is used indicating electrical potential.

Resistance is wrong because it is the measure in OHMS of resistance to the flow of electricity. '

Current refers to the flow of electricity.

Voltage refers to the electrical difference between two points (Positive and Negative).

Read more on this question on the following page(s): 6-42

T5A11 - (N)

What type of current flow is opposed by resistance?

Correct Answer is "D" - **All of these choices are correct**

All types of current can be affected by resistance. This includes DC (Direct Current), AC (Alternating Current), and RF (Radio Frequency Current).

Resistance exists everywhere. In components called "Resistors" designed for this purpose, and even bare wire such as used in power lines, antenna feed lines, and antennas.

Read more on this question on the following page(s): 6-41

T5A12

What describes the number of times per second that an alternating current makes a complete cycle?

Correct Answer is "D" - **Frequency**

The number if times per second that alternating current makes a complete cycle is referred to as FREQUENCY. The unit of measure for this is the HERTZ abbreviated as HZ. AC Power operates at a frequency of 60 Hz. The calling frequency for the 2-Meter ham radio band is 144.56 MHz. (146,520,000 Hertz)

Read more on this question on the following page(s): 6-42

T5B01

How many milliamperes is 1.5 amperes?

Correct Answer is "C" - **1500 milliamperes**

For this type of question you need to remember the metric designations and how they relate.

Milli represents one-one thousandth (1/1000), So converting amperes to milliamperes is a simple matter of multiplying the number, 1.5 by 1000 to get a result of 1500 milliamperes.

Remember milli represents 1/1000.

Read more on this question on the following page(s): 6-16

T5B02 - (M)

Which is equal to 1,500,000 hertz?

Correct Answer is "A" - **1500 kHz**

This is a good test for your understanding of the sizes. In our answers we are given options in Kilohertz, Megahertz, ad Gigahertz. We need to do some math for each to see which is correct.

- Kilo (1,000 or thousand)
- Mega (1,000,000 - Million)
- Giga (1,000,000,000 - Billion).

We need to convert our 1,500,000 number to each of these to see which answer is correct.

- First - 1,500,000 - Divide by 1,000 (Kilo) to get the value in Kilohertz. In this case, the number would be 1,500 kHz.
- Next - 1,500,000 - Divide by a Million to get the value in MHz. In this case, the number would be 1.5 MHz.
- Next - 1,500,000 - Divide by a Billion to get the value is GHz. In this case the number would be 0.0015 GHz.

Of these numbers, only one of them matches - "A", 1,500 kHz or 1500 kHz.

Read more on this question on the following page(s): 6-18

T5B03
Which is equal to one kilovolt?

Correct Answer is "C" - **One thousand volts**

The metric measure of "kilo" is short for one-thousand. So a Kilovolt will equal one thousand volts.

Read more on this question on the following page(s): 6-16

T5B04
Which is equal to one microvolt?

Correct Answer is "A" - **One one-millionth of a volt**

Don't get confused with Milli which is one one-thousandth. Micro is a measure of one-one millionth - a tiny fraction, 1/1,000,000. The measure of a million is MEGA so answer B is wrong. Remember - Micro is one Millionth.

Read more on this question on the following page(s): 6-16

T5B05
Which is equal to 500 milliwatts?

Correct Answer is "B" - **0.5 watts**

A measure of a Milli is one one-thousandth, or .001. In doing the math, 500 x .001 = .5, so .5 watts is your answer.

Remember - Milli is one thousandth.

Read more on this question on the following page(s): 6-16

T5B06 - (M)

Which is equal to 3000 milliamperes?

Correct Answer is "D" - **3 amperes**

A milliamperes is one one-thousandth. Remember Milli is 1/1000. So, when we multiply 1/1000 x 3,000, our result is 3,000/1,000 which equals 3/1, or 3. Our answer is 3 Amperes.

Remember a milli is 1/1000.

Read more on this question on the following page(s): 6-16

T5B07 - (M)
Which is equal to 3.525 MHz?

Correct Answer is "C" - **3525 kHz**

Our units are MEGA-Hertz. Mega is the measure of 1,000,000 (One Million). So if we multiply this out, 3.525 x 1,000,000 is equal to 3,525,000 Hertz. DON'T BE FOOLED BY ANSWER D - That looks like the answer but it is not because the measure in D is "kHz", not Hertz. Since all of our answers are in kHz, we need to convert 3,525,000 Hertz to kHz. If we devide 3,525,000 by 1,000 which is equial to 1-kHz, our answer is 3525 kHz, which is our answer in "C".

Read more on this question on the following page(s): 6-18

T5B08 - (M)
Which is equal to 1,000,000 picofarads?

Correct Answer is "B" - **1 microfarad**

Remember the order of your metric units!

- 1 farad = 1,000 millifarads (mF)
- 1 milli-farad = 1,000 micro-farads (µF)
- 1 micro-farad = 1,000 nano-farads (nF)
- 1 nano-farad = 1,000 pico-farads (pF)

Therefore 1,000,000 pico-farads = 1,000 nano-farads = 1 micro-farad

Recommendation: This is a memorization question for most of us.

Read more on this question on the following page(s): 6-16, 6-17

T5B09
Which decibel value most closely represents a power increase from 5 watts to 10 watts?

Correct Answer is "B" - **3 dB**

Decibels are the measure that Ham operators use to compare signal strength or measure gain in antenna signal strength. Decibel measurement is a logarithmic unit. Explained another way - Decibels (dB) is a ratio of two power values. In this case, 3 dB is our answer as it is the logarithmic ratio for the doubling of power.

- A dB gain of 2 equates to increasing power - Multiple by 1.585 - In this case an increase from 5-watts to about 7.92-watts.
- A dB gain of 3 equates to a doubling of power - In multiply by 2 - in this case an increase from 5 watts to 10 watts.
- A dB gain of 5 equates to increasing power - multiply by 3.162 - In this case from 5-watts to 15.81-watts
- A dB gain of 6 equates to quadrupling of power - multiply by 4 - In this case an increase from 5-watts to 20-watts.
- A dB gain of 10 equates to increasing of power by a factor of 10 - multiply by 10 - In this case an increase from 5-watts to 50-watts.

If your reducing power, then you will use s negative (-) value in your dB rating and you would be dividing rather than multiplying.

https://www.electronics-notes.com/articles/basic_concepts/decibel/neper-to-db-conversion.php
http://www.arrl.org/files/file/A%20Tutorial%20on%20the%20Decibel%20-%20Version%202_1%20-%20Formatted(1).pdf

Read more on this question on the following page(s): 6-7

T5B10
Which decibel value most closely represents a power decrease from 12 watts to 3 watts?

Correct Answer is "C" - **-6 dB**

Decibels are the measure that Ham operators use to compare signal strength or measure gain in antenna signal strength. Decibel measurement is a logarithmic unit. Explained another way - Decibels (dB) is a ratio of two power values. In this case, -6 dB is our answer as it is the logarithmic ratio for the decreasing of power.

If your reducing power, then you will use s negative (-) value in your dB rating and you would be dividing rather than multiplying.

Read more on this question on the following page(s): 6-7

T5B11
Which decibel value represents a power increase from 20 watts to 200 watts?

Correct Answer is "A" - **10 dB**

Decibels are the measure that Ham operators use to compare signal strength or measure gain in antenna signal strength. Decibel measurement is a logarithmic unit. Explained another way - Decibels (dB) is a ratio of two power values. In this case, 10 dB is our answer as it is the logarithmic ratio for the doubling of power.

Read more on this question on the following page(s): 6-7

T5B12
Which is equal to 28400 kHz?

Correct Answer is "D" - **28.400 MHz**

For this answer we need to look at the measure of what these values are in - kHz or MHz. Remember that kHz is a measure of 1000 hertz. Megahertz is a measure of one million hertz. So, first - how many Hertz is 28400 kHz? Multiply this by a thousand, and we are looking at 28,400,000 hertz. This is 28-million, 4-hundred thousand hertz. Now looking at our answers, only "D" represents this answer. Our answer is 28.400 MHz.

Read more on this question on the following page(s): 6-18

T5B13 - (M)
Which is equal to 2425 MHz?

Correct Answer is "C" - **2.425 GHz**

Looking at our question, let's break this down to write it out fully. 2425 MHz - This is two thousand, four-hundred and 25 thousand MHz which written out is 2,425,000,000 Hertz. With our first digit being in the Gigahertz range, and it only being a single digit, then only answer "D" could match - It is a single digit in the Gigahertz range. Our answer is 2.425 GHz.

Read more on this question on the following page(s): 6-19

T5C01
What describes the ability to store energy in an electric field?

Correct Answer is "D" - **Capacitance**

For this question we need to remember that we are looking for a description that describes our ability to store energy - Let's look at each of these answers.

Inductance is the tendency of an electrical conductor to oppose a change in the electric current flowing through it. Most often related to coils.

Resistance is the measure of the opposition to current flow in an electrical circuit most often related to resister components.

Tolerance is the reference to the permissible deviation a component has from its specified value.

Capacitance refers to the ability of a component (Capacitor) to store energy in an electric field.

In this question capacitance refers t the ability to store energy in an electric field. Think of a capacitor which canto function as a battery for very short periods.

Read more on this question on the following page(s): 6-37, 6-41

T5C02
What is the unit of capacitance?

Correct Answer is "A" - **The farad**

This is going to be a memorization question - one of the questions best memorized. The answer here is Farad. Farad is how we measure capacitance.

The Ohm is a measure of resistance.

The Volt is the measure of the difference in electrical potential between two points.

The Henry is the measure of inductance of a coil.

Read more on this question on the following page(s): 6-26

T5C03
What describes the ability to store energy in a magnetic field?

Correct Answer is "D" - **Inductance**

"Inductance" is the ability to store energy in a magnetic field - Measured in "henrys" and usually in coils or transformers.

Capacitance is the ability to store energy in an ELECTRIC field - Usually in capacitors and measured in farads.

Resistance is the opposition of electrical current, usually in resistors and measured in Ohms.

Inductance in the ability to store energy in a magnetic field - usually in a coil or transformer, measured in henrys.

In electrical engineering, admittance is a measure of how easily a circuit or device will allow a current to flow.

Read more on this question on the following page(s): 6-41

T5C04
What is the unit of inductance?

Correct Answer is "C" - **The henry**

This is going to be a memorization question - one of the questions best memorized. The answer here is Henry. Henry is how we measure Inductance.

- The Coulomb (symbolized C) is the standard unit of electric charge in the International System of Units (SI).
- The Farad is the measure of Capacitance.
- The Ohm is a measure of resistance.
- The Henry is the measure of inductance of a coil.

Read more on this question on the following page(s): 6-27

T5C05
What is the unit of impedance?

Correct Answer is "D" - **The ohm**

Resistance is the opposition of electrical current in a circuit. Impedance is also a form of resistance, but against the flow of Alternating Current in a circuit.

Volt is the measure f the difference in electrical charge between two points.

Ampere is a measure of electrons flowing through a circuit.

The coulomb is the International System of Units (SI) unit of electric charge.

The Ohm is the measure of resistance in an electrical circuit.

Read more on this question on the following page(s): 6-37

T5C06

What does the abbreviation "RF" mean?

Correct Answer is "A" - **Radio frequency signals of all types**

RF is the abbreviation for Radio Frequency.

Read more on this question on the following page(s): 6-15

T5C07 - (N)

What is the abbreviation for megahertz?

Correct Answer is "D" - **MHz**

The abbreviation for Megahertz is MHz. Remember - Big "M". big "H", little "z". The abbreviation for Hertz is Hz.

Read more on this question on the following page(s): 6-17

T5C08 - (M)

What is the formula used to calculate electrical power (P) in a DC circuit?

Correct Answer is "A" - **P = E x I**

Power formulas are very important to memorize. Knowing the formulas and how they relate will assist you in being able to answer many of the questions in the test.

In this case, Power is represented with a "P'. It is a multiplication result of the Voltage, represented with an "E" and electrical current represented with "I". So, our formula is P = E x I.

If you recall your Algebra from school, you can use the principals from Algebra to alter your formula to account for any of the values we need based on having any two of the three values.

Read more on this question on the following page(s): 6-37

T5C09
How much power is delivered by a voltage of 13.8 volts DC and a current of 10 amperes?

Correct Answer is "A" - **138 watts**

Using out Power formula of P = E x I, we can easily calculate this answer. In our example, voltage (E) is 13.8 volts, and our Amperes (I) value is 10-amps. By calculating this, out, 13.8 x 10 = 138. Our Power value (P) is 138 (watts).

Read more on this question on the following page(s): 6-10

T5C10
How much power is delivered by a voltage of 12 volts DC and a current of 2.5 amperes?

Correct Answer is "B" - **30 watts**

This is another question where we use out basic power formula of P = E x I. In this case, we have a voltage of 12-volts, and by multiplying by our amperes value of 2.5, we get our answer. P = 12 x 2.5, or our answer of 30. Our total power is 30-watts.

Read more on this question on the following page(s): 6-8

T5C11 - (M)
How much current is required to deliver 120 watts at a voltage of 12 volts DC?

Correct Answer is "B" - **10 amperes**

In this problem, we are going to use our basic power formula of P = E x I, but we are going to invert it to work based on the two values we have which are Power and Volts. Our inverted formula is I = P / E.

I = 120 / 12; so, our answer is I = 10.

Read more on this question on the following page(s): 6-8

T5C12 - (M)
What is impedance?

Correct Answer is "A" - **The opposition to AC current flow**

Impedance and Resistance are often confused as they both have similar characteristics. Both are opposition to current within a circuit, however Impedance is specific to AC flow in a circuit and can be found in coils and transformers.

Read more on this question on the following page(s): 6-65

T5C13 - (M)
What is the abbreviation for kilohertz?

Correct Answer is "D" - **kHz**

This is a memorization question. The abbreviation of kilohertz is kHz - Lower case "k", uppercase "H", lower case "z". As you can see from the answers, case is important.

Read more on this question on the following page(s): 6-17

T5D01 - (M)
What formula is used to calculate current in a circuit?

Correct Answer is "B" - **I = E / R**

The formular to calculate current is an inverted version of our ohms law formula which is E (voltage) = I (amps) x R (resistance) or E = I x R. In this case, since we are trying to calculate for current, we invert our formula to be I = E / R.

In our Ham test and studies, we use "E" as an abbreviation for voltage instead of "V". Both are correct but are used by different standards. Also - in our power calculation formulas we are always multiplying or dividing. In answers C & D, both of those answers are using addition or subtraction, so we can ignore those answers immediately.

Let's review our four possible answers. Remember the answer must be a based on our core formula of "E = I x R".

- We know that "I" will have to be on the left side of our formula because this is the value we are solving for.
- Any valid formula will use multiplication of division in the formula, so addition and subtraction is not a valid possibility. This rules out "C" and "D".
- Since we are solving for current, and our base formula solves for "E = I x R", then the left portion of our formula MUST be a division action.
- Based on the top three points, only "B" is valid as it is out only option using division on the left side of our formula. I = E / R/

https://www.fluke.com/en-us/learn/blog/electrical/what-is-ohms-law
Read more on this question on the following page(s): 6-9

T5D02 - (M)
What formula is used to calculate voltage in a circuit?

Correct Answer is "A" - **E= I x R**

Using the Ohms Law formula we can calculate what our voltage is by calculating the amount of current passing through the resistance value - E = I x R. This is an important formula to memorize.

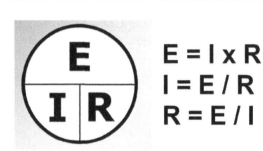

- Answer "B" is not correct because the formula is wrong using division instead of multiplication.
- Answers "C" and "D" are not correct because they both use addition or subtraction which is not used in our formulas.

Read more on this question on the following page(s): 6-9

T5D03 - (M)
What formula is used to calculate resistance in a circuit?

Correct Answer is "B" - **R = E / I**

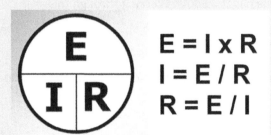

The formula for calculating resistance is a variation of our formula for calculating voltage which is "E = I x R". In this case, since we are calculating for Resistance, we need to invert the formula. Our inverted formula here is: "R = E / I".

Read more on this question on the following page(s): 6-9

T5D04
What is the resistance of a circuit in which a current of 3 amperes flows when connected to 90 volts?

Correct Answer is "B" - **30 ohms**

We use the variance of our Ohms law formula, "E = I x R" which is "R = E / I".

Working through this as:

R = 90 (volts) / 3 (Amps);   R = 90 / 3;

R = 30. So, our answer is 30 ohms.

Read more on this question on the following page(s): 6-10

T5D05

What is the resistance of a circuit for which the applied voltage is 12 volts and the current flow is 1.5 amperes?

Correct Answer is "C" - **8 ohms**

We use the variance of our Ohms law formula, "E = I x R" which is "R = E / I". Working through this as:

R = 12 (volts) / 1.5 (Amps);   R = 12 / 1.5;

R = 8. So, our answer is 8 ohms.

Read more on this question on the following page(s): 6-10

T5D06

What is the resistance of a circuit that draws 4 amperes from a 12-volt source?

Correct Answer is "A" - **3 ohms**

We use the variance of our Ohms law formula, "E = I x R" which is "R = E / I". Working through this as:

R = 12 (volts) / 4 (Amps);   R = 12 / 4;

R = 3. So, our answer is 3 ohms.

Read more on this question on the following page(s): 6-10

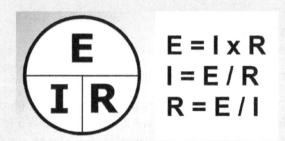

T5D07

What is the current in a circuit with an applied voltage of 120 volts and a resistance of 80 ohms?

Correct Answer is "D" - **1.5 amperes**

We use the variance of our Ohms law formula, "E = I x R" which is "I = E / R". Working through this as:

I = 120 (volts) / 80 (Ohms);   I = 120 / 80;

I = 1.5. So, our answer is 1.5 Amps.

Read more on this question on the following page(s): 6-10

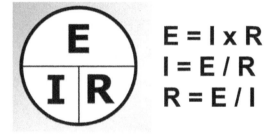

T5D08

What is the current through a 100-ohm resistor connected across 200 volts?

Correct Answer is "C" - **2 amperes**

We use the variance of our Ohms law formula, "E = I x R" which is "I = E / R". Working through this as:

I = 200 (volts) / 100 (Ohms);   I = 200 / 100;

I = 2. So, our answer is 2 amperes.

Read more on this question on the following page(s): 6-10

T5D09
What is the current through a 24-ohm resistor connected across 240 volts?

Correct Answer is "C" - **10 amperes**

We use the variance of our Ohms law formula, "E = I x R" which is "I = E / R". Working through this as:

I = 240 (volts) / 24 (Ohms);   I = 240 / 24;

I = 10. So, our answer is 10 amperes.

Read more on this question on the following page(s): 6-10

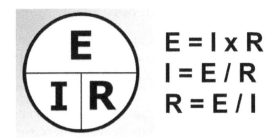

T5D10
What is the voltage across a 2-ohm resistor if a current of 0.5 amperes flows through it?

Correct Answer is "A" - **1 volt**

Here we use the Ohms law formula, "E = I x R":

E = 2 (ohms) x 0.5 (amps);   E = 2 x 0.5;

E = 1. So, our answer is 1 volt.

Read more on this question on the following page(s): 6-11

T5D11
What is the voltage across a 10-ohm resistor if a current of 1 ampere flows through it?

Correct Answer is "B" - **10 volts**

Here we use the Ohms law formula, "E = I x R":
E = 10 (ohms) x 1 (amps);   E = 10 x 1;

E = 10. So, our answer is 10 volts.

Read more on this question on the following page(s): 6-9

T5D12
What is the voltage across a 10-ohm resistor if a current of 2 amperes flows through it?

Correct Answer is "D" - **20 volts**

Here we use the Ohms law formula, "E = I x R":

E = 10 (ohms) x 2 (amps);   E = 10 x 2;

E = 20. So, our answer is 20 volts.

Read more on this question on the following page(s): 6-9, 6-10

T5D13 - (N)

In which type of circuit is DC current the same through all components?

Correct Answer is "A" - **Series**

There are two types of circuits - Serial and Parallel. In a series circuit, all components are connected end-to-end with no "Forks" in the circuit which would split the current.

A series circuit in which there is no forking, the same current runs through all components.

In a parallel circuit, the current splits at each branch depending on the resistance of the branch. If both sides of the forked path have the same resistance or impedance, then the current splits evenly. If the resistance is different between each branch, then the current splits proportionally based on the split values.

Read more on this question on the following page(s): 6-36

T5D14 - (N)

In which type of circuit is voltage the same across all components?

Correct Answer is "B" - **Parallel**

There are two types of circuits - Serial and Parallel. In a parallel circuit, the current flows through one or more forks or branches in the circuit. Across each branch, the voltage will be the same though the current flow (amps) will vary depending on the resistance of each branch.

For those of us familiar with circuit design, we may realize a problem with this question. The question states the voltage would be the same across all components. In reality - no - though the voltage will be the same across all branches. For instance - If you have a circuit with parallel 3 branches, and each branch has a total resistance of 100 ohms. If each branch has a single 100-ohm resistor, then this question and answer are 100% correct.

But - Let's say we have a circuit where 2 of the branches each contain a 100-ohm resistor and our voltage is 12-volts. But - the third branch has two resistors each of which are 50-ohms. In the first two branches, the voltage across each resistor will be 12-volts, but in the third branch the voltage will be 6-volts across each resistor totaling 12-volts.

Read more on this question on the following page(s): 6-36

T6A01

What electrical component opposes the flow of current in a DC circuit?

Correct Answer is "B" - **Resistor**

This is a memorization question.

- A Resistor is an electrical component that opposes the flow of current in a DC circuit.
- An inductor is a component that opposes the flow of current in an AC circuit.
- An inverter is a circuit that converts DC power to AC power.
- A transformer is use to step AC voltage up or down (120v to 240v, or 240v down to 120v for instance)

Read more on this question on the following page(s): 6-25

T6A02

What type of component is often used as an adjustable volume control?

Correct Answer is "C" - **Potentiometer**

This is a memorization question.

- A Potentiometer is an electrical component that can be used as an adjustable volume control. (Volume dial).
- A fixed resistor has a single set value that opposes DC current.
- A Power resistor is used to safely convert large amounts of energy into heat.
- A transformer is used to step AC voltage up or down (120v to 240v, or 240v down to 120v for instance)

Read more on this question on the following page(s): 6-35

T6A03

What electrical parameter is controlled by a potentiometer?

Correct Answer is "B" - **Resistance**

A potentiometer is a type of resistor that allows you to adjust the value of the resistance in the component by literally dialing up or dialing down the resistance value.

Read more on this question on the following page(s): 6-26

T6A04

What electrical component stores energy in an electric field?

Correct Answer is "B" - **Capacitor**

In an Electric field, a Capacitor acts as a miniature battery in a circuit holding power for a short period. A varistor is an electronic component with an electrical resistance that varies with the applied voltage. An inductor is a simple electronic component that is simply a coil of wire that can store energy in a magnetic field. A diode is an electronic component that allows current to flow in only one direction and blocks flow from the opposite direction.

T6A05

What type of electrical component consists of conductive surfaces separated by an insulator?

Correct Answer is "D" - **Capacitor**

- A Capacitor can act as a miniature battery by holding a charge - it consists of two conductive surfaces that are separated by an insulator. The insulator prevents current in a DC circuit from passing through. In a DC circuit a capacitor electrically looks like an open circuit. In an AC circuit, the capacitor appears as a short.
- A resistor is a component that blocks current in a DC circuit.
- A potentiometer is a component that is an adjustable resistor with a varying resistor value.
- An oscillator is a circuit which produces a continuous, repeated, alternating waveform without any input.

Read more on this question on the following page(s): 6-26

T6A06

What type of electrical component stores energy in a magnetic field?

Correct Answer is "C" - **Inductor**

- An inductor, also called a coil, choke, or reactor, is a passive two-terminal electrical component that stores energy in a magnetic field.
- A varistor is an electronic component with an electrical resistance that varies with the applied voltage.
- A Capacitor is a component that can hold an electrical charge acting as a small battery.
- A diode is a component that allows current to flow in only one direction.

Read more on this question on the following page(s): 6-27

T6A07

What electrical component is typically constructed as a coil of wire?

Correct Answer is "D" - **Inductor**

- An inductor is a simple device that is constructed as a coil of wire that has the ability to store energy in a magnetic field. Inductors include coils, chokes, or transformers.
- A Switch is a physical device that breaks or makes a wire connection possible, opening or closing the circuit.
- A Capacitor is a component that can hold a charge similar to a small battery.
- A Diode is a device that allows current to flow in only one direction.

Read more on this question on the following page(s): 6-27

T6A08 - (N)

What is the function of an SPDT switch?

Correct Answer is "C" - **A single circuit is switched between one of two other circuits**

SPDT is short for SINGLE-POLE-DOUBLE-THROW switch - This is a switch that allows a circuit to be switched between one of multiple other circuits.

Read more on this question on the following page(s): 6-26

T6A09

What electrical component is used to protect other circuit components from current overloads?

Correct Answer is "A" - **Fuse**

A fuse is a special wire that is inserted in a circuit that allows only a limited amount of current to pass across it before burning out. Rather than allowing too much current to cross the circuit creating a fire hazard, the fuse will melt in a controlled manner and kill the power flow before a fire or hazard occurs.

Read more on this question on the following page(s): 6-28

T6A10
Which of the following battery chemistries is rechargeable?

Correct Answer is "D" - **All these choices are correct**

There are several types of batteries that can be recharged. All these types can be recharged. Different chemistries have different results. Lead-acid is the type of battery used in vehicles and deep-cycle and marine batteries. Lithium-ion based batteries are most expensive but also provide the highest energy storage capacity.

Read more on this question on the following page(s): 6-28

T6A11
Which of the following battery chemistries is not rechargeable?

Correct Answer is "B" - **Carbon-zinc**

A carbon-zinc battery is a one-use battery chemistry that cannot be recharged. If recharged there is a very high chance that the battery will leak or possibly explode.

Read more on this question on the following page(s): 6-28

T6A12 - (N)
What type of switch is represented by component 3 in figure T-2?

Correct Answer is "A" - **Single-pole single-throw**

A Single-pole single-throw switch is an "On/Off" switch allowing power to be cut off in a circuit.

Read more on this question on the following page(s): 6-25

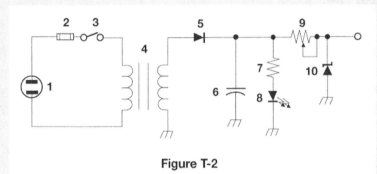

Figure T-2

T6B01 - (N)
Which is true about forward voltage drop in a diode?

Correct Answer is "A" - **It is lower in some diode types than in others**

A diode acts in some ways like a switch - allowing current to pass through in one direction and not the other direction. This action does have a cost, however. The diode is not like a piece of wire with no resistance - as current passes through there is a slight voltage drop across the diode. The amount of the voltage drop is dependent upon the material the diode is made up of. In a silicon diode the drop across the diode is about 0.6 to 0.7 volt. Other materials however have less voltage drop. Schottky diodes can be rated as low as 0.2 V, germanium diodes 0.25 to 0.3 V.

LEDs are also a form of a diode with red or blue light-emitting diodes (LEDs) having voltage drop values of 1.4 V and 4.0 V respectively.

Read more on this question on the following page(s): 6-25

T6B02
What electronic component allows current to flow in only one direction?

Correct Answer is "C" - **Diode**

A Diode is an electronic component that allows current to flow only in one direction acting as a wire when current flows in one direction and blocks the flow of current in the other direction.

- A Resistor is a component that opposes current flow in a DC circuit.
- A fuse is a component that acts as a wire connection until the flow of electrical current exceeds the amperage rating of the fuse, then it burns out to prevent damage to the circuit or a fire hazard.
- A Diode is an electronic component that allows current flow in one direction and blocks current flow in the opposite direction.
- A Driven element is a portion in a directional antenna that is the energized element of the antenna connected to the radio.

Read more on this question on the following page(s): 6-25

T6B03 - (M)
Which of these components can be used as an electronic switch?

Correct Answer is "C" - **Transistor**

A transistor is an electronic component that can act as an electronic switch. It has three legs on it. Two of the three legs are connected to a circuit with the third leg acting as a switch control opening or closing as power is applied to it. For instance, with no power applied the transistor may act as an open circuit. When power is applied, the circuit is closed and current flows through the transistor.

Additionally a transistor can also act as an amplifier - allowing more current to flow through as power is increased.

- A Varistor is a Variable Resistor and never acts as a switch - but it is dependent on voltage to control it.
- A Potentiometer is a physical dial that is also a variable resistor but is not dependent on a voltage.
- A thermistor is a type of resistor whose resistance is strongly dependent on temperature, more so than in standard resistors.

Read more on this question on the following page(s): 6-33

T6B04
Which of the following components can consist of three regions of semiconductor material?

Correct Answer is "B" - **Transistor**

Transistors are comprised of three regions of semiconductor material that allow the transistor to act as a switch or an amplifier. Two legs of the transistor are connected to a circuit so that they can act as a closed connection. As power is applied to the third leg of the transistor, the transistor acts as a switch effectively closing the circuit allowing current to flow through the other two legs. If the transistor is being used as an amplifier, then as power is gradually increased to the control leg, the amount of current increases proportionally to the amount of power applied to the third leg.

Read more on this question on the following page(s): 6-25

T6B05 - (N)
What type of transistor has a gate, drain, and source?

Correct Answer is "B" - **Field-effect**

A Field Effect Transistor (FET) is a three-terminal Active semiconductor device, where the output current is controlled by an electric field generated by the input voltage. FETs are extensively used in Integrated Circuits (ICs) due to their compact size and significantly lower power consumption.

- A Varistor is a variable resistor that requires a voltage to be applied to function.
- A bipolar transistor allows a small current injected at one of its terminals to control a much larger current flowing between two other terminals, making the device capable of amplification or switching.
- Tesla Effect is not a valid thing.

Read more on this question on the following page(s): 6-25

T6B06
How is the cathode lead of a semiconductor diode often marked on the package?

Correct Answer is "B" - **With a stripe**

Diodes are tiny devices. In order to mark the diode's cathode's lead a stripe is used on one side of the diode.

Read more on this question on the following page(s): 6-32

T6B07 - (N)
What causes a light-emitting diode (LED) to emit light?

Correct Answer is "A" - **Forward current**

A LED is a diode with the same properties in that current only flows in one direction. When current is flowing in the forward direction the LED then emits light. Otherwise, with current in the opposite direction the current is blocked, and no light is emitted. DC or AC current could be applied. Current flowing in the forward direction will pass and power the LED. Current flowing in reverse will be blocked and the LED will not light.

LEDs are manufactured in several different colors and used as indicator lights.

Read more on this question on the following page(s): 6-26

T6B08
What does the abbreviation FET stand for?

Correct Answer is "D" - **Field Effect Transistor**

FET is an abbreviation for FIELD EFFECT TRANSISTOR. FETs are often used for weak signal amplification – such as for amplifying wireless analog or digital signals. This is a memorization question.

Read more on this question on the following page(s): 6-34

T6B09
What are the names for the electrodes of a diode?

Correct Answer is "C" - **Anode and cathode**

The names for the electrodes of a diode are Anode and Cathode. A Diode only has two sides only.

- Plus and Minus are not references to the charge points of a battery.
- Source and drain are references to two of the three connection points of a three-legged transistor with the third leg being the Gate.
- For a BJT (Bipolar junction transistor) the terminals are named emitter, collector and base.
- For a FET (Field effect transistor) the terminals are named source, gate and drain.

Read more on this question on the following page(s): 6-32

T6B10 - (M)

Which of the following can provide power gain?

Correct Answer is "B" - **Transistor**

A transistor can not only work as a switch, but it can act as an amplifier as well. When you read in our question power gain, we are seeing we are looking for a device that can act as an amplifier.

- A transformer can increase or decrease voltage, but it also alters our current flow so that the power does not amplify. In fact, due to losses of the transformer, we will actually lose some power.
- A reactor, also known as a line reactor, is a coil wired in series between two points in a power system to minimize inrush current, voltage notching effects, and voltage spikes.
- A resistor is an electronic component that opposes the flow of current in a DC circuit.

Read more on this question on the following page(s): 6-34

T6B11

What is the term that describes a device's ability to amplify a signal?

Correct Answer is "A" - **Gain**

When we read the word gain in a question - we are looking for a reference to amplification or an amplifier. Likewise, the ability to amplify a signal means we are getting a level of GAIN with more power.

Gain is measured in decibels (dB) and is used in measuring power amplification, RF Signal amplification, and noise levels.

All three of our questions deal with asking what decibel levels represent what levels of increase (Gains) or decrease (Loss) in power. For these questions, here is a chart that you should try to memorize:

- To INCREASE your power by a factor of 2 (2x), your dB Gain will be 3dB.
- To INCREASE your power by a factor of 4 (4x), your dB Gain will be 6dB.
- To INCREASE your power by a factor of 10 (10\x), your dB Gain will be 10 dB
In addition to measuring, we also have measurements in loss that are represented by a Negative dB value (-3 dB for instance). For losses:

- A LOSS of power by a factor of 2 (Half), your dB LOSS will be -3dB.
- A LOSS of power by a factor of 4 (One-Quarter), your dB LOSS will be-6 dB.
- A LOSS of power by a factor of 10 (One-Tenth), your dB LOSS will be-10 dB

Read more on this question on the following page(s): 6-29

T6B12 - (N)

What are the names of the electrodes of a bipolar junction transistor?

Correct Answer is "B" - **Emitter, base, collector**

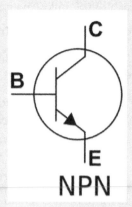

The bipolar junction transistor (BJT) is a current-controlled electronic device main employed for amplification and switching purpose with three terminals called emitter, base, and collector.

A Transistor can act as a switch or amplifier. Current flows between the conductors to the top and bottom of the transistor, while current applied in the left-side conductor controls the flow of current and controls the switch or amplifier functions.

Read more on this question on the following page(s): 6-25

T6C01

What is the name of an electrical wiring diagram that uses standard component symbols?

Correct Answer is "C" - **Schematic**

A schematic is a "Blueprint" for electronic circuits that maps out all components used in the circuit through diagrams and all electrical connections. Using a schematic you can tell how components are electrically connected.

- A "Bill of materials" is simply a listing or inventory of items - it may or may not be a complete list of components and does not show how the components are electrically connected.
- A connector pinout is a display, chart or table that lists what each connection of a specific device is for. It does not show how components are connected together.
- A Flow chart displays how process flows work but does not specific connections or components of a circuit.

Read more on this question on the following page(s): 6-35

DIAGRAM PROBLEMS
Use Figure T-1 here for problems T6C02 thru T6C05.

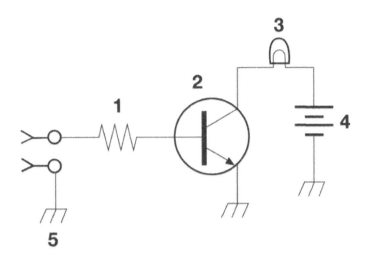

T6C02
What is component 1 in figure T-1?

Correct Answer is "A" - **Resistor**

Component 1 is the drawing representation of a resistor in a schematic.

Read more on this question on the following page(s): 6-35, 6-36

T6C03
What is component 2 in figure T-1?

Correct Answer is "B" - **Transistor**

Component 2 is the drawing representation of a TRANSISTOR in a schematic.

Read more on this question on the following page(s): 6-35, 6-36

T6C04
What is component 3 in figure T-1?

Correct Answer is "C" - **Lamp**

Component 3 is the drawing representation of a LAMP (Lightbulb) in a schematic.

Read more on this question on the following page(s): 6-26, 6-35, 6-36

T6C05
What is component 4 in figure T-1?

Correct Answer is "D" - **Battery**

Component 4 is the drawing representation of a BATTERY in a schematic.

Read more on this question on the following page(s): 6-26

DIAGRAM PROBLEMS
Use Figure T-2 here for problems T6C06 thru T6C09.

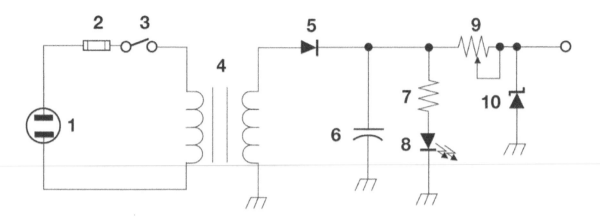

T6C06
What is component 6 in figure T-2?

Correct Answer is "B" - **Capacitor**

Component 6 is the drawing representation of a CAPACITOR in a schematic. A Capacitor acts as a small DC battery capable of storing power.

Read more on this question on the following page(s): 6-26, 6-35

T6C07
What is component 8 in figure T-2?

Correct Answer is "D" - **Light emitting diode**

Component 8 is the drawing representation of a LIGHT EMITTING DIODE (LED) in a schematic. Note the difference between the symbol of an LED with a LAMP.

Read more on this question on the following page(s): 6-26, 6-35

T6C08
What is component 9 in figure T-2?

Correct Answer is "C" - **Variable resistor**

Component 9 is the drawing representation of a VARIABLE RESISTOR in a schematic. Note that the symbol looks like a resistor however has a center-point line to the middle of the resistor indicating that this is a resistor with a value that can change.

Read more on this question on the following page(s): 6-26, 6-35

T6C09
What is component 4 in figure T-2?

Correct Answer is "D" - **Transformer**

Component 4 is the drawing representation of a TRANSFORMER in a schematic. Transformers can be used with AC power to step UP or step-DOWN voltage. Transformers often iron and contain windings on each side of the transform that are isolated from each other electrically and each contains a number of windings on it. To step up or increase the voltage there will be a differing number of windings on each side. The ratio of the windings to each other determine how the electricity is increased or decreased.

For instance – If a transformer has 100 windings and 100-volts coming in on one side, and the transformer has 200 windings on the other side, then the ratio is 100:200 or 1:2. The voltage will step up accordingly from whatever the input voltage is to twice based on the ration (1:2) – so we would have 200 volts on the side of the transformer with 200 windings.

Read more on this question on the following page(s): 6-27, 6-35

DIAGRAM PROBLEMS: Figure T-3
Use figure T-3 here for problems T6C10 & T6C11

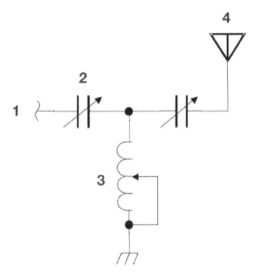

T6C10
What is component 3 in figure T-3?

Correct Answer is "D" - **Variable inductor**

Component 3 is the drawing representation of a VARIABLE INDUCTOR in a schematic.

Read more on this question on the following page(s): 6-27

T6C11
What is component 4 in figure T-3?

Correct Answer is "A" - **Antenna**

Component 4 is the drawing representation of an ANTENNA in a schematic.

Read more on this question on the following page(s): 6-27

T6C12 - (N)
Which of the following is accurately represented in electrical schematics?

Correct Answer is "C" - **Component connections**

Electrical schematics always display the components in a circuit and equally as important displays the component connections. Schematics do not display wire lengths or physical appearance.

Read more on this question on the following page(s): 6-35

T6D01
Which of the following devices or circuits changes an alternating current into a varying direct current signal?

Correct Answer is "B" - **Rectifier**

A rectifier is a device that converts an oscillating two-directional alternating current (AC) into a single-directional direct current (DC). The rectifier is designed to basically cut an AC output in half - either the top or bottom half. Following other components and more complex circuit design can be used to flatten out the output into a more normal DC power output.

Read more on this question on the following page(s): 6-30

T6D02
What is a relay?

Correct Answer is "A" - **An electrically controlled switch**

A relay is a switch that is controlled by applying an electrical current to it. When the electrical current is applied to one set of terminals on the relay, and magnetic field is applied that closes the relay which closes another separate circuit. This allows a wide range of capabilities from being able to energize a more powerful circuit than the side of the relay you are applying energy through, to being able to create a remote switch that can be controlled remotely of through a timer.

Read more on this question (T6D02) on the following page(s): 6-30

T6D03 - (N)

Which of the following is a reason to use shielded wire?

Correct Answer is "C" - **To prevent coupling of unwanted signals to or from the wire**

With shielded wire, there is an outer shield which wraps around an inner wire and helps to protect or reduce noise and unwanted signals from being sent along the inner wire. Shielded wire is most often used in Antenna feed line - protecting the feed line from emitting radio signals or also preventing unwanted signals from reaching into the wire causing interference or noise that can be heard on the receiving radio.

Read more on this question on the following page(s): 6-62

T6D04

Which of the following displays an electrical quantity as a numeric value?

Correct Answer is "C" - **Meter**

A meter is used to test for electrical values or component values. For instance - A Volt-meter allows for the testing of voltage levels. An Ammeter allows for the measuring of electrical current.

- A potentiometer is a type of variable resistor where the value of the resistor is controlled through a physical dial allowing you to literally dial-up or dial-down the resistance value.
- A Transistor is a component that can be used as an electrical switch or amplifier.
- A Relay is a switch that is controlled by applying an electrical current on one set of terminals, thus magnetizing and closing another set of terminals that can pass a higher level of current.

T6D05

What type of circuit controls the amount of voltage from a power supply?

Correct Answer is "A" - **Regulator**

This one can be easy to remember when you realize in the question that what is being asked is about a type of circuit that CONTROLS the amount of voltage. Another way of saying this is to ask where type of circuit can REGULATE the voltage from a power supply. In our answers, "A" stands out as it is a REGULATOR - It would make sense that a REGULATOR and REGULATE or CONTROL something.

- An OSCILLATOR is a circuit that creates an oscillating signal at some set frequency.
- A Filter is a circuit that can filter out certain frequencies, such as limiting frequencies or filtering out noise.
- A Phase inverter is a circuit that creates an inverted of flipped signal that is opposite from the incoming signal.

Read more on this question on the following page(s): 6-31

T6D06 - (M)

What component changes 120 V AC power to a lower AC voltage for other uses?

Correct Answer is "B" - **Transformer**

A transformer is a pair of coils placed adjacent to each other in a package with a different number of wire windings on each side of the transformer. By altering the ratio of the windings between the two sides of the transformer (100 windings on one side for instance with 200 windings on the other side) we are able to step up our AC voltage or step it down based on the relationship of the windings.

- A Variable capacitor is a capacitor whose value can be changed through an electrical or mechanical method
- A Transistor is a solid-state component that can be used either as a switch or an amplifier.
- A Diode is a component that allows current to pass through in one direction and blocks current flow in the other direction.

Read more on this question on the following page(s): 6-27

T6D07

Which of the following is commonly used as a visual indicator?

Correct Answer is "A" - **LED**

A visual indicator would be a component that produces a visual indication of a condition - such as a status light, like a power light. Of the devices listed here, only "A" - LED can do that. A LED is a Light-Emitting Diode that produces a light when on.

- A FET is a FIELD EFFECT TRANSISTOR - A type of Transistor but gives no visual indication of its operational status.
- A Zener Diode is a type of diode that allows current flow in only one direction, but again gives no visual indication of its status.
- A Bipolar transistor is again another type of transistor with no visual indication of its operational status.

Read more on this question on the following page(s): 6-26

T6D08

Which of the following is combined with an inductor to make a resonant circuit?

Correct Answer is "D" - **Capacitor**

A resonant circuit can be a circuit as simple as a coil and a capacitor that can be used as a filter tuned to a specific frequency. A Resonant circut is also referred to as a "Tuned" circuit or aka a "LC" circuit. (L is an abbreviation for a coil, C an abbreviation for Capacitor). They can be used as oscillators, filters, tuners and frequency mixers.

Read more on this question on the following page(s): 6-26

T6D09
What is the name of a device that combines several semiconductors and other components into one package?

Correct Answer is "C" - **Integrated circuit**

Integrated circuits are packages that contain multiple semiconductor components all in one single chip package. These allow for entire devices to be built onto a single chip for specific purposes.

Read more on this question on the following page(s): 6-31

T6D10
What is the function of component 2 in figure T-1?

Correct Answer is "C" - **Control the flow of current**

Component 2 in T-1 is an NPN Transistor. The NPN Transistor has three pins on it - The Collector (C), Base (B), and Emitter (E). By applying current to the Base of the transistor, we can either turn on the flow of current between the Collector and the Emitter like a switch, or by adjusting the current up or down we can use the transistor as an amplifier increasing the power in increments in proportion to the amount of power being applied to the base.

Read more on this question on the following page(s): 6-35, 6-36

T6D11 - (M)
Which of the following is a resonant or tuned circuit?

Correct Answer is "A" - **An inductor and a capacitor in series or parallel**

By creating a circuit with an Inductor and a Capacitor in either series or in parallel, we are building a resonant or tuned circuit designed to operate at a particular frequency depending upon the values of the components used in the circuit.

Read more on this question on the following page(s): 6-26

T7A01
Which term describes the ability of a receiver to detect the presence of a signal?

Correct Answer is "B" - **Sensitivity**

What this question is asking about is the ability of a receiving radio to be able to pick up a signal, which could be a weak signal. The sensitivity of a receiver determines the ability of the receiver to pick up a weak signal.

- Linearity is the design of an amplifier in which the output signal is directly proportional, but increased, to the input signal.
- Selectivity is the ability of a radio receiver to select between specific frequencies without getting overlaps.
- The total harmonic distortion (THD or THDi) is a measurement of the harmonic distortion present in a signal.

T7A02 - (M)

What is a transceiver?

Correct Answer is "A" - **A device that combines a receiver and transmitter**

The word Transceiver is derived from the words Transmitter and Receiver. A transceiver is a device that combines both of these functions into one device. Though radios that we use today are always combined systems, in early ham radio a Transmitter and a Receiver were often two different pieces of equipment.

T7A03

Which of the following is used to convert a signal from one frequency to another?

Correct Answer is "B" - **Mixer**

A mixer is a circuit that can take a signal and convert it between frequencies. Two signals are applied to a mixer, and it produces new signals at the sum and difference of the original frequencies.

- A phase splitter, phase-inverter circuit combines the characteristics of a common emitter amplifier with that of a common collector amplifier.
- An Inverter is a device that converts a DC Signal or power source to an AC signal or power source.
- An Amplifier is a device designed to increase an output signal based on an input signal.

T7A04

Which term describes the ability of a receiver to discriminate between multiple signals?

Correct Answer is "C" - **Selectivity**

"Selectivity" is the ability of a receiver to be able to discriminate between multiple incoming signals. This is NOT to be confused with Sensitivity which refers to the ability of a receiver to detect weak signals.
(See question T7A01 above)

T7A05

What is the name of a circuit that generates a signal at a specific frequency?

Correct Answer is "D" - **Oscillator**

An oscillator circuit is one that generates a signal at either an audio or radio frequency. An oscillator can be as simple as a LC circuit with an inductor and capacitor to determine the frequency to be generated. Oscillators can be used to create frequencies which are used to transmit on as carrier waves.

T7A06

What device converts the RF input and output of a transceiver to another band?

Correct Answer is "C" - **Transverter**

A transverter is a radio frequency device that consists of an upconverter and a downconverter in one unit. These are used in transceivers to change the range of frequencies that a transceiver can use for communication.

- A High-pass filter is a filter that can remove frequencies below a particular frequency allowing higher frequencies to pass.
- A Low-pass filter allows frequencies below a certain frequency to pass while blocking frequencies above that level.
- A Phase-inverter is A circuit or device that changes the phase of a signal by 180°.

Read more on this question on the following page(s): 6-31

T7A07 - (M)

What is the function of a transceiver's PTT input?

Correct Answer is "B" - **Switches transceiver from receive to transmit when grounded**

The PTT for many radios is a simple button that activates the Push-To-Talk function. But - The PTT input is also a line that, when grounded, puts the transceiver into transmit mode and allows broadcasting. This line connection would be used when connected to a computer, modem or remote controlling device.

T7A08

Which of the following describes combining speech with an RF carrier signal?

Correct Answer is "C" - **Modulation**

"Modulation" is the action of overlaying and combining a verbal signal such as your voice over an RF Carrier signal. The variances that occur in the new modulated signal will produce the same voice signal on the receiving radio allowing your voice to be heard.

In Ham radio we use multiple types of modulation, the most common of which are:

- FM – Frequency Modulation where the frequency varies to carry the voice or data signal. Most commonly used with 70-cm and 2-meter radios with new ham operators. Also, the modulation used with GMRS, MURS, FRS, and VHF Marine Radio. Also used with FM Broadcast radio, and Television broadcast.

- AM - Amplitude Modulation is where the amplitude of the signal varies to carry the voice or data signal. Most common with Ham Radio HF band use, but also used on VHF and UHF bands with radios that support this modulation type. AM Modulation is also used with AM Broadcast radio, Airband radios used in aircraft and airport ground control, and also CB Radio. A variance of AM modulation is SSB (Single Sideband).

- PM- Phase Modulation is a third type of modulation with similarities to FM, however more frequently used for forms of digital communications and not used for voice transmissions (Rarely).

T7A09
What is the function of the SSB/CW-FM switch on a VHF power amplifier?

Correct Answer is "B" - **Set the amplifier for proper operation in the selected mode**

On some radio amplifiers there is a mode switch for SSB/CW-FM modes because the power amplifier has different criteria it must operate under depending upon what type of signal it is amplifying.

T7A10 - (M)
What device increases the transmitted output power from a transceiver?

Correct Answer is "B" - **An RF power amplifier**

A RF Power amplifier is used to increase the Radio Frequency power being broadcast out of a transceiver for a stronger radio frequency signal.

Read more on this question on the following page(s): 6-31

T7A11
Where is an RF preamplifier installed?

Correct Answer is "A" - **Between the antenna and receiver**

An RF amplifier connects directly between the output of a radio transmitter and to the antenna. The outbound signal from the transmitter then becomes the incoming signal to the amplifier, and the amplifier feeds a more powerful signal out to the antenna.

Read more on this question on the following page(s): 6-32

T7B01
What can you do if you are told your FM handheld or mobile transceiver is over-deviating?

Correct Answer is "D" - **Talk farther away from the microphone**

Over-deviation is often caused by simply talking too close to the microphone. This sounds like muffled or distorted audio. To correct, simply move the microphone farther from your mouth.

T7B02
What would cause a broadcast AM or FM radio to receive an amateur radio transmission unintentionally?

Correct Answer is "A" - **The receiver is unable to reject strong signals outside the AM or FM band**

If your ham radio signal is being heard on an AM or FM radio, the problem most likely is the receiving radio's inability to reject signals that it may be picking up that are outside of the AM or FM frequency bands. This would be a problem with the receiving radio.

T7B03

Which of the following can cause radio frequency interference?

Correct Answer is "D" - **All these choices are correct**

Radio frequency interference can come from many sources.

- Fundamental Overload - Where the transmitted signal is so powerful that receiving radios are unable to filter it.
- Harmonics can occur when the transmitting radio broadcasts on frequencies that are not the intended broadcast frequency, often one or more frequencies.
- Spurious Emissions which can include harmonic emissions, parasitic emissions, intermodulation products.

T7B04 - (N)

Which of the following could you use to cure distorted audio caused by RF current on the shield of a microphone cable?

Correct Answer is "D" - **Ferrite choke**

Ferrite chokes are passive electronic components that can suppress high frequency signals. These can be attached to a power wire, or a transmission cable to assist in suppressing RF interference. The choke is often a Snap-On device that simply is attached to the power cable or transmission wire.

T7B05

How can fundamental overload of a non-amateur radio or TV receiver by an amateur signal be reduced or eliminated?

Correct Answer is "A" - **Block the amateur signal with a filter at the antenna input of the affected receiver**

If the problem with fundamental overload is occurring it is often occurring on a receiver, the best solution to resolve the problem at the receiver by installing a filter on the antenna input of the radio receiver.

Fundamental Overload is NOT a transmitter problem - It is A problem at the receiver. Remember this fact. All of the other answers are referring to solutions on the transmitter which are not correct.

T7B06

Which of the following actions should you take if a neighbor tells you that your station's transmissions are interfering with their radio or TV reception?

Correct Answer is "A" - **Make sure that your station is functioning properly and that it does not cause interference to your own radio or television when it is tuned to the same channel**

If your neighbor is telling you that he is receiving interference from your ham station, understand that the problem could likely be a problem with his receiver. But - you do need to check your radio station and make sure that it is operating properly. There are problems that your radio could have, and you do need to verify that your own radio is not causing the problem. A good starting point to verify your own radio or television is not picking up the interference.

T7B07

Which of the following can reduce overload of a VHF transceiver by a nearby commercial FM station?

Correct Answer is "D" - **Installing a band-reject filter**

If you have a VHF Transceiver that is picking up overload from a close by FM commercial station, you could install a band-reject filter onto your radio that is tuned specifically to the frequency range of the FM station and block the incoming frequency.

Read more on this question on the following page(s): 6-34

T7B08

What should you do if something in a neighbor's home is causing harmful interference to your amateur station?

Correct Answer is "D" - **All these choices are correct**

There are multiple steps you can take including ALL of the steps listed here.

1. Work with your neighbor to identify where the interference is coming from.
2. Be polite - If he has something that is causing the interference then it is an FCC violation.
3. Best to work together to resolve than to escalate.
4. Check your own station and make sure it is operating properly.

T7B09 - (N)

What should be the first step to resolve non-fiber optic cable TV interference caused by your amateur radio transmission?

Correct Answer is "D" - **Be sure all TV feed line coaxial connectors are installed properly**

If you have a Fiber optic system it will not pick up RF interference. If your TV is using coaxial cable as a feed line in and it is receiving interference the very first thing you should check is the quality of the coaxial connectors that are installed in the cable before attempting to add any type of filter to the antenna input or any type of preamplifier to boost a weak signal. The problem may be as simple as a lose connector.

Read more on this question on the following page(s): 6-62

T7B10

What might be a problem if you receive a report that your audio signal through an FM repeater is distorted or unintelligible?

Correct Answer is "D" - **All these choices are correct**

There are multiple causes that can affect your audio signal passing through an FM repeater. These include:

1. Your transmitter may be slightly off frequency causing a distorted signal.
2. Batteries in the radio may be low causing poor transmission.
3. You may be in a bad location with some, or all your signal being blocked.

T7B11

What is a symptom of RF feedback in a transmitter or transceiver?

Correct Answer is "C" - **Reports of garbled, distorted, or unintelligible voice transmissions**

RF Feedback can occur when your radio's transmitter output is picked up in the microphone of your radio. This RF Feedback can cause garbled, distorted or unintelligible voice transmissions.

T7C01

What is the primary purpose of a dummy load?

Correct Answer is "A" - **To prevent transmitting signals over the air when making tests**

A dummy load is a large capacity resistor that is attached to the antenna output of your radio instead of a regular antenna. The dummy load will absorb your signal without it being broadcast over the air allowing you to performing testing on your radio. Tests such as SWR tests with an SWR meter can be performed with use of a dummy load without worrying about the signal being broadcast and heard.

Read more on this question on the following page(s): 6-60

T7C02

Which of the following is used to determine if an antenna is resonant at the desired operating frequency?

Correct Answer is "B" - **An antenna analyzer**

- An antenna analyzer is a testing tool that allows you to test the quality and performance of your antenna. For this question - Remember both the question and the answer have the word "ANTENNA" in them.
- The VTVM is a highly sensitive voltmeter that uses a vacuum tube for heightened sensitivity.
- A Q Meter is a piece of equipment used in the testing of radio frequency circuits.
- A frequency counter is a device which can read a frequency being transmitted.

Read more on this question on the following page(s): 6-66

T7C03 - (N)

What does a dummy load consist of?

Correct Answer is "B" - **A non-inductive resistor mounted on a heat sink**

A dummy load is made up of a large non-inductive resistor which absorbs the radio signal, and a heat sink which dissipates heat that is generated in the process. Dummy loads come in different sizes, from small sizes designed to be used with low-power handheld radios, to large dummy loads in paint cans called a "Cantenna".

Read more on this question on the following page(s): 6-59

T7C04

What reading on an SWR meter indicates a perfect impedance match between the antenna and the feed line?

Correct Answer is "C" - **1:1**

An SWR meter displays "Standing Wave Ratio" which gives a performance ratio reading for your antenna. The SWR meter is attached to the output of the radio antenna, then the antenna is attached to the SWR meter allowing the meter to perform the reading "In-Line". The best possible SWR ratio will be a "1:1" ratio. As the ratio goes up, this indicates poorer performance of the antenna.

For instance - A 1:1 ratio is best, while a 1.5:1 is still considered good though not as good. As the ratio continues to rise, poorer performance comes from the radio-antenna combination with more power loss occurring from the antenna feed line and the antenna. If the ratio rises above 2:1, such as 5:1 or 9:1 you should make adjustments to bring the ratio down or you are putting your transmitter at risk for damage.

Read more on this question on the following page(s): 6-66

T7C05

Why do most solid-state transmitters reduce output power as SWR increases beyond a certain level?

Correct Answer is "A" - **To protect the output amplifier transistors**

SWR is the measure of how well the impedance matches between radio transmitter and the antenna. When the impedance between radio transmitter and antenna match you will get the most efficient transfer of power to the antenna and the best transmission results. With the lower SWR ratio and the impedance match is best, your power transfer is the best and you have little reflection of power back from the antenna.

When the SWR ratio is high then the impedance is mismatched. A poorly matched impedance results in reflection back from the antenna and back to the transmitter. When this occurs damage to the transmitter and output amplifier could occur. To avoid this, many solid-State transmitters will reduce power output as the SWR ratio increases to prevent damage from reflected power.

T7C06

What does an SWR reading of 4:1 indicate?

Correct Answer is "D" - **Impedance mismatch**

An SWR reading of 4:1 is high and indicates a poor impedance match between the radio transmitter and the antenna. This high of an SWR meter reading indicates an **Impedance Mismatch**.

Read more on this question on the following page(s): 6-66

T7C07

What happens to power lost in a feed line?

Correct Answer is "C" - **It is converted into heat**

Power lost in a feed line to a poor impedance match (A bad SWR measurement) is converted into heat.

Read more on this question on the following page(s): 6-63

T7C08 - (M)
Which instrument can be used to determine SWR?

Correct Answer is "D" - **Directional wattmeter**

The Directional Wattmeter is a separate type of device from the SWR meter that measures power flow between the transmitter and antenna in one direction. Forward power is the power from the transmitter and reflected power is power that is being reflected back from an improperly matched feed.

So - Two devices that can be used to measure SMR are the SWR meter and the Directional Wattmeter. Since the SWR meter is not an option in our choices, the answer is Directional Wattmeter.

Read more on this question on the following page(s): 6-66

T7C09 - (M)
Which of the following causes failure of coaxial cables?

Correct Answer is "A" - **Moisture contamination**

Coaxial cable failure can result in poor transmission, reception, RF interference, and other problems affecting the quality of radio operation. The most common cause of these types of failures comes from moisture contamination of the coaxial cable. For this reason, you should thoroughly seal all connections in the cable.

Read more on this question on the following page(s): 6-64

T7C10
Why should the outer jacket of coaxial cable be resistant to ultraviolet light?
Correct Answer is "D" - **Ultraviolet light can damage the jacket and allow water to enter the cable**

Ultraviolet light in sunlight can cause the outer jacket of the cable to crack and allow water and moisture to enter into the cable which will call a variety of performance problems and potentially failure of the feed line to the antenna. It can also cause higher SWR readings which could result in damage to the transmitter.

Read more on this question on the following page(s): 6-64

T7C11
What is a disadvantage of air core coaxial cable when compared to foam or solid dielectric types?

Correct Answer is "C" - **It requires special techniques to prevent moisture in the cable**

An Air-core coaxial cable is a special type of coax cable that requires special techniques in handling the cable to prevent moisture from building up in the cable. Air core coaxial cable has the dielectric insulation between the braid and center conductor supported by a partially hollow plastic spacer.

Read more on this question on the following page(s): 6-63

T7D01
Which instrument would you use to measure electric potential?

Correct Answer is "B" - **A voltmeter**

Electric Potential is measured in VOLTS. A voltmeter is the tool for measuring voltage between two points.

Read more on this question on the following page(s): 6-42

T7D02

How is a voltmeter connected to a component to measure applied voltage?

Correct Answer is "B" - **In parallel**

A voltmeter is connected in Parallel to a component that it is measuring voltage across. It is important that the voltmeter not break the circuit - It will be passively taking measurement across to read the voltage running across the two points. Understand that if you have a circuit that runs off a particular voltage power supply, such as from a 12-volt battery, the voltage across some components will not necessarily be that voltage. It could be of lower voltage or higher voltage.

Read more on this question on the following page(s): 6-42

T7D03 - (M)

When configured to measure current, how is a multimeter connected to a component?

Correct Answer is "A" - **In series**

Measuring current is very different from measuring voltage. For a measurement of current, or amperage, the meter must be connected in SERIES in the circuit. You must break the circuit and allow the current to flow through the meter for a reading on the meter.

Read more on this question (T7D03) on the following page(s): 6-43

T7D04

Which instrument is used to measure electric current?

Correct Answer is "D" - **An ammeter**

Electrical current is also known as Amperage. If you can remember this then there is only one answer - An Ammeter is used to measure electrical current.

When measuring amperage (Current) you can use two methods - One is to break the circuit and add the meter in series so that all current actually flows through the meter, or use a clamp meter that clamps around the wires and measures current through sensing the magnetic field and measures the current based on what is known as the Semiconductor Hall effect.

https://housetechlab.com/how-to-measure-dc-amps-with-a-clamp-meter/

Read more on this question on the following page(s): 6-42

T7D05 - (Deleted from Exam)

How is an ohmmeter connected to a component to measure its resistance? - QUESTION REMOVED

Correct Answer is "A" - **In parallel**

This question has been removed from the test, but the question pool was not renumbered. This is the reason it was still included in this study book.

T7D06

Which of the following can damage a multimeter?

Correct Answer is "C" - **Attempting to measure voltage when using the resistance setting**

Not setting a multimeter to the appropriate mode can damage your meter. In our possible answers there are only two answers that fit this - "A" and "C". If you are using the meter to measure voltage but have it in the resistance setting the power flowing into the meter is likely to damage it. Measuring resistance while the meter is in the voltage setting will not have a damaging effect because there will be no power flowing through the meter measuring across a resistor.

Read more on this question on the following page(s): 6-44

T7D07

Which of the following measurements are made using a multimeter?

Correct Answer is "C" - **Voltage and resistance**

Both voltage and resistance can be measured with a multimeter.

- Impedance and Reactance are calculated, not measured, though you can measure some aspects of these.
- Signal strength is measured with an "S Meter".
- Since A & B are both incorrect, then "D" is also incorrect.

For more visit this website: https://42electronics.com/blogs/learn-more/using-a-multimeter

Read more on this question on the following page(s): 6-42

T7D08 - (N)

Which of the following types of solder should not be used for radio and electronic applications?

Correct Answer is "A" - **Acid-core solder**

This is a Tricky question because it is similar to the T7D08 question from the old radio pool, but it is the opposite.

Acid-core solder contains an acid in it that can easily damage small metal components as would be found in Ham radio components. This is the correct answer.

Rosin-core solder is the preferred type of solder to use. It contains a rosin-flux which helps to eliminate oxidation.

T7D09 - (M)

What is the characteristic appearance of a cold tin-lead solder joint?

Correct Answer is "C" - **A rough or lumpy surface**

If solder is not properly applied, such as not brought up to the appropriate temperature, not enough flux is applied, or the solder is disturbed during the setting process it may result in a rough, lumpy or grey surface.

T7D10 - (N)

What reading indicates that an ohmmeter is connected across a large, discharged capacitor?

Correct Answer is "A" - **Increasing resistance with time**

When an ohmmeter is attached across a discharged capacitor, the capacitor will first appear to have low resistance as the capacitor begins to charge. Over time as the capacitor builds up a charge the resistance will increase. The capacitor will pass the current freely while it is discharged and over time as it charges it will stop passing current as it builds a higher resistance value.

T7D11

Which of the following precautions should be taken when measuring in-circuit resistance with an ohmmeter?

Correct Answer is "B" - **Ensure that the circuit is not powered**

Resistance is measured with an ohmmeter. To measure resistance, you must measure it in an unpowered circuit. Measuring in an energized circuit will result in having incorrect measurements and may result in damage to your meter.

T8A01

Which of the following is a form of amplitude modulation?

Correct Answer is "C" - **Single sideband**

Amplitude modulation (AM) is used in ham radio most commonly on the HF frequencies. Single Sideband radio (SSB) is a form of modulation where the main carrier and either the upper side or the lower side of the original AM signal are removed. SSB radio allows less power to be used for transmitting.

T8A02 - (M)

What type of modulation is commonly used for VHF packet radio transmissions?

Correct Answer is "A" - **FM or PM**

For this question, let's first understand that we are talking about VHF radio where the most common form of modulation is FM. This leads us to answer "A" - **FM or PM**.

T8A03

Which type of voice mode is often used for long-distance (weak signal) contacts on the VHF and UHF bands?

Correct Answer is "C" - **SSB**

Single Sideband (SSB) modulation can be used for long distance communication in the VHF and UHF Bands. This is because SSB requires the least power and less bandwidth than full AM modulation, it is better used for longer distance communication. Though as techs we will become familiar with using handheld radios and mobile radios as our primary radio types, and these radios use FM modulation, we won't be using AM modulation as commonly in the VHF and UHF bands. Also remember that VHF and UHF bands are "Line of Sight", however you can still use these bands for communications using AM modulation and SSB modulation.

On the 10-Meter band which new Technicians do have partial access to, access is limited to AM use and not FM use. To use 10-meters therefore you will need a radio compatible with AM modulation.

T8A04 - (M)
Which type of modulation is commonly used for VHF and UHF voice repeaters?

Correct Answer is "D" - **FM or PM**

The most common form of modulation used by repeaters is FM, or Frequency Modulation. Another form of modulation that can also be used is Phase Modulation, or PM.

- AM modulation is most commonly used with HF communication not using repeaters, but rather direct radio-to-radio comms.
- SSB Modulation is a form of AM modulation, again not used with repeaters.
- PSK is Phase-Shift-Keying - A computer soundcard-generated radio teletype mode.

T8A05
Which of the following types of signal has the narrowest bandwidth?

Correct Answer is "C" - **CW**

CW is short for "Continuous Wave", also known as morse code. It is a series of tones used to communicate. Since it is not as complex as voice communication it requires less bandwidth. Only 150 Hz is required in bandwidth for CW. CW modulation is basically just "On" or "Off" signals and does not have levels of power needed to correspond to signaling such as what voice would require.

T8A06
Which sideband is normally used for 10-meter HF, VHF, and UHF single-sideband communications?

Correct Answer is "A" - **Upper sideband**

When using SSB radio, only the Upper or Lower sideband are used removing the center carrier as well as the other sideband channel during use. For HF frequencies, VHF and UHF the UPPER Sideband only is used. LSB is used in frequencies that are below 10-MHz.

T8A07 - (M)
What is a characteristic of single sideband (SSB) compared to FM?

Correct Answer is "C" - **SSB signals have narrower bandwidth**

SSB has a much narrower bandwidth and requires less power to transmit. It is used more commonly in HF radio than it is in VHF or UHF.

T8A08
What is the approximate bandwidth of a typical single sideband (SSB) voice signal?

Correct Answer is "B" - **3 kHz**

The bandwidth of an SSB signal is approximately half of what a regular AM modulation bandwidth it, which is about 6-kHz. In SSB, both the carrier signal and one of the two sidebands are stripped away from the signal. This leaves about 3-kHz as used bandwidth.

Read more on this question on the following page(s): *6-24*

T8A09
What is the approximate bandwidth of a VHF repeater FM voice signal?

Correct Answer is "C" - **Between 10 and 15 kHz**

The bandwidth of an FM modulated signal is between 10-kHz and 15-kHz.

Read more on this question on the following page(s): 6-79

T8A10 - (M)
What is the approximate bandwidth of AM fast-scan TV transmissions?

Correct Answer is "B" - **About 6 MHz**

An AM fast-scan signal has a bandwidth of about 6-MHz. In this question we need to remember we are asking about fast-scan TV transmissions. A TV Transmission takes much more bandwidth than does simple voice. For this reason, our measurement is in MEGAHERTZ (MHz) rather than kilohertz as we measure our voice bandwidth levels.

Read more on this question on the following page(s): 6-22

T8A11
What is the approximate bandwidth required to transmit a CW signal?

Correct Answer is "B" - **150 Hz**

CW, short for Continuous Wave, is Morse Code. CW uses the least bandwidth to transmit on. CW is also known as Morse Code.

Read more on this question on the following page(s): 6-24

T8A12 - (N)
Which of the following is a disadvantage of FM compared with single sideband?

Correct Answer is "B" - **Only one signal can be received at a time**

FM has some disadvantages compared to AM and SSB. One of the disadvantages is referred to as "Capture Effect" which is where an FM receiver has a tendency to capture only one FM station. This is one reason why Air Band radio which operates in the VHF band uses AM modulation - It allows even weaker signals to be heard in the background.

Another disadvantage to be aware of is that FM modulation requires much more bandwidth over SSB.

T8B01
What telemetry information is typically transmitted by satellite beacons?

Correct Answer is "C" - **Health and status of the satellite**

Satellite beacons will normally transmit their operational status and health condition information which can be received by anyone capable of receiving it - with or without a license.

T8B02
What is the impact of using excessive effective radiated power on a satellite uplink?

Correct Answer is "B" - **Blocking access by other users**

When transmitting it is expected that you should use only the amount of power necessary to reach the other station. Excessive power will bock other transmissions. This is also the case when communicating with a satellite - excessive power use will block access to the satellite uplink by other users.

T8B03
Which of the following are provided by satellite tracking programs?

Correct Answer is "D" - **All these choices are correct**

Satellite tracking programs are incredibly useful for ham operators in providing information needed to communicate with those satellites. Information that you can commonly derive through software includes:

- Maps with real-time position information of the satellite
- Time, azimuth, and elevation of the start, maximum altitude, and end of a pass.
- Satellite transmission frequency including effects of Doppler shift.

The answer to this question is that **All of the choices are correct**.

T8B04
What mode of transmission is commonly used by amateur radio satellites?

Correct Answer is "D" - **All these choices are correct**

Amateur radio satellites can use multiple modes of transmission including

- SSB
- FM
- CW/data

T8B05
What is a satellite beacon?

Correct Answer is "D" - **A transmission from a satellite that contains status information**

A satellite beacon is simply a transmission from a satellite that contains status information about the satellite. The status information may include Health and status of the satellite.

Read more on this question on the following page(s): 6-79

T8B06

Which of the following are inputs to a satellite tracking program?

Correct Answer is "B" - **The Keplerian elements**

An "Input" is information that is entered into a program for tracking satellite information. The name of the inputs being added are "The Keplerian Elements" named after Johannes Kepler who lived from 1571-1630. These are his laws planetary motion which include the parameters that define the orbit of a satellite.

Read more on this question on the following page(s): 6-81

T8B07

What is Doppler shift in reference to satellite communications?

Correct Answer is "C" - **An observed change in signal frequency caused by relative motion between the satellite and Earth station**

Doppler Shift or "The Doppler Effect" is an effect with moving satellites as they approach your position from orbit, pass overhead, and then move away from your position. This effect will, depending upon frequencies and bands being used, cause a deviation in the actual frequency you are using for uplink/downlink. The shift in frequency may be +/- 3kHz on 2-Meters, or +/- 10 kHz on 70-cm band.

Read more on this question on the following page(s): 6-80

T8B08

What is meant by the statement that a satellite is operating in U/V mode?

Correct Answer is "B" - **The satellite uplink is in the 70-centimeter band and the downlink is in the 2-meter band**

In this question, the reference to U/V is referring to UHF/VHF bands. When communicating to a satellite in U/V mode, then the Uplink frequency (You transmitting to Satellite) is using either the VHF or UHF band, and then downlink (Satellite transmitting to you) is using the opposite band from the uplink band. Of our answers, only one of our answers references these two bands.

Read more on this question on the following page(s): 6-80

T8B09

What causes spin fading of satellite signals?

Correct Answer is "B" - **Rotation of the satellite and its antennas**

Spin Fading is caused by the spinning of the antennas on a satellite as the satellite spins in orbit. During these spins the antenna position changes so that it alters between being optimum for your connection to the satellite and then not being optimum as the antenna rotates away from you. This can result in what appears to be a fading in and out of signal strength. If the antenna is a directional then the effect becomes more so than if the antenna on the satellite is omnidirectional.

Read more on this question on the following page(s): 6-80

T8B10 - (M)
What is a LEO satellite?

Correct Answer is "D" - **A satellite in low earth orbit**

LEO is short for "Low Earth Orbit" - These are satellites typically between 250 and 2000 kilometers in altitude.

Read more on this question on the following page(s): 6-79

T8B11 - (M)
Who may receive telemetry from a space station?

Correct Answer is "A" - **Anyone**

As with any ham radio function, anyone can receive and listen - only licensed techs however can transmit. The correct answer is **Anyone**.

Read more on this question on the following page(s): 6-81

T8B12
Which of the following is a way to determine whether your satellite uplink power is neither too low nor too high?

Correct Answer is "C" - **Your signal strength on the downlink should be about the same as the beacon**

For his one let's look at all of the answers individually to rule them out or acknowledge the right one.

- "A" - This one references looking at your signal strength report in the telemetry data - Wrong because the telemetry data is not immediately available as a reference. This data would be available at a time AFTER you are trying to communicate.
- "B" - Wrong because distortion from a downlink signal can be caused by many things, not just power going up.
- "C" - In this answer, the beacon that is being referred to is a beacon signal coming from the satellite. Using this signal, you can compare the signal strength of the beacon signal to the strength of the downlink and if they are the same then your power level is right or close to right.
- "D" - Wrong because we know "A" and "B" are wrong.

Read more on this question (T8B12) on the following page(s): 6-80

T8C01
Which of the following methods is used to locate sources of noise interference or jamming?

Correct Answer is "C" - **Radio direction finding**

Radio Direction finding is a skill many hams learn through a gaming event called "Fox Hunting". This involves using portable radios and directional based antennas to locate the direction and source of a remote signal. The fox hunter looks for the remote source by pointing the directional antenna in different directions and listening for the strongest signal which should be received when pointing the antenna in the direction of the source.

This can be a useful skill allowing a radio operator to find sources of noise interference or to locate illegal ham operators either operating without a license or calling willful interference.

T8C02

Which of these items would be useful a hidden transmitter hunt?

Correct Answer is "B" - **A directional antenna**

A directional antenna performs better by picking up weak signals better when pointed in the direction of the radio signal, or allowing the radio to receive the signals in a noticeably stronger manner when pointed to the radio source.

Read more on this question on the following page(s): 6-56

T8C03

What operating activity involves contacting as many stations as possible during a specified period?

Correct Answer is "D" - **Contesting**

Ham operators play many games that have a goal of developing essential skills. One of these games is "Contesting" in which the ham operators have a challenge to make as many contacts as possible during a specific time Window. Though this can be run on any ham band, it is most often performed on HF bands where the radio operators are making contacts radio-to-radio and not through use of repeater systems. The relative short range of VHF/UHF make contesting not as popular on those upper bands.

T8C04

Which of the following is good procedure when contacting another station in a contest?

Correct Answer is "C" - **Send only the minimum information needed for proper identification and the contest exchange**

In radio contesting the goal of the contest is to establish as many contacts as possible - so you don't want to dilly-dally around in conversation. Send only the minimum information needed for proper identification and the contest exchange.

- "A" - Signing in with only a partial call sign is not information for proper identification.
- "B" - Contacting the station twice or multiple times is wasting time - If the other station needs clarification of your information, he will ask for it during the first time, plus he may not be reachable a second time.
- "D" - Wrong since A & B are wrong.

T8C05

What is a grid locator?

Correct Answer is "A" - **A letter-number designator assigned to a geographic location**

A grid locator is a grid system that exists throughout the world based on global coordinates which offer a general location of a station and allow for estimated mapping of distances and areas. Winlink uses the grid location system to identify your location and help to identify possible relay stations you could connect to under various frequencies.

Grid locations are used in Winlink to identify your location and nearby servers to connect to for relaying of Winlink email.

T8C06

How is over the air access to IRLP nodes accomplished?

Correct Answer is "B" - **By using DTMF signals**

IRLP nodes over ham radio communication are accessed via Dual Tone Multi-Frequency (DTMF) keypad controls. DTMF utilizes the 10-digit keypad on your ham radio to transmit tones just like the tones you hear on your numeric keypad of your telephone. The DTMF keypad allows you to send tones over the air by using the dial pad on the radio as you press the PTT button, thus sending tone codes to the remote equipment.

T8C07

What is Voice Over Internet Protocol (VoIP)?

Correct Answer is "D" - **A method of delivering voice communications over the internet using digital techniques**

VoIP is a standard that is popular today in Internet based telephony and internet- based communications system. If allows a voice to be digitized and transferred across the internet. This is a system that is also available in digital ham radio modes to transmit your communications from one digital radio to another. Many government agencies including national and local are moving towards digital radio to get better clarity and optimized use of the bandwidth allowing more voice channels over the same frequencies.

T8C08

What is the Internet Radio Linking Project (IRLP)?

Correct Answer is "A" - **A technique to connect amateur radio systems, such as repeaters, via the internet using Voice Over Internet Protocol (VoIP)**

IRLP - the Internet Radio Linking Project - Is a method by which repeaters can be connected to each other through a VoIP connection through the Internet and allows multiple repeaters in multiple locations to work as one. This has the ability to create larger radio networks in a geographical area than can be covered with just a single repeater.

Read more on this question on the following page(s): 6-71

T8C09 - (N)
Which of the following protocols enables an amateur station to transmit through a repeater without using a radio to initiate the transmission?

Correct Answer is "D" - **EchoLink**

EchoLink is an application that can be installed on a computer, tablet or smartphone that can be used to access a repeater if the repeater is EchoLink connected. Using a smartphone, you can use the smartphone as a portable radio with all of your communications running through Cellular data to the remote repeater no matter how far across the state, country, or even across the world you may be. Echolink requires you to be validated with an appropriate call sign before you can log in and use it.

Read more on this question on the following page(s): 6-71

T8C10 - (N)
What is required before using the EchoLink system?

Correct Answer is "C" - **Register your call sign and provide proof of license**

Echolink can ONLY be used once you have registered your call sign with the Echolink system, and you provide proof of being a licensed ham radio operator. Proof is as simple as a copy of your ham radio licensed sent by E-mail to review.

Read more on this question on the following page(s): 6-71

T8C11
What is an amateur radio station that connects other amateur stations to the internet?

Correct Answer is "A" - **A gateway**

In general, a gateway is a device that connects dissimilar systems. This can be said for a ham radio connection, or also in data/network communications.

- A repeater is a radio receiver/transmitter that rebroadcasts an incoming radio signal out for much farther distance.
- A Digipeater is a Digital Repeater that repeats data packets rather than voice traffic.
- A Beacon is a radio station that broadcasts our status information as a one-way transmission.

T8D01
Which of the following is a digital communications mode?

Correct Answer is "D" - **All these choices are correct**

All of the modes listed are digital communications modes. Packet Radio is a mode that allows computers to exchange data over a radio. IEEE 802.11 is a set of specifications for implementing a WLAN on the 900-MHz, and several GHZ BandsFT8 is a mode that uses the computer's soundcard during communications.

Read more on this question on the following page(s): 6-70

T8D02 - (N)
What is a "talkgroup" on a DMR repeater?

Correct Answer is "B" - **A way for groups of users to share a channel at different times without hearing other users on the channel**

A "Talkgroup" is a way with DMR radio radios to allow radio operators to communicate with each other through a repeater without other users not in the talk group hearing you, and without you being able to hear others in other talk groups.

Read more on this question on the following page(s): 6-72

T8D03 - (N)
What kind of data can be transmitted by APRS?

Correct Answer is "D" - **All these choices are correct**

APRS is short for AUTOMATIC PACKET REPORTING SYSTEM which is capable of transmitting several types of data over a radio system. An APRS module can be connected to an analog radio or APRS can be implemented in some types of digital radios including some DMR handheld radios. Data types that can be used in APRS include GPS Position data, Text messages, and Weather data.

APRS Modules are often used for tracking delivery vehicles, and also for weather stations.

Read more on this question on the following page(s): 6-70

T8D04
What type of transmission is indicated by the term "NTSC?"

Correct Answer is "C" - **An analog fast-scan color TV signal**

NTSC is short for "Never-The-Same-Color" and is the standard used to encode colors in analog fast scan color TV signals. If you can remember that NTSC is related to color, there is only one answer that has the word "Color" in it which is "C".

T8D05
Which of the following is an application of APRS?

Correct Answer is "A" - **Providing real-time tactical digital communications in conjunction with a map showing the locations of stations**

APRS is commonly used for providing real-time tactical digital communications such as GPS location information, such as tracking delivery vehicles, or used in weather stations reporting weather data real-time.

Read more on this question on the following page(s): 6-70

T8D06
What does the abbreviation "PSK" mean?

Correct Answer is "B" - **Phase Shift Keying**

PSK is Phase Shift Keying - A method of sending data digitally by changing the phase if the signal being transmitted.

Read more on this question on the following page(s): 6-74

T8D07 - (M)
Which of the following describes DMR?

Correct Answer is "A" - **A technique for time-multiplexing two digital voice signals on a single 12.5 kHz repeater channel**

DMR is short for Digital Mobile Radio - is one of several methods of Digital Radio. Of all digital radio systems, DMR is the only one that uses time-multiplexing techniques to facilitate two 12.5-MHz voice transmission signals to be forwarded through a repeater using the same 12.5-MHz channel.

- "B" is easy to discard because DMR is NOT a position tracking system.
- "C" is easy to discard also because it is not a logging system.
- "D" is more difficult as it may sound accurate.

The trick to this answer however is that DMR is the only digital mode that uses Time Multiplexing making "A" the correct answer.

Read more on this question on the following page(s): 6-72

T8D08
Which of the following is included in packet radio transmissions?

Correct Answer is "D" - **All these choices are correct**

Packet radio is a digital communications method sending packets of data. It has error detection using a "Check Sum" which is a calculation of the data in the packet stored as a verification check - if the check does not match the calculation, then an error in transmitting has occurred. Packet radio also contains a header that contains the call sign of the station that the information is being sent to. Packet radio also contains an automatic repeat request in case of error.

All of the choices for this question are correct.

Read more on this question on the following page(s): 6-74

T8D09 - (M)
What is CW?

Correct Answer is "D" - **Another name for a Morse code transmission**

CW is short for "Continuous Wave" (aka: Morse Code) requiring as little as 150-Hz of bandwidth.

Read more on this question on the following page(s): 6-70

T8D10
Which of the following operating activities is supported by digital mode software in the WSJT-X software suite?

Correct Answer is "D" - **All these choices are correct**

WSJT-X Software Suite is computer software that is used for weak-signal radio communication. It can be used for Earth-moon-earth radio transmissions, for weak signal propagation beacons, and for meteor scatter radio communications. All of these are radio methods that involve bouncing radio signals and will result in weaker signals being received back.

Read more on this question on the following page(s): 6-73, 6-74

T8D11 - (M)
What is an ARQ transmission system?

Correct Answer is "C" - **An error correction method in which the receiving station detects errors and sends a request for retransmission**

ARQ is short for AUTOMATIC REPEAT REQUEST (Not Repeater - Repeat). It is an error correction mechanism for data transmissions. It uses acknowledgements sent back by the receiver and timeouts for reliable data transmission over unreliable communication methods.

Read more on this question on the following page(s): 6-74

T8D12 - (M)
Which of the following best describes an amateur radio mesh network?

Correct Answer is "A" - **An amateur-radio based data network using commercial Wi-Fi equipment with modified firmware**

A mesh network uses modified WiFi equipment to establish a network using Ham frequencies that can also operate at higher power levels under Ham radio rules. As operating at higher power you can establish a linked set of WiFi routers operating for miles under line-of-sight communications.

http://oemcomm.org/ham-mesh-network-primer/

Read more on this question on the following page(s): 6-72

T8D13 - (M)
What is FT8?

Correct Answer is "B" - **A digital mode capable of low signal-to-noise operation**

FT8 is a relatively new digital mode that operates well for weak signal communications.

Read more on this question on the following page(s): 6-73

T9A01
What is a beam antenna?

Correct Answer is "C" - **An antenna that concentrates signals in one direction**

A beam antenna, also known as a directional antenna, uses a directional signal with gain to transmit stronger into a single direction and to receive weaker signals than would otherwise be possible in the direction that the antenna is pointing in. Examples of directional antennas include the YAGI and DISH antennas - both popular and easily recognizable.

T9A02 - (M)
Which of the following describes a type of antenna loading?

Correct Answer is "A" - **Electrically lengthening by inserting inductors in radiating elements**

For optimal tuning an antenna needs to be the correct length based upon frequency the antenna is being used for. To shorten an antenna but keeping the same electrical length of the antenna, a coil or inductor can be added to the antenna. For instance - Let's consider a CB radio antenna which works on a wavelength in the 11-meter band. The wavelength of an 11-meter radio wave is about 36 feet. This makes a 1/4 wavelength antenna about 9 feet, and a 5/8 length antenna 22.5-feet. Too long of antenna for practical use on a vehicle, however winding the antenna in a coil can allow the antenna length to be shorter while keeping the electrical length long for best performance.

Read more on this question on the following page(s): 6-59

T9A03
Which of the following describes a simple dipole oriented parallel to Earth's surface?

Correct Answer is "B" - **A horizontally polarized antenna**

Running parallel to the earth's surface requires that the antenna being mounted above ground but flat horizontally mounted. This is considered a horizontal polarization. A Dipole antenna is an antenna that is fed from the middle with leading out away from the middle connection point of the feedline.

Read more on this question on the following page(s): 6-49

T9A04 - (M)
What is a disadvantage of the short, flexible antenna supplied with most handheld radio transceivers, compared to a full-sized quarter-wave antenna?

Correct Answer is "A" - **It has low efficiency**

The shorter antennas that come with many handheld radios is optimized for UHF frequencies,, however is incredibly inefficient for many frequencies such as 2-meters which require an antenna with an electrical length of about 19" to work better.

Read more on this question on the following page(s): 6-14

T9A05 - (M)

Which of the following increases the resonant frequency of a dipole antenna?

Correct Answer is "C" - **Shortening it**

A Dipole antenna is an antenna that has two separate conductive segments of equal length that are fed from the center by the radio feedline. Shortening the feed point of the Dipole antenna will increase the resonance of the antenna.

Read more on this question on the following page(s): 6-13, 6-58

T9A06 - (N)

Which of the following types of antennas offers the greatest gain?

Correct Answer is "D" - **Yagi**

Antenna's with the greatest level of gain are Directional antennas. These types of antennas are best for picking up weak transmissions and also for contacting far away radio systems or repeaters. Of the antennas listed below, only one is a directional antenna - the Yagi antenna.

- A Dish antenna is another type of directional antenna.
- The 5/8 wave vertical antenna is a good performing vertical antenna popular for VHF/UHF use but is omnidirectional.
- The Isotropic is another type of omni-directional antenna. as is the J pole antenna.

Read more on this question on the following page(s): 6-56

T9A07 - (M)

What is a disadvantage of using a handheld VHF transceiver with a flexible antenna inside a vehicle?

Correct Answer is "A" - **Signal strength is reduced due to the shielding effect of the vehicle**

A car will act like a metal box - absorbing the radio signals being transmitted, and likewise the car will block radio signals reaching to the handheld radio. For good mobile operation you need to get the antenna OUTSIDE of the car - use a Mag-mount antenna, a trunk mount, roof mount or some other form of external antenna.

The metal in the vehicle will act as a FARADY cage to a degree by absorbing the signal transmitting from the radio if the antenna is inside the car and will block signal from the outside to a degree also.

T9A08

What is the approximate length, in inches, of a quarter-wavelength vertical antenna for 146 MHz?

Correct Answer is "C" - **19**

This is a calculation question. The formula for wavelength is:

wavelength = Speed of light (Meters) / Frequency (Meters)

Wavelength = 300,000,000 / 146,000,000;   Wavelength = 300 / 146

Wavelength =2.05479 Meters.

Now we need to calculate for inches.

1-Meter = 3.28 Feet, so we can convert our meters to feet as follows:

Wavelength (Feet) = 2.05479 * 3.28;   Wavelength (Feet) = 6.73971.

Now we need to convert this into inches simply by multiplying by the number of inches per foot (12).

So, our wavelength in inches = 80.87652 inches.

Lastly, we need to calculate a quarter wavelength, so we simply divide by 4.

80.87652 / 4 = 20.21913 inches.

When calculating our "Ideal" length, we take our final number of 20.2 inches (Rounded to one decimal places)
and multiply by 0.95. In this case, 20.21 x 0.95 comes out to 19.1995 inches (19.2).

Of our answers, 19 inches is the closest answer, so our answer is "C".

Read more on this question on the following page(s): 6-12

T9A09

What is the approximate length, in inches, of a half-wavelength 6-meter dipole antenna?

Correct Answer is "C" - **112**

This is a calculation question. The formula for wavelength is:

Wavelength = Speed of light (Meters) / Frequency (Meters)

Wavelength = 300,000,000 / 50,000,000;   Wavelength = 300 / 50

Wavelength = 6 Meters.

Now we need to calculate for inches.

1-Meter = 3.28 Feet, so we can convert our meters to feet as follows:

Wavelength (Feet) = 6 * 3.28;   Wavelength (Feet) = 19.68

Now we need to convert this into inches simply by multiplying by the number of inches per foot (12).

Our wavelength in inches = 236.16 inches.

Lastly, we need to calculate a Half wavelength, so we simply divide by 2.

236.16 / 2 = 118.08 inches.

When calculating our "Ideal" length, we take our final number of 118.1 inches (Rounded to one decimal places) and multiply by 0.95. In this case, 118.1 x 0.95 comes out to 112.195 inches (19.2).

Now of our answers, 112 inches is the closest answer, so our answer is "C".

Read more on this question on the following page(s): 6-13

T9A10

In which direction does a half-wave dipole antenna radiate the strongest signal?

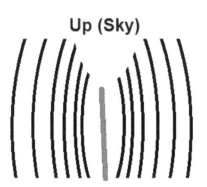

Correct Answer is "D" - **Broadside to the antenna**

In a half wave dipole antenna, the strongest signals always radiate BROADSIDE to the antenna. If the antenna is vertically polarized such as most VHF/UHF antennas, the radiation will move out to the sides from the antenna. This explains why using your handheld radio it is always best to hold the radio with the antenna straight up and down for best performance.

Read more on this question on the following page(s): 6-49

T9A11
What is antenna gain?

Correct Answer is "C" - **The increase in signal strength in a specified direction compared to a reference antenna.**

Antenna gain is a measured increase in signal strength. Some antennas have more gain than others - and directional antennas such as Yagi and Dish antennas have even more gain that apply in the direction in which the antenna is being directed.

Gain is measured in Decibels (dB).

Read more on this question on the following page(s): 6-59

T9A12 - (M)
What is an advantage of a 5/8 wavelength whip antenna for VHF or UHF mobile service?

Correct Answer is "A" - **It has more gain than a 1/4-wavelength antenna**

A 5/8 wavelength antenna has a higher gain than a 1/4 wavelength antenna and will result in better performance.

Read more on this question on the following page(s): 6-58

T9B01 - (M)
What is a benefit of low SWR?

Correct Answer is "B" - **Reduced signal loss**

A low SWR reading indicates a better impedance match between the radio transmitter and the antenna. The lower the SWR and better the impedance match, then the less the signal loss will be radiating from the radio transmitter.

Read more on this question on the following page(s): 6-66

T9B02 - (M)
What is the most common impedance of coaxial cables used in amateur radio?

Correct Answer is "B" - **50 ohms**

In Ham radio, 50 ohms is the impedance value for coaxial cables. There are several types of cable that can be used including RG-58, RG-8. RG-8u, LMR-400 and others as well.

Never use other ohm rated cable, such as a 75-ohm or 93-ohm cable should never be used for ham radio.

T9B03

Why is coaxial cable the most common feed line for amateur radio antenna systems?

Correct Answer is "A" - **It is easy to use and requires few special installation considerations**

Coaxial cable is relatively easy to use and requires few special installation needs. As a shielded cable, it provides a level of shielding from RF Interference and noise. For ham radio there are several types of coaxial cable that all have 50-ohm impedance but have different qualities at different frequencies. RG-58 is the most common and well known, and also cheapest coax cable type used in Radio work. Other types such as RG-8 and LMR-400 work with less signal loss at higher frequencies but are more expensive cable types.

Read more on this question on the following page(s): 6-63

T9B04

What is the major function of an antenna tuner (antenna coupler)?

Correct Answer is "A" - **It matches the antenna system impedance to the transceiver's output impedance**

An antenna tuner is an electronic interface that connects between a transmitter and an antenna to tune the antenna to the transmitter to obtain the lowest impedence possible. The antenna tuner is most likely to be used with HF radios and not with VHF/UHF Mobile radios or handheld radios. An Antenna tuner allows an unmatched antenna to be matched to the radio for best performance.

Read more on this question on the following page(s): 6-75

T9B05 - (M)

What happens as the frequency of a signal in coaxial cable is increased?

Correct Answer is "D" - **The loss increases**

Coaxial cable has a different impedance for different frequencies, meaning that it works best at specific frequencies. In Ham radio, the lower the frequency, the lower the impedance and the lower the signal loss. As the frequency of a Radio signal increases, so does the loss. Different types of coaxial cable will react differently. RG-58 coaxial cable is a much poorer performer than RG-8 or LMR-400. If your cable distance is long, use the better types of cable for better performance.

Read more on this question on the following page(s): 6-63

T9B06

Which of the following RF connector types is most suitable for frequencies above 400 MHz?

Correct Answer is "B" - **Type N**

Different types of coax connectors work better at different frequencies. The traditional PL-259/SO-239 connectors found on most coax cables for ham radio work best for HF and VHF frequencies. For UHF Frequencies, particularly frequencies above 400-MHz a Type N connector works best.

T9B07 - (M)
Which of the following is true of PL-259 type coax connectors?

Correct Answer is "C" - **They are commonly used at HF and VHF frequencies**

The PL-259/SO-239 types of connectors are most often used for HF and VHF frequencies. Frequencies at above 400-MHz more often use a Type "N" connector.

Pictured here to the right is a PL-259 connector that plugs into a SO-239 connector. The PL-259 connectors are common on your coax feed line while the SO-239 is the connection on your radio.

T9B08 - (N)
Which of the following is a source of loss in coaxial feed line?

Correct Answer is "D" - **All these choices are correct**

Using coax cable for feed line requires proper installation and care for proper use. There are several things that can cause problems with your signal - Water intrusion into the Coaxial cable, High SWR, and multiple connectors in the line such as when coax lines are spliced together.

T9B09
What can cause erratic changes in SWR?

Correct Answer is "B" - **Loose connection in the antenna or feed line**

Erratic readings when using an SWR meter often come from loose or bad feed line connections.

Read more on this question on the following page(s): 6-64

T9B10 - (N)
What is the electrical difference between RG-58 and RG-213 coaxial cable?

Correct Answer is "C" - **RG-213 cable has less loss at a given frequency**

RG-58 is a popular type of coaxial cable often used in CB Radio and Ham Radio. The problem with this cable type though is tied to higher loss that is in the cable - More so at higher frequencies. As the length of cable increases so does the loss making a low-loss cable more important. RG-213 has a lower loss, particularly at higher frequencies such as VHF/UHF.

Read more on this question on the following page(s): 6-63

T9B11
Which of the following types of feed line has the lowest loss at VHF and UHF?

Correct Answer is "C" - **Air-insulated hardline**

There are several types of feed lines that can be used to connect your radio to your antenna. As often is the case, the best is also the most expensive. In this case, an Air-insulated hardline happens to be the best, and the most expensive, used often in commercial installations for VHF/UHF frequencies.

- 50-ohm flexible coax is a lesser expensive coax used and has a variety of losses depending upon the particular type of cable.
- A Multi-conductor unbalanced cable has several conductors within the same cable but is not the lowest loss cable.
- A 75-ohm flexible cable is the incorrect impedance, and also is a less expensive cable with higher loss.

Read more on this question on the following page(s): 6-63

T9B12 - (N)
What is standing wave ratio (SWR)?

Correct Answer is "A" - **A measure of how well a load is matched to a transmission line**

Standing Wave Radio - aka SWR - Is the measure of how well the antenna load is matched to the transmitter. A low SWR, such as 1:1, is ideal. The higher the SWR reading, the less efficient the impedance match and the higher the loss in signal.

Read more on this question on the following page(s): 6-64

T0A01
Which of the following is a safety hazard of a 12-volt storage battery?

Correct Answer is "B" - **Shorting the terminals can cause burns, fire, or an explosion**

A 12-volt battery does have some hazards. But the voltage is also low enough to provide a good level of safety. Voltage itself does not become hazard until the DC voltage reaches a level of about 50 volts or higher. Though the batteries are not highly dangerous to the touch at 12-volts, there are extreme hazards if the two terminals touch which would allow extremely high levels of current to pass between the terminals. The energy that could pass is so high that it could, and most likely would lead to fire, burns or an explosion.

12-volts is not high enough of a voltage to provide an electrical shock. Also - RF emissions are not emitted from batteries.

Read more on this question on the following page(s): 6-46

T0A02
What health hazard is presented by electrical current flowing through the body?

Correct Answer is "D" - **All these choices are correct**

The human body carries and uses electrical current. As such, outside electrical current that interferes with the body's own electrical patterns can create hazards for us. Excessive electrical current can cause injury by heating tissue. It may also disrupt the normal electrical functions of cells and may cause involuntary muscle contractions.

T0A03 - (N)
In the United States, what circuit does black wire insulation indicate in a three-wire 120 V cable?

Correct Answer is "B" - **Hot**

In the US, the black wire indicates a "Hot" wire, while white is neutral, and green is ground.

Read more on this question on the following page(s): 6-38

T0A04 - (M)
What is the purpose of a fuse in an electrical circuit?

Correct Answer is "B" - **To remove power in case of overload**

A fuse is designed to burn out and remove power in case of an overload. It is a safety feature designed to prevent fires. Never use a fuse that carries a higher rating than what the circuit is designed for.

T0A05
Why should a 5-ampere fuse never be replaced with a 20-ampere fuse?

Correct Answer is "C" - **Excessive current could cause a fire**

Replacing a small-rated fuse with a larger rated fuse can be a fire hazard and can allow too much current to flow creating a fire.

Read more on this question on the following page(s): 6-28

T0A06
What is a good way to guard against electrical shock at your station?

Correct Answer is "D" - **All these choices are correct**

There are multiple steps you can take to reduce the risk of electrical shock.

1. Using three-wire cords and plugs for all AC powered equipment provides a ground line.
2. Connecting all AC power station equipment to a common safety ground.
3. Installing mechanical interlocks in high-voltage circuits. The Interlock switch is for your home power panel and prevents back feeding or improper connection of alternative power into the home.

T0A07 - (M)
Where should a lightning arrester be installed in a coaxial feed line?

Correct Answer is "D" - **On a grounded panel near where feed lines enter the building**

Arresters should be installed as close a possible to the equipment to be protected, often at the point where the coax cable enters the building. They can also be installed near the antenna for additional protection.

Read more on this question on the following page(s): 6-64

T0A08 - (M)
Where should a fuse or circuit breaker be installed in a 120V AC power circuit?

Correct Answer is "A" - **In series with the hot conductor only**

The key to this answer is "In Series" and "Hot Conductor". You can only have the fuse installed in series with a hot conductor - Not with Neutral conductors. It must be in series - Never in Parallel. If the fuse or circuit breaker were installed in parallel, then there would be an unprotected path that could be a hazard. The fust must be in series with the path that is at risk.

Read more on this question on the following page(s): 6-28

T0A09
What should be done to all external ground rods or earth connections?

Correct Answer is "C" - **Bond them together with heavy wire or conductive strap**

Ground rods should be bound together with heavy wire or conductive strap so that they have a shared path to ground and your ground is common. Waterproofing ground rods is not necessary. Also - Keeping them far apart is not necessary - it is best to have them bound together for a single path to ground. Ground rods cannot be tuned - there is no RF component to them.

Read more on this question on the following page(s): 6-62

T0A10 - (M)
What hazard is caused by charging or discharging a battery too quickly?

Correct Answer is "A" - **Overheating or out-gassing**

On the Ham radio test - This question is going to apply to common Lead-acid cells where there is a higher concern with rapidly charging or rapidly discharging of batteries. In that case there can be an out-gassing issue and an overheating issue on the batteries. There is no output ripple issue, and no half-wave rectification issue, nor any memory effect issue.

Now days often Lithium based batteries are used more often. Lithium batteries more rapidly charge and have no gassing issues at all. A Lithium based battery has a different set of risks though these are minimalized using LiFePO4 chemistry.

Read more on this question on the following page(s): 6-46

T0A11 - (M)
What hazard exists in a power supply immediately after turning it off?

Correct Answer is "D" - **Charge stored in filter capacitors.**

Capacitors are "Mini Batteries" that are capable of holding a level of charge for hours after power is removed from the circuit. When working with a power supply that has had its power removed, never assume there is no power still in the unit. DC Filters, Power transformers, and diodes have not residual charge after power is removed.

Read more on this question on the following page(s): 6-28, 6-29

T0A12 - (N)
Which of the following precautions should be taken when measuring high voltages with a voltmeter?

Correct Answer is "B" - **Ensure that the voltmeter and leads are rated for use at the voltages to be measured**

Of the answers available, the real risk is using a meter and leads on a voltage level higher than what the meter and the leads may be rated for.

Read more on this question on the following page(s): 6-28, 6-29

T0B01 - (N)
Which of the following is good practice when installing ground wires on a tower for lightning protection?

Correct Answer is "C" - **Ensure that connections are short and direct**

Ground wires should be installed as short as possible and as directly as possible. Avoid any sharp bends in the wire and avoid excess lengths in wires.

Read more on this question on the following page(s): 6-62

T0B02 - (N)
What is required when climbing an antenna tower?

Correct Answer is "D" - **All these choices are correct**

Safety is critical when climbing antenna towers. All possible precautions should be taken.

- Have sufficient training on safe tower climbing techniques
- Use appropriate tie-off to the tower at all times
- Always wear an approved climbing harness

Read more on this question on the following page(s): 6-61

T0B03

Under what circumstances is it safe to climb a tower without a helper or observer?

Correct Answer is "D" - **Never**

Safety is ALWAYS critical with tower climbing - It is NEVER acceptable to do any tower work alone. Always have a helper or an observer.

Read more on this question on the following page(s): 6-61

T0B04

Which of the following is an important safety precaution to observe when putting up an antenna tower?

Correct Answer is "C" - **Look for and stay clear of any overhead electrical wires**

When raising any type of antenna tower, or even a simple antenna pole, always make sure you are clear of any electrical wires that may be around. Also - Make sure that when you raise a pole or tower, that if it were to fall in ANY direction that there are no overhead power wires or hazards can be hit.

Read more on this question on the following page(s): 6-61

T0B05 - (N)

What is the purpose of a safety wire through a turnbuckle used to tension guy lines?

Correct Answer is "B" - **Prevent loosening of the turnbuckle from vibration**

A turnbuckle will vibrate over time. Use of a safety wire in the turnbuckle prevents it from loosening.

T0B06

What is the minimum safe distance from a power line to allow when installing an antenna?

Correct Answer is "D" - **Enough so that if the antenna falls, no part of it can come closer than 10 feet to the power wires**

When raising an antenna or antenna tower, it is important to make sure that if the antenna or tower falls in any direction, that it will not fall against a power line. It is recommended that you have at least a ten-foot additional gap for safety.

Read more on this question on the following page(s): 6-61

T0B07

Which of the following is an important safety rule to remember when using a crank-up tower?

Correct Answer is "C" - **This type of tower must not be climbed unless it is retracted, or mechanical safety locking devices have been installed**

A tower that can be extended can be a crank-up tower. These types of towers can easily collapse if appropriate safety precautions are not taken. Never attempt to climb a crank-up tower unless appropriate safety steps are taken to insure it will not collapse under your weight.

Read more on this question on the following page(s): 6-61

T0B08

Which is a proper grounding method for a tower?

Correct Answer is "D" - **Separate eight-foot ground rods for each tower leg, bonded to the tower and each other**

For best grounding, each tower leg should have a separate eight foot ground rod attached to it and tightly bonded to the tower as well as each other. You want the ground to be as tightly set as possible.

Read more on this question on the following page(s): 6-62

T0B09

Why should you avoid attaching an antenna to a utility pole?

Correct Answer is "C" - **The antenna could contact high-voltage power lines**

Never attach an antenna to a utility pole that has electrical lines running on it. This is an incredible danger if the antenna touches the power line. If you have a utility pole that has no power or utility lines running on it, then that is not the same danger. The danger comes with mixing an antenna on a pole with any type of utility on it.

Read more on this question on the following page(s): 6-61

T0B10

Which of the following is true when installing grounding conductors used for lightning protection?

Correct Answer is "C" - **Sharp bends must be avoided**

Grounding lines should always be as short and direct as possible. ALWAYS avoid sharp bends in your grounding conductors.

Read more on this question on the following page(s): 6-62

T0B11

Which of the following establishes grounding requirements for an amateur radio tower or antenna?

Correct Answer is "B" - **Local electrical codes**

All rules and regulations are dictated and controlled by your own local electrical codes.

The FCC dictates radio regulations, not electrical rules. The FAA has oversight over tower heights near airports or where aircraft are in question, and Underwrite Labs makes recommendations but again, no oversight in local electrical rules.

T0C01

What type of radiation are radio signals?

Correct Answer is "D" - **Non-ionizing radiation**

This is a memorization answer. Radio signals are Non-ionizing radiation.

T0C02

At which of the following frequencies does maximum permissible exposure have the lowest value?

Correct Answer is "B" - **50 MHz**

50-MHz is in the 6-Meter band and is a frequency that has most hazardous risk to the human body, therefore has the lowest amount of exposure time that can be allowed. This is a memorization answer.

Read more on this question on the following page(s): 6-24

T0C03 - (N)

How does the allowable power density for RF safety change if duty cycle changes from 100 percent to 50 percent?

Correct Answer is "C" - **It increases by a factor of 2**

The duty cycle of a radio transmitter is the amount of time that the transmitter is on and pushing a signal out vs. the amount of time that no transmission is occurring. If a transmitter is transmitting 50% of the, we have a 50% duty cycle. If it is transmitting only 20% of the time, we have a 20% duty cycle. And a 100% duty cycle indicates we are constantly transmitting. If we were to cut in half our duty cycle, then we double the amount of allowable exposure time.

T0C04
What factors affect the RF exposure of people near an amateur station antenna?

Correct Answer is "D" - **All these choices are correct**

There are several factors that affect the RF exposure of people near an amateur station antenna. All of the following are included:

- Frequency and power level of the RF field
- Distance from the antenna to a person
- Radiation pattern of the antenna

T0C05
Why do exposure limits vary with frequency?

Correct Answer is "D" - **The human body absorbs more RF energy at some frequencies than at others**

As the answer states - the human body absorbs more RF energy at certain frequencies than at others. 50-MHz tends to be the frequency that our bodies are most sensitive to.

Read more on this question on the following page(s): 6-24

T0C06
Which of the following is an acceptable method to determine whether your station complies with FCC RF exposure regulations?

Correct Answer is "D" - **All these choices are correct**

There are several methods to ensure your station complies with the FCC RF exposure rules.

- By calculation based on FCC OET Bulletin 65
- By calculation based on computer modeling
- By measurement of field strength using calibrated equipment

T0C07 - (M)
What hazard is created by touching an antenna during a transmission?

Correct Answer is "B" - **RF burn to skin**

If a radio antenna is putting out a lot of power, there is a danger that you could get an RF burn by touching the antenna. This is not a danger on low-power radios, but with your license you will have the ability to push hundreds of watts, up to 1500 watts of power.

T0C08 - (M)

Which of the following actions can reduce exposure to RF radiation?

Correct Answer is "A" - **Relocate antennas**

If you have a high-power radio pushing out RF radio signals over an antenna, the risk will be where the power is coming out - at the antenna. Since the antenna is the component that causes the risk, the best way to avoid or reduce exposure to RF radiation is to relocate the antenna.

Read more on this question on the following page(s): 6-68

T0C09

How can you make sure your station stays in compliance with RF safety regulations?

Correct Answer is "B" - **By re-evaluating the station whenever an item in the transmitter or antenna system is changed**

Whenever you make a change to your radio station you should evaluate if the changes you are making will have any effect in compliance or safety. The FCC does not care about any one specific change in your station.

A High SWR will create a risk to your transmitter but is not a compliance issue.

T0C10

Why is duty cycle one of the factors used to determine safe RF radiation exposure levels?

Correct Answer is "A" - **It affects the average exposure to radiation**

The higher the duty cycle, and the higher the percentage of time that the transmitter is active, the higher the RF Radiation exposure levels. Likewise, the lower the duty cycle the less RF Radiation is being broadcast and the lower the radion exposure levels are.

T0C11

What is the definition of duty cycle during the averaging time for RF exposure?

Correct Answer is "C" - **The percentage of time that a transmitter is transmitting**

A transmitter that is always broadcasting has a 100% duty cycle. If the transmitting is occurring half the time, then you have a 50% duty cycle. If transmitting a quarter of the time, then you have a 25% duty cycle.

T0C12 - (M)
How does RF radiation differ from ionizing radiation (radioactivity)?

Correct Answer is "A" - **RF radiation does not have sufficient energy to cause chemical changes in cells and damage DNA**

RF radiation is radiation emitted from your radio antennas where ionizing radiation is radiation that can be sourced from x-rays, ultraviolet light and high exposure to sunlight. RF does not have the same destructived effect as ionizing radiation. In fact, it is a form of non-ionizing radiation. Even though RF radiation is not dangerous in the same way as ionizing radiation, it is still a risk that can create RF Burn.

T0C13 - (N)
Who is responsible for ensuring that no person is exposed to RF energy above the FCC exposure limits?

Correct Answer is "B" - **The station licensee**

The station licensee is the owner of the station - The person who holds the license and who is responsible for making sure the station is in proper operating condition. This includes making sure that the antenna is proper, station power is within legal limits, and that no dangerous RF energy exists.

Read more on this question on the following page(s): 6-68

Chapter 6 – Ham Radio Discussions

Welcome to section 8 of our course book. This section is designed to cover 9 different ham radio topics that are on the tests with. We will drill into each topic and cover certain areas with more explanation than we provided in the earlier section of this book "Practice Test Answers & Explanations". In our coverage of the topics we will cover only as deep as we need to explain the questions on the test and to provide you an understanding of how we reached the answers. For instance – In part 5 of this section we will cover *"Electricity Basics – Power and Voltage, Formulas and Concepts"* and we will go deep enough for an understanding of the topics as they apply to the test, but we will not drift outside of the Ham Test topics.

As explained in the Introduction, the design of this book is to work well for "Leaping" back and forth through sections, providing extra explanation and support for those areas you may need while many readers may be able to skip sections or chapters. If you have a strong electrical knowledge already then, some sections you may wish to skip while other sections may be needed to work through for better topic understanding.

The answers that are provided for the questions in this chapter may not be in the exact wording as they are on the actual test but will be identified with the test question in parentheses and will carry the overall meaning of the question and answer. In the questions & Answers section of this book where the questions are listed with the exact wording and explanation of the answer, the page were the problem is found in this chapter will also be provided there.

6.1 – Terms and Definitions covered in this Chapter

Before we delve deeply into the sections of this chapter which will cover several technical topics, I want to provide a list of terms and definitions that will be used throughout the technical course that you may run across during testing, and that you will run across during studying. Understanding exactly what these terms mean will help you greatly during studying for the exam.

CIRCUITS

Amplifier	A Device, circuit, or component that amplifies an inbound signal. Amplifiers can be applied to Radio Signals to boost the power of the outbound signal or could be as simple as a transistor boosting the power through the circuit.
Parallel Circuit	A Circuit in which components are in parallel to each other and current flows in different paths, not necessarily through all components. The voltage across each parallel path is the same though it may be different across components of the same paths.
Schematic	A Schematic is a drawing that shows the components of a circuit and how each of the components are connected in the circuit.

Series Circuit	A Series Circuit is a circuit in which multiple components are connected end-to-end and the same current flows through all of the components. The voltage levels aross each component will vary depending upon how the components are valued and interact within the circuit.

COMPONENTS

Band Pass Filter	A filter which allows a specific band or set of frequencies to pass through. All frequencies outside of the value of the Band-Pass filter are blocked.
Band Reject Filter	A filter which rejects frequencies within a specific range. All other frequencies are allowed to pass unobstructed. Useful if you are picking up a specific frequency from a powerful source bleeding through your radio causing interference.
Conductor	Usually, Metal such as a wire. A component or material that allows the free flow of electricity. Different conductors have different characteristics. For instance - Copper is an excellent conductor. Aluminum is also a good conductor but can be a fire hazard if it overheats whereas copper could heat to a much greater amount before being problematic.
Diode (Component)	An electronic component that allows current flow in one direction.
Gauge	Thickness of wire. The higher the number the thinner the wire. Not on the test but related to some topics.
Insulator	A Material or wire cover that blocks the flow of electricity. Used to prevent electrical shorts or for safety from electrical shock.
Transistor (Component)	A component that can be used as an amplifier magnifying a current through it or as a switch controlling the on/off actions of the current flowing through it. The transistor has three electrodes - one of which in the middle is the control and the other two through which the current flows.

MEASUREMENTS

Decibel (dB) – Power Gain	When used relative to power the Decibel is a measure of power gain.
Decibel (dB) – Signal Gain	When used relative to RF antenna design, the Decibel represents a signal gain or loss. For example - A directional antenna will have a high level of signal gain in one direction such as forward while having a signal loss in the reverse direction.
Decibel (dB) – Volume/Noise	When used relative to Audio measurements, the Decibel is used to measure how loud something is. High dB level values indicate a loud noise such as from a loud generator or engine while a low dB level indicates a low-volume noise such as a hum.
Gigahertz (GHz)	A measure of Hertz in the 1-billion range. 1-Billion hertz is a Gigahertz (GHz)
Henry	A measure of inductors such as a coil often used in an AC Circuit such as an oscillator circuit.

Hertz (Hz)	A Hertz is a single complete cycle of AC power or and RF frequency signal. In the US the AC power grid operates at 60 hertz. In Radio/RF Terms, the number of Hertz of a radio wave is the frequency of the radio signal. For instance - Calling frequency on 2-Meters is 146.52 million Hertz. (MHz)
Kilohertz (kHz)	Kilo is 1000, so 1-Kiloherts is 1,000 Hertz.
Megahertz (MHz)	Mega is 1,000,000 or 1-Million hertz.
Meter	A Measure of length which is 3.28 feet. Radio wavelengths are measured in Meters. For instance - A radio signal said to be in the 2-Meter radio band is said to be about 2-meters in length. Exact wavelength depends on specific frequency. (146.52-MHz is 2.04 Meters)
Speed of Light	How fast light travels. For all RF calculations, the speed of light is 300,000,000 Meters per Second.

POWER REFERENCES

Alternating Current (AC)	Alternating Current (AC) is current moving through the grid or an electrical circuit that alternates from positive to negative in voltage value. A Sinewave is used to represent the flow of alternating current. AC current commonly comes from the power grid to provide electrical power into your home.
Ampere (Power)	Ampere is the measure of electrons moving through a wire or circuit. Think of the current measurement equivalent to the measure of the amount of water flow through a pipe - NOT the pressure but rather the amount that flows through the pipe.
Capacitance	The ability of a component or circuit to store electromagnetic energy. A Capacitor is the best example.
Current	Current is the measure of electrons moving through a wire, circuit, or component.
Direct Current (DC)	Direct Current (DC) is current that moves through a wire, circuit or component at a steady voltage level. Think of the battery that provides electrical power to the accessories and lights in your car from a 12-volt battery.
Electrical Field	An electrical field is an electrically charged field that can occur such as in a battery, circuit, or capacitor. Discharge of an electrical field can provide a shock if touched, and results in the flow of electricity.
Farad (Capacitance)	Farad is the measurement of capacitance, or how much a capacitor can store.
Gain (Power)	Gain as it relates to power is the measured increase in power such as through an amplifier or transistor.
Impedance	Impedance is the resistance of an electrical circuit, component, or wire to RF energy. Impedance values can vary based upon the frequency of the RF signal. For instance - Coaxial Cable will have a lower impedance value at low RF frequencies, and higher impedance at higher RF frequencies making it important to use the appropriate type of coaxial cable based on the frequencies being fed through it.

Inductance	A property of an electric circuit by which an electromotive force is induced in it by a variation of current either in the circuit itself or in a neighboring circuit
Magnetic Field	A magnetic field that can form around an object or component such as an inductor. Magnetic fields have the characteristic of attracting or opposing metal objects to the point of pulling or pushing metal objects physically to or away from the magnetic field.
Ohm (Power)	The Ohm is the measure of the volume of resistance to electricity. Used to indicate the level of resistance of an electrical component to current. Also used to measure impedance which is the opposition to electrical current in an AC circuit or resistance in a wire or cable.
Power	The electrical measure in Watts of how much electrical capacity is available based upon the voltage and current available in the source. Measured as $P = E \times I$ where P is Power, E is the Voltage or Electrical Potential, and I is the current amount. For instance, a 12.8v LiFeP04 battery that can produce 100 Amps of current steadily over an hour has 12.8 x 100 watts of power, or 1,280 watt-hours of power.
Resistance	Opposition to current in an AC or DC Circuit. The most common component that creates resistance directly is the Resistor. Other components, such as the Inductor or coil, can create resistance in an AC circuit however in a DC circuit will not create resistance.
Sinewave	An up-and-down movement of electrical current or RF energy.
Volt (Power)	The Volt is the measure of Electrical Potential between two points and is represented in all of our formulas with "E", short for electrical potential. Another common abbreviation is "V" but is not used in the formulas you will see on all of the test questions.
Watt (Power)	Watt is the combined measure of power based on multiplying the Electrical Potential (E) by the Current (I) and is represented in formulas with the abbreviation of "E". The formula for power is $P = E \times I$.

RADIO REFERENCES

CW	CW is short for Carrier Wave and is otherwise known as MORSE CODE. The Carrier wave reference comes from referencing a continuous carrier wave turned on or off for a signal represented by "Beeps" as heard over a speaker or "Clicks".
dipole antenna	A Dipole antenna is an antenna that is sized based on the frequency being transmitted or received and is fed from a feed point in the middle of the antenna. A Half-wave dipole antenna will feed from the center going to two separated wires each 1/4 wavelength long. Visually like a capital "T" with the center vertical line representing the feed line and each leg of the top being a separate wire feeding out in opposite directions. Popular among HF frequencies but can be used on any.
Gain (RF Signals)	Gain as it relates to RF signals is the increase in effective RF signal in our out such as measured through a directional antenna. (Yagi and Dish antennas for instance).

Line-of-sight	Line of Sight references the fact that many frequencies normally operate outwardly based on visual site. An antenna broadcasting a thousand feet up will have a much greater distance it can travel as it will match the ability to "See" farther whereas an antenna broadcasting 5' above the ground will have a shorter distance it can "See" and reach.
phone	Phone in our pool questions is a reference to "Voice" communications where the operator speaks through a microphone and listens on the transceiver's speaker, rather than CW which is a series of beeps or a Digital mode which sounds more like organized static.
Polarization	As it applies to Antennas, the polarization of antenna relates to the horizontal or vertical orientation of an antenna. As signals process through the antenna, the signals radiate outwardly and broadside (From the sides) of the antenna. A horizontally polarized antenna will best radiate signals up through the atmosphere for better opportunity for atmospherics skip. A Vertically polarized antenna will radiate signals outward across the ground to the horizon. Two stations trying to communicate will have better results if both utilize the same polarization of their antennas.
RF	RF is short for Radio Frequency.
SSB	SSB is short for Single-Side Band used in AM Modulated radio where the carrier wave and one of the two side bands are removed, and only a single side band is used. Some clarity is lost, however more power is applied to just the one sideband allowing greater power efficiency for longer distances.
Wavelength	Wavelength is the length of a radio frequency signal in Meters.

Most of the terms that are listed above will be referenced at some point in the upcoming topical sections about to be covered.

6.2 – Math Calculations

Math is one of the more intimidating topics for many individuals studying for the test. But – Keep these three important points in minD.

1. The test will consist of only a small number of math questions – 7 or less. You could literally miss every single math question on your test and still walk away passing.

2. Understanding the math problems is easier if you memorize and understand the formulas. Several of the formulas are actually quite simple, so we will review the formulas and how to apply them here, and we will focus on the more likely used formulas such as calculating Power.

3. Lastly – there will be some questions that are just easier to memorize. Decibels for instance was one of the more difficult topics for me when I tested, but there are a very small number of Decibel questions

in the possible pool. So, you may find it easier to memorize those few questions and not worry about having to do math or formulas in that area.

Electrical Abbreviations

Let's first review the electrical abbreviations that will be used in the formulas on the test. It is important to understand what these abbreviations are and eliminate any possible confusion. The confusion that can occur is that in some cases there are multiple abbreviations for the same thing. In electronics school I always learned that the abbreviation for VOLT is "V". However, in Ham Radio we use "E" as the abbreviation for VOLT which is short for "Electromagnetic Force" which is an older definition and the abbreviation that is used in the OHM's Law formulas. ***Voltage is the term used to describe the force that causes electron flow (T5A05)***.

Other abbreviations which are used in the Ham Test for power and formulas are:

E	Voltage / Electromagnetic Force (Based on Ohm's Law Abbreviations)
I	Current (Which is the measurement in Amps)
R	Resistance (Measurement in Ohms)
P	Power (Watts)
AC	Alternating Current (House power)
DC	Direct Current (Power from Batteries)
RMS	Root Mean Square – Which is effective voltage from House AC style power.
V	Voltage – Electrical Potential as measured across two points
PEP	Peak Envelope Power
dB	Decibel – Measurement of Power Gain or Power Loss

- http://www.ka3pmw.com/general%20lesson%2004.pdf
- https://www.fluke.com/en-us/learn/blog/electrical/what-is-ohms-law

6.2.1 – Decibel Problems – Power and Signal Loss and Gain

Decibels are used to measure power signal loss and gain and is the standard for a measure in Antennas and in Cable performance for power transfer. For the test, there are only three possible questions that you may get that touch on Decibels. Though this is an important concept to understand, and we will cover the details of the concept in some depth shortly, I feel that covering the depth and details of how decibels work as well as the formulas for just four possible questions would create confusion. For that reason, we're going to look at the questions that are on the test and cover the basics for the Decibel problems.

All three of our questions deal with asking what decibel levels represent what levels of increase (Gains) or decrease (Loss) in power. For these questions, here is a chart that you should try to memorize:

To INCREASE your power by a factor of 2 (2x), your dB Gain will be	3 dB
To INCREASE your power by a factor of 4 (4x), your dB Gain will be	6 dB
To INCREASE your power by a factor of 10 (10x) , your dB Gain will be	10 dB

In addition to measuring, we also have measurements in loss that are represented by a Negative dB value (-3 dB for instance). For losses:

A LOSS of power by a factor of 2 (Half), your dB LOSS will be	-3 dB
A LOSS of power by a factor of 4 (One-Quarter), your dB LOSS will be	-6 dB
A LOSS of power by a factor of 10 (One-Tenth), your dB LOSS will be	-10 dB

These are the three possible questions you may see in the test:

(T5B09):
Which decibel value most closely represents a power increase from 5 watts to 10 watts? 3 dB

(T5B10):
Which decibel value most closely represents a power decrease from 12 watts to 3 watts? -6 dB

(T5B11):
Which decibel value represents a power increase from 20 watts to 200 watts? 10 dB

For the Emergency Operator or Prepper, here is what you really need to understand about Decibels. Decibels is a measure of gain or loss. We will most often see these readings in antennas or feed lines in the manner of signal gain we can get out of one antenna vs. another antenna, so a larger dB gain in one antenna will mean a better performance from that antenna over another. In coaxial cable such as use in feed lines from a radio transmitter to the antenna, the greater the dB Gain the greater the loss in signal going through from the radio to the antenna.

For Antennas, directional antennas are one type of antenna that will offer a gain in signal strength for the direction that the antenna is being directed in. If you are on the edge of the range to a repeater, you could use a Yagi or Dish antenna pointed in the direction of the repeater to help boost your radio signal to the repeater, creating a better connection to the repeater.

For Coaxial cables used for feed lines, you will want to keep the dB Loss that is shown as a specification for the cable as low as possible. You also need to be aware that the dB loss in coaxial cable will vary depending upon the frequency of your radio signal through the coax. In most coax cables, dB loss at HF frequencies is much lower than it is at VHF frequencies, and at UHF frequencies the loss increases even more. We will discuss this more in the Section 7 chapter for Antennas and Coax.

6.2.2 - Electrical Power Calculations – Watts, Volts, Current and Power
The next area where Math problems will be most prevalent at is with basic power calculations and power conversions. In this category of questions, we are using two values of power – Voltage (E), Current or Amps (I), and Power Calculation (P) to determine the third value. This is all based on the basic power formula

which is represented as "P = E x I". In these equations, "P" represents total "Power" which is represented in **Watts**; "E" represents "Electromagnetic Force" or Voltage represented in **Volts**; and "I" represents our total current or "Amperage" represented in **Amps**.

Base FormulA. P = I x E;

In this formula we calculate I times E and our result is P

Alternate versions:

I = P / E;   In this formula we divide P by E and our result is I

E = P / I;   In this formula we dide P by I and our result is E

P = I x E

The graphical circle is in the base formula format which is P = I x E. The first value that we are trying to solve for, P, I or E, is always placed on the left side of our problem. On the right side of our problem are the other two values for which we should have known values for. In these problems you will always need two of the three values to be known to solve for the third. For instance:

Question (T5C10): How much power is delivered by a voltage of 12 volts DC and a current of and a DC Current of 2.5 Amps?

In this question we will use the original Power formula of P = I x E.

P = (12 volts) x (2.5 Amps);   P = 12 x 2.5;   P = 30

So, our **answer for (T5C10) is 30**, and since power is measured in watts, our actual answer is 30 watts. Now let's look at a variation of this problem where we are going to solve for I (Amps) instead of P (Power).

Question (T5C11): How much current is required to deliver 120 watts at a voltage of 12 volts DC?

In this question we are going to modify our formula. Instead of P = I x E, we are solving for I, so we use the formula I = P / E.

I = (120 watts) / (12 volts);   I = 120 / 12;   I = 10

So, our **answer for (T5C11) is 10**, and since current is measured in Amps our actual answer is 10 Amps.

OHM's Law Calculations

Using the "Ohms Law Formula Circle" on the next page, we will use a similar formula which will allow us to calculate for Volts (E), Current (I), or Resistance if we know two of the three values. It uses a similar circle formula as we are using in our Power formula above, however, is not the same formula.

Base FormulA. E (Volts) = I (Current) x R (Resistance);
In this formula we calculate I times R and our result is E

Alternate versions:

I = E / R;   In this formula we divide E by R and our result is I

R = E / I;   In this formula we divide E by I and our result is R

$$E = I \times R$$

This graphical circle for the OHMS Law formula is very similar to our Power Circle. In both we are using Voltage, aka Electromagnetic Force (E) and Current (I) as two of our known values. But in this one we are using Resistance measured in Ohms as our third known value. Let's take a look at a couple of our test questions to work through the formula.

There are (3) variations of this formula which are:

- *(T5D01) – The formula to calculate the current in a circuit is I = E / R*
- *(T5D02) – The formula to calculate Voltage in a circuit is E = I x R*
- *(T5D03) – The formula to calculate Resistance in a circuit is R = E / I*

Memorize the **OHMS LAW** circle shown here to the right and you should be able to remember these variations.

(T5D11) What is the voltage across a 10-ohm resistor if a current of 1 amperes flows through it?

In this question we are going to use our base formula of E = I x R to get our answer.

   E = (1 Amps) x (10 Ohms);   E = 1 x 10;   E = 10

So, **our answer for (T5D11) is 10**, and since Volts or Electromagnetic Force is measured in Volts, our answer is 10 Volts.

(T5D12) - What is the voltage across a 10-ohm resistor if a current of 2 amperes flows through it?

In this question we are going to use our base formula of E = I x R to get our answer.

   E = (2 Amps) x (10 Ohms);   E = 2 x 10;   E = 20

So, **our answer for (T5D12) is 20**, and since Volts or Electromagnetic Force is measured in Volts, our answer is 20 Volts. Now let's look at a variation of this problem.

(T5D09) - What is the current through a 24-ohm resistor connected across 240 volts?

In this question we are going to use a variation of our formula in the form of I = E / R for our answer.

I = (240 volts) / (24 Ohms);   I = 240 / 24;   I = 10

So, our answer we are looking for is 10 and since current is measured in Amps; **our answer is 10 Amps.**

(T5C09) - How much power is delivered by a voltage of 13.8 volts DC and a current of 10 amperes?
Using the formula where P = E x I, we simply multiply 13.8 x 10 to get our answer **of 138-watts.**

(T5D04) - What is the resistance of a circuit in which a current of 3 amperes flows when connected to 90 volts?
Using the variation of the OHMS formula where R = E / I, we divide our voltage (E) which is 90 by our current (I) which is 3 to find that our resistance will be **30 ohms.**

(T5D05) – What is the resistance of a circuit for which the applied voltage is 12-volts, and the current flow is 1.5 amperes?
Using the variation of the OHMS formula of R = E / I, we divide our voltage (E) which is 12 by our current (I) which is 1.5 to find that our resistance will be **8 ohms.**

(T5D06) – What is the resistance of a circuit that draws 4 amperes from a 12-volt source?
Again, we are going to use our OHMS formula of R = E / I, dividing out voltage (E) which is 12 by our current (I) which s 4 to find that our resistance is **3 ohms.**

(T5D07) – What is the Current in a circuit with an applied voltage of 120-volts and a resistance of 80-ohms?
In this question we are using a different variation of our Ohms formula. For this, the variation we are solving for is going to be I = E / R. We divide our voltage (E) of 120-volts by our resistance of 80 ohms (R) to get our current which will resolve to **1.5 Amperes**. (120 / 80 = 1.5)

(T5D08) – What is the current through a 100-ohm resistor connected across 200-volts?
We will use the same formula we used above in T5D07 which is I = E / R. The formula will be I = 200 (E) / 100 (I) or
"I = 200 / 100" which resolves to **2-Amperes.**

(T5D10) – What is the voltage across a 2-ohm resistor if a current of 0.5 amperes flows through it?
In this question the variation of the OHMS formula we will use is E = I x R. Plugging our numbers into it will give us the formula of I = 0.5 (I) x 2 (R) which solves to 1, so our answer is **1-Volt**.

For the Prepper and Emergency Operator, having a solid understanding of Power will help in planning for emergency operations and planning proper battery and power sources to make sure you are able to stay on the air. For instance – It is easy to understand you need a 12-volt battery. But – if you are limited to using a small 10-amp/hour battery and your radio is drawing 15-amps, it is important not only to understand how long your battery will last you, but also to understand charging options to keep your battery charged and your radio on the air. It would be easy to under power your radio needs if you don't understand how much power you will need for your radio. Use of a radio for 2-5 minutes an hour for a remote operator just using the radio for status and updates is much different than for a Net Control operator who may be on the radio 30 or 45 minutes each hour relaying information between stations and passing messages. Also understanding the power needs you have to keep batteries charged, lights on, and radios operating will help you know if you are going to be able to get by with a couple of solar panels producing power during the day, or if you need to have some form of generator that can produce power 24-hours a day but will require fuel for operation.

6.2.3 - Frequency Calculations
Our next big area of Math calculations comes in with frequency calculations. Here we are determining our wavelength in meters of a particular frequency, or determining our frequency based on a known wavelength. Why is this important, besides being included on the tests?

Understanding the relationship between frequency and wavelength is important in planning proper antennas for your radio. While it is easy to go out and purchase an antenna for your radio, you may find a need at some point to be able to stand up a home-brew antenna for mounting higher in the air for better performance, or for even building a directional antenna to squeeze more radio range for your station to a repeater or another operator that may be outside of your radio's normal range. Knowing the lengths for the elements you will need for your antenna based on frequencies you will be transmitting on is necessary to be able to hope for good performance.

Fortunately, our formula we will be using here is simpler than our Power and Ohm's law formulas because we already know one of our three values in the formula – ***the speed of light which is 300,000,000 meters per second (T3B11)***. This value will be represented by "c". Knowing this then we will only need to have one of our other two values – the wavelength (Represented with the "λ" symbol) as measured in Meters, or the Frequency (f) we will be operating on also measured in Megahertz. Our formula therefore that we will be using is:

$$\lambda = c / f$$

Some other values we will need to know include:

Speed of light in Meters:	300,000,000 Meters per second
Conversion of Meters into Feet:	1 Meter = 3.28 Feet
Conversion of Feet to Inches:	1 Foot = 12 inches
Conversion of Meters to Inches:	1 Meter = 39.36 Inches
Optimal length of an antenna to the calculated length:	About 5% shorter, so take your final number and multiply by 0.95 for your answer.

REMEMBER – The Velocity of a Radio wave traveling through free space is the speed of light, or 300,000,000 meters per second (T3B04). Let's look at some of the actual questions on our tests and work through the answer.

(T9A08) - What is the approximate length, in inches, of a quarter-wavelength vertical antenna for 146 MHz?

We know here that one of our three values, the speed of light in METERS will always be 300,000,000. That leaves only frequency or wavelength that we need to solve the problem. Our question gives us our frequency of 146 MHz which when written out as a long number is 146,000,000 Hz. So then, our formula should look as follows:

$$\lambda = c / f; \qquad \lambda = 300,000,000 / 146,000,000; \qquad \lambda = 2.054794520547945 \text{ Meters.}$$

For simplicity let's round to 2 decimal places, so our answer is 2.05 Meters. Now – We need to convert this into feet and inches.

If you can remember that 1 Meter = 3.28 feet, then our next calculation is:

Feet = (2.05 Meters) x 3.28;   Feet = 6.724 Feet

And next let's convert our number of feet, 6.724 into inches as follows:

Inches = 6.724 x 12;   Inches = 80.688 Inches.

We now know our wavelength is 80.7 inches rounded off to 1 decimal. But out question is not asking for the wavelength in inches. No – it is asking for the length in inches of a quarter-wavelength vertical antenna. So, we need to divide our answer of 80.7 by four:

Quarter Wavelength = 80.7 / 4;   Quarter wavelength = 20.175 inches.

Now – This is important – as our last step we need to multiply our answer by 0.95 for optimal length, so now we do this:

Quarter wavelength x 0.95;   20.175 x 0.95 = 19.16 inches

In this question, the closest answer is 19 inches. So – We will select 19 inches as our answer. Let's look at a second similar question that is in our test.

(T9A09) - What is the approximate length, in inches, of a half-wavelength 6-meter dipole antenna?
This is very similar to the prior example. We know the formula of "$\lambda = c / f$". We know that the constant value for the speed of light is 300,000,000. So, we need either the frequency or the wavelength. For this question since we are calculating for 6-Meter band, we will use the base frequency for the 6-meter band. In this case that is 50,000,000 Hz. Our formula should look like:

$\lambda = c / f$; $\lambda = 300,000,000 / 50,000,000$; $\lambda = 6$ Meters.

Now let's convert this to feet and then inches:

Feet = 6 x 3.28;   *Feet = 19.68 Feet;*

And now to inches...

Inches = 19.68 feet x 12;   *Inches = 236.16 inches.*

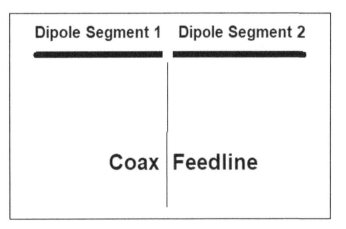

Now – Looking back at our question, we are looking for the length, in inches, of a half-wavelength dipole antenna. A dipole antenna is an antenna that has a feed point from the radio transmitter in the middle. Think of a "T" where the feed line comes up through the middle and then connects to the two-dipole segment. Each dipole segment is ½ of the length of the total. In our question, we are looking for a half-wavelength antenna, so half of our 236 inches of our full wavelength will be 118 inches.

Since our ideal length will be 95% of what our calculated answer is:

Ideal length = 118 x 0.95;   *Ideal length = 112.1 inches*

So, this gives us our answer of 112 inches.

With Dipole Antennas – The best way of increasing the resonant frequency of a Dipole antenna is by shortening it (T9A05).

> *On the test there are only two questions where these calculations need to be made, though there are others that refer to the formula. Unlike the Decibels questions where I did not cover the process in depth, the need to understand this concept for antenna building is critical. You simply cannot build a good antenna without knowing these calculations, and in the event of an emergency you may need to build one for better reception. A good antenna can be built out of spare parts – MacGyvering it so to say. Extension cords, picture wire, or other types of unshielded cable. There is still more to making the connection from the coax to the antenna wire which we won't cover here, but understand this formula is critical to calculating proper antenna length.*

The Relationship between Frequency and Wavelength

Another topic to understand is how frequency and wavelength are related. As the frequency rises, which is measured in **Hertz**, the wavelength in inches or meters goes down. This is the topic of question **(T3B05)** which says, "**As the wavelength gets shorter the frequency increases".** With higher frequencies you have more cycles per second, which equates to shorter wavelength in a single cycle. This is a natural occurrence of cramming more cycles into the same period. Likewise, as the frequency goes down, the wavelength gets longer. Longer wavelengths have much better ability to reflect through the atmosphere – these are our HF frequencies. Higher frequencies could be considered "Sharper" and tend to reflect much less. If you think of higher frequencies (VHF, UHF) as "Sharper" it is easier to think of these frequencies "Cutting" through the atmosphere with less reflection.

(T9A04) asks "What is a disadvantage of the short, flexible antenna supplied with most handheld radio transceivers, compared to a full-sized quarter-wave antenna? The answer to this question is **"It has low efficiency".** Let's drill into this topic briefly.

Most handheld radios come with an antenna that is about 7-inches long. A 70-cm wavelength, the full-wavelength is about 27.5 inches, so a ¼ wavelength antenna is about 6.88 inches. Remember I said the antennas are about 7", so these HT antennas are ¼ wavelength UHF 70-cm Antennas.

For the 2-Meter frequencies, the general full-wavelength is about 78.72 inches, meaning a ¼ wavelength is about 19.68 inches. This makes the antenna on the HT radio less than a 1/10 wavelength. Because this is so much shorter than even the ¼ wavelength 19.68 inches, it is highly inefficient. So, the question is referring to the size being inefficient for many uses. Instead use of an antenna designed for 2-meters would be much better. A ¼ wavelength 2-Meter antenna will also be close to a 5/8 wavelength so even at UHF frequencies the 2-Meter antennas will do at least an adequate job.

But remember – For the best performance you are always going to do best with an antenna properly sized for the specific frequency you are working.

6.2.4 – Metric Conversions and Metric Calculations

HERTZ, KILOHERTZ, and MEGAHERTZ

Hertz is the standard measure of 1 cycle per second of a Radio Frequency (RF) signal and is identified as the unit measurement for frequency (T5A06). (RF is the abbreviation for Radio Frequencies of all types – (T5C06). As a technician, the frequencies you will be receiving permissions in are all in the Megahertz range, which are millions of hertz. On the lower frequency side you will be able to transmit in the 10-MHz range, moving up into the higher bands.

On the test, the references you will need to remember are:

1. Hertz – One cycle per second, abbreviated as (**Hz**)
2. Kilohertz – One thousand cycles per second, abbreviated as (**kHz**). AM Radio stations for instance. As a licensed Tech you will NOT have permissions in the kHz range.
3. Megahertz – One Million cycles per second, abbreviated as (**MHz**). Think here of FM Music stations, Television Stations. Your primary bands are going to be VHF/UHF frequencies measured in MHz.

Remember these are magnitude math changes so you will need to be performing, so you need to keep in mind the following conversions:

- A Kilo is short for 1,000, so 1-Kilovolt = 1,000 volts
- Milli is short for 1/1,000, so 1 millivolt = 1/1000 or .001 volt; 1,000 millivolts = 1.0 volt; 500 millivolts = ½ volt.
- Micro is short for 1/1,000,000 so 1 microvolt = 1/1,000,000 volts or .000001 volt.
- A Pico is 1 trillionth and is only used in one question.

Table 8-1: Metric Measure values

Mnemonics	Prefix	Symbol	Magnitude		Magnitude
the	Tera	T	10	12	1,000,000,000,000
great	Giga	G	10	9	1,000,000,000
mighty	mega	M	10	6	1,000,000
king	Kilo	k	10	3	1,000
Hector	hecto	h	10	2	100
died	Deka	da	10	1	10
unexpectedly	Unit	-	1		1
drinking	Deci	da	10	-1	-10
chocolate	centi	c	10	-2	-100
milk	Milli	m	10	-3	-1,000
Monday	micro		10	-6	-1,000,000
night	Nano	n	10	-9	-1,000,000,000
pictures	Pico	p	10	-12	-1,000,000,000,000

Converting between Measures

There will be several possible questions related to the conversion of unit measures. For instance – 57000 Hertz is equal to how many kilohertz? Or converting kilohertz info megahertz. Likewise, there will be several questions that require the conversion of amps to milliamps, watts into milliwatts, or farads into picofarads. You will need to know your metric conversions for these. Most of the questions will be relatively easy, though some will toss you measure units that are unusual and will throw you off.

Here are some examples:

(T5B01) - How Many milliamperes is 1.5 Amperes?

In this question we are being asked to convert Amperes to Milliamperes. Using the table on the next page and understanding that our Ampere is a single unit and milli is equivalent to $1/1000^{th}$ of a single unit we can multiply our given number of 1.5 by 1,000 to get 1500 milliamperes.

Our answer is 1,500 milliamperes.

(T5B03) – Which is equal to one kilovolt?
 If you remember that a kilo is equal to 1,000, then you will know that *one kilovolt equals one-thousand volts.*

(T5B04) - Which is equal to one microvolt?
Again, we can look at our table to see that the measure "micro" is equal to 1/1,000,000 of a single unit. So, our answer for this one is *One One-Millionth of a volt.*

(T5B05) – Which is equal to 500 milliwatts?
If you remember that Milli is 1/1000 or one-thousandth, and that 1 of any value (1-watt) then 500 milliwatts is 500/1000 watts, *or our answer of 0.5 watts* (1/2 watt).

(T5B06) – Which is equal to 3000 milliamperes?

Here since one milliampere is 1/1000 amps and we are multiplying by 3000, then what we have is 3000 milliamperes which divided by 1,000 is 3. **So, our answer 3 *amperes*.**

(T5B08) - Which is equal to 1,000,000 picofarads?

This is probably the most difficult in this category on the test because of the way you need to convert it. For this, since none of the answers were in single-unit measure (Farads) then we were going to have to do conversions to find fractional possibilities.

First, let's convert 1,000,000 picofarads to farads – simply divide by 1,000,000 and we get 1/1,000,000 farads. So, looking at our chart, we look to see which measure is in the millionths. Here we can see that would be "micro" – So 1/1,000,000 is one-micro farad. ***Our answer here is one Micro Farad***.

- 1 farad = 1,000 millifarads (mF)
- 1 millifarad = 1,000 micro-farads (µF)
- 1 microfarad = 1,000 nano-farads (nF)
- 1 nano-farad = 1,000 picofarads (pF)

We have to remember here that our order is: Farad, then Millifarad, then Microfarad, then Nano-farad. Remembering this, 1,000,000 picofarads = 1,000 nano-farad and 1,000 non-farads = 1-microfarad.

Special comment for problem (T5B08) *– If you can remember that there is only 1 question in the pool that touches on farad size conversion – you can just memorize "1-microfarad" as the proper answer. You will be focusing on remembering a lot for the test, so just remember "1-Microfarad" rather than this multi-level magnitude conversion.*

6.2.5 - TEST PROBLEMS DEALING WITH FREQUENCIES AND WAVELENGTH

In the prior pages we focused on math related problems that were focuses on energy values. The question pool also covers several questions that are related to frequency conversions between different magnitudes (Hertz to Kilohertz, Kilohertz to Megahertz, etc.). before we look at these problems, let's remember these points when talking about frequencies:

1. The term HERTZ represents a single full wavelength cycle. When we talk abut the frequency in hertz, we are talking about how MANY of the wavelength cycles occur each second.
2. The speed of light is a constant that is used in some formulas (Not all) which is 300,000,000 meters per second.
3. Abbreviations are CASE sensitive - Remember that the case is sensitive for the abbreviations.
4. Hertz is abbreviated **Hz** – uppercase H, lower-case z.
5. ***kilohertz is abbreviated kHz (T5C13)*** – lower-case k, uppercase H, lower-case z.
6. ***Megahertz is abbreviated MHz (T5C07)*** – upper-case M, upper-case H, lower-case z

(T3B06) – The formula for converting frequency to approximate wavelength in meters is:

Wavelength in Meters = 300 divided by the frequency in megahertz

For this question – we don't use the full 300,000,000 meters per second because the number is already in millions (300 million). Our frequency in Megahertz is also in millions, so we cancel out the additional zero's.

(T5B02) - Which is equal to 1,500,000 Hertz?

Relatively simple here – We need to multiply out 1,500,000 by positive measure values to see where we have a match. As a hint – Our Frequency measures are usually in Hertz (Which the question already gives us), Kilohertz, Megahertz or Gigahertz. So – Using Kilo, Mega and Giga, which of these give us a whole number or greater value (Greater than 1)?

  A. 1,500,000 Hertz = 1,500 Kilohertz   (divide 1,500,000 by 1000)
  B. 1,500,000 Hertz = 1.5 Megahertz   (divide 1,500,000 by 1,000,000)
  C. 1,500,000 Hertz = 0.0015 Gigahertz (divide 1,500,000 by 1,000,000,000)

Since we are looking for a value of 1 or greater, only A or B above would qualify. In our possible answers in the question, only 1500 kHz would be a match. VERY IMPORTANT – Make sure you pay attention to the measurements being used – In this question, we have (2) answers with 1500 in the answer – Only one though is "kHz". **Our answer here is 1500 kHz.**

(T5B07) – Which is equal to 3.525 MHz? This question is very similar to the above question in that we need to know our measurements and do the conversions. First – Our value of 3.525-MHz is equal to 3,525,000 Hz. Our options are:

  - 0.003525 kHz (Which when multiplied by 1000 comes out to 3.525 Hz)
  - 35.25 kHz   (Which when multiplied by 1000 comes out to 35,250 Hz)
  - **3525 kHz**   (Which when multiplied by 1000 comes out to 3,525,000 Hz)
  - 3,525,000 kHz (Which when multiplied by 1000 comes out to 3,525,000,000 Hz).

So, the answer as to which equals 3.525-MHz is **3525-kHz.**

(T5B12) – Which is equal to 28400 kHz? Again, we covert all of our frequencies to Hertz values. 28,400-kHz x 1000 is equal to 28,400,000 Hz. So which of our answers equals this?

  - 28.400 kHz   (Which multiplied by 1000 equals 284,000 Hz) – Multiply by 1000 because this value is in kHz
  - 2.800 MHz   (Which multiplied by 1 million equals 2800000 Hz) - Multiply by one million because this value
                       is in MHz)
  - 284.00 MHz   (Which multiplied by 1 million equals 284,000,000 Hz)
  - **28.400 MHz**   (Which multiplied by 1 million equals 28,400,000 Hz)

Our answer is **28.400 MHz**

(T5B13) – Which is equal to 2425 MHz? Again, we convert all our frequencies to Hertz values. 2,425-MHz (One Million is equal to 2,425,000,000). Which of our answers equals this?

- 0.002425 GHz (Multiply by 1 billion (1,000,000,000) to get 2,425,000 Hz)
- 24.25 GHz   (Multiply by 1 billion (1,000,000,000) to get 24,250,000,000 Hz)
- **2.425 GHz**   (Multiply by 1 billion (1b,000,000,000) to get 2,425,000,000 Hz)
- 2425 GHz   (Multiply by 1 billion (1,000,000,000) to get 2,425,000,000,000 Hz)

Our answer is **2.425 GHz.**

In these questions that we have reviewed above and all of which are in the question pool of 411 questions, what I recommend is converting all into straight Hz values, so they are all at the same magnitude. Then make your comparisons. With a calculator this should be very quick. You are not likely to get more than one or two of these frequency conversion problems and remember that the test is limited to only 7 at most math questions.

6.3 - Frequency Bands Explained

I have seen enough new hams and students asking questions about bands and being confused about their meaning. A ham radio "Band" is a group of related frequencies within a specific range that have similar characteristics. So frequency ranges are often referred to as a "Band" which is equivalent to a range of frequencies that share their approximate wavelength in meters (T3B07). Privileges for ham radio operators are given in specific bands. As a "Technician" you will have access to the following bands:

- **10-Meter HF Band – Partial access to this band only, 28.000 MHz – 28.500 MHz (T1B01)**
  As a Tech you will only have partial access to this band. General and Extra level operators have full access which runs from 28.000-MHz to 29.700-MHz. This is an HF band and has HF characteristics including some longer distance capabilities and better ability to reflect through the atmosphere than do VHF and UHF frequencies. Also – As a technician you will be limited in transmitting power on the 10-Meter band to 200-watts. As a General license holder or an Amateur Extra license holder, you power limitation is 1500-watts.

- 6-Meter VHF Band – Full access to this band, 50.0 MHz to 54.0-MHz. **The frequency range of 50.0-MHz thru 50.1 MHz and 144.0-MHz thru 144.1 MHz are available for CW use only (T1B07).**

- 2-Meter VHF Band – Full access to this band, 144.0 MHz to 148.0-MHz. This is a very popular tech-level band available on handheld radios and often used with repeaters. **The frequency range of 50.0-MHz thru 50.1 MHz and 144.0-MHz thru 144.1 MHz are available for CW use only (T1B07).**

- 1.25-Meter VHF Band – Partial access from 222.0 MHz to 225.0 MHz limited to 25-watts. This band is available on some handheld radios though for best use would require an antenna specific to this band. ***Note: The frequencies from 219 to 220-MHz in the 1.25-Meter band are available to amateurs for the use of Fixed Digital Message forwarding systems only (T1B05).***

- 70-cm UHF Band – Full access to this band, 420.0 MHz to 450.0-MHz. This is the second most popular band for Techs working from Handheld radios and heavy repeater use.

Additionally, Techs also have full access to the following bands which are higher in frequencies. These frequencies are not commonly available on handheld or mobile radios and as higher UHF frequencies will have distance limitations. Not all of these have "Band" names but rather are referred to by frequency range.

Following is a list of the higher frequencies in the UHF band that the new Technician has access. These are, for the most part, specialty bands that experimenters or special use operators will use:

- 33-cm Band – 902-MHz to 928-MHz
- 23-cm Band – 1240-MHz to 1300-MHz
- 2300-2310 MHz UHF
- 2390-2450 MHz UHF
- 3300-3500 MHz
- 5650-5925 MHz
- 10.0 – 10.5 GHz
- 24.0 – 24.25 GHz
- 46.0 – 47.2 GHz
- 76.0 – 81.0 GHz
- 122.25 – 123.0 GHz
- 134.0 – 141.0 GHz
- 241.0 – 250.0 GHz
- All above 275 GHz

6.3.1 - General Characteristics of the Bands
In general, the characteristics that may be asked about on the tests refer to the following:

- ***HF Bands – 3-MHz to 30-MHz (T3B10)*** - Longer wavelength and lower frequencies.
These bands work best for long-distance/non-repeater communications, and do not function on handheld radios. They are available on both mobile radios and base radios. Radios operating with these frequencies are more expensive though there are some mobile radios that do operate in the 6-Meter and 10-Meter bands as FM radios that are in the $200 and up range.

These frequencies propagate through the atmosphere allowing longer distance communication without the need for repeaters. For most HF frequencies (Except for 10-Meters) a "General" license is required to operate. In many cases, the best emergency radio operation will work from HF frequencies since no repeater operation is needed. The propagation characteristics for most HF radio operation will work best for longer distance – but it needs to be understood that short-distance communication often is poor unless a special antenna is needed such as an NVIS antenna (Near Vertical Incidence Skywave – Not on the test).

Note: Though not considered "Ham Radio" – CB Radio operates near frequency ranges – Specifically in the 11-Meter band. CB Radio has poor performance and quality when compared to Ham Radio HF communications due to:

- Lower Power – Only 4-watts regular operation, 12-watts SSB operation. HF Radio operates usually in the 50 to 1500-watt power levels. (Legal power limits – There are many illegal operators).
- Usually vertical polarized antennas (Straight up) so atmospheric propagation does not occur.

- *VHF – 30-MHz to 300-MHz frequencies (T3B08)* - Shorter wavelengths than HF, higher frequencies. VHF is "Line of Sight" and only extends beyond the curvature of the earth in a limited range. Though these frequencies can extend beyond the curvature of the earth, they are more easily blocked by obstacles – Trees, Vegetation, Homes, Buildings, Cars, Hills, Mountains, etc. FM Radio and Television stations (TV Channels 2 thru 13) broadcast in these frequencies, so think about radio station range in your car as you move away from a radio station.

The 2-Meter and 1.25-Meter frequencies can be found on most handheld radios, though the 1.25-Meter frequency on far fewer. Distance communications is most often through repeaters with VHF Radios. 6-Meters also is a VHF frequency ranging from 50 to 54-MHz and is available on some mobile radios.

2-Meter frequency wavelengths are 2-Meters in length which equates to 2-Meters * 3.28 (Feet/Meter) length in feet (6.56 feet). In inches this comes out to 6.56 ft x 12 = 78.72 inches. A typical handheld radio antenna is ¼ wavelength, so about 19 inches in length.

- *UHF – 300 to 3000 MHz Frequencies (T3B09)* –Shorter wavelengths/higher frequencies than VHF. Commercial use of UHF includes television channels 16 and higher that tend to have lesser quality than the VHF channels. These are also line-of-sight and more easily blocked by obstacles including vegetation, hills, mountains, cars and buildings. UHF frequencies are also often range-extended through radio repeaters.

The 70-cm frequencies (420 to 450-MHz) can be found on most handheld radios. 70-cm frequency wavelengths are 70-cm in length (.7 Meters * 3.28 = 2.296 feet). In inches this comes out to 27.552 which gives us a ¼ wavelength antenna length of about 6.88 inches making these great antenna lengths for handheld radios.

So be sure to remember:

A. *HF is 3-MHz to 30-MHz (T3B10)*

B. *VHF is 30-MHz to 300-MHz (T3B08)*
C. *UHF is 300-MHz to 3000-MHz (3-GHz) (T3B09)*

Edge of Band Use

In the test pool there is one specific question that we need to understand deals with use of the edge frequencies in a band. For instance – The VHF 2-Meter band operates between 144.0-MHz and 148.0-MHz. What happens if we set our transceiver exactly to 148.0 MHz? When you're transmit from an Analog 2-Meter radio, you are using 25-kHz of bandwidth with your carrier frequency being set right dead center of the frequency you are using. So, if you are transmitting on 148.0-MHz, your signal transmits 12.5-kHz below 148.0-MHz and 12.5-kHz ABOVE 148.0-MHz. This means you are transmitting between 147.875-MHz and 148.125-MHz. So, you are transmitting ABOVE the 148.000 MHz frequency which is not allowed. But – This is not the only reason.

(T1B09) - Why should you not set your transmit frequency to be exactly at the edge of an amateur band or sub-band?

- *To allow for calibration error in the transmitter frequency display*
- *So that modulation side bands do not extend beyond the band edge*
  (Explanation of this is discussed above)
- *To allow for transmitter frequency drift*
  (The transmitter could easily drift off frequency)

Because all the options for this question in the pool are correct, the correct choice is *"All these choices are correct".*

AM Fast Scan TV Transmissions
A more unusual use, but a use that will be available to you as a technician, will be the use of Fast-Scan TV transmissions. Fast-Scan TV is a method of sending broadcast full-motion pictures over short distances using UHF and microwave bands. For the test, the only question you will need to remember for Fast-Scan TV Transmissions is that *the approximate bandwidth of the AM Fast-Scan Transmission is about 6-MHz (T8A10).*

6.3.2 - Phone and CW Operation

There will be several questions on the test for Phone and CW operation. Here are some things to understand about these concepts:

A. Phone operation refers to "Voice" operation – Holding down the PTT button and just talking. In many bands there are certain frequencies within the band reserved for phone operation which is the most common use of the frequencies.

B. CW operation refers to Morse Code. CW is short for Continuous Wave and is the tones that you hear in rapid succession on the radio at times. When communicating on a repeater you will often hear these tones. Repeaters are required to identify themselves every few minutes and CW is one allowable method that is quick and cannot be confused with a caller. Many bands have specific frequencies that are dedicated to CW-Only use and there are questions on the test for these.

    a. In VHF 6-Meters, 50.0 to 50.1-MHz is reserved for CW Only
    b. In VHF, 144.0 to 144.1-MHz is reserved for CW only

C. CW communication requires less bandwidth to communicate with since it uses a simple continuous tone. The bandwidth needed is only 150-Hz (Not kHz) which is tiny. It can also transmit and be received with less power.

D. Knowledge of CW in how to use it used to be required on tests however is not any longer.

E. ***In the HF bands, a new technician will ONLY have Phone/Voice privileges in the 10-Meter band. (T1B06)***

6.3.3 – Notes about the 6-Meter Band

There are several questions on the test specific to use of the 6-Meter band. Here are some points to understand about 6-Meters.

A. ***6-Meter band runs from 50.0 to 54.0-MHz. (T1B03)***

B. ***Due to the length of the wavelength for 6-Meters, if you are trying to bounce a signal off a meteor during a meteor shower, 6-Meters is the best band for this. (T3C07)***

C. ***6-Meters along with 10-Meters will work better than other bands you have access to as a technician for long-distance communication through the atmosphere during sunspot activity due*** *to longer wavelengths. (T3C10)*

D. *In the category of safety and RF Radiation exposure, the human body is most sensitive to the 6-Meter wavelengths than any other wavelengths. This is simply because the human body will absorb more radiation at these frequencies than others. (T0C02 & T0C05).*

The 6-Meter band is still VHF but has longer wavelengths and therefore will have some longer distance opportunities from the higher frequencies. As a technician, you will also have access to a portion of the 10-meter band which will offer even greater distance opportunity. Check out chapter 9, section

6.3.4 – SSB Notes

"Single-Side-Band", or SSB, is a capability of AM Modulation where the radio signal carrier and one of the two side bands are removed from being transmitted. In most radios that new TECHNICIANS will be using, most of these radios are FM modulated radios. (Handhelds, Baofengs, etc). But – If you have an AM capable radio, such as a more expensive all-band radio, you can broadcast using AM modulation and therefore can utilize side bands and try to work some longer distance communication.

If you are communicating using Side band communication (Which only uses a part of the signal and can focus more power out on that partial signal) you would use the UPPER side band for UHF, VHF and 10-meter frequencies. *In Other HF frequencies below 10-Meters you would normally utilize LOWER SIDE BAND. (T8A06)*

When communicating with sideband you are only utilizing a part of the band – and cutting out the other side band and the actual carrier. *Doing so allows you to reduce the width of the full voice signal to only 3-kHz for voice (T8A08).* Remember from our CW notes above, *if you were communicating with CW instead of Voice you would be communicating with a bandwidth as little as 150-Hz. (T8A11).*

6.3.5 – Calling Frequencies

Each radio band has certain frequencies that are considered "Calling Frequencies". This means – If you are in an unfamiliar area and need calling out, then these are the frequencies to try first. Also – If you are an emergency radio operator, then these are frequencies you should be monitoring in case someone is trying to reach out for help. Calling frequencies are NOT the same as channels in channelized radio such as CB Radio, but they are the closest things because they are known values. You could consider calling frequencies similar to "CB Channel 9 and 19" for road emergencies and for travel information. Calling frequencies on 2-Meter and 70-CM are:

- *2-Meters – 146.520 MHz (T2A02 & T1B04)*
- 70-cm – 446.000 MHz (Not on the test)

6.4 - Symbols & Components

Before taking the test, you should study and have a basic understanding of all the various components that may be discussed on the test and that are in the reference schematics that are going to be covered on the test. There will only be 3 schematics that are covered in the pool, so you may very likely NOT see but only one of two of them. In the table below you will find the components that are possibly in the schematics.

6.4.1 – Components Schematic Images

Table 7-2 - Components

Diagram#	Item #	Component / Description	Schematic Diagram
T-1	1	**Resistor** A resistor provides opposition to DC current in a circuit. A resistor is a ceramic component that is marked with painted color lines to indicate the value of resistance. Resistor values are measured in OHMs. ***Resistors oppose the flow of current in a DC Circuit (T6A01).***	
T-1	2	**Transistor** A Transistor can act as a switch or amplifier. Current flows between the conductors to the top and bottom of the transistor, while current applied in the left-side conductor controls the flow of current and controls the switch or amplifier functions. ***Transistors contain three separate regions of semiconductor material (T6B04).*** ***A Field Effect Transistor has three connections – Gate, Drain and Source (T6B05).*** ***A Bipolar Junction Transistor has three connections referred to as Emitter, Base and Collector (T6B12).*** Transistors are measured by their voltage, amperage, and by design for specific purpose.	
T-2	3	**Single-Pole Single-Throw Switch (SPST)** ***A simple switch used to apply and terminate power in the circuit. (T6A12)*** Switches including SPST and SPDT switches are measured by the voltages and amperage they can support.	

Not on Diagram	-	**Single-Pole Double-Throw Switch (SPDT)** *The SPDT switch is commonly used to allow a single circuit to be switched between one of two other circuits (T6A08).*	
T-1	3	**Lamp** *A DC power light, not to be confused with an LED. (T6C04)* A Lamp is a bulb such as an incandescent bulb. They are measured based on voltage and size or purpose.	
T-1	4	**Battery** *A DC Battery with a (+) and (-) Terminal (T6C05).* A DC Battery can be any of a wide variety of battery types.	
T-2	6	**Capacitor** *A Capacitor which can store power even after the power is removed from the circuit (T6C06). Capacitors work in circuits to store energy in an electric field, working often as a miniature battery (T6A04). Capacitors are made up of conductive surfaces separated by an insulator (T6A05).* *Capacitors can be used along with inductors to make resonant circuits (T6D08). A Resonant tuned circuit can be made with a capacitor and an inductor used in a series or parallel circuit (T6D11).* *The unit of measure of a capacitor is the Farad. (T5C02)*	
T-2	8	**Light Emitting Diode (LED)** *A type of one-directional diode that emits light as current passes through it (T6C07). A LED is a type of Diode that emits light when forward current passes through it (T6B07). An LED is commonly used as a visual indicator such as a power indicator (T6D07).*	
T-2	9	**Variable Resistor (Varistor)** *A Potentiometer, such as a radio volume dial. (T6C08)* Variable resistors are measured in Ohms. *A Potentiometer is often used as an adjustable volume control (T6A02).* *The Potentiometer controls the electrical parameter known as RESISTANCE in a circuit (T6A03).*	

T-2	4	**Transformer** *Transformers are used to step-up/step-down AC voltage (T6C09).* *A Transformer is used with AC voltage to "Step-Up" or "Step-down" the voltage based on the windings on each side of the transformer. For instance – If a transformer has 200 windings on one side (Side A), and 100 windings on the other side (Side B) and passes 120-volts through side "A" then the voltage steps down to 60 volts on side "B". (T6D06)*	
T-3	3	**Variable Inductor** *Often used in an LC circuit, the value of the inductor can be adjusted as needed to tune the circuit (T6C10).* *The unit of measure for Inductors is The Henry (T5C04)*	
T-3	4	**Antenna** *The Antenna symbol representing the antenna on a transmitter or receiver. (T6C11)*	
Not On Diagrams	-	**Diode** The diode is an electronic component that allows the flow of data in only one direction. Current flows forward through the diode when the voltage rises above a certain level depending on the diode and blocks current when the voltage applied is of the opposite value. Using this characteristic, a diode or block of diodes can be used to convert AC power into DC power.	
Not on Diagrams	-	**Inductor** The Inductor is a coil added to a circuit that looks like a straight piece of wire to DC power, but for Alternating current it will create impedance and *Inductors can store energy in a magnetic field that is created as electricity passed through (T6A06).* *Inductors are typically constructed as simple coils of wire. (T6A07)*	

FUSES AND CIRCUIT BREAKERS

Fuses and Circuit breakers are protective components that are used in devices to prevent electrical overload from occurring. They both perform the same function – Creating an open circuit that removes power or current from an active circuit, however they function in two different manners. *The purpose of the fuse is to remove power or current from the circuit in the case of an overload by melting and creating a gap in the circuit (T0A04) And to protect other circuit components from current overloads (T6A09)*. Once a fuse blows it, the old destroyed fuse must be removed from the device and replaced with a new one. The circuit breaker does the same function however the reaction time can be slower which could lead to some damage before the circuit opens. Even so, circuit breakers have the advantage that they can simply be "Flipped" back on quickly without the need to replace. This is what makes circuit breakers the common protection for electrical overloads in the home. (Some homes may still use fuses but these now days are highly uncommon.) *Fuses and Breakers are always installed in series with the HOT conductor only (T0A08)* in both AC and DC Circuits. Circuit breakers which are usually installed in your panel box for the house for instance, are still in series between your household outlets and the outside power feed into the house.

Fuses are sized based upon the amount of current that can safely pass through them. These sizes are in current and based on voltages – though the more important size rating is the Amps that the fuse will allow to pass. *NEVER USE THE WRONG SIZED FUSE. For instance – Using a 20-amp fuse in place of a 5-amp fuse will allow more current than is safe to cross over the fuse and cause damage. Excessive current could easily cause a fire in the device (T0A05)*.

6.4.2 - Circuits

This section will cover several types of "Circuits" which are assemblies made up of two or more electronic components that perform a very specific purpose. The circuit systems we are covering here may be parts of a system used for a larger system, such as a power supply which could stand on its own or be embedded within a radio, device, or may be parts of a larger system. Some may even be component "Packages" such as Integrated Circuits where multiple components are built into a single component to perform a function. Integrated Circuits, or "IC" circuits are computer chips or combined components that come in a single chip or package that perform a function but have multiple components such as micro transistors, capacitors, inductors, and other components all in one neat clean package.

6.4.3 – Power Supplies

A Power supply may be integrated into an appliance or device, such a home computer, television, or appliance. For most Ham Radios, the power supply is often an external device that the radio can be plugged into. Typical Ham Radio power supplies provide a "12-volt" power supply to the radio. For mobile mount radios, the mobile radio will connect into the vehicles 12-volt (Which is actually 13.8-volts) power supply. For most base model radios designed to work from a desk, the radios will plug into an external power supply which provides 12v/13.8v or DC power.

(T0A11) – What hazard exists in a power supply immediately after turning it off?

This question is designed around the idea of opening up a power supply to attempt a component level repair if the power supply fails. When you read in this book about Capacitors, we mention that capacitors will hold a charge and store electrical energy in them. As such, when the power supply is disconnected from it's normal power input, the capacitors in the power supply may still hold an electrical charge, thus **the hazard that exists is from the charge stored in the filter capacitors (T0A11)**.

(T4A01) – Which of the following is an appropriate power supply rating for a typical 50-watt output mobile FM transceiver?

For this question, the key is that they are asking for the power supply rating for a MOBILE transceiver. Mobile transceivers are all designed to work from your vehicles DC power system. Though we refer to these as "12-volts" the actual typical voltage is 13.8-volts which is what our car alternators put out to maintain the charge on a 12-volt battery. When the vehicle is running, the voltage should read 13.8-volts even though the battery voltage level may drop when the car is shut off. The current drain for a 50-watt mobile radio is 12-amps. Because of this, a 50-watt radio plugged into the cigarette lighter will try and pull more amperage at 12-amps than our cigarette lighter/accessory outlet is designed for (10-Amps) and you will blow a fuse. When installing a mobile radio you need to run the power either directly to the battery, or to a power point in the car capable of providing 12-amps of power. When running wire – MAKE SURE TO USE A LARGE ENOUGH GAUGE TO CARRY THE CURRENT. I like to use a heavier 10-gauge wire just in case.

So – Our answer to this question is that **an appropriate power supply for a 50-watt mobile radio should provide 13.8-volts at 12-Amps of current (T4A01)**. If you are using a mobile radio in your home, plan for a 12-volt based power supply that can provide this level of amperage.

RF POWER METER

An RF Power Meter reads the amount of power being pushed out from your transmitter through the feed line and out through the antenna. The SWR Meter is an example of this. **When using an RF Power meter, the meter should be installed in the feed line between the transmitter and the antenna (T4A05)**.

GAIN IN RELATION TO POWER

Elsewhere in this chapter we talk about GAIN as it applies to the magnification of our effective RF strength with antennas. Another area where the term "Gain" is used is in electrical power and refers to the power magnification that is performed through a device such as an Antenna amplifier, Power amplifier or transistor. The amount of gain is measured in decibels. A Power amplifier is often used by a radio to amplify the signal strength being broadcast. Baofeng Tech has power amplifiers that can be installed in a car for instance and used with smaller handheld radios to boost the wattage output from the common 5-watts up to as much as 40-watts out. So, in question **(T6B11) when asked what the term that describes a device's ability to amplify a signal, the answer is "Gain"**.

RECTIFIERS

A rectifier is a component circuit that is used to product DC power from incoming AC Power. This is a circuit that is used by a power supply for our home-based ham radios that allows the 120-volt AC power to be converted in to 12-volt DC power. The rectifier circuit shown here to the right often has (4) one-way diodes that allow current to flow in only one direction. When the AC current is flowing in a positive direction then the voltage passes through the rectifier through one pair of diodes. When the voltage reverses into the negative direction then the first pair of diodes cuts off the current flow but the other pair then allow it. As this continues, then we tend to have a power pattern that appears more like the power pattern below

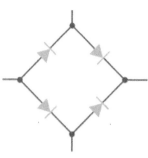

A 4-Diode Rectifier

instead of the AC sine-wave pattern we are more familiar with. Using capacitors and other components we are able to smooth this out to a clean DC power source. We also use other components in the power supply to drop the power levels from the 120-volts that come in from our grid power source to a 12-volt power level that is required by our radio. In question *(T6D01), A Rectifier is the answer for a device or circuit that changes an Alternating Current (AC) into a varying Direct Current (DC) signal* as shown below, then using other components such as capacitors to smooth the power level out.

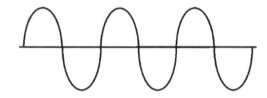

A Power AC Wave before being adjusted through a rectifier circuit

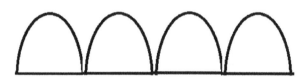

An AC Power pattern after being processed through a Rectifier.

RELAYS

A Relay is a device or component that can be used as an electrically controlled switch (T6D02). A common relay component is a device that contains a magnet which normally is not active at all – no magnetic charge. When an electrical current is applied through the relay switch, the magnet in the switch is energized (Electromagnet) and then at that point the magnet pulls down a switch that closes and allows current to flow through the other side. So the relay actually is two switches – one side activated by an electromagnet and the other

side being a Single-Pole/Single-throw switch that closes when the magnet energizes. The relay can be used either as a remote switch allowing remote control of a system by controlling the power flow, or it can be used to allow a small power applied to the relay to close a switch capable of allowing a much greater level of power to flow through the other side.

REGULATOR

Earlier we talked about a RECTIFIER in a DC Power supply that can be used to convert AC power into DC power. *A Regulator is another part of a power supply that is used to control the voltage coming from a power supply (T6D05).* It literally regulates the power out of the power supply making sure that it comes out at a proper power level – Not too low, and not too high.

OSCILLATORS

An Oscillator is a circuit that generates a signal at a specific frequency (T7A05) for use as a transmitting frequency for your radio or can be used also as a part of a filter. The oscillator can be as simple as this 2-component LC Tank circuit shown to the right here with a single capacitor and a single inductor or can be much more

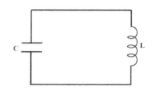

complex. The oscillator can generate an oscillating repeating frequency based on the values of the components used.

INTEGRATED CIRCUIT (IC)

We mentioned an Integrated Circuit (IC) above in this section as a device that combines several semiconductors and other components into a single package (T6D09). As shown here to the right, the IC circuit looks like a simple computer chip – but in fact can be entire devices such as radio receivers or specialized circuits in one tiny package.

TRANSVERTER

A Transverter is a device that converts the RF Input and output of a transceiver from one radio band to another (T7A06). This can be used to change the messages being transmitted between bands to extend their range or to transmit the signals that may work better in an instance for some reason. One example of a transverter would be a cross-band repeater which takes an incoming radio signal (Such as on VHF) and retransmits it on another band (Such as UHF) to extend the signal range or make the signal available on another band which may have more favorable characteristics.

RF POWER AMPLIFIER

An RF Power Amplifier is a device that increases the transmitted power output from a transceiver (T7A10). This device will attach from the output of transmitter where the feedline connects, amplifies the power output, and then feed through the normal feedline out to the antenna. Baofeng Tech sells a unit that will boost the 5-watt output from a handheld radio to 40-watts providing a better output signal from a vehicle without the need for a full mobile radio. On many radio bands a Power RF Amplifier can be used to boost output power up to 1500-watts PEP.

RF PRE-AMPLIFIER

An RF Preamplifier is a device that increases the incoming signal to a better-quality signal for reception by the radio receiver. *The RF Preamplifier is installed between the antenna and the receiver (T7A11).* Remember for the test that the "RF PRE" amplifier is used for the receiver where the "RF AMPLIFIER" is used for transmitting.

DIODES

Diodes are electronic components with the unique quality that they allow current to flow in only one direction (T6B02). This allows the diode to be used as a sort of electronic switch and used in circuits such as Rectifiers for converting AC power into DC power. Though the diode generally looks like a piece of wire allowing most of the current to flow through it, as power moves forward through the diode there is a voltage drop that occurs it.

A standard Diode diagram with Anode and Cathode (Right), a picture of a diode with a painted stripe at the top (Middle), and a Zener Diode with Anode and Cathode (Right)

For the test, understand that the forward Voltage drop across a diode is lower in some types of diodes than it is in others (T6B01). For instance, a diode composed of Silicon has a voltage drop when current is flowing forward through it of 0.7 volts. A germanium composed diode however has a lower voltage drop of only 0.3 volts. This may not be important at higher voltage ranges but if operating at a low voltage level this does become more significant.

In the images above we see pictures on the right and left that are schematic representations of two types of diodes, a regular diode and a Zener diode which allows current flow in both directions. *Both of the schematics show the Anode and Cathode locations which are the names for the two electrodes of the diode (T6B09).* In the center image we see a picture of a diode. Notice in the picture that there is a stripe at the top of the diode. *The stripe on a diode represents the CATHODE of the diode (T6B06).*

TRANSISTORS

Transistors are the components that revolutionized electronics by giving us the ability to use small discrete components for small and low-power amplification and switching purposes instead of the much larger and power- hungry vacuum tubes that were used in the past. Fast-forward decades later and all electronics are composed of components where thousands or tens of thousands of tiny transistor and silicon components are manufactured into integrated circuits allowing all of the miraculous functions we have from simple switches to the computing power of our smart phones. For the purpose of the Technician's test, we want to focus on just a few points that the test will touch on. Let's first look at two common types of transistors, the silicon PNP and NPN transistors as shown in the images below.

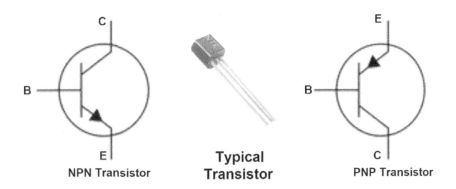

NPN Transistor   Typical Transistor   PNP Transistor

For purposes of the test, we are not going to drill into the differences between the PNP and NPN transistors or how they are composed – instead we will focus on the topics needed for the test. Know however the following:

- Transistors have Three terminals.
- The Base (B) is the center terminal which controls current through the other two terminals, the Collector (C) and Emitter (E).
- The Collector Terminal (C) where current flows from.
- The Emitter (E) where current flows out from.
- The transistor can be used as a "Switch" by supplying power to the base or shutting off power to the base – An On or Off function.
- The transistor could also be used as an amplifier meaning that as power is slowly increased to the base then the amount of power flowing through the collector and emitter adjusts proportionally to that power applied to the base.
- Depending upon the type of transistor being used the three terminals may also be referred to as *Source, Gate* and *Drain*. BJT Transistors (Bipolar Junction Transistors) have emitter, base and collector as terminal names. For FET Transistor the terminals are *Source, Gate* and *Drain*.

With these characteristics listed, let's look at the questions about transistors on the test.

- ***(T6B03) – A Transistor can be used as an electronic switch (T6B03).*** This means that the transistor can be used as a simple On-Off device allowing the flow of current through two of the terminals of the transistor when power is applied to the center terminal (Base) it will turn on the flow of power between the other two terminals – the collector and the emitter.

- ***(T6B08) - The abbreviation FET is short for FIELD EFFECT TRANSISTOR (T6B08).*** The FET is a type of transistor that uses an electric field to control the flow of current. For FET Transistor the terminals are named *Source, Gate* and *Drain.*

- ***(T6B10) – The TRANSISTOR can provide power gain.*** Here we are given a list of electronic components – Transformer, Transistor, Reactor, and Resistor. The Transformer will increase AC power from one side of the transformer to the other, but this is a Transformation or Conversion process – Not a process considered "Gain". The Reactor is another name for an Inductor which has the ability to store energy in a magnetic field but not amplify it. The resistor limits the flow of current in a circuit. The only choice we have that performs an amplification function resulting in power gain is the Transistor.

FERRITE CHOKES

A Ferrite choke is a solid component made up of some type of metal such as Iron, Manganese, Manganese Zinc, Nickel zinc or some combination that can be used to help eliminate interfering signals that may be getting picked up by wiring such as microphone cable or other cable. Sometimes a microphone cable will pick up interference from the transmitter that causes problems with the quality of your voice signal being transmitted. Often by attaching a ferrite choke around the microphone cable or wrapping loops in the cable through the choke the interference can be eliminated. In question ***(T7B04) the reader is asked, "Which of the following could you use to cure distorted audio caused by RF current on the shield of a microphone cable?".*** The answer for this question is **Ferrite Choke.**

BAND REJECT FILTER

Another tool that you can use to help clean up noise and signal problems is a Band Reject Filter. These filters are designed to allow the passing of most radio frequencies unaltered, however they will filter out and "Reject" frequencies that sit within a particular frequency range. These may be used if you are located somewhere such as near a commercial radio or television tower that is broadcasting in a particular frequency and that broadcast is creating problems for you. By installing a Band Reject Filter for the frequencies causing problems, you will be able to filter out all incoming signals in that frequency range that are causing problems for you allowing normal operation in all other bands. Question ***(T7B07) specifically asks "Which of the following can reduce overload of a VHF transceiver by a nearby commercial FM Station?*** The answer you are looking or is **Installing a Band Reject Filter.**

The opposite of the Band-Reject filter is called a Band-Pass filter which operates just the opposite. The Band-Pass filter allows ONLY the frequencies within a particular band or frequency range to pass through and blocks all others.

6.4.2 – Schematic Diagrams used in the Ham Radio Technician Test

Following are the schematic diagrams that are used in the test. *A Schematic diagram is an electrical wiring diagram that uses standard component symbols to show how the components are electrically connected (T6C01 & T6C12)*. The numbers and diagram numbers correspond to the components listed in table 7-2.

Table 7-3: Schematic Diagrams

Components in this diagram are:

1. Resistor (T6C02)
2. *Transistor* (T6C03) *Controls the flow of current* (T6D10)
3. Lamp (T6C04)
4. Battery

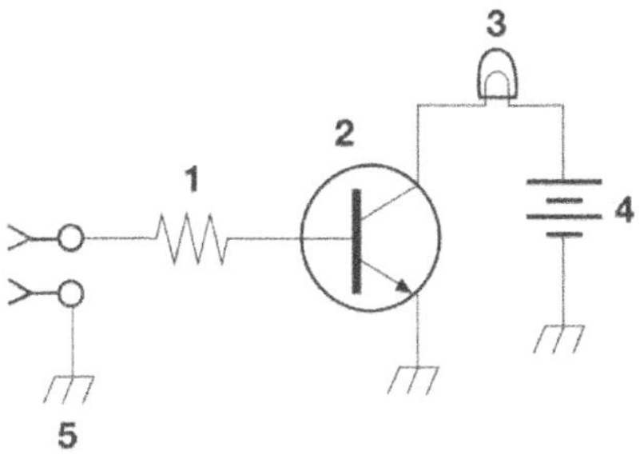

Figure T-1

Components in this diagram are:

1. Non-Polarized Male Connector
2. Closed Connection Link
3. Switch
4. *Transformer* (T6C09)
5. Diode
6. *Capacitor* (T6C06)
7. Resistor
8. *Light Emitting Diode* (T6C07)
9. Variable Resistor (T6C08)
10. Zener Diode

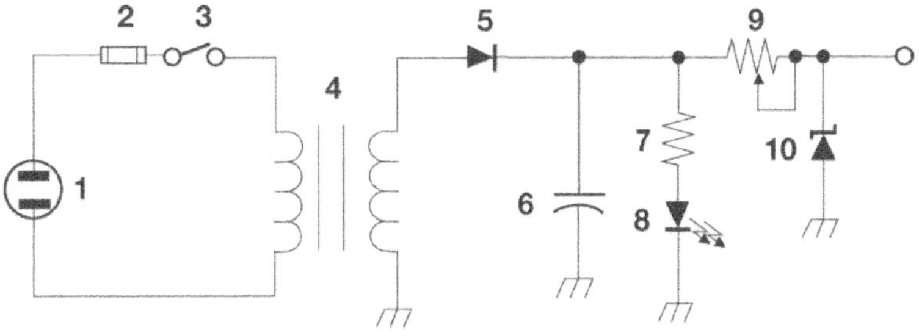

Figure T-2

Components in this diagram are:

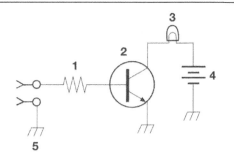

5. Resistor (T6C02)
6. **Transistor** (T6C03) **Controls the flow of current** (T6D10)
7. Lamp (T6C04)
8. Battery

Figure T-1

Series & Parallel Connections in a circuit

Components in a circuit can be connected in two ways – Series or Parallel. Components that are connected in series are connected such as the Resistor R-1 and Resistor R-2 are shown in Figure to the right here. These two components are connected end-to-end with the same current flowing through both components. **In a Series circuit the DC current is the same in all components (T5D13).**

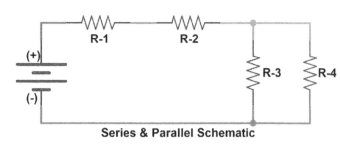

Series & Parallel Schematic

Here the voltage will vary among the components but adds up across all components to the total voltage across the circuit. In the same diagram, Resistor R-3 and Resistor R-4 are shown in Parallel. In Parallel component layout, the current actually forks and follows two separate paths. **In a Parallel circuit, the current forks but the voltage remains the same across all branches of the circuit (T5D14).** In this case, the

current that comes from the Positive battery terminal and flows through R-1 and R-2 then splits following two separate paths through R-3 and R-4 back to the battery's negative (-) terminal. The use of Series or Parallel connections to a circuit depends upon the circuit design and purpose.

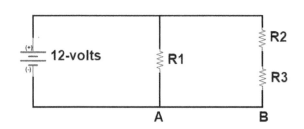

Note about question T5D14 on the pool – The question states that the voltage stays the same across all components in the circuit. This may be true in a simple parallel circuit where there is only one component in each parallel branch. But if the parallel branch contains multiple components, then the voltage will vary across components though it WILL remain the same across each parallel branch.

In the schematic here above, if R1, R2 & R3 are all 1000-ohm resistors, then the voltage across branch "A" and branch "B" will be the same – 12-volts. In Branch "A" which has a single component, the voltage across R1 will be 12-volts. In Brach "B" however, the voltage across R2 will be 6-volts, and the voltage across R3 will be 6-volts which total 12-volts which is the voltage across the entire branch.

6.4.3 – Component units of measure

There are several components in the test pool that have unique measurement units.

Table 7-4: Electrical Units of Measure for various component types

Ampere "A"	***The Amp is abbreviated in our formulas with the letter "I" and is the measure of electrical current. (T5A01)***
Farad "F"	The Farad is a unit of measure for capacitance. The symbol for Farads in formulas is "F". ***Capacitance is described as the ability to store energy in an electric field (T5C01)***.
Henry "H" / "L"	The Henry is the unit of measure for Inductance and is abbreviated with the letter "H". In the formula for a tuned circuit (Aka LC Circuit) the letter "L" represents the value of Henrys.
Ohm "Ω"	The Ohm is the measure of resistance in a resistor. ***The Ohm is also the measure of impedance (T5C05)***. The abbreviation used for Ohms is the Omega symbol - "Ω"
Volt/ Voltage	The Volt is the measure of electrical potential and is abbreviated either with "V" short for Volt, or with "E" short for Electrical Potential. In the formulas used on the Technician's tests, "E" is the abbreviation that is used.
Watt	***The Watt is the measure of electrical power (T5A02)*** and is the measure that is used in identifying how much power a radio can transmit with. The abbreviation for watt is "W" and is represented in the formulas for power used on the test as "P". For example: ***$P = E \times I$ where P is power in Watts, "E" is Electrical Potential (Volts) and "I" is the abbreviation for Current Intensity (Amps) (T5C08)***.

6.5 - Electricity Basics

This section will cover several basic topics that need to be understood for the Tech license exam. Though the section is titled "Electricity Basics" we will not cover other electrical topics that are covered elsewhere in this chapter.

6.5.1 – Basic Concepts

In this section we are going to discuss electricity basics only as far as the topic applies to the Technician Examination. We will discuss the measures of power and how they relate to each other. Many of these topics such as our covering of formulas have been touched on in our section for Math calculations. Many of the questions in the pool of 411 questions cover formula-based topics that require an understanding of what the concepts of electricity and power are.

AMPERAGE & CURRENT (I)

Amperage and Current are the measure of the flow of electrons running through a device (T5A03), circuit or component. Current is the overall reference to the flow of electrons while Amperage is the actual measure of the number of electrons in movement. Our power formulas we measure current in AMPS represented in our math formulas with "I". The flow of electricity can be thought of in the same way as how water flows through a pipe. The water moves through the pipe at a specific flow rate. The volume that flows through a circuit is measured in amperage.

VOLTAGE & ELECTRICAL POTENTIAL (E)

Voltage is the Electrical Potential of electricity in a circuit. Looking at our comparison to water flowing through a pipe, you can think of voltage as being equivalent to the pressure of water flowing through a pipe. When the voltage level increases the same amperage flowing through the circuit moves more rapidly. Voltage will be measured between two points with a Voltmeter or a Multimeter such as between the positive and negative terminals of a battery. You can also measure voltage drop over a component which tells you how much voltage that component is using. Measuring across two terminals of a resistor will give you the voltage drop across that resistor component.

POWER AND WATTAGE (P) & (W)

Power is the combination of voltage and amperage flowing through a circuit and is measured with the formula of "P = E x I". Wattage is the actual term we use for the power flowing through a device or circuit. To increase the power flowing through a deice we can either increase the amperage or we can increase the voltage. For instance, if we have a device that needs 120 watts to operate, it could operate either using 120 volts electrical potential with an amperage rate of 1-amp, or it could operate using 12-volts electrical potential with 10-amps flowing through it. So, both of these combinations work:

120-watts = 120-volts x 1-amp   or   120-watts = 12-volts x 10-amps

And in our formula P = E x I, P represents the 120-watts that is our total power. Of course, all of this is tied in with how the circuit or device is designed, but I wanted to show you the relationship between voltage and amperage, and how they relate together for the measurement of power. By increasing one or the other, you will increase the total power.

Back to our analogy of water flowing through pipes. Increasing our pipe from a 2-inch pipe to a 4-inch pipe while allowing the water to flow through the pipe at the same rate of 2-PSI, we will increase the total amount of water flowing through the pipe. Likewise – if we keep the same 2-inch pipe and increase our water pressure to 4-psi, then we are again increasing the total amount of water flowing each minute.

In our analogy here, the pipe is equivalent to our electrical conductors that Amps flow through. The pressure of the water flowing through our pipes is equivalent to our voltage level. Increasing our Amp flow or our Voltage flow increases our total power flowing through the circuit. The total amount of water is a result of the pressure and volume of water flowing through out pipes.

CONDUCTORS & INSULATORS

Conductors are pathways made of Metals that allow the flow of electricity. On circuit boards, these may be layered onto the boards directly. More commonly we use conductors that are wires that are connected between two points allowing electricity to flow between those points. Think of battery cables, power cables, or extension cables. Some types of metals perform better than others for the conducting of electricity. One of the best metals is Copper. Another popular metal is Aluminum, however high levels of current through aluminum wiring can heat the wiring beyond a safety level creating a fire hazard. As the current you are moving through the conductor increases, the need to increase the size of the metal to allow more amperage to pass through. Think of a thick car battery cable – these are thick to allow a high amperage to move from the battery to the car during the vehicle's startup, whereas a very thin wire can be used to connect a 9-volt battery to a fire alarm detector because the amps used is comparatively very low. *Metals are generally good conductors of electricity because they have many free electrons in their materials (T5A07)*.

Insulators are materials that can be used to block the flow of electricity. In the case of our wires and extension or power cords, the rubber cover that protects the wires also blocks the flow of electricity. Other insulators that will block the flow of electricity include Glass, Ceramic, plastics, paper, and rubber. *Glass is considered to be a good electrical insulator (T5A08)*.

A few point that I would like to cover here about wire conductors that you need to be aware of for the test.

- Thickness or Gauge of wire – Heavy gauge wire will transfer electricity better than thinner wires but are more expensive in cost. For Ham radio, our wire lengths will probably be short so thicker would be better of wire size to use. If working with something like solar where our wire lengths can get bigger, we want to balance performance and cost of the wire, so the gauge of wire becomes important.
- Thickness of wire is measured in Gauges. The higher the gauge, the thinner the wire. The lower the gauge of wire, the thicker the wire should be.
- Low gauge/thick wire is better for higher currents (High Amps). Think of your car battery cable – The car battery provides a high number of cranking amps to the car for starting, so a thick wire is used.
- High gauge/thinner wire works for low power uses – Think of the battery connectors to a 9-volt battery in a small radio.

- Some wire such as Copper works better as an electrical conductor than others. Aluminum wire, while adequate for some uses, can catch fire if overloaded and should be used with caution for some applications.
- Electrons moving through wire actually travel along the outside of a conductor, not through it. This is one reason a larger wire works better – more surface area.
- Wires do have resistance – Running power long distances can result in power transfer loss due to the resistance in the conductor. Thinner wires are going to have more resistance than thicker wires.
- When conducting electricity, thicker wire should be used for short-distance low-voltage (12v) applications while longer-distance/higher voltage (120v) applications can more likely use a smaller/higher gauge wire.
- For grounding purposes, flat straps are recommended for use because they have greater surface area for the transfer of electricity. *For bonding at RF, Flat copper strap is the preferred conductor (T4A08)*.
- Because of the higher power requirements of many transceivers, *Short heavy-gauge wires are used for a transceivers DC power connection to minimize voltage drop when transmitting (T4A03)*. This is because when the transceiver starts transmitting, much more power is pulled from the power supply at once.
- The standard color codes for DC power is to use RED for the Positive connection to the battery, while using BLACK as the negative or Ground connection to the battery.
- The standard color codes for AC power in the United States depends on the voltage level (120/240), and the phase type. For the test – remember *that the BLACK wire insulation for 120-volt three-wire cable is for HOT (T0A03).*

RESISTANCE & IMPEDANCE

Both resistance and impedance are the opposition to current flow in a circuit. *The measure of electrical resistance is measured in Ohms (T5A04)* but differ as to how they apply in a DC circuit or an AC circuit. In a DC Circuit resistance is most often found in the use of components such as resistors that are used to limit the flow of electricity. Components like a variable resistor can be used in devices to adjust the level of resistance that is being applied allowing control over the flow of electricity. A volume control for instance in a radio can be adjusted to increase or reduce the power flow directly affecting the volume.

Impedance is more complex as it applies to both AC electrical power, and RF energy coming out of your radio. AC electricity from our power outlets in your home at 60 Hertz, and RF Radio signals are similar in that they have positive and negative ranges. RF radio signals however are wireless radio signals operating at much greater frequencies than the relatively slow AC Power. Instead of resistors which provide opposition to our electrical current or radio waves, in an AC or RF circuit we see inductors and coils as providing this opposition.

As impedance is the opposition to RF signals, then impedance becomes a significant factor in radio transmissions. Coaxial cable contains an impedance characteristic which creates an opposition to our radio signals going out from our radio, through the coaxial feed lines, and out to our antenna. Different types of coaxial cable will have difference impedance at differing frequencies. A poorly chosen type of coaxial cable can easily consume most of our power from a radio leaving little signal to get out through our antenna. For instance – a 5-watt radio connected to an outdoor antenna through 100-feet of low-quality coaxial cable may lose most of its signal through the impedance of the cable. Note that the impedance values of various cable will also vary depending upon the frequency you are transmitting. Typically, impedance increases as frequency increases meaning that a coaxial cable that works fine for CB radio or 10-Meter band radio may work horribly for VHF or UHF frequencies.

CAPAITANCE AND INDUCTANCE

Both Capacitance and Inductance are characteristics that can allow the storing of energy. ***Capacitance is the ability to store energy in an ELECTRIC Field (T5C01)*** and is stored in circuits or components such as capacitors in a way in which the energy can be measured through a voltmeter. If you attach a capacitor across the positive and negative leads of a battery, a charge will build up in the capacitor where the capacitor is storing energy and acting as a small battery even after the battery is removed. Note for the test – ***Capacitance is related to an Electric Field and storage of energy through capacitors.***

Inductance is the ability to store energy in a MAGNETIC field (T5C03) and is stored in components such as inductors or coils. Inductance is more difficult to measure with a multimeter, however, can be measured through a multi-step process which we will not cover here. Note that for the test however, you must remember that ***Inductance is related to a Magnetic Field and storage of energy through Inductors.***

On the Test:

Question ***T5A11*** on the test asks specifically about the type of current flow that is opposed by resistance. In fact, there are sever which include:

- Direct current (DC Current from Batteries usually)
- Alternating current (AC Current coming in from the grid)
- RF Current (Radio waves and Radio Frequency energy being transmitted)

For this question, the answer is ***All of these choices are correct (T5A11)*** as there are multiple types of current that will be apposed to resistance, whether that resistance is a result of components like resistors, from power transmission lines, or from the impedance found in RF Transmission and Feed lines such as coax cable.

6.5.2 – AC & DC Power

Power is the measure of the rate in which electrical energy is used (T5A10) and is a result of the voltage and amperes being multiplied (P = E x I). Power comes in two flavors for use to power our devices – AC or Alternating Current, or DC short for Direct Current.

Alternating current is delivered to your home as a form of electrical power that varies in voltage levels from a positive 120-volts to a negative 120-volts in a sine-wave pattern at a frequency of 60 cycles per second (T5A09). Frequency is the number of times per second that an alternating current makes a complete cycle (T5A12). AC power originates from the power company and is distributed to neighborhoods through power lines at a much higher voltage levels ranging from hundreds of kilowatts and stepped down in voltage the closer the power gets to your home at multiple levels until it comes into your home at 120-volts or 240-volts.

DC power or Direct Current is power that operates at a steady voltage level such as the power which comes out of a battery or from a 12-volt power supply that converts AC alternating current power (120v) into steady DC power. Most ham radios, including home base radios, operate from 12-volt based DC Power. For installing into a car or truck this is simple – we just tap into the vehicle's 12-volt power system. If running a radio from the house though, we can either power our radio from a 12-volt battery, or we can get a power supply that plugs into our AC power and gives is a 12-v steady output power.

6.5.3 – Measuring Tools – Meters & Other Testing Tools

A multi-meter is an electronic measuring tool that is used to measure voltage, amperage, resistance in ohms, and sometimes functions such as continuity and transistor testing (T7D07). Multi meters are multiple meter types rolled into single packages. There are two general types of multi meters – Digital and Analog and each can be purchased for as little as $10 or less at a local Walmart or on Amazon. A good multi-meter should be a part of everyone's home tool kit allowing you to check most commonly AC power from home power outlets (Taking appropriate safety steps of course) or DC power levels for batteries used in appliances or devices around the house.

Today's multi-meters are designed to serve multiple functions; however, you can still find single-use meters. **A Voltmeter for instance is an instrument meant to measure electrical potential between two points (T7D01). Another instrument called an Ammeter is dedicated to measure electric current (T7D04).**

For Ham Radio you will mostly be using a multi-meter for testing battery voltages. This is done by touching the positive and negative leads of the meter to the positive and negative leads of the battery being tested. **Taking measurements of voltage is always done in PARALLEL to the battery or the component that is being measured (T7D02).** You can take a voltage measurement across non-battery components such as a resistor to measure what the voltage drop across the component is. Most meters will allow the measuring of both DC and AC voltages – Make sue you set the meter to the correct position and value, however. The meters generally have a range for the measurements you are trying to measure such as 2v, 20v, 200v, or 200v DC

Power, or AC power in differing ranges, Ohm (Resistance) ranges in different ranges, and Amperage ratings in differing ranges. Many meters can also do diode tests, continuity testing for shorts with audible tones, and other types of testing.

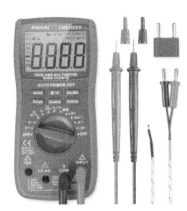

AstroAI Digital Multimeter with Lead kit   GB Instruments Analog Multimeter

Measuring Amperage and Voltage

Many meters can measure both amperage and voltage. As mentioned above, the measuring of voltage is performed by touching the positive and negative leads across a component in PARALLEL to the component. When measuring amperage, this is performed differently in that you must actually "Break" the circuit path and ***attach the meter in SERIES with the meter acting as a component allowing the current to flow through the meter for measurement (T7D03)***. Alternatively, you could use a "Clamp" style ammeter as shown below to measure current. With this meter, a clamp is unobtrusively placed around the wire that the current is flowing through to get a current reading for the circuit. These types of meters have a high accuracy and are non-evasive with their interaction with the circuit – you don't have to interrupt the circuit if there is a wire that you can get the clamp around.

As a precaution, when measuring high voltages with a voltmeter always ensure that the voltmeter and leads are rated for use at the voltages being measured (T0A12). Taking readings from an improperly rated meter could result in shock or death.

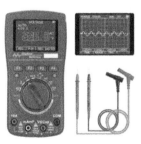

KAIWEETS Digital Clamp Meter   Handheld Oscilloscope Multimeter

Another type of meter that I want to mention, but is NOT covered on the test, is an Oscilloscope Meter as shown on the previous page. These meters are tremendously useful for testing the AC quality of a low-frequency power source, such as the AC power coming out of the wall outlet. I have one of these meters. They measure standard AC and DC voltages just fine, and mine can measure capacitance values as well as AC quality. Where I use it is with working with generators and solar power inverters to verify the quality of the AC power coming out of the power sources. A poor-quality AC power source that is off frequency can create problems with sensitive electronics or devices with inductive motors such as refrigerators and pumping equipment. The need to know the quality of the AC power coming out is critical for the safe operation of some types of equipment.

When using a Multimeter always pay attention to what you are doing and the settings of the meter. Having a meter set to take one type of measurement but hooking it up for another can damage the meter. For instance, **attempting to measure voltage with a multimeter when the meter is set to resistance could damage the meter (T7D06)**.

6.6 - Basics on Batteries

Batteries are a topic of importance for the Ham Radio. On the test however, there are only a small number of questions that are related to batteries, so we are going to discuss topics surrounding those particular questions with some expansion on batteries.

6.6.1 - Battery Chemistry

There are several types of chemistries that can be used in production of batteries. On the test you will be asked about a few, and whether they are rechargeable or not. In Ham radio, batteries are what power our radios, from the 12-volt batteries in our vehicles, to the Lithium batteries often found in our handhelds, or even battery packs comprised of AA or AAA batteries used also for handheld radios. Ham Radios that are stationary desk models for the home often feed from a 12-volt battery source which could be directly from a battery, or more often from a 12-volt power supply which transforms AC wall outlet power into 12-volt power.

For battery chemistry topics, following are touched on in the questions poo:

- Nickel-metal hydride (NiMH)
  A rechargeable battery chemistry popular for high current drain applications used in digital cameras and other high-drain applications. These batteries contain less energy than Lithium-ion based batteries but are also less expensive.

- Lithium-ion
  A rechargeable battery chemistry that has become most popular with high-energy power needs. There are several various types of Lithium based batteries with different characteristics. Though not the most powerful, LiFePO4 based batteries do provide a highly stable and safer chemistry option than some other Lithium battery solutions. Some Lithium battery chemistries can be highly hazardous if the battery is pierced or damage creating a high fire risk. LiFePO4 batteries are much safer and popular for some radio use, solar use, and even Electric Vehicles. Many Lithium batteries can be drained to near 0 with no harm to the battery.

- Lead-acid
  A rechargeable battery chemistry that is based on use of lead plates and a chemical or acid to allow the battery to hold a charge. This is an older design of battery first developed in 1859 by French scientist Nicolas Gautherot. The Lead-Acid battery design stores less energy than newer battery designs, however the low cost of the battery keeps it as a popular solution for uses ranging from car starter batteries, to solar energy storage, and marine use. Popular are 12-volt large format batteries used in cars and other motorized vehicles.

- Nickel-cadmium
  A rechargeable battery chemistry using nickel oxide hydroxide and metallic cadmium as electrodes. These batteries store energy at a lower voltage level – 1.2v instead of 1.5v for instance in smaller battery packages. Though the hold a lower voltage level than other types of batteries they still can supply high surge currents and are a popular battery chemistry used for many applications such as cordless telephones, emergency lighting, and remote-controlled electric cars, airplanes, and boats.

- *Carbon-zinc (T6A11)*
  The only Non-rechargeable chemistry that is touched on in the test. These one-use batteries are still popular for low-energy uses such as remote controls, and store about one-eighth of the energy that popular alkaline batteries store, however are very inexpensive batteries.

On the test there are only two questions talking about battery chemistry:

- *(T6A10) - Which of the following battery chemistries is rechargeable?*
  For this question, you are given three battery types all of which are rechargeable and a fourth answer which is correct – "*All these choices are correct*".

- *(T6A11) - Which of the following battery chemistries is not rechargeable?*
  For this question we are looking at "*Carbon-Zink*" which is the only battery chemistry in our list which is NOT rechargeable.

6.6.2 – Battery Safety

Mishandling of batteries can result in a variety of dangers. Flooded batteries which require water or battery acid to be added can give off poisonous fumes that can be deadly in a closed environment. High-capacity batteries such as many types of Lithium based batteries can be fire hazard and even explosive. Any type of battery can present a shock when shorted, especially when the battery is a larger high-energy battery such as a 12-volt car battery or solar battery.

In the pool you will have a limited number of questions that you will need to be ready for – in fact we have just two possible questions that touch on battery safety:

- **(T0A01) - Which of the following is a safety hazard of a 12-volt storage battery?**
  The answer is **"Shorting the terminals can cause burns, fire, or an explosion".**

  When working with larger batteries such as 12-volt car batteries, and even more so with larger Lithium based batteries which hold much more power, one of the biggest risks comes from accidentally shorting the terminals of the batteries together. This will cause a rapid discharge of energy that can spark and easily cause a fire hazard. Batteries such as Lithium Batteries can be such a risk that airlines have implemented special safety requirements for the transport of any such batteries. You can carry b, batteries on flights with you, however care must be taken.

  Consider the danger that could occur when using a simple all-metal wrench such as the one shown here to the right to tighten or loosen a battery cable from a 12-volt car or solar lithium battery. If the wrench is long enough and crosses both terminals you will have a high-energy short that can very easily start a fire or result in the battery exploding. Take extreme caution and if possible, use wrenches where the handles are insulated.

- **(T0A10) - What hazard is caused by charging or discharging a battery too quickly?**
  The answer is "**Overheating or out-gassing**".

  This problem relates more to Lead-Acid batteries and batteries that have a chemical reaction that can produce gasses. In RV and Campers, care must be taken where batteries for the campers are stored in case they are a type which can produce gas that could get into the camper cabin at night or when individuals are enclosed. Batteries can also overheat creating a fire hazard if overcharged or charged too quickly.

6.6.3 – Battery Performance

Performance of a battery depends on how the battery is used, chemistry of the battery, discharge and charging cycles, storage and operating temperatures, and age of the battery. In my classes and books on Solar Power and Emergency Power I cover these topics extensively, but for the purpose of studying for the test we are only going to cover the two questions that are discussed on the test.

- *(T4A09) - How can you determine the length of time that equipment can be powered from a battery?*
*The answer is "**Divide the battery ampere-hour rating by the average current draw of the equipment**".*

This is important for sizing a battery for use. For example – If you are planning an emergency radio station for use in a shelter during a hurricane, you need to be able to estimate how long a battery of a particular size will last you based on your setup. If you have a base radio which has a power draw of 10-amps when transmitting, and you have two batteries – one with a 7-amp/hour rating and the other with a 20-amp/hour rating, how much time transmitting would each battery provide?

This is calculated as follows:

1. Determine the Amp-hour rating of the batteries. In this case we have 7ah and 20ah.
2. Divide each by the amp draw while transmitting.

Amp-Hour Rating of Battery	Amp-Hours Transmitting	Formula	Multiplier	Answer = Multiplier x 60 (for Minutes)
7-ah	10	7 / 10	0.7	0.7 x 60 Minutes = 42 42 Minutes Transmitting Time
20-ah	10	20 / 10	2.0	2.0 x 60 Minutes = 120 120 Mins Transmit Time (2-Hours)

In this problem we are not calculating non-transmitting time (Receiving or monitoring). But it gives us a rough estimate of our battery lifetime. In this solution by the way – If we have a method of charging our battery while it is still being used, such as from a solar panel or even a gas generator, then the 7-ah battery could still work well. I use one in a portable radio kit with a 25-watt mobile radio due to the smaller battery size and weight.

- **(T4A11) - Where should the negative power return of a mobile transceiver be connected in a vehicle?**
  The answer here is "At the 12-volt battery chassis ground".

  This question deals more with performance of the radio when properly powered of connected. The 12-volt chassis ground should have the same ground point as the negative point on the 12-volt battery or power source. Note that just connecting to metal in the vehicle does not necessarily equate to 12-volt ground. But - If in your vehicle it does, then this will be an acceptable point to attach your negative power return to.

6.7 - Antenna Basics and understanding Radio Range concepts

Antennas are a highly important topic for the new Ham Radio operator to understand. In this portion of Section 7 of this book, we are going to first cover the topics that are covered on the test related to antennas, and we are also going to go into some more depth later about Antennas. When given the choice on a radio setup to increase power or improve your antenna, the effort should be made into improving your antenna every time. A Handheld radio used within a vehicle will get poor performance but adding an antenna using a trunk mount, magnet mount or some other permanent mount will make a huge difference in being able to both receive signals and in being heard when transmitting. Adding more power will do very little when attempting to get your signal out of your radio or into it from the outside.

For a home base radio, either using a base model radio, a mobile radio being used as a base, or even a handheld radio, extending your antenna away from obstructions and high in the air will also make a huge difference in making contacts and getting distance out of your radio. Every HF radio needs a good antenna preferably mounted outdoors or designed for use in the attic or designed for best use with the radio based on frequency and bands being operated.

6.7.1 - Antenna Polarization

Antenna Polarization is the topic of the direction in which the antenna is mounted for the best signal performance coming off it. Typically, an antenna is mounted either vertically (Up and down) or horizontally (Parallel to the ground). When a signal comes off an antenna, it broadcasts off the antenna ***Broadside*** to the antenna. This means if the antenna is vertical such as shown below, the signals move out to the side directions. They do not broadcast up towards the atmosphere (Not the strongest signals). If the antenna is mounted horizontally as shown in the second example, as most HF antennas for long-range communication will be, then the signals transmit up into the atmosphere and down into the ground. The signals transmitting up can then be reflected from the ionosphere to a distant location. The signals that broadcast down to the ground will bounce back up into the atmosphere again for reflection in the atmosphere.

Note: A Horizontally mounted antenna needs to be raised a particular height above the ground varying by the frequencies it is transmitting for best performance.

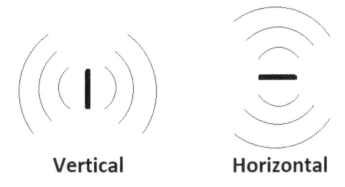

Vertical   **Horizontal**

A Half-wave dipole for instance radiates its strongest signal BROADSIDE to the antenna (T9A10).

The antenna polarization normally used for long-distance CW and SSB contacts on the VHF and UHF bands is ***Horizontal as this polarization offers the best opportunity for long distance communication (T3A03)***.

A Dipole antenna is an antenna that has its feed point in the center of the antenna. The signal feeds out of the transmitter through the feed line where it comes to the antenna, and then feeds out to two separate elements. Dipole antennas are more common with HF radio frequencies, but can be used with VHF and UHF also. A simple dipole oriented parallel to the Earth's surface will have a ***Horizontal Polarization since it is in fact running parallel to the ground. (T9A03)***.

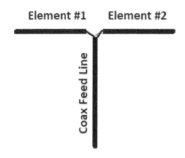

When two operators are communicating with each other the best radio reception and performance will occur when both operators are working with antennas using the same polarization. Think of it this way – If you are talking to your buddy on VHF frequencies with your antenna in a vertical position (Vertically polarized), your signals are strongest moving out in a sideways direction. But if he has laid down his handheld radio so it is operating with the antenna in a horizontal direction, then as your radio signal crosses his antenna it will not cross the antenna to the broadside of his antenna, and his signals will not cross your antenna to the broadside. In fact, a weaker signal will be crossing both of your antennas providing both of you with weaker communications signals. Question ***(T3A04) specifically asks What happens when antennas at opposite ends of a VHF or UHF line of sight radio link are not using the same polarization,*** which the answer is ***"Received Strength is reduced"***.

6.7.2 - UHF/VHF Line of Site – Understanding Radio Distance Limits

Note: This Section topic is mostly unaddressed on the Technician test, but I am including it here to bring an understanding of the real radio capabilities you will have as a Tech level licensed operator.

This is an area that I intend to go beyond the questions in the test for. Real radio capabilities are a topic that I have found too many new ham operators do not have a proper understanding about. Many new hams get their license and have their new BaoFeng handheld radios, and they think they can jump on the airwaves and start chatting with radio operators' long distances away. This is wrong.

Under the right circumstances, and with the use repeaters, you could get ranges of dozens to hundreds of miles talking with others. But – when operating in simplex mode, which is radio to radio mode, using a simple handheld radio you should expect ranges typically of 1 to 3 miles. More in some cases where geography and conditions align properly, and much less in many conditions such as urban use or where your geography includes dense plant life, buildings or homes, hills, and mountain areas.

Both VHF and UHF frequencies are considered "Line of Site" frequencies. This means as they travel out from your radio, they generally transmit straight out until they are blocked or reach the point of the earth's curvature. Though there can be some reflection through the atmosphere at these frequencies it is less common. Radio signals at UHF and VHF frequencies tend to travel out through the atmosphere and not reflected back. They can though reflect from buildings or other obstructions sometimes allowing reflected signal communication possible.

Line of Sight Radio and Antenna Height

Most radio operates at a level of "Line of Sight" meaning direct distance from antenna to antenna. Depending upon frequency you are working in, some frequencies are more rigid to line of sight than others, but all follow this rule with some twists depending on frequency. As your frequency increases, such as into the VHF and UHF Frequencies, this rule becomes more rigid.

What we are referring to by line of sight is how the radio signal transmits from point to point taking the curvature of the earth into account. Though trees, buildings and other natural as well as man-made obstacles to make a difference, generally we are here referring to the curvature of the earth and significant obstacles such as mountains,

So, what is our line of site from a handheld radio?

Take a person standing in the open holding a handheld radio (Position C in our diagram on the next page). The normal curvature of the earth dictates that the line of sight with the antenna raised at five feet above the ground will be almost 3 miles (2.75 miles from position C to position A) from that point to the farthest point where the earth curves. Beyond that point falls below the curvature of the earth. If a second person is standing 3 miles beyond that point with his antenna 5 feet above the curvature of the earth, then together their antennas are seeing each other at 5.5 miles apart (Position C to position C). After that signal loss becomes great. ***Keep in mind – This is under PERFECT conditions. Perfectly flat surface, absolutely no obstacles, good clear day with no bad weather.***

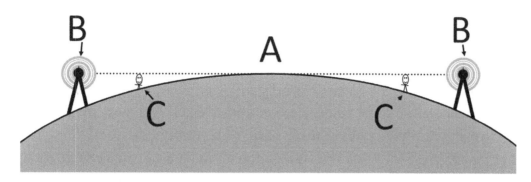

horizon(km) = 3.569 x (Square Root of Antenna height(meters))

Here is how we work through this formula. We will assume you are standing with your antenna 6 feet in the air, and so is your buddy.

1. First, we need to divide antenna height in feet by 3.28 to get our height in meters. This comes out to 1.524 Meters.
2. Next the square root of 1.524 comes out to 1.235.
3. Multiply 1.235 by 3.569 to get our distance in Meters. This comes out to 4.432.
4. Finally multiply 4.432 by 0.621371 (KM to Miles formula) to get our distance in miles. This is comes out to 2.754 miles – The distance from you to the curvature. You and your buddy can talk 2x this distance, or 5.5 miles apart.

A formula calculator for calculating distance can be found online on the Ham Universe website at:

https://www.hamuniverse.com/lineofsightcalculator.html

So, is 5.5 miles the range limit? Nope.

If you are talking to another radio operator from radio to radio, often referred to as simplex radio operation (Both users transmit and receive on the SAME frequency without a frequency offset) then, well, yes, 5.5 miles would be the limit. Increasing the height of either antenna will extend this distance either by directly raising the antenna or by standing at a higher level (Balcony of a building, on top of a building or tower, on a hill, or on a mountain) then the range will increase. Radio operators talking from high points, such as mountain to mountain with large distances between them but no obstacles (50 miles for instance) can communicate on low wattage radios (5 watts for example) quite well. Again though, this depends on the height of your antenna and obstacles in between both radios. Talking to another radio operator at 50 miles from the peaks of two mountains or high hills with direct line of sight communicating is common.

In our example on the previous page, we have two tall antennas which each have a height of 25 feet. If I am communicating to that station and my antenna is 5 feet high, then our combined range we can communicate from is about 9 miles (25 Feet gives a distance to the radio horizon of 6.1 miles plus my range of 2.75 miles at 5 feet high). If we both have 25' raised antennas our range is just over 12 miles.

Though we have this formula for measuring out our theoretical radio horizon, we need to understand the following points also about VHF and UHF wavelengths:

- The radio horizon for VHF and UHF signals more distant than the visual horizon **under perfect conditions** because the Atmosphere can refract radio waves slightly (T3C11). We must stress however that this is under perfect conditions which brings us to our second point which is…
- The radio horizon for VHF and UHF are rarely met due to common obstructions which absorb and limit our radio range – Homes, Cars, Forests & Vegetation, Hills, Mountains, etc. all cut down our true radio range when working with simplex signals (Not communicating through a repeater) for VHF & UHF frequencies.
- UHF radio signals are also rarely heard beyond the radio horizon because these UHF signals do not usually propagate through the ionosphere (T3C01) – Higher frequencies are "Sharper" frequencies that cut through the atmosphere.

For more online of sight radio distance calculations visit HamUniverse.com at:
http://www.hamuniverse.com/lineofsightcalculator.html .

Enter Repeater Systems.

In radio, repeaters can be used to extend the range of your radio communication. A radio operator standing with an antenna height of 5 feet talking to a repeater with an antenna on a tower that is 500' in the air (A Commercial tower) can talk at a range of about 30 miles (27 Miles for the repeater, about 3 miles for my handheld). In my own area of Florida, I communicate throughout much of the Tampa Bay area through a repeater on an antenna at 875 feet in the air from almost 40 miles away. And since that repeater is part of a 5-repeater network, I frequently talk to other radio operators over 100 miles away! We will talk more about repeaters in section 7.11 of this chapter, and more in chapter 8 when we discuss locating repeaters.

Characteristics of Radio Frequencies

Lastly, we need to discuss and understand the differing qualities of radio signals communicating at differing frequencies. We just spoke about "Line of Sight" where radio signals like to travel in straight lines. But radio signals at lower frequencies have more of an ability to bounce or reflect around the curvature of the earth or bounce from the atmosphere than do higher frequency radio signals.

The ability of a radio wavelength to bounce or travel around the curvature of the earth or through the atmosphere is called Propagation. Propagation is what allows an AM radio signal to travel hundreds of miles or allows a HAM radio operator to communicate across the country or across continents, even to travel part way around the world. Many factors play into propagation such as solar activity and weather conditions. This allows a radio operator one day or one minute to reach several thousands of miles away, and then right after they will lose that contact and not be able to reach them again.

Propagation is common with low-frequency radio waves which have longer wavelengths. In fact, it is a characteristic of these lower frequency. This leads to the rule by the FCC for AM Broadcast stations to have to reduce their power at night after the sun goes down and the atmosphere is more conducive to radio signal propagation traveling further. Otherwise, this would cause bleed-over effects between radio stations at night if power were not reduced.

Propagation is what allows shortwave broadcasters to transmit extreme distances to other countries. This is how stations such as "Voice of America" can transmit to foreign countries who are not allowed to hear our news, and why other countries including Russia, China, North Korea and Cuba have radio broadcasts targeting to the United States.

As the frequencies increase and the radio wavelengths shorten, the ability to bounce reduces and radio waves better penetrate structures (To a degree). Thus, our cell phone signals work better indoors than longer radio wave signals. In radio communication, this is also why VHF does slightly better for communicating outdoors and UHF tends to slightly better indoors.

An excellent analogy I once heard is as follows. Imagine walking through a building holding a stick that is 6.72 feet long and holding it without turning it. This is the length of a 2-meter VHF wavelength. You keep bumping into things and hitting things. Now walk with a stick that is just 2.21 feet long – the length of a 70-cm UHF wavelength. It is much easier to move throughout the building with the short stick than the long stick.

UHF signals (Short stick) penetrate buildings better than VHF frequencies (Long stick). So, while this sounds better, the reverse is true of a signal's ability to propagate outside. A VHF signal generally travels farther outdoors where there are few obstacles. And likewise, by dropping into the HF bands with even lower frequencies, our distance further increases. This allows 6-meter and 10-meter radios to communicate farther outdoors without repeaters.

6.7.3 – Radio Signal Interference, Propagation

Let's say we are trying to communicate out using our radio to another station at some distance. There are several factors we need to understand to know if we are going to be able to reach a long distance, and how we need to be set up. As this test is for the Technician's exam, we won't be working much with HF frequencies, but you do need to understand some of the characteristics of all the bands, particularly VHF and UHF frequencies.

In section 6.7.2 above, we discussed Line-of-sight radio wave transmission which is dominant with VHF and UHF frequencies. We touched on geography being a big issue – Trees and vegetation, mountains, hills and valleys, buildings and clutter in suburban areas are a huge hindrance. UHF and microwave signals have a problem with vegetation referred to as *Absorption which blocks and consume radio signals (T3A02)*. *Anther condition that could cut down on your radio range, particularly in Microwave frequencies, is Precipitation (T3A07)*. Fog, rain, and atmospheric conditions can affect some frequency bands more than other bands. For instance – *many bands are affected by both fog and rain, though some bands such as 6-meter and 10-meter, are affected to a very little degree (T3A12)*.

Radio waves can also reflect from surfaces creating a bounce effect. Sometimes *use of a directional antenna might enable your station to communicate to a distant repeater off a reflected signal that is indirect from direct line of sight to the repeater (T3A05)*. Reflection of a signal can also cause a phenomenon referred to as *Multi-path Propagation* where radio signals bounce and may result in reaching the same destination through different paths.

Problems this can cause include:

- *VHF signal strengths sometimes varying greatly with only a slight move of the antenna of a few feet (T3A01).*
- *Data Transmissions can result in an increase in error rates due to radio waves received at slightly different times from multiple paths (T3A10).*
- *Another signal problem that can occur if one of the operators is moving such as while driving, is a problem called "Picket Fencing" also caused by multipath propagation (T3A06).*

The Earth's Ionosphere

As a licensed technician, most of your work will be done with VHF (2-Meter, 1.25-Meter) and UHF (70-cm plus others) frequencies. You will have access to the full range of the 6-Meter band as well as some frequencies in the 10-Meter band, but the handheld radios and mobile radios most popular usually do not work with these bands. Even so, the test covers discussions about signal propagation through the earth's atmosphere which is very important to understand.

First, propagation through the atmosphere occurs in the primarily in the ionosphere, the layer of the atmosphere that is generally 30-miles to 600-miles above the surface and includes the thermosphere as well as parts of the mesosphere and exosphere. This is the area of the atmosphere where ionization occurs from solar radiation and where auroras typically occur. Radio signals can reflect through the ionosphere at certain frequencies. *Propagation through the Ionosphere will refract or bend HF and VHF Frequencies best and not UHF Frequencies (T3A11)*. The way I always have thought of this – as frequencies increase, they get "Sharper" and cut through the atmosphere. Lower frequencies are much duller and bounce out of the Ionosphere. *In general, between HF and VHF frequencies, Long-distance ionospheric propagation is more common with HF frequencies than VHF frequencies (T3C02)* though it does occur at times with VHF frequencies. There are two types of propagation that are covered on the test:

- *Sporadic "E" Propagation is most commonly associated with occasional strong signals on the 10, 6, and 2-meter bands from beyond the radio horizon. (T3C04)*

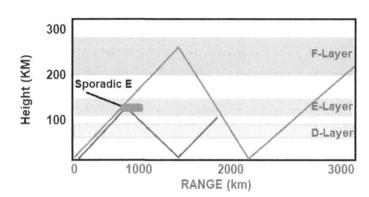

- Sporadic "F" Propagation where most frequency bands including HF frequencies reflect through.

Though VHF frequencies don't often propagation through the "F" region, here are some exceptions covered on the test:

- *10-Meter band can often propagate from dawn to shortly after sunset during periods of high sunspot activity (T3C09).*

- *6 & 10-Meter bands may provide long-distance communications via the ionosphere's F region during the peak of the sunspot cycle (T3C10).*

Unusual Propagation

This topic covers certain topics on the test that I consider "Unusual" because you won't likely ever use them as a technician, but that you should know as a Ham operator.

Tropospheric Ducting is a topic that needs to be understood. This is a condition where a layer in the atmosphere forms usually from a weather front moving through and creates an opportunity for radio signals to be propagates to a much greater range through this layer than normal. *Tropospheric ducting can result in the propagation of VHF and UHF frequencies for 300-miles or more is caused by conditions such as weather frontal*

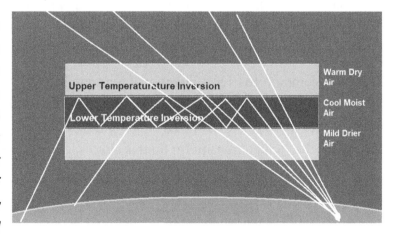

boundaries when warmer temperatures occur higher in the atmosphere than the temperatures at lower levels creating layers of air stacked allowing for the propagation extensions to occur (T3C06, T3C08).

https://3fs.net.au/tropospheric-propagation/

Another topic that you may see a question on is on Auroral backscatter. Auroral backscatter occurs when there is greater solar activity such as from solar flares or storms that interact with the atmosphere creating greater Northern and Southern light activity. **When this occurs the opportunity for VHF signal propagation at greater distances increase through those signals are distorted and signal strength varies considerably (T3C03)**. When this type of activity occurs, there is opportunity for increased VHF activity and at the same time HF propagation is affected and often blocked out.

The last unusual propagation subject that is in the question pool is about Meteor Scatter. This is the opportunity to bounce radio signals from meteors during a meteor shower. The one single question on the test that you may see is about which band is best suited for communicating via meteor scatter which happens to be 6-Meters.

https://www.electronics-notes.com/articles/antennas-propagation/auroral-backscatter-propagation/basics.php

6.7.4 - Directional Antennas

A Directional antenna, also known as a "Beam" antenna, is an antenna that concentrates signals into a single direction for better performance and working with weak signals in that one direction (T9A01). One type of directional antenna you will recognize immediately is the satellite dish antenna. The satellite dish allows the antenna to be pointed in a single direction and pick up weaker signals that regular omnidirectional antenna might miss. **Another type of directional antenna that offers better performance and greater gain than an omnidirectional antenna is a Yagi antenna (T9A06)**. On the test, question T9A06 compares the Yagi antenna to a 5/8 vertical wave, an Isotropic, and a J-Pole antenna, all of which are Omnidirectional antennas with the Yagi being the only directional antenna. (The Isotropic Antenna is a theoretical antenna that is a single point in space that radiates out in all directions equally).

Another common use for a directional antenna by many ham operators is use in games. **One game – a hidden transmitter hunt, uses a directional antenna that is pointed in various directions allowing the operator to identify the strongest signal based on the direction the antenna is pointing (T8C02)**. Another name for the Hidden transmitter hunt is also called a "Fox Hunt".

Some types of directional antennas are listed below, though only the Yagi is discussed on the test:

Parabolic Dish Antenna The Dish antenna using the reflective dish to capture or reflect out the radio waves in a specific direction. These can be found used in Ham radio, and many other types of communications. These are well known for Satellite communications as well as radio telescopes that are peering deep into space.	
Yagi Antenna The Yagi antenna will be one of the more used antennas in Ham Radio for directional use. It is an antenna with multiple elements of differing sizes that radiates in one specific direction. The rear element is the longest and is referred to as the reflector. The next shortest is the driven element where your antenna feed line connects. At least one shorter element extends out to the end of the antenna which acts as a director refining your signal. At least one director is needed, though often multiple directors can be added providing more focus. As additional directors are added they each are shorter in length as they move closer to the end of the antenna.	
Quad Antenna The Quad Antenna is another form of a directional antenna which consists of a single driven element (Connected to your radio via Feed line) and multiple parasitic elements. With a quad antenna each element is square or round offering operation in multiple polarizations.	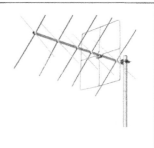

6.7.5 – Antenna Length & Gain/Loss

Antenna Length

To understand the topic of why antenna length is important and how it can affect your radio signal's gain or loss, let us take a moment to discuss RESONANCE. Resonance in ham radio refers to how well the radio wave performs through a particular length of antenna wire. With an antenna, the degree of how well the radio signal works is related to how well matched the actual length of the antenna is to the wavelength of the radio signal. If they are matched perfectly, then there should be no signal loss (Theoretically) coming from the signal and moving through the antenna. This would be an SWR reading of 1:1. If they are slightly mismatches, then our SWR reading starts to rise and our efficiency of the antenna starts to drop. The efficiency loss results in a signal loss which will dissipate as heat in the feed line and antenna As the mismatch grows we will have a higher SWR reading and less efficiency. Think of using a CB radio antenna for a VHF signal – or a VHF antenna for a GMRS radio signal. The frequency differences create a mismatch, higher SWR, and problems. In some cases these problems, when great, could result in damage to the transmitter.

Note on Dipole Antennas – The best way of increasing the resonant frequency of a Dipole antenna is by shortening it (T9A05).

When talking antenna lengths for good SWR and efficiency, the antenna does NOT have to be the full length of the wavelength. For example – a CB Radio antenna, if matched to the full wavelength in the 11-meter band would be 36' feet in length. When is the last time you saw a truck on the road with a 36' antenna? Instead, we will use a fractional length antenna. Here are some common lengths for different radio bands. The 11-Meter band is CB Radio and not a Tech Operator privilege, but many who are familiar with CB radio may be familiar with these antennas.

Meters - Full Wavelength	11-Meter (CB)	10-Meter	6-Meter	2-Meter	70-cm
Feet - Full Wavelength	36.08	32.8	19.68	6.56	2.296
Inches - Full Wavelength	432.96	393.6	236.16	78.72	27.552
Feet - Half Wavelength	9.02	8.2	4.92	1.64	0.574
Inches - Half wavelength	108.24	98.4	59.04	19.68	6.888
Feet - 1/4 Wavelength	2.255	2.05	1.23	0.41	0.1435
Inches - 1/4 Wavelength	27.06	24.6	14.76	4.92	1.722
Feet - 5/8 Wavelength	22.55	20.5	12.3	4.1	1.435
Inches - 5/8 Wavelength	270.6	246	147.6	49.2	17.22

A few points of note:

- We are adding the 5/8 wavelength antenna because ***the 5/8 wavelength is a length that performs better than half-wavelength and quarter-wavelength antennas and is very popular (T9A12).***

- The actual length of an antenna does not need to be the electrical length – A longer antenna with an electrical length for a half-wave or 5/8 wave, or even full wave can be created by using a coil to have the proper electrical length. A CB Radio antenna such as a "Firestik" has a longer electrical length than the actual antenna length by wiring the antenna around a fiberglass rod allowing a shorter physical antenna to be used – Highly useful for the longer lengths of CB Radio wavelengths.

- The use of a coil is a form of *Antenna Loading. Antenna Loading is the act of electrically lengthening the antenna by inserting inductors in radiating elements (T9A02)*.

- The relationship between 70-cm antenna lengths and 2-Meter lengths is almost 1/3 – 0.35 – allowing a 2-Meter antenna to work generally well for 70-cm wavelengths. This depends however on the exact lengths and the antenna design. For best performance, use an antenna that is designed for the band you are operating on.

- Many antennas are tunable – Meaning you can fine tune the length of the antenna for specific frequencies for best performance. To do this, you should use an SWR meter for verification.

Antenna Gain

Gain when related to antennas refers to the ability of an antenna to radiate and perform better in one direction when compared to a reference antenna (T9A11), thus performing better communicating with stations in that direction. An excellent example of this is with a Yagi antenna. When a Yagi antenna is pointed in one direction, North for example, it will have a higher gain when communicating in that direction meaning it will receive weaker signals and will transmit farther. It will outperform an omnidirectional antenna which operates the same in all directions.

Note: A reference antenna is a theoretical antenna that is a single point in space that, if it existed, would radiate a signal out equally in all 3-dimensions from its origin point.

In the direction of south however, it will have poorer performance in that direction for both receive and transmit, and will not operate as well as a omnidirectional antenna.

Antenna gain of an antenna such as a Yagi or Dish antenna make those designs of antennas best when communicating with a remote repeater. With television signals, these types of antennas will pick up television stations from the direction they are pointing much better than a pair of rabbit ears. This is why Yagi antennas are popular for television use, and dish antennas are popular for Satellite use.

6.7.6 - Antenna Dummy Load

This is a quick topic but needs a little explanation. There are only two questions on the test related to Dummy loads, so we will cover both of those quickly here with a brief explanation of what a dummy load is. *A Dummy load is a non-inductive load mounted on a heat sink (T7C03)* that can absorb the transmitting signal from a radio transmitter and dissipate that signal out as heat. These loads are used to connect to a transmitter instead of an antenna so that the transmitter sees an appropriate load and testing of the transmitter does not either create a signal going out through your antenna when you are testing and allows a safe outlet for the power from your transmitter that could otherwise damage your radio if no antenna were connected. Basically, you can do transmission testing without sending out a signal, though at a very short distance you would still be able to pick up the signal. Per question *(T7C01)*, **The purpose of a dummy load is to prevent transmitting signals over the air when making tests.** Below are two examples of dummy loads you may run across:

A 50-watt Dummy load with a PL-259 connector

This dummy load can be connected to the back of any radio that uses a SO-239 connector on it, or with the proper adapters it can be used with any handheld radio. The load will absorb up to 50-watts of power allowing safe testing of the radio.

The "Cantenna" style dummy load

This load is made using a Paint can and large resistors with appropriate heat sinks for dissipating up to 1000-watts of power from a high-power radio setup.

6.7.7 - Antenna Poles / Installation

As has been mentioned before, if given a choice between power and antenna, antenna makes more of a difference in your being able to communicate. And with the antenna, best placement of the antenna is critical. If you are operating a handheld with an antenna on the handheld radio it simply will not perform as well as if you remove the antenna and attach an external antenna such as a car mag-mount antenna to the radio, or an antenna specifically designed for outside operation and pole mounting. You will usually need an adapter to go to the radio – Usually a SO-239 connector to either a SMA adapter for your radio (Baofengs for instance) or a SO-239 to BNC, depending on the radio antenna connection.

SO-239 Female to SMA Female adapter

SO-239 Female to SMA-Female Cable Adapter

When setting up an external antenna for use with a handheld, mobile, or base ham radio, getting as much height as possible is always beneficial as well as being as clear from obstructions as possible. This can lead to options of mounting an antenna on your roof, on a long, tall pole, or even using a small tower for getting height. When doing so there are going to be several issues which you must remember that are specifically covered on the test.

1. When putting up an antenna tower, **look for and stay clear of any overhead electrical wires (T0B04)**. While this may sound simple enough, as you are extending a pole or tower into the air it can be easy to forget that your closer to wires with an extended pole than you are with the pole collapsed.

2. When standing up a pole or antenna, the minimum safe distance from a power line during installation of the antenna is **so that if the antenna falls, no part of it can come closer than 10 feet to the power wires (T0B06).** This means – If your pole falls with the antenna on the pole, there should be at least a ten feet distance from any utility wire. If the pole falls due to being knocked over, it could travel several feet crossing a hot wire creating a hazard.

3. Always avoid attaching an antenna to a utility pole as **the antenna could contact high-voltage power lines (T0B09)**. As mentioned in #2 just above, crossing a live wire could create a tremendous hazard for any active radio operator or could create a fire through the antenna or feed line.

When installing an antenna in such a way as to get more height, you could opt to mount the antenna on the roof of your home or your radio shack, on a pole such as a simple painter's pole, an isolated utility pole, or some type of antenna tower. If using a utility pole, we would assume this to be a newly installed pole with NO other service running to it and isolated a safe distance from any other pole with any type of powered lines or utility service. There are three specific questions on antenna towers on the test.

When climbing a tower, there are multiple items that are always required – Question **(T0B02)** touches on this and the answer is **All these choices are correct.** The choices given and the safety requirements are:

- Have sufficient training on safe tower climbing techniques.
- Use appropriate tie-off to the tower at all times.
- Always wear an approved climbing harness.

In addition, recognize that climbing an antenna tower – even a small one, can be incredibly dangerous. You always should have a helper or observer to monitor you in case you have a mishap – a fall, or an equipment malfunction that could trap you on the tower. **NEVER climb a tower without a helper or observer (T0B03).** Some types of towers are "Crank-Up" towers. These towers use multiple segments that can be cranked up to an extended height for better performance. **This type of tower must not be climbed unless it is retracted, or mechanical safety locking devices have been installed (T0B07)**. A collapse with this type of tower while an individual is on the tower could easily result in the loss of a limb or a very serious injury. Always – Safety First.

The test also covers three questions related to proper electrical grounding of a radio tower. The rules in your area that cover the requirements for grounding are always **covered by the Local electrical codes** (T0B11). The test also covers two specific questions on grounding for towers. These are:

- **(T0B01)** – This happens to be a new question for the 2022-2026 question pool. When installing ground wires on a tower for lightning protection, **Always ensure that connections are short and direct.** The reason is that lightning or electrical surges will try to travel the shortest distance possible. Unnecessary length or bends in the wire may result in electrical current following another route to ground.

- **(T0B08)** – The proper grounding method for a tower is to use **separate eight-foot ground rods for watch tower leg that are bonded to the tower and to each other.** This assumes you are using a tower with multiple leg segments such as the one pictured here to the right. By bonding the ground rods together, you are insuring you have a shared ground connection for each of the tower legs. **All external ground rods or earth connections should be bonded together with heavy wire or electrical strap (T0A09). When installing grounding conductors for lightning protection, remember that sharp bends must be avoided (T0B10).** A sharp bend in the conductor may produce an impedance looking like a wire coil allowing the current running through the grounding conductor to look for a path with less impedance creating a possible arc.

6.8 – Coax Cable & Feed Lines

Coaxial cable is the cable type we use to move our signals from our radios to our remote antennas. Of course, if you are using a handheld radio, you may consider this to be a non-issue, but even with a handheld radio, by using a remote antenna such as a Mag-mount antenna in the car or an external antenna for your home or camp site, then the use of Coaxial cable will become more of a need to understand for performance. Let's cover some quick facts about coaxial cable:

- Coaxial Cable is a shielded cable that has a signal wire at the core and a shield that wraps around the core signal wire **to prevent coupling of unwanted signals to or from the wire (T6D03)**. This means a cleaner signal without interference both in and out, and less chance of signal being heard on radios, televisions, or cordless telephones. If you are having interference problems such as TV interference, the first thing you should do is **be sure all TV Feed line coaxial connectors are installed properly (T7B09)**.

- All coaxial cable that is used for amateur radio is a 50-ohm cable (T9B02). This is different from the 75-ohm coaxial cable used wiring up for television use. The 75-ohm coax should never be used for ham radio as it will simply not perform well at all. 50-Ohm cable is not as commonly available as 75-ohm cable. You will not find it in Home Depot or Lowes. Instead, you could find it at Truck stops, CB Radio shops, or many marine supply stores that sell VHF Marine radios and antennas. *Coaxial cable is the feed line for amateur radio antenna systems because it is easy to use and requires few special installation considerations (T9B03).*

- Not all coax cable is the same. The most common at many places such as truck stops is an RG-58 coaxial cable – But this cable has poor performance at VHF and UHF frequencies. *As the frequency of a signal in coaxial cable is increased, the loss increases (T9B05).* This means that a coaxial cable that may be adequate for lower frequencies, such as CB radio which functions in the 27-MHz (HF) frequencies, as the frequencies increase such as in our 2-Meter VHF frequencies (144-148 MHz) or our 70-cm frequencies (420-450 MHz) then our losses increase and our performance drops. *Power that is lost in our feed lines is converted into heat (T7C07)* and does not go out as signal through our antenna.

- Better quality cable (And more expensive) such as RG-8, RG-8u, RG-213, LMR-400 or others should be used for better power transfer performance and less signal loss. Depending on the distance you are running the cable, you should check the specifications of the cable. RG-58 is a poor choice even for distances as little as 25-feet. Imagine you are using a 5-watt radio to connect to an antenna raised 20 feet in the air – a cheap coax may absorb most of your power where a more expensive cable will allow most of your signal to transmit. On the test, question *(T9B10) specifically asks the difference between RG-58 and RG-213 cables, which is RG-213 had less loss at a given frequency (T9B10)*. At HF frequencies such as CB Radio and 10-Meters there won't be as much difference, but the difference is high at UHF frequencies.

- As mentioned, different types of coax work differently at different frequencies. For commercial use, there will be types of coax that are used that are not practical for amateur operator use. One of these is *Air Coaxial Cable which requires special techniques to prevent moisture in the cable (T7C11)*. This may include the need to maintain air pressure in the length of the coax to keep water moisture from penetrating into the cable which can be expensive. This was much more common years ago before the extensive use of Fiber Optic cable. *Air Insulated Hardline is a coaxial feed line that has the lowest loss at VHF and UHF frequencies (T9B11).*

Air Insulated Hardline Coax – Has a plastic winding around the center core, otherwise an air core for insulation. This type of Coax requires special tools and special handling for use.

Coax is not the perfect cable. There are several problems that can occur when using coaxial cable as your feed line. ***Moisture contamination is one of the most common causes of failure with coaxial cable (T7C09)***. Moisture contamination occurs when water or moisture seeps into the cable through breaks in the outer shield, or through poor connections at the coaxial connectors. If you are going to be using coaxial cable in locations where it will be exposed to sunlight – remember that sunlight includes ultraviolet light. ***Ultraviolet light can damage the jacket and allow water to enter the cable (T7C10)***.

In the next section of this chapter, we are going to talk about SWR. When using an external antenna, it is good to use a SWR meter to make sure that our impedance match between our transmitter and our antenna is proper to avoid excessive signal loss. ***One problem that can occur and can cause erratic changes in our SWR readings comes from loose connections in the antenna or the feed line running to our antenna (T9B09)***.

One last question in the test pool related to coaxial cable deals with lightning arrestors. ***The lightning arrestor is used to intercept electrical static and current coming from our antenna and should be installed on coaxial feed line on a grounded panel near where feed lines are entering the building (T0A07)***. When a lightning surge occurs, the intent is that the current from the surge is diverted through the arrestor to ground protecting the equipment. This is the intent – however a big enough lightning strike still may pass through and to your equipment. For this reason, you should avoid operating during storms and disconnect your antenna line when not in use from the radio.

6.9 – SWR & SWR Meters

Standing Wave Ration (SWR) is a measure of how well a load is matched to a transmission line (T9B12). SWR Meters are used to measure power coming out of your radio transmitter to your antenna, and to measure the impedance match from the transmitter to the antenna. With some SWR meters both the power levels and the impedance match can read at the same time. Other meters may work better for some types of testing than others, such as the Gam3Gear meter shown here to the right which is a good digital meter for handheld radios such as the Baofeng radio used by many preppers and emergency operators, as well as many new hams.

In using an SWR meter for antenna tuning, you will see the term **Impedance** very often. For clarity, ***Impedance is the opposition to AC Current flow in an AC Circuit (T5C12),*** but it is also the resistance that a radio wave has moving through a coaxial feed line to the antenna. The amount of impedance that you may be seeing is dependent upon multiple factors including the frequency (Impedance grows as frequency goes up), the quality of the coaxial cable, and the tuning of the antenna (Which often is how well the antenna length resonates with the frequency being transmitted through it).

The SWR meter connects in between the output of the radio and the antenna or the antenna feed line. If your work with your radio will including using external antennas connected even to a handheld radio, then picking up an inexpensive SWR meter can be quite useful.

Below are two popular SWR meters that are both priced in the $50 to $100 price range. The MFJ-844 shown on the left is an analog meter which can be switched between SWR mode and Power mode.

MFJ-844 Analog SWR Meter

SURECOM SW-102 Digital Meter

In the image to the right here is the digital output from the Surecom digital meter. In the display we can see the following:

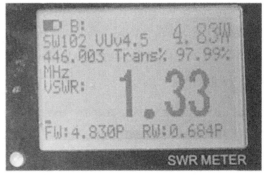

- Frequency (446.003 MHz)
- RF Power (4.83-Watts)
- VSWR (1.33)

All these properties will display simultaneously making this digital meter a very useful tool, particularly if you are operating multiple radios using multiple antenna configurations.

In the image below, we have a Baofeng radio connected to our Surecom SWR meter, then connected to a "Stubby" antenna. When we press our PTT button, the SWR meter provides us our reading. In the SWR reading that is being displayed, the lower the value (1.0 being perfect for this digital meter). The higher the reading, the more out of balance the impedance will be and the greater the chances for problems with your ability to transmit, or even damage to your transmitter. On the radio test, a low SWR reading is indicated by a 1:1 ratio with a higher ratio of 1.5 being less ideal, and a high ratio of 1:3, 1:4, or higher being even less ideal. *A meter reading on an SWR Meter that indicates a perfect impedance match between the antenna and feed line would be 1:1 (T7C04). A meter reading of 4:1 would indicate an impedance mismatch (T7C06).* Such a mismatch could result in actual damage to the transmitter. Always try for the lowest SWR reading possible. *The benefit or a low SWR will be reduced signal loss (T9B01).*

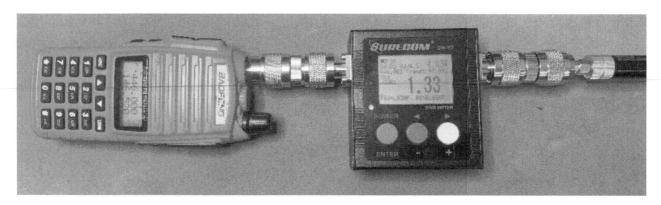

More Resources for SWR:

https://www.robkalmeijer.nl/techniek/electronica/radiotechniek/hambladen/qst/1959/04/page24/index.html

When selecting an accessory SWR meter there are two things you need to consider – The Frequency range you will be reading, and the power level at which the measurements will be taken (T4A02). Most meters work only within specific frequency ranges – HF meters for instance and meters that will read VHF/UHF frequencies. They may also be designed for only a set power limit – many do not work on higher power levels and may be damaged if too much power is applied.

Directional Wattmeter

Another instrument that can be used to accurately measure the wattage passing through a feed line is the Directional Wattmeter (T7C08). This instrument is more accurate (And more expensive) than the SWR Meter running up into several hundreds of dollars for higher quality model meters.

Another tool that you must be aware of is the **Antenna Analyzer**. The Antenna Analyzer is a testing device that can indicate the resonant frequency and VSWR by outputting a signal frequency while looking at the amplitude of the signal both forward and the power being reflected back. Traditional analyzers can run several hundred dollars though some new devices called "Nanometers" can be used to track signal quality and can be purchased for under $100. Question *(T7C02) asks "Which of the following is used to determine* *if an antenna is resonant at the desired operating frequency?".* The answer to this question is *An antenna analyzer.*

6.A - About your License

In this section we are going to talk about some of the topics about being licensed and what it means. For covering this section, we are going to simply list on the test related to licensing and rules and give a brief explanation of each issue.

Each licensed ham operator receives a call sign. That call sign follows a format of:

- One or two characters at the beginning that indicate your region location. Older call signs were one character but those ran out.
- A single digit number (0-9) which is your region number.
- Two or three character suffix – 2 Characters for Amateur Extra level operators (Old call signs may have only a single character) and three characters for Tech and General operators.

For the test, all you need to remember is that the sample question (T1C05) is asking about a proper format for a call sign. The answer is the SAME format as what you will receive when you get your call sign. Two Alpha-1 Number-3 Alpha, or 2x1x3. Only one answer will match that. If you can remember 213 you will have that question understood.

Once you pass your test you will NOT be yet able to transmit on the radio – you MUST wait until your name appears in the FCC database before you can transmit on the air (T1A05).

As soon as your operator license does appear in the FCC's license database you may transmit on the amateur radio bands for the license level you are assigned (T1C10). This usually occurs within 2-weeks so you will need to be patient.

Once you receive your license it will be good for Ten years before you need to renew it (T1C08). After the ten-year period is up you will need to renew it by paying a fee.

The grace period for renewal is two years (T1C09).

During the grace period you are NOT permitted to transmit on the radio (T1C11).

Proof that you have a valid FCC issued primary/operator license comes from the license appearing in the FCC ULS Database (T1A05).

When transmitting on the air you need to remember – *You must identify yourself at least every ten minutes during and at the end of the transmission (T1F03).* Start off by identifying yourself and keep track of your time. At the end of your conversation ALWAYS identify yourself.

If you happen to have friends and wish to start a club of your own – you can! **For a club station license grant you must have at least four members (T1F11)**. But – getting your own call sign for your club could be useful for club events where you may have multiple individuals operating using the club's call sign as they rotate on duty.

By the way – You are as a licensed operator required to maintain your address and contact information with the FCC.

License Levels

As a new operator you will be at the entry level point – The Technician level. A few years ago there used to be a NOVICE level which was the entry level, and an ADVANCED level after the general. A few years ago both of these were dropped. **Today there are three Ham Radio license levels in the United States – Technician, General and Amateur Extra (T1C01). No matter what level license you obtain in the U.S., there will only be ONE license grant held by any operator with privileges increasing for you as you test at higher levels (T1A04).**

The transmitting frequency privileges of the amateur station are determined by the class of operator license held by the control operator (T1E04). In this case, you as the license holder are referred to as the control operator. **At No Time can a technician license holder be the control operator of a station operating in the Amateur Extra or General class band segments (T1E06).** This includes operating as a radio operator during an emergency event. **Amateur station control operators are only permitted to transmit outside of their frequency privileges of their license class in situations involving the immediate safety of human life or protection of property (T2C09).**

The Station Licensee

There are a few questions on the test referring to the station licensee. This means the owner of the radio station. If you are the licensee and your radio is being used for emergency contact, then you are the station licensee. **As the station licensee, you must designate who will be the control operator if you step away (T1E03). When you are the station licensee (Radio owner) and another licensed person is operating the radio, BOTH you (Station licensee) and the Control operator are responsible for proper operation of the station (T1E07).** Also – **The station licensee is the individual responsible for proper safety performance of the station and ensuring that no person is exposed to RF energy above the FCC exposure limits (T0C13).**

If exposure to RF Radiation is a risk one of the easiest actions that you can take is to Relocate the Antenna(s) causing the problem (T0C08).

Radio Transmission Power

The power that you transmit at are dependent upon the level of license you have, and on the band which you are operating on. As a general rule of thumb, with exceptions of course, the maximum power that a ham operator can broadcast with is 1500 watts of power. That is a lot of power to be working with. As I said however – there are exceptions. Here are some of the exceptions:

10-Meter Band	*Technician level operators are limited to 200-watts broadcasting power on HF Band segments (T1B11).* As it happens, the only HF band that Techs are allowed to voice-broadcast on is the 10-Meter band.
VHF Frequencies ABVE 30-MHz	*Except for some specific restrictions, Technicians can use up to 1500-watts of power on frequencies above 30-MHz (T1B12).*
HF Bands other than 10-Meters	Technicians have CW/Morse Code privileges on some additional HF bands such as 80-Meters, 40-Meters, and 15-Meters but are limited to only 200-watts of operational power.

FCC Topics on the Test

On the 2022 to 2026 pool there are three additional questions which directly ask about FCC Rules that you need to understand – but these are pretty straight forward.

- *(T1C04) – What may happen if the FCC is unable to reach you by Email?*
  If the FCC cannot contact you by email – including contact at times other than license expiration, they may revoke or suspend your operator's license. Communication is highly important. This is a new question on the test because it deals with communication by **EMAIL**. Applicants are now required to have a valid Email address on file for communication.

- *(T1D01): With which countries are FCC-licensed amateur radio stations prohibited from exchanging communications?*
  Any country whose administration has notified the International Telecommunication Union (ITU) that it objects to such communications. As of March, 2022, the FCC has no countries banned on their list, though there are countries that make it illegal for their population to use Ham Radios. For a current status of this rule check the FCC website at https://www.fcc.gov/wireless/bureau-divisions/mobility-division/amateur-radio-service/international-arrangements

- *(T2C01): When do FCC Rules NOT apply to the operation of an amateur station?*
  The FCC rules ALWAYS apply. This one is easy to remember – The FCC Rules ALWAYS apply. The most common challenge to this is – Can a non-ham operator use a ham frequency during an emergency or operate outside of their band privileges. But this rule does fall under an FCC Rule in that during an

emergency where life or property are at risk then non-allowed frequencies or bands can be used. BUT – And this is a big but – Be prepared to show that you were in this situation – otherwise fines and penalties can be applied.

6.B – Digital Radio Modes

Digital Radio covers a range of topics in Ham Radio that will cover one of the following topics:

- Digital Radio systems, such as DMR – Where the voice signal is digitized and transmitted for a clearer signal with more information that can be sent.
- Computer based software that uses ham radio to broadcast signals more efficiently than voice-based radio (Winlink for example for E-mail).
- CW over Ham Radio (Yes, CW is the *FIRST* digital mode). **CW is another name for Morse Code (T8D09)**.
- Wireless Local Area Networking (Connecting of computers such as under IEEE 802.11)

There are a lot of areas that we can cover, but as we are focused on specifically topics related to the Technician exam, let's *focus* on those questions.

In the most basic, question **(T8D01)** asks for an example or examples of Digital Communications Modes. Under the structure of that question, the answer of **All these choices are correct** covers:

- Packet radio – A form of radio communications transmitting packets of data. Can be used with software or hardware devices such as APRS to transmit weather and GPS data.
- IEEE 802.11 – Connecting of computer and network systems over wireless radio networks.
- FT8 – A digital mode that uses a computer's sound card to code and decode signals over radio.

Digital Modes can include the use of software to transmit voice or data or can cover the use of electronic interfaces to connect devices to a radio for transmitting of data. Once such interface is APRS which is short for *Automatic Packet Reporting System*. **APRS can provide real-time tactical digital communications in conjunction with mapping tools to show the locations of APRS enabled stations (T8D05)**.

These APRS systems can be used to transmit (T8D03):

- GPS position data through connection of a GPS Module
- Text messages
- Weather data

Digital Radio and Computers

In the age of computers and the Internet, digital radio is also deeply embedded into working with computers to transit over ham radio. Some methods use terminal-type modes on a computer to actually transit life data, allowing the operator at one station to key in their message and it is displayed on other stations. Other methods of digital radio using computers can be seen using WinLink which is an Email-over-Ham Radio system. A user at a remote station that has no internet connection uses a terminal and a ham radio setup to send email messages out. In this case, the messages are transmitted to a Winlink server that is located at remote location hundreds or even thousands of miles away, and the email is routed out onto the Internet through a gateway system. You email then can be received at its normal destination. Likewise, you are able to receive email, though not at your regular email address. Winlink users have their own Winlink email accounts, so you won't be able to communicate through your normal email address.

Winlink has become a preferred method for passing many types of communication during emergency events. The accuracy and speed of transmission is much higher than through voice communication. Messaging must pass through a Winlink terminal, so they must be handled by a Winlink registered user.

Echolink is another popular digital communications method which can function in several ways. Echolink runs either from a computer or smart phone and allows voice communication through VOIP Voice-Over-IP). **VOIP is a method of delivering voice communications over the Internet using digital techniques (T8C07)**. You may be using VOIP today without realizing it. VOIP is used on internet home phones and some add-on applications for your smart phone allow you to use VOIP services from your cell phone. (Zello for instance).

When you log into Echolink, you can broadcast through your computer or smartphone to another Echolink user or to a repeater at a remote location connected via Echolink. You actually do not need a radio if you have a computer terminal. If you do have your radio, it may be possible to connect your radio to the computer and have your radio act like a gateway device. Then you can use a second radio that is within radio range to communicate through your computer to remote locations anywhere in the world also using Echolink. You could be in your garage, out in the yard, or anywhere within radio range and reachable by ham radio from anywhere in the world. **Echolink is the protocol that enables an amateur station to transmit through a repeater without using a radio to initiate the transmission (T8C09)**. The Echolink software and system are only available to licensed ham operators. **To use Echolink, you must register on the Echolink website and provide your registered call sign as well as proof of your license, usually in the form of a scanned or faxed copy of your actual license (T8C10)**.

Connectivity via computer is performed through some form of computer interface. **Signals used in a computer-radio interface for digital operation mode are Receive Audio, Transmit Audio, and Transmitter keying** (T4A06). The interface used can be an external box that connects between your radio and computer, or some more expensive radios may actually have built-in interfaces that will connect to your computer, usually through a special cable. **The connections run from the radio's speaker connection to the computer's "Line In" or Microphone sound card port, and the radio's Mic connection to the computer's "Line Out" or speaker port (T4A07)**.

The Internet Relay Linking Project (IRLP) is a technique to connect amateur radio systems, such as repeaters, via the internet using Voice Over Internet Protocol (VoIP) (T8C08). This is an effective method to allow multiple repeaters located in different areas to act as one large system covering a much larger area.

Another form of "Digital Communications" is what is called an Amateur Radio Mesh Network. *The Mesh Network is an amateur-radio based network using commercial wi-fi equipment with modified firmware (T8D12)*. The Mesh Network uses Ham frequencies for communication and thanks to the privileges of the ham operators, can operate at greater power levels than otherwise possible on these ham frequencies. Links between nodes can extend for miles based on the line-of-site conditions.

6.B.2 – Digital Radio Hardware

DMR – Digital Mobile Radio

Digital Mobile Radio, or DMR, is one of the most popular forms of Digital Radio systems in the United States and is covered with several questions on the test. DMR is a digital radio mode using mostly handheld radios operating radio to radio, radio to DMR Repeater, or radio through "Hotspot" and through the internet to other hotspots or repeaters. *Using a Digital mode hotspot, a DMR Radio operator can connect via digital voice through the hotspot and communicate through the Internet (T4A10)*. Unlike Analog radio, DMR digitizes your voice and transmits it digitally over the airwaves and possibly through the internet to remote destinations. DMR is not the only digital radio method, but it is the only one covered on the test. Other popular digital radio methods include P.25 (Popular with government agencies), TMPR, NXDN, System Fusion and others.

What is unique about DMR radio is that it uses time multiplexing to allow two 12.5 kHz signals to communicate over the same frequency that older analog ham radio uses (T8D07) – you can connect two voice channels over the same 25-kHz frequency as an analog radio use. *DMR also uses "Talk Groups" to organize radio users allowing radio operators to share a channel at different times without having to hear other users on the channel (T8D02). Talk groups use a group identification code entered in the radio to allow the radio to filter out other conversations other than other users in the same talk group (T4B09). The access information for repeaters and talk groups is stored in a "Code Plug" on the radio (T4B07).* The code plug is a programmed configuration – not a hardware device. The code plug can be stored on your computer and even shared with other DMR radio users allowing multiple users to have the same programmed radio configuration. *With DMR, accessing a specific group of stations through the digital voice transceiver is done by entering the groups Identification number (T4B09).*

When moving to digital radio systems such as DMR, there are a number of advantages over traditional analog radio which include:

- Better voice and communication quality
- Lower bandwidth – DMR uses 12.5 kHz bandwidth vs. 25-kHz as used with analog radio using Time Multiplexing to share the frequency with two channels.

- Ability to use a "Hotspot" – A small puck-sized radio receiver that receives your radio signal and can communicate across the Internet. Think of a Hotspot as a repeater in your pocket.
- As these are digital devices and computerized – they can support many more channels and groups for programming. Some support several thousand programmable channels.
- Most models are backwards compatible with analog radios, so one radio can serve two functions.

Not everything is better, however. Some of the downsides, many of which are minor, include:

- More expensive radio equipment (Starting usually around $200).
- Slightly smaller transmission footprint – Same power but once the quality drops the signal will no longer be repeated.
- More difficult to program and operate – But also much more powerful. Due to higher difficulty, when I teach classes I tend to focus strictly on analog radios.
- More complex and expensive support gear may be needed – Digital Hotspot, more specialized repeaters. (Hotspots may cost from $100 to $200 or more)
- Many repeaters and all hotspots will be dependent upon Internet connectivity. During a disaster or emergency, loss of the Internet is more likely to impact capabilities

DMR Digital repeaters support "Talk Groups" which you can access by programming your radio with the appropriate group ID or code (T2B07). For DMR, groups of users are grouped based on color codes which must match the repeater color code for access. (T2B12) Color codes act the same as a PL/CTCSS Toner or a DCS code does for analog radio. There are 15 separate "Color Codes" that can be used by DMR Radio operators to connect to various repeaters. Without setting to the proper code, you will not be able to communicate through the repeater.

6.B.3- Digital via Software

FT8 is an extremely weak-signal digital narrow-band mode that uses only 50-Hz of bandwidth and is capable of low signal-to-noise operation (T8D13). It is not a software package itself, though it is a mode that is used by software packages for weak-signal communication which can be used when talking long distances and propagation may be weak. *When using software such as WSJT-X which uses FT-8 mode for communication, the transceiver's audio input and output are connected to the computer's audio input and output (T4A04).*

WSJT-X is one of several software programs amateur operators can use for digital communications using a computer and ham radio. It is an open-source application that uses multiple modes such as FT-8 to perform weak-signal communication. *Activities that are supported by WSJT-X include: (T8D10)*

- *Earth-Moon-Earth*
- *Weak signal propagation beacons*
- *Meteor scatter*

In the current test pool, question (T8D10) specifically asks which of these above modes are supported, the answer of which is "All of these choices are correct" as WSJT-X supports all these activities.

Packet Radio is another digital radio communications method that is used by ham radio operators to send packets of data via radio similar as to how packets of data are passed on the Internet. Question *(T8D08) specifically asks what is included in packet radio transmissions include all of the following:*

- Each packet contains a check sum that permits error detection.
- Each packet contains a header that contains the call sign of the station to which the information is being sent.
- Each packet also includes an automatic repeat request in case of error.

ARQ, short for AUTOMATIC REPEAT REQUEST, is an error correction method in which the receiving station detects errors and sends a request for retransmission (T8D11). This system is used by digital systems communicating by using acknowledgements sent back by the receiving station to indicate that the message was properly received. If the sending station does not receive the acknowledgement when expected it will retransmit the message until it is acknowledged, or a determined timeout period is reached.

The last of the Digital communications questions we need to cover is PSK which is short for Phase-Shift-Keying (T8D06). PSK is a DIGITAL modulation method which transfers data by changing the phase of a constant frequency reference signal (Carrier signal). PSK is only one of several digital modulation methods but is the only one that is covered on the test. As you study Ham Radio you will or will have studied other modulation methods – most commonly FM (Frequency Modulation) and AM (Amplitude Modulation).

Frequency Modulation (FM) is used commonly with handheld radios and radios in the UHF-VHF bands. FM provides a better-quality voice signal by modulating the frequency of the signal and is common with 2-Meter and 70-cm Ham radio, Marine VHF, GMRS, MURS, 6-Meter, 10-Meter, and most repeater operation.

Amplitude Modulation is most used in HF frequencies but also may be used in VHF and UHF bands as well. Single-Sideband (SSB) is a transmission mode common using AM modulation where the carrier wave and one sideband are stripped from the signal being transmitted so that more output power can be applied to the one sideband being sent out. Airband Aircraft radio, operating in the VHF frequencies, uses Amplitude Modulation for communication operating. A benefit of AM operation is the allowance of radio signals to mix – if two stations are transmitting you may hear both at the same time overlapping. Though this can cause distortion, it does allow the hearing of the signals indicating there is a second signal. With FM Modulation, the stronger signal dominates cutting off the weaker signal entirely.

6.C – Repeater Concepts

For the new Technician, it is important to understand when you get your Ham radio license, most of your distance communications are going to be dependent upon the use of some sort of repeater. For analog and emergency operators, your dependence on repeaters with only a Tech license will be high. Next you must realize that the repeaters, to remain operational in an emergency, will be dependent upon power, fuel, and in some cases with backbone connected repeaters the Internet (Unless they use a backbone RF connection).

As a Tech you will also have access to the full 6-Meter band which will open some additional capabilities, and a portion of the 10-Meter band which will open more opportunities for longer range radio communications. But you will need a radio capable of communicating in 6-Meter and 10-Meter bands as there are far fewer radios that handle these bands that are in the new-ham starting price range. Once you get into full capability HF style radios with VHF/UHF capabilities you will have more options, but as most new technicians usually start off budget sided you may have few if any options. (A starter HF radio with new equipment will start in the $1500 to $2000 range, as you plan for the radio, power supply, antenna tuner, antenna and coaxial feed line).

An Antenna tuner is a device you can add to your radio (Usually HF Radios) that matches the antenna system impedance to the transceiver's output impedance (T9B04). This can be done automatically or by tuning the Antenna tuner with an actual physical dial. Using an antenna tuner allows a radio operator to be able to use an antenna that is not ideal for the frequency band you are transmitting on. You may not get the best signal out, but by matching the impedance through the tuner you will protect your transceiver from damage that could occur through use of an unmatched antenna, and you will get performance better than without the antenna tuner.

A repeater which you will most likely need to learn about quickly once getting licensed for use as a Tech license holder is a radio station that follows automatic control (T1E08). It falls into use with other stations as a station that can automatically retransmit the signals of other amateur stations, all of which include Repeater, Auxiliary, or Space Stations (T1D07). We will talk more about Satellites later in this chapter. *The Repeater Station is the only type of amateur station that simultaneously retransmits the signal of another amateur station on a different channel or channels (T1F09).*

As you will learn when studying for your exam – All stations must have a control operator – But who is the control operator that is an automatic station that runs all the time? This rule is met by requiring the repeater to be remotely controlled by one or more administrators for the repeater that can remotely shut it down if necessary. This could be done through remote control over the Internet, or through DTMF codes from a handheld radio. But – *Who is accountable if a repeater inadvertently retransmits communications that violate FCC rules? In this case it is the control operator of the originating station that violated the rules – Not the operator of the repeater (T1F10).*

I have met far too many new hams who receive their license without understanding their capabilities. So, let's just knock them out here:

- New techs working 70-cm and 2-meter on handheld radios will typically have a 1-3 mile range using FM modulation with the stock antenna, and a higher power mobile radio will have more, all dependent upon your location and conditions   .
- If you have a radio that does 6-meters or 10-meters, then you may have a bit more range. Most mobile radios that do 6-meter/10-meter do so using FM modulation. That means no SSB and not very good propagation. A radio that does AM modulation will work better for distance.
- Using repeaters you CAN get distances of dozens to hundreds of miles – This is TOTALLY dependent on the quality, configuration, and capabilities of the specific repeater or repeater system. This includes height, location, line-of-sight, and networked (Meaning back-boned to multiple repeaters) or stand-alone. *A Linked Repeater network is the definition when a network of repeaters are connected in which signals received by one repeater are transmitted by all the repeaters in the network (T2B03).*
- An emergency operator or someone looking to use these repeaters for emergency operation can participate and help out during an event. In my area of Florida, we have many hams that will operate on one of multiple repeaters during an event. Likely loss of one or more repeaters may occur due to antenna falling or lack of power, but not all repeaters will go down.

What is needed to know about to connect to a repeater? Well, there are several parameters on your handheld radio or mobile radio that will need to be set correctly for your radio to work properly with a repeater. Just setting the frequency is not enough. Most repeaters we use and that will be covered on the test are DUPLEX repeaters. This means the repeater uses one frequency to transmit out, and another to listen on for folks that are trying to communicate with the repeater. There are SIMPLEX repeaters which work on a single frequency. They listen for your message, store and record it, then once you finish talking, they play your message back. Kind of odd to listen to, but these repeaters are not as popular. They tend to be low-cost (Some under $100) and can be used for some emergency short-range uses or for preppers, but they are not used on commercial towers. For more on these, look at the section for SIMPLEX REPEATERS in the next chapter.

On a duplex repeater, the frequency that the repeater lists as its frequency is the frequency that it is transmitting on. When you program your radio to that frequency you can hear any repeater traffic. But – That is NOT the frequency that it is listening for you on. If you find the repeater's listening frequency, you will still not be heard unless your radio is programmed to transmit the appropriate DCS or CTCSS tones which act as a "Secret Handshake" to tell the repeater you are intentionally trying to communicate with it. This helps the repeater keep the "Riff-Raff" out – It keeps it from activating by anyone who just broadcasts on that particular frequency.

So – what parameters are needed to operate on a repeater?

- Repeaters Published frequency – This is the frequency the repeater transmits OUT on.
- ***CTCSS sub-audible tones transmitted with the voice signal for Analog repeaters – This is the "Handshake" that occurs telling the repeater you are intentionally communicating with it and opens up the squelch of the receiver (T2B02).*** If not heard, the squelch keeps the repeater from hearing your signal.
- Some repeaters will use a DCS digital code to control opening the squelch – Similar to how CTCSS works but using a digital code instead of a tone.
- If using DMR Radio you will need to set the DMR Color code to identify which talk group you are communicating with.
- ***Repeater Offset – This is a programmed offset that is the difference between the repeaters transmit (Output) frequency and it's listening (Input) frequency (T2A07).***
  In the U.S., the common repeater offset in the 2-meter band is plus or minus 600-kHz (T2A01).
  In the U.S., the common repeater offset in the 70-cm band is plus or minus 5.0-MHz. (T2A03)
- The offset direction – This is one of three options:
  - Positive – Meaning the receive frequency is ABOVE the transmit frequency by the amount set in the Frequency Offset amount above.
  - Negative – Meaning the receiving frequency is BELOW the transmit frequency by the amount set in the Frequency Offset amount above.
  - None – Meaning your radio will transmit and receive on the same frequency (Simplex).

Troubleshooting your radio when it won't work with a repeater is a common problem. In most cases it simply means that you have missed on of the following steps in programming your radio:

- You have not properly set the offset amount. This allows the radio to calculate the transmit frequency from the receive frequency. Remember the frequency you key into your radio is YOUR radios Receive/Input frequency, which happens to be the repeater's Transmit/Output frequency.
- If the repeater is using CTCSS Tones (Also referred to as PL tones in some cases) then you may not be using the proper tone. The repeater will be using a specific CTCSS tone *IF* it is using CTCSS Tones. Your tone settings must match.
- If the repeater is using DCS tones which are digital codes, then you may not be using the proper DCS tone.
- If the repeater is using DMR Color codes (For a DMR repeater) then you may not be using the right code
- Lastly, you must be using the same frequency offset as the repeater. The offset tells the repeater that when calculating for the frequency to listed in on (And that you will be transmitting on), then that frequency will be ABOVE or BELOW its frequency.

If a repeater is programmed to use 442.550 as it's frequency and this is advertised, then that means the repeater is transmitting on 442.550 and that is what you need to set your radio to – Your listening frequency. Let's say the offset is 5.0 MHz (Standard in the US). Then the offset could be 5.0 MHz ABOVE or BELOW 442.550-MHz. That means the listening frequency for the repeater, which would be your radio's transmit frequency would be calculated to either 447.550 MHz (Above) or 437.550 MHz (Below). In the U.S. we mostly use a (+) Positive offset, so you need to set your radio to Positive offset which will set up to use 447.550 MHz – 5.0 MHz ABOVE the repeaters transmit frequency (Your receive frequency).

There is only one question on the test for this troubleshooting:

(T2B04): If you are unable to connect to a repeater whose output you can hear then it is likely for one of these reasons:

- **Improper transceiver offset**
- **You are using the wrong CTCSS tone**
- **You are using the wrong DCS code**
- **All these choices are correct**

On the test, the correct answer is "All these choices are correct".

Knowing these parameters for the repeater you are going to communicate with and how to program your radio for them will allow you to use that repeater. Because every radio is different, we are not going to go over that, though in the next chapter we will for the Baofeng Radio. One recommendation we will make – Get a software application to program your radio with. I use Chirp on several different radios though I also have radios not compatible with it. A good software application will allow you to program many channels quickly and will allow you to back up your radio and store the configuration electronically.

When properly programmed, your radio will listen to the repeater on the frequency your set your radio to and that is being displayed on the radio. When transmitting, if you look at the radio display it will display a different frequency – The offset frequency which is also the frequency that the repeater should be listening to. (This assumes you are using the proper CTCSS or DCS codes).

One function of your radio used for troubleshooting is called the radio's "Reverse Mode" which allows you to LISTEN on the repeater's INPUT frequency instead of the repeater's OUTPUT frequency (T2B01) – The opposite of how you normally interact with the repeater. This is a useful function if you are at or near the repeater's physical location and are troubleshooting to determine if a signal is reaching the repeater.

Who determines the frequencies of the Repeaters?

When the owner of a repeater is planning to put up the repeater, they coordinate with the Volunteer Frequency Coordinator recognized by local amateurs (T1A08). The Volunteer Frequency Coordinator is a group selected by amateur operators in a local or regional area whose stations are eligible to be repeater or auxiliary stations (T1A09).

Using the repeater

When using the repeater, the appropriate way to call another station on a repeater if you know the other station's call sign is to **say the station's call sign, then identify with your call sign (T2A04)**. **If you are listening on a repeater and looking for any contact, this is done by stating your station's call sign followed by the word "monitoring" (T2A09)**. If you hear this, feel free to jump in and talk to them.

Frequency Bandwidth on a repeater

When using ham radio your radio in Analog mode normally uses 25-MHz of bandwidth for a voice transmission. For digital DMR Radio, the voice bandwidth is 12.5-kHz, which is half of what analog radio uses. Analog radios typically also use 25-MHz on Ham frequencies for SIMPLEX radio communication – That is radio-to-radio. But – What is the bandwidth use of a repeater?

Question (T8A09) in the question pool asks this question. The approximate bandwidth of a VHF Repeater FM Voice signal is between 10-kHz and 15-kHz.

6.D – Let's talk about Satellites

The last topic we are going to cover in this chapter relates to space satellites and the use of satellites. **A Satellite is defined by the FCC Part 97 rules as "An Amateur Station located more than 50-kM above the earth's surface" (T1A07).** This includes anything from a limited operation radio station or repeater in orbit, to the International Space Station (ISS). Another term you may see on the test is for a "LEO". **LEO is an abbreviation for LOW-EARTH-ORBIT (T8B10)** and may include a satellite that is normally at an altitude of 1000-km or less, though the number is not clearly defined for the test.

A Beacon is defined under the FCC Part 97 rules as an amateur station transmitting communications for the purpose or observing propagation or related experimental activities (T1A06). A beacon is usually a one-way radio transmitter. By listening for a beacon, you can observe the quality of your signal and the direction of the signal gaining highly useful information. By knowing the location of the beacon, you can also determine both your ability to receive the beacon's radio transmission, and how well you can hear that signal. **A Satellite Beacon is a transmission from a Satellite that contains status information (T8B05).**

As a technician licensed amateur operator, you will be able to use satellites for communication – primary from the aspect of testing your range and capabilities. You can reach satellites with a radio as simple as a handheld radio unit using an appropriate directional antenna. In addition, **any amateur holding a technician class or higher license can communicate with a satellite on the ham bands and also can communicate with the International Space Station (ISS) on VHF, UHF or any allowable bands per your license (T1B02)**. The ISS routinely operates on VHF/UHF frequencies for ham communication.

Satellites can operate in many ham modes. ***Common Ham modes include SSB, FM, and CW/Data. Question T8B04 in the pool questions is properly answered with "All of these choices are correct".*** Commonly a satellite may operate on multiple frequencies, allowing one frequency for uplink (Receiving) communication and another frequency for downlink (Transmitting) communication. ***When a satellite is said to be operating in U/V mode, this means that the satellite uplink is in the 70-cm band and the downlink is in the 2-Meter band (T8B08).***

During Satellite communication you may experience different types of conditions which will affect the quality of your communication. Some of these conditions include, but not necessarily are limited to the following:

- ***Doppler Shift (T8B07)***
  Doppler Shift is referred to as an observed change in signal frequency caused by relative motion between the satellite and earth station. This means as the satellite is moving in orbit towards you or away from you, the motion of the satellite may cause a slight shift in frequency for your communication. This could result in your need to alter your frequency slightly to maintain the communication.

- ***Spin Fading (T8B09)***
  Spin Fading is a distortion that can occur caused by the rotation of the satellite and its antenna. As the satellite spins in orbit moving toward or away from you, the spinning will point the antenna towards you, then away, then towards, and continue to repeat creating a fading effect.

When communicating with a satellite as with ground communication, you should only use as much power as needed to reach the satellite. Overpowering your signal may result in the blocking of other communicators trying to also reach the satellite. Test question (***T8B12)*** asks ***"A Way to determine whether your satellite uplink power is neither too low nor too high"***, of which the correct answer is ***"Your signal strength on the downlink should be about the same as the beacon"***. But – How do you tell? This question is directed towards the communication to a satellite which has an uplink and a separate downlink frequency. As the satellite operates, it will usually be broadcasting a CW beacon. As you transmit your signal, you will then be able to receive your signal back on the receiving frequency (Which is also transmitting the beacon signal). You can compare the quality of the beacon signal to your signal being broadcast back and adjust your power up or down based on the quality of the beacon and your re-transmitted signal. ***Remember – Use only the amount of power you need to and do not overpower.***

Satellites & Software

We have just discussed that you can communicate with satellites when you get your new license. But – How do you find them?

Well – There's an App for that! In fact, there are multiple software applications that do that. I'm not making recommendations for any, but at the end of this section I do include a reference that will. Satellite tracking software, if running from your computer, tablet, or smartphone, use several characteristics as input factors for satellite tracking. ***These elements used by satellite tracking software programs are known as The Keplerian Elements (T8B06) and include the following:***

- Epoch
- Orbital Inclination
- Right Ascension of Ascending Node (R.A.A.N.)
- Argument of Perigee

- Eccentricity
- Mean Motion
- Mean Anomaly
- Drag (optional)

Exact details of what these are can be found at AMSAT's website at the following link:

https://www.amsat.org/keplerian-elements-tutorial/

These factors are used by the software to determine which satellites you may be able to reach from your location along with where and when you should be able to reach the satellite in orbit. The software can provide you several important pieces of information including:

- Maps showing the real-time position of the satellite track over Earth
- The time, azimuth, and elevation of the start, maximum altitude, and end of a pass
- The apparent frequency of the satellite transmission, including effects of Doppler shift

Pool question (T8B03) specifically asks about what information can be provided by software of which the answer is "All these choices are correct".

Telemetry is information that is health and status information about a satellite or space station usually transmitted by the satellite or space station and is available to anyone for receiving (T8B11). This is information used by tracking software, as well as the Keplerian Elements data, for tracking the software.

For more information about Satellites with Ham Radio, as well as recommendations for software, antennas, and details on specific satellite capabilities, visit AMSAT.ORG's website at https://www.amsat.org/ .

Chapter 7 – Not on the Test

In this chapter we are going to cover a variety of topics that may not be covered on the Ham radio tech exam and could actually be skipped in it's entirety, however I am expanding by including many topics here that will give you a better overall grasp of Ham radio and to help you with topics you may need to know soon after getting licensed.

7.1- Finding Repeaters for VHF/UHF Talking

We have already talked about repeaters earlier in the book. But now we want to have some focus on these wonderful devices and make sure you understand just how important they are.

I live in Florida. Between June and December, we live in Hurricane country – always aware and ready just in case. (August through October are the most active months). For Ham operators, there are two types of Ham use around hurricane season. HF Radio allows an operator to set up anywhere and using either a traditional HF radio antenna, or what is referred to as an NVIS antenna for short-range HF, a ham operator can communicate without the need for repeaters. (NVIS is Near Vertical Incidence Skywave)

But – add a repeater network and now we immediately increase our local-use capabilities, and we grow our pool of volunteers. Most of the shelters around the Tampa Bay area where I live are within range of a repeater with a handheld radio. And during Hurricane Michael in 2018 when the panhandle was devastated, all the repeaters stayed up and operational allowing hams to still communicate from their handheld radios even though cellular systems were devastated for weeks. Line cuts had effectively ruined most cellular networks for over two weeks except for one. (Some networked repeaters were disconnected from the network but still remained operational for local use).

Full Duplex Repeaters are electronic frequency repeating devices that receive a signal on one frequency and retransmit on a second frequency simultaneously. Usually, these frequencies are slightly offset. In the VHF band the normal offset is 600 kHz + or – from the primary frequency, and in UHF the offset is 5Mhz + or - from the primary frequency. This means that if you program your radio to receive on 449.125 MHz with an offset of (-) 5Mhz, then the radio will transmit on 444.125-MHz. This offset allows the repeater to listen on one frequency, 444.125-Mhz and then immediately retransmit on 449.125-MHz to all other operators. You won't hear the transmission of course because you have your microphone keyed and are talking, but all other operators will hear you. This is what allows for "Live" communication – no delay between your speaking and others hearing you.

In addition to having offset frequencies, you also will have to program your radio with a tone to use as a "Squelch Tone". This is a tone that the repeater specifically listens for to know to repeat the incoming signal. There are a number of standard CTCSS Squelch tones that your radio can be set for and which tones to use are depending on the settings of the repeater you are using. (Radio Menu items 11 & 13 cover these tones)

CTCSS RADIO TONES

67.0	82.5	100.0	123.0	151.4	186.2	225.7
69.3	85.4	103.5	127.3	156.7	192.8	229.1
79.9	88.5	107.2	131.8	162.2	203.5	233.6
74.4	91.5	110.9	136.5	167.9	206.5	241.8
77.0	94.8	114.8	141.3	173.8	210.7	250.3
79.7	97.4	118.8	146.2	179.9	218.1	254.1

In most cases these tones will be published by the club or organization that runs the repeater for public use. But – If the club or organization chooses to not publish the tone that is their option. Some radios can detect and set themselves for the specific PL tone being used. Other radios may have a scanning function to allow your radio to identify the tone being used.

If you are programming from CHIRP and perform a Repeater Book query using chirp, in nearly all cases the proper tone will be pulled and programmed for you.

Repeater Planning & Repeater Coordinators

The frequencies used by repeaters in an area will be coordinated by a "Repeater Coordinator", which is an organization that tracks and plans all repeaters in a geographic area. It is the responsibility of the Repeater Coordinator to track the power, location, and frequency of all repeaters as well as the tones being used, and then to assign out frequencies and tones as well as any other information to repeater operators wishing to stand up a new repeater. This coordination is meant to prevent conflict between repeaters. Frequencies and settings are reused in an area normally. In Florida we have many repeaters on the same frequencies and tones, however the repeater coordinator ensures that these are not located within proximity of each other thus preventing confusion and communications overlaps.

The repeater itself is located within a data center or communications center cabinet. The repeater is connected to antennas which are mounted as high as possible. Popular locations include the tops of tall buildings, or on antenna towers running from a few hundred to several hundred feet (Or over a thousand feet) in the air. These are shared towers where multiple antenna systems are located which may include community Television and Radio station antennas. The higher the better for us because the repeaters we use are VHF/UHF frequency based – Line-of-Sight. The greater the height, the greater the range we can talk.

To get more details about specific repeaters or repeater networks try looking for them on one of these websites:

1. Radio Reference
   https://www.radioreference.com/

2. RepeaterBook.com
   https://repeaterbook.com/

3. LiveCentral.com
   http://www.levinecentral.com/repeaters/google_mapping.php

4. Amateur Radio Newsline
   https://www.arnewsline.org/repeater-list

5. CHIRP
   https://chirp.danplanet.com/projects/chirp/wiki/Home

I am including Chirp because you can run the Query function in Chirp and pull a list of repeaters based on county or distance from your location. That list can be exported for use later and even printed.

Repeater Cost

If you are wondering about how much it costs to get a **Professional** Full-Duplex repeater up and running, the cost usually starts at over a thousand dollars and heads up from there. Repeaters are sophisticated hardware that go well beyond that of your handheld radio or mobile radio. The filtering for a full-duplex repeater is performed by a high-quality Duplexer which makes it possible for the repeater to be able to filter the received signals and transmitted signals for simultaneous work on the same antenna system. The cost to maintain a repeater is high also – Requiring specially trained personnel to climb the towers, when necessary, at a high cost to the repeater owner. (For repeaters mounted in a professional/commercial tower system).

If you are wanting to experiment with a repeater, then there is a low-cost solution to allow you to connect two radios together and configure them as repeaters. These are definitely "Amateur" repeaters and may work for temporary use but would not make a good permanent solution. I have one that I have used in training classes and even camping trips with other Hams. See the end of this chapter for more on this.

SIMPLEX Repeaters

If you do want to play with repeaters at an entry-level stage, there is an inexpensive repeater solution that you can get into for around a hundred dollars that may interest you. In this case, enter the SIMPLEX Repeater. These are quite simple devices in comparison to the complex Full Duplex repeaters that we have been talking about, and function at a much more basic level.

With a simplex repeater, a small device is set up with a radio. The radio can be your handheld radio (You will need a specific interface cable based on the radio). The device is attached to the radio through a cable which runs from the Mic/Speaker connector on your radio into the small simplex repeater, often just the size of a bedroom alarm clock/radio. The radio is placed on a frequency in Simplex mode – same frequency for both receives and transmit, and then the repeater is plugged in. When the radio receives a communication from someone, it simply records the message coming in and then when finished it re-transmits the message out on the same radio.

For you – the person sending the message, this is odd because immediately after you speak your message into the radio, then the repeater plays back your message in your voice. For others that are within hearing distance of your radio they will also hear your message twice – the first time when you originally sent it and the second time when the message goes back out. But for anyone else not in range of your radio they will only hear you once.

Just like a Full-duplex repeater, you can set your radio and simplex repeater up with a raised antenna which improves the transmission range. I have two types of antennas I use for this purpose – One is a military style pole tower with eight 4-foot fiberglass poles that can be raised up to 32' in the air. I also have then a lightweight 8' painters' pole that I can attach for a total height of 40', then the antenna is added.

Based on the formula we covered in a prior chapter about radio horizons, this extends my radio range out as follows:

Radio Horizon (In Km) = 4.12 x √Height (In Meters) - and 40 Feet in our example = 12.2 Meters, so:

Radio Horizon (Km) = 4.12 x √12.2;   and √12.2 = 3.49

Radio Horizon (Km) = 4.12 x 3.49;   therefore

Radio Horizon (Km) = 4.12 x 3.49 which equals 14.38 km

14.38 km x .621 = 8.92 Miles

So, if looking for a way to deploy a short-term emergency repeater, I can do this relatively easily with my Handheld radio! Now this will require some cable and antenna adapters to get the antenna up and operating from our radio which we will cover in a later chapter. There are other factors to think about such as length and type of feed line which can consume a handheld radio's transmitting power.

Besides an external device to have for working as a repeater, I need to also mention that you can use some models of radios as simplex repeaters without the need for any additional hardware. Though this is a capability that is beyond the capabilities of most radios, I do happen to own a more advanced radio by Baofeng Tech which is their DMR 6x2 radio (A Firmware updated Anytone 828). Though this is a DMR Digital radio, the radio also works fine as an analog radio. Advantages of this radio include being able to store 4,000 channels, being able to group channels together, and having advanced functions such as a simplex repeater built in. That's right – I can set this radio up without anything additional as a small simplex repeater (For DMR).

If you decide you would like to play with setting up a simplex repeater, two models which I am aware of are:

1. SURECOM makes several types of small repeaters. All will require one to two radios for use for receiving and transmitting. The models they make are in both DUPLEX and SIMPLEX.

2. ARGENT makes a small simplex repeater that can be used with a single radio for simplex repeater operation. I have had better success with this repeater for SIMPLEX operation.

You will find that for a technician level Ham operator, that repeaters are the best tool you can to expand your range and use of your new radio. If you do fall into the Prepper community, then a simple simplex repeater may be something that interests you for extending your radio's operational range in an area where you may be with others.

Definitions: SIMPLEX, DUPLEX, and Cross-Band Repeaters

SIMPLEX Repeater: This is a small device that connects to your radio and records incoming messages digitally. The message then is immediately re-broadcast back out on the same radio that received the signal.

Characteristics include:

- Cheaper (1 Radio, 1 Antenna, 1 Repeater box)
- Simpler – Works well with SIMPLEX, no Offsets or Shift settings
- Users have to listen to their own message after transmitting, so better for short messaging back and forth.
- Works with all HAM radios and can work with GMRS Radios as well.

DUPLEX Repeater: This type of repeater has two components – Receiver and Transmitter. In a small device such as we built it requires two radios and can require two antennas. A Professional quality Duplex repeater can cost $1,000 or more – These are the most common types you will find readily available to connect to.

Characteristics include:

- More expensive and complex than a Simplex repeater.
- More equipment.
- Can work with 1 or 2 antennas – With 1 Antenna you will need a Duplexer.
- Filtering requirements for single-band 1-antenna repeater are for high quality – high-quality duplexer will be needed ($$$).
- Works with all HAM radios and can work with GMRS Radios as well as long as the radios support CTCSS, Shift Offset, etc)

Cross-Band Repeater: This repeater is a DUPLEX repeater however it uses two separate bands for Receive and Transmit. By using two bands we are receiving and transmitting with significant frequency separation allowing Duplex repeater functions to occur in simpler radio systems.

Characteristics include:

- DUPLEX capabilities with less expensive equipment than a professional DUPLEX Repeater.
- Many Mobile transceivers can perform this function.
- Easier to work with 1 antenna.
- Radios have to support Dual-Monitoring to operate on two frequencies at the same time. Single-receiver/channel transceivers will not work with a cross-band repeater.

What happens when the power or Internet goes out to Repeaters?

In the event of a wide-spread power outage what happens to a repeater or a repeater network? Most amateur ham repeaters are run by clubs. Most are also set up with some type of backup power – either a UPS for a short-duration power outage, or with a Generator to provide longer duration power since a generator can be refueled.

But the establishment of backup power is totally up to the repeater operators. In a repeater network, you will likely have a good backup power plan established. As a part of the network, the repeaters are more critical and noticed in the event of a failure. A responsible repeater owner participating in a network will likely take this into account and provide a backup contingency plan.

But what about if communications or the Internet goes down? For independent repeaters, loss of communications or the Internet will not make too big of a difference. Independent repeaters work alone where they extend the range of VHF/UHF radio communications. But – If the repeater is a part of a multi-repeater coordinated network, and if the repeaters are connected via a back-bone Internet connection, then in most cases the repeaters will drop into an "Independent" mode where they still work, but each as an independent repeater covering a very localized area.

In my area of Florida, there is a very well-known multi-repeater network heavily used for casual communications as well as emergency planning and emergency coordination. This repeater network has an Internet backbone for synchronizing all repeater transmissions across the area. If a failure in the Internet does occur, then repeaters not able to connect will then work as independent local repeaters.

The reason this is important to understand is so that you know that the dependence on a repeater for extending your range works only as well as the current situation. Repeaters are wonderful devices but factor the possibility of not having access to these into your emergency plans. Without access to a repeater, your next best solutions will be:

- Assembling and readying an external antenna, best on a pole, for extending your radio range.
- Purchase and set up a 25-watt or 50-watt mobile radio with an appropriate antenna for more power and range.
- Consider taking your license to the next level – A General license allows you to get a HF Radio which allows for communication over much greater distances (Hundreds to Thousands of miles).

7.2 - Battery Box – Power Solutions for Portable operation

For my own power solutions, I have settled on three separate solutions which can provide me enough power to last through a short or extended power outage and power all my communications needs. These may not be the solutions you need, however an explanation of my own solutions and why I am using them will help you to understand options you may want to consider looking at. The descriptions of the designs are basic. Look for my book to be released on simple Battery Based Power solutions with detailed plans, or you can find plans online through google and YouTube.

Solution 1: Solar Generator

I have settled on using an Inergy Apex Solar Generator to provide limited AC Power, up to 550-watts of sustained output as well as 12-volt and USB power out. The key features that I look at in any solar generator are:

- Power levels out – Mine can spike to 1500-watts for about 5 minutes, then sustain 550-watts. This is enough for a quick 2-minute zap with the microwave, though I would prefer if re-purchasing at least 1000-watts sustained.

- Lithium based battery – This is a MUST. Lead-Acid batteries are much heavier and have much less power. Use only a Lithium based battery solution (My Recommendation).

- Pure Sinewave Output – Critical for any type of sensitive equipment. This is the standard but be sure on this specification.

- Solar Charge Capacity – How much solar can the system take in. Mine supports up to 500-watts in, which is about what I would consider as a minimum. Many units support only 100 watts or less. **BASE THIS ON YOUR NEED**. If the unit charges too slowly you will not be able to have it charged up during the next day before nightfall.

- Power Outlets – Mine supports (6) 120-volt outputs (12.5 Amps Max combined), (2) 12-volt accessory ports, and (4) USB ports.

This first solution was my first solar generator and will provide a decent amount of power for some use, including refrigeration and lighting. The problems with this solution which led to additional solutions stemmed from the 1-kWh battery. During a full power outage this would not last overnight with some lighting and keeping my refrigerator running. The charging capacity is good allowing me to fully recharge it the next day, but by middle of the night it would run out of energy.

By creating the two battery solutions I have listed coming up I can remove some of the load as well as being able to add my larger 1.4-kW batteries as additional charging sources for this unit thereby giving me plenty of power to keep minimal devices on through the night. I need to note that the battery expansion from Inergy for the Apex never materialize and therefore I designed my own solution at half the price with more power, though the charging is slower as my expansion connects through the Solar Charge port instead of through the battery expansion port.

The Inergy Apex 1500-watt Solar Generator (Now Discontinued) Offers up to 1500-watt AC Out, plus multiple DC Power options & Solar Recharging. Many manufactures now produce similar devices requiring no gasoline.

Solution 2: Simple 12-volt LiFeP04 Battery Box

I have built two of these but will only describe one here as the first I built had design flaws, which was the reason for building the second.

The components I used are:

- 12.8 Volt, 36-Amp/Hour LiFeP04 Battery from Amazon ($130)
- 12-volt Cigarette Lighter Port from Amazon ($8)
- 12-volt Voltmeter from Amazon ($6)
- Plastic Ammo case from Harbor Freight ($12)
- 12-volt Keyed Power switch from Harbor Freight ($7)
- Wiring and Anderson Connectors for Radio power and external power expansion ($20)
- 600-amp Battery Buses for power distribution (Very small, $10)

Simple 12-volt Power box with 12-volt accessory port, 12-volt digital meter, & power out via Anderson Connectors popular for Ham Radio use.

The design for this unit came from the need for me to be able to power all 12-volt appliances in my camper, mostly while opening it and doing maintenance. It also provides more than enough power for my radio kits and can be simultaneously recharged from solar panels, though my normal charging method is simply from a Lithium Charger purchased from Amazon for about $30.

Thanks to the battery I have used, the battery provides plenty of power for short-duration needs including powering my entire camper and operating the slides on the camper. The battery is small at only 36-Amp/Hours, but it is very light weight making this battery system very portable and easy to use. Among the lessons I learned while building this system from my first are:

1. Not to cram too much into the Ammo box – In the first I included a PWM charge controller which made working space tighter in the box.
2. Not to include 12-volt or other outlets in the hinged top – The wiring became very sensitive to the opening and closing of the top causing wires to pull loose. The use of the lid for wiring in the first design was due to limited working space in lesson #1.
3. Not to use Lead-Acid Batteries – In my first design I used (2) 20-amp/hour Lead Acid batteries in parallel which in dimensions were the same as the newer LiFeP04 battery. But – They are heavy. And

with Lead Acid you can only discharge 50% of the total charge before damage. With the LiFePO4 I can discharge 90% and the battery will be safe.

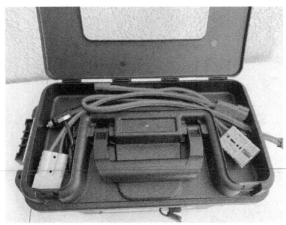

The Top storage is used for storing various connection adapters used for radios or even plugging into my camper for 12-volt utility power.

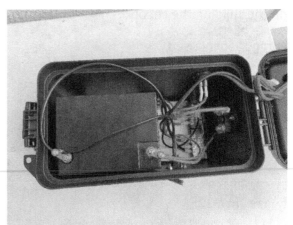

A Look inside shows the battery on the left side, and most of the wiring to the right. All power outlets are fused for protection of over draining the battery

A Key to making the Mounting all work

This was not my first battery box attempt. The biggest changes I made between my first and second were:

1. To first use a piece of 1x6 PVC board that I taped to be bottom of the box with double-sided 3M tape. This kept me from having to drill through the plastic to secure mounts and connectors – I could mount these into the PVC board instead.

   I have found working with PVC board is great – it can be picked up at your local Home Depot or Lowes and works better than wood in that double sided tape will stick extremely well to it. I use 3M Double sided tape or Gorilla tape usually found in the paint area of your home improvement store. Silicon adhesive also works well as well as screws.

2. I avoided attaching any outlets or connections to the lid that opened. Each time I would open or close the original box, the stress and movement of the wires encouraged the pulling of wires which at times unplugged outlets and worse created lose wires that could short. I do add a Red/Black Zip wire from the battery or fuse panel with an Anderson connection at the end that is loose and can be fed out to a radio or other device for powering.

Solution 3: Best - 1.4kWh LiFeP04 Battery in a "Pelican" Case

This solution for me does prove third time is the charm. The goal of this system was to provide larger capacity for my radio and communications needs, and also to fill a larger power need for more than a few hours in my RV Camper.

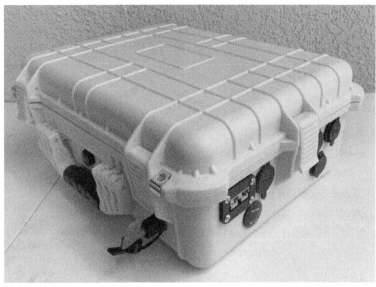

For this solution I made the following changes from my second solution:

1. Batteries – I used higher capacity 3.2v LiFeP04 batteries in a 12.8-volt configuration. Each of the (8) batteries I used provide 55-AH f energy for a total of 1.4 kWh of energy. ($220)

This "Pelican Case" battery system has 1.4kWh of power, internal BMS, On/Off switch 12-volt power meter, and several types of DC Power Ports.

2. Case – I upgraded to a Pelican-style case from Harbor Freight for better protection of the battery and electronic components. ($50)

3. BMS – I used a Battery Management System which is a circuit board installed with the system that limits the power in and out to the battery, and also provides balancing and protection of the battery cells. This added over $120 to the cost of the system but greatly protects the system also. ($120)

4. More Ports – Bigger case allowed me to establish more ports. This new unit has (2) 12-volt ports, (2) USB Ports, (2) Standard Anderson Connector ports (For Ham Radios up to 20-Amps each), a single 50-Amp Anderson port (Larger wires & Connector), a 12-voltmeter, and several fuses for each type of port. ($50)

5. A 60-Amp circuit-breaker added to the unit to limit the power out of the larger Anderson connection, though the BMS also has limit protection designed into it. ($10)

6. Wiring and Buses for wiring management ($20)

The "Pelican Case" power box with a 300-watt Pure Sinewave inverter to the 12-volt accessory plug. I can connect a 500-watt PS power inverter or a 750-watt inverter via the 50-amp rectangular Anderson Power port.

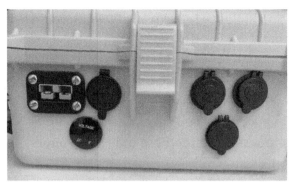

Power outlets include, from top-left row to right (1) 50-Amp Anderson Outlet, (2) Dual 45A Anderson outlets (Dust cover on), (3 & 4) Dual 12-volt car Accessory outlets. On the second row from left to right: (5) 12-voltmeter and lastly we have a dual USB port installed. All have dust covers on.

Here to the right is the internal view of the 1.4-kWh Pelican Battery unit. I am using (8) 60280 55-ah 3.2v LiFePO4 batteries from BatteryHookup.com.

On top of the batteries, I mounted a BMS (Battery Management System) which regulates the charging and discharging of the battery system. It also has a Bluetooth module allowing me to monitor and manage the power from my iPhone, even allowing me to remotely turn it on or off. I also have a physical heavy-duty keyed power switch installed. Power also runs through a 100-amp circuit breaker to protect from over current.

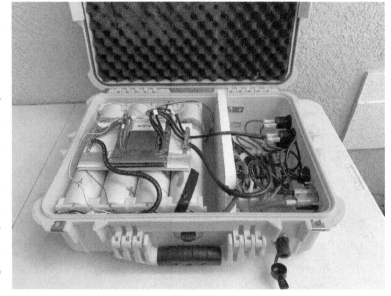

No AC Outlet or Charge Controllers for solutions #2 & #3

If you did not notice from my notes on the 2nd and 3rd solutions, I did not include any AC Outlets, Power Inverters, or Solar chargers in these second solutions. This was because the focus of both solutions was to provide 12-volt power out for radios and camper use, and to provide DC power out which can be easily derived from the 12-volt batteries.

If I need AC power from either 12-volt battery box, I have both a 300-watt and a 500-watt Pure-sinewave Inverter which I can connect to either the 12-volt Cigarette lighter accessory outlet, or to the 50-amp Anderson accessory outlet. (For the 500-watt inverter I would only use the 50-amp outlet of the larger battery box).

For charging I would use my Lithium compatible Renogy PWM Charge controller to interface from external batteries into the battery boxes, or I could plug either battery box directly into my camper's MPPT Charge controller. I have mounted both the 500-watt Pure-sinewave inverter and the Renogy PWM Charge controller into a separate plastic Ammo box for cleanliness while my 300-watt Pure sinewave inverter can connect through the 12-volt cigarette lighter outlets which both allow up to 15-amps of power out (A Car cigarette outlet is typically limited to 10-amps).

As this book is focused on the topic of communications, I have included this appendix for reference only and will not go deeper into the power system designs. But I do stress that you need to take power capabilities into mind when planning your solutions – a reason I wrote two separate books specifically on the topics. Both books go much, much deeper into depth on the topic and do include planning and specification topics on fuel-based generator solutions.

In Summary

All of the battery power solutions I have shown above will work to provide power for an emergency radio, and in some cases other devices. At a minimum a 12-volt car or marine battery would work with a method to recharge it either from a gas generator or solar panels.

Solar Generators which provide both 12-volt power and some level of AC power are more available in recent years from Harbor Freight, Home Depot, Wal-Mart or Costco. Costs are down to as little as about $300 to start or more – just make sure you can recharge these. A Gasoline generator is a good option but does require the fuel to run and can bring unwanted attention if running at night.

7.3 - BaoFeng Programming for Repeaters

In this chapter we are going to review the process for hand programming a handheld radio. This is an important skill which is covered in all manuals and may be needed if operating during an emergency where there is either no internet or no computer to use for computer programming. For the example I am going to use the popular Baofeng Handheld radio, which is very popular with new hams, Emergency operators (As a backup radio) and Preppers. The following instructions have been pulled out of my popular book, "*So, You just bought a Baofeng Radio... Now What?*" which goes over the use of these radios for new ham operators and preppers.

So, you have your Baofeng Radio. You have mastered being able to talk to others in Simplex mode – That is where you and the other radio user are talking and listening on the same frequency. But – Simplex mode is limited. You will likely be limited to between 1 and 3 miles of range even with an updated and external antenna on one of these handhelds.

But fear not – There is an easy way to get from dozens to hundreds of miles of range from your little handheld radio. That answer comes from Repeaters. A club or commercial repeater is a device that is located hundreds of feet up on a building or an antenna tower. If you are living in a mountain area, then you may find repeaters that are located thousands of feet up on a tower that is on the top of a tower. Most repeaters will have a 25-mile range as a rough estimate assuming no extreme repeater heights are possible. This means that I can stand in one location talking to a repeater 25 miles away from me to another operator 25-miles on the other side of the repeater, totaling 50 miles apart.

Repeaters operate on the principle of using two frequencies slightly offset. Most repeaters are extremely expensive units with the ability to filter and re-transmit out on the same antenna or two antennas physically close to each other and on different nearby frequencies. A UHF repeater that is advertised for instance to operate on a frequency of 442.550 MHz actually operates on two frequencies. The 442.550 MHz frequency is the TRANSMITTING frequency of the repeater, and also the RECEIVING frequency of your handheld radio. So, it operates on two frequencies at the same time.

Your handheld radio, when properly programmed, will actually transmit on what is called an "Offset Frequency", or a frequency that is offset to the frequency of the repeater. For UHF that standard offset value is 5.0 MHz (VHF Offset amount is 600 kHz or 0.6 MHz).

What does this mean? It means that when your radio is properly programmed to receive on a frequency of 442.500 MHz which is the transmitting frequency of the repeater, then you radio will TRANSMIT on an offset frequency of 447.550 (5.0 MHz *above* the receiving frequency). And guess what – That repeater that is transmitting on 442.550 MHz is receiving on the 447.550 MHz frequency. Two different frequencies. So, your properly programmed ham radio is working on opposite frequencies for transmitting and receiving from the repeater.

Now that we understand that your radio and the repeater are using two different frequencies, we need to now realize that the repeater operates so fast that it takes the radio signal it is receiving on 447.550 MHz from John 25 miles away from the repeater and 50 miles away from you, and it almost immediately begins retransmitting that signal back out on 442.550 MHz which you can then hear on your radio. So, you are not hearing John directly – you are hearing John from the repeater. If John were standing 100 feet away from you and looking at you across the field talking to you on his radio, you are still hearing him through the repeater, not from his radio **IF** you and John are using the repeater to talk. Now in that case the preferred communication method would be SIMPLEX where you and John are talking directly to each other. If you use the repeater then everyone within a 25 to 50-mile radius is listening to you both talking. Not a very private conversation. (Even in simplex mode your conversation is not private, but the range of those who can hear you is limited to the power you are putting out and the capability of your radio. Set your radio to 1-watt of power and you will be limited to only a short distance.

So here we can see the importance of repeaters. I almost exclusively communicate on repeaters for my operation. Unless I am volunteering for a community event using radios, or I am communicating with friends camping or on a hike. I use repeaters.

NETWORK REPEATERS

Now let's take repeater operation a step further. You now understand that a repeater has a general range of 25 miles or more. Also, realize that repeaters communicate using two frequencies – one for transmitting to your receiving radio, and another frequency that receives your transmitting frequency (And others as well). But what about more range? Here in my home in Tampa Florida I can communicate on the NI4CE Repeater system 200 miles from point to point. On another repeater network, SARNET, I can communicate from Pensacola in the panhandle of Florida down into the Keys – A distance of over 700 miles (Driving) and a drive of over 11 hours. I can talk on the radio network, with some gaps in between, for the full drive.

Repeaters can be interconnected by creating a backbone connection between the repeaters. In this configuration, when one repeater receives a communication then that communication is forwarded out the backbone and retransmitted on all repeaters simultaneously. The type of backbone connection can vary – from and internet-based backbone, to microwave radio transmitters beaming between repeater towers. Regardless of the technology used, for you this means a wider communication range for you when talking through a network connected repeater system.

Both repeater networks I described above are frequently used in storm season when emergency communications teams with ARES-RACES spin up. As operators are placed in evacuation centers. If power is lost in an evacuation and regular communications fails, then in most cases these repeaters will continue to allow communication between evacuation centers and the county EOC center. (In most cases backup power and repeater operation will outlast the worst of the storm system.) In 2018 when Hurricane Michael struck the panhandle of Florida and county government communications failed – deputies and emergency services dispatched without radio, Ham operators and the SARNET repeaters continued to operate. (Though the repeater backbone did go down, each repeater continued to operate as independent repeaters).

RADIO TONES AND OFFSETS

Before moving to programming our radios for repeater use, I want to explain two more important aspects that need to be understood.

Radio tones are sub-audible tones that are transmitted with your communication to the repeater. Analog ham radio on VHF and UHF can be set to transmit no tone, or to transmit a sub-audible tone ranging from just 67 hertz up to 254.1 hertz. These tones act as keys to the repeater of sorts – if you are transmitting the same tone signal from your radio that the repeater is expecting to hear from a valid transmission, then the repeater accepts your communication and re-transmits it out on its transmitting frequency for everyone to hear. If the tone is not correct, then your transmission is completely ignored. This explains why many individuals try to talk through a repeater you may be hearing others talking on, but they seem to ignore you when you talk back. You are not transmitting the correct tone, so they do not hear you. PL Tone is also referred to as CTCSS Tone (Continuous Tone Coded Squelch System).

> Both CTCSS tones and PL tones refer to audible tones used in radio systems. "PL" is short for "Privacy Line" and was a trademarked version of tones used by Motorola. CTCSS is a generic reference to the same audible tone process. Today these terms are often used interchangeably.

Another tone system that some repeaters use is DCS which stands for Digital Coded Squelch. This is a digital method that sends a digital code to the repeater to confirm operation between radio transmitter and repeater. Because DCS uses digital codes, there are more code signals available for use in areas where repeaters may overlap coverage. DCS is a newer coding method and not as commonly used on amateur repeaters.

The Radio Offset value as explained earlier in this chapter is the amount of the frequency difference between the transit and receive frequencies. In our above UHF example, we used a 5-MHz difference between the repeater's transmit frequency of 442.550 MHz and it's receive frequency of 447.550 MHz. As also mentioned, our VHF offset frequency value is 600-kHz, or 0.6-MHz. But – what about the direction of the offset? Is the offset amount above or below the receive frequency on your radio? Keep in mind that both of our frequencies, one for transmit and the second for receive, must always remain within the frequency limits of the band you are working in. With a transmit frequency of 442.550 MHz then you could technically go 5-MHz above or 5-MHz below the 442.550-MHz.

In the US the rules for offset direction are:

70-cm Band	442.000 MHz – 445.000 MHz	+ 5 MHz - Positive Offset
70-cm Band	447.000 MHz – 450.000 MHz	- 5 MHz - Negative Offset
2-Meter Band	145.200 MHz - 145.500 MHz	-600 kHz - Negative Offset
2-Meter Band	146.610 MHz - 146.970 MHz	-600 kHz - Negative Offset

2-Meter Band	147.000 MHz - 147.390 MHz	+600 kHz - Positive Offset

These rules are not set in concrete and apply in the US only. However, they are generally followed by Ham Operators and Repeater Operators.

We have now talked about Transmit and Receive frequencies, offset amounts, offset direction, and Tone signals. Now we are going to use all this information to apply it to programming our Baofeng radios for a repeater. Above I mentioned the NI4CE Repeater network that is located in West-Central Florida. We will use one of those repeaters as a model for our programming by hand of our Baofeng radio.

The specifications I am going to use for the repeater are:

Transmit Frequency (Downlink) (Your radio's RECEIVE frequency)	442.550 MHz
Receive Frequency (Uplink) (Your radio's TRANSMIT frequency)	447.550 MHz
Uplink/Transmit tone	100.00 Hz
Downlink/Receive tone	100.00 Hz
Offset Amount	5.0 MHz
Offset Direction	+ (Positive)

Before we start programming, we want to look at the Menu settings on our radio that we will be programming to affect these changes.

Menu Option #	Purpose
11: R-CTCS	Receive CTCSS/PL Tone. Setting this value will tell the radio not to play a transmission over the speaker UNLESS it is transmitting this tone frequency.
13: T-CTCS	Transmit CTCSS/PL Tone. This tells the Baofeng radio to TRANSMIT the tone you set with your radio transmission. Matching this to the repeater will tell the repeater you are intending your message to that repeater.
25: SFT-D	Shift Direction – "+", "-", or no shift. Use No shift when transmitting simplex (Usually to another radio directly) and to a repeater use the value that matches the repeater.
26: Offset	The frequency offset is the amount of offset used to communicate to a repeater. For UHF this is 5.0 MHz, for VHF we use 600 kHz. (In the US).
27: Mem-CH	ADD Memory Channel – We will use this menu option to store our frequency into a memory channel for recall when we are working in Channel Mode.
28: Del-CH	DELETE Memory Channel – We may not use this. If you find a channel to delete then this menu option will be used to clear that channel.

To program our Baofeng radio, these are the ONLY settings that we will need to program. We will also need to confirm an empty channel on our radio to insert our new programming into. To do this, follow these steps:

1. Turn your radio on and place it in CHANNEL mode. *On the UV82 and similar models this is done by holding the MENU button down while turning the radio on while the radio speaks "Channel Mode"*

*(You may have to do this twice). On the BF-F8HP/UV-5R use the [**VFO/MR**] button.*

2. Next, we need to find an empty channel. In channel mode, key in 127 to see if channel 127 is empty. If it is empty the radio will go directly to channel 0. If it occupied the radio will jump to 127. You need to find an empty channel that can be used. Following I will use 127 to program for the upcoming programming example.

Deleting a Memory Channel

Follow these steps to delete an occupied channel if necessary. Because the Radio times out of MENU mode in about 10 seconds, so a delay in executing steps will result in the menu timing out and you will need to restart.

1. Press the [**MENU**] button to enter Menu mode.

2. Key in [**2**]-[**8**]-[**MENU**] to go to MENU Delete Channel Mode and you will hear "DELETE CHANNEL".

3. Quickly key in the channel number you are going to delete. For instance, for channel 127 key in [1]-[2]-[7] and press [MENU] to confirm. This will delete the settings of channel 127.

Programming our Repeater settings into our Baofeng Radio Channel

Now that we know the channel number we are going to use to program and we have all our settings, let's program out radio. For this to occur, remember that the radio will time out if you stop the programming process for 10 seconds, so need to make sure we know all our values when we start – no pausing during the process.

Radio in Frequency Mode	Radio Receive Frequency	442.550 MHz
Menu 11 = R-CTCS	Receive CTCSS Tone	100.00 Hz
Menu 13 – T-CTCS	Transit CTCSS Tons	100.00 Hz
Menu 25 – SFT-D	Shift Offset Direction	+ (Positive)
Menu 26 – OFFSET	Offset Value	5.0 MHz (005.000)
Menu 27 – MEM-CH	Add Memory Channel	Ch 127

1. Place the radio in FREQUENCY mode. (Remember we cannot set up a channel in Channel mode for programming).

2. Enter the frequency 442.550.

3. Set the Receive CTCSS tone by keying [**MENU**]-[**1**]-[**1**]-[**MENU**] and you will hear "CTCSS". Quickly key in "100" to set 100-Hz and press [**MENU**] to save the setting. You will hear "CONFIRM".

4. Set the Transmit Tone by keying [**MENU**]-[**1**]-[**3**]-[**MENU**] and you will hear "CTCSS". Quickly key in "100" to set 100-Hz and press [**MENU**] to save the setting. You will hear "CONFIRM".

5. Set the Frequency Offset Direction now by keying [**MENU**]-[**2**]-[**5**]-[**MENU**] and you will hear "FREQUENCY DIRECTION". Quickly use the [**UP**]/[**DOWN**] buttons to select "+" for a positive offset direction.

6. Set the Frequency Offset Amount now by keying [**MENU**]-[**2**]-[**6**]-[**MENU**] and you will hear "OFFSET FREQUENCY". Quickly type in "005 000" to set the offset frequency amount of 5.0-MHz, then press [**MENU**] to confirm and you will hear "CONFIRM".

7. We will now save our newly programmed channel. Press [MENU]-[2]-[7]-[MENU] and you will hear "MEMORY CHANNEL". Quickly type in "127" and press [MENU], then you will hear "CONFIRM".

This will have completed the programming steps. Now turn your radio off, then back on. Place it in Channel mode and key in "127". You should be able to communicate with the repeater if you are within transmission range of the repeater. In most case you will find it easier to receive and hear conversations on the repeater than to reach the repeater. Receive range is much greater than transit range. On most repeaters, if you transmit to the repeater simply with a signal check message such as "STATE-YOUR-CALL-SIGN Requesting a signal check". If someone hears your signal, they will likely response. Even if you do not get a response, if the repeater hears your signal it may trigger the repeater to broadcast the repeater identification. If your signal is not strong enough to reach the repeater, even though you may be hearing others communicating on the frequency, they may not hear you.

Options for being able to be better heard by the repeater try one of the following:

1. Reposition yourself – Just by moving outdoors, away from obstacles, or in a better position you may be able to reach the repeater.
2. Replace your antenna. Try going to a better antenna. A long whip, a Signal Stick, A Nagoya antenna, or even attaching an external antenna such as a car mag-mount antenna.
3. Gain height. Try communicating from a higher position or use an antenna that is mounted on a pole or in a tree.

What about programming a SIMPLEX Channel?
A simplex channel can be programmed with the same steps however you will NOT need to program a frequency offset amount (Menu 26) or a frequency offset direction (Menu 25). In addition, you most likely will not want to program Receive CTCSS (Menu 11) or Transmit CTCSS (Menu 13) for CTCSS Tone settings. So here is a simplistic instruction for SIMPLEX Programming:

1. Place the radio in FREQUENCY mode. (Remember we cannot set up a channel in Channel mode for programming).

2. Enter the frequency 442.550.

3. Insure the Receive CTCSS tone is off by keying [**MENU**]-[**1**]-[**1**]-[**MENU**] and you will hear "CTCSS". Quickly key in "0" to turn off Receive CTCSS and press [**MENU**] to save the setting. You will hear "CONFIRM".

4. Insure the Transmit Tone is off by keying [**MENU**]-[**1**]-[**3**]-[**MENU**] and you will hear "CTCSS". Quickly key in "0" to turn off Transmit CTCSS and press [**MENU**] to save the setting. You will hear "CONFIRM".

5. Turn off Frequency Offset Direction now by keying [**MENU**]-[**2**]-[**5**]-[**MENU**] and you will hear "FREQUENCY DIRECTION". Quickly use the [**UP**]/[**DOWN**] buttons to select "OFF" to turn off the offset direction.

6. Set the Frequency Offset Amount now by keying [**MENU**]-[**2**]-[**6**]-[**MENU**] and you will hear "OFFSET FREQUENCY". Quickly type in "000 000" to set the offset frequency amount of 0 (No Offset), then press [**MENU**] to confirm and you will hear "CONFIRM".

7. We will now save our newly programmed channel. Press [MENU]-[2]-[7]-[MENU] and you will hear "MEMORY CHANNEL". Quickly type in "127" and press [MENU], then you will hear "CONFIRM".

These steps will program your SIMPLEX channel into the radio.

How did I find the repeater setting values?
There are multiple methods of looking up a repeater channel values. Here are three:

- Go to the club site that operates the repeater. In most cases they will post this information directly onto their website.
- Go to a website called REPEATERBOOK.COM. Here you can do a repeater search by state and town. You can go to the details of the repeater to get all the programming information and in many cases can also find out the actual location of the repeater.
  You can also download the Repeater Book app for iOS or Android to use on a mobile phone or tablet. This is my preferred method while out-and-about of on-the-fly repeaters. The App uses your current locations to provide a list of repeaters nearest to you.

- CHIRP Programming Tool – Chirp allows you to perform a proximity query (Miles from a zip code) and a Political query (State/County). Then select the band you are looking for – 2-Meters or 70-centimeters for our Baofeng radio – and you will be provided a list of repeaters. If you are using CHIRP to program your radio, then it is easy to copy the returned results into channels for your radio before uploading the configuration back to your radio. We will touch on CHIRP in the next chapter.

BIDDLE'S HAM RADIO STUDY GUIDE - TECHNICIAN LICENSE 2022-2026

7.4 - Better Antennas for better performance

The Antenna is, in my opinion, the most important upgrade you can get for your radio. After getting the radio and starting to use it you will want to consider replacing that stock antenna with something better. Also – Let's cover using a simple Mag Mount antenna in a variety of ways to get a stronger signal out.

First things First – the SMA Antenna Mount

Handheld radios come with a variety of antenna mounts, ranging from screw-type SMA Antenna mounts to BNC usually on the top of the radio. Both my Yaesu and Baofeng radios use a screw-type SMA Connector, though they use different genders on the SMA connector. Now this is fine and works generally well, but the first thing I do to all of my radios when I get them is to install a SMA to BNC Adapter on the radios themselves.

The factory antenna mount and antenna that is using SMA connectors

A SMA to BNC Adapter screws onto the SMA Mount and allows a BNC Antenna to be added to the radio. Convenient for quick swaps of antenna.

The benefit of adding a SMA-to-BNC adapter to the radio is to allow a quick swap of the antenna and not worrying about mis-threading of the antenna onto the radio. Now electrically this is another connection so there is a slight drawback, but I enjoy the convenience of a quick antenna swap such as when I jump into my less-frequently used car that has a Mag-Mount antenna on it.

Consider if you want to do this to your radio because if you do, you will then want to make sure any new antennas you purchase have a BNC connector to the radio rather than a SMA.

Nagoya Antenna

There are multiple antennas that you can get and put onto your radio in replacement of the stock antenna that comes with most handheld radios which can improve the performance of your radio. For less than

$20 you can get a Nagoya NA-771 which is a 15.6-inch whip antenna that will operate better for both VHF and UHF with your radio. The Nagoya can be ordered from Amazon and is also available through all Ham radio stores including GigaParts.com and Ham Radio Outlet. Be sure to select the proper base on the new antenna for your radio as the same antenna is available in multiple base types (SMA & BNC). Nagoya has several good models of their antennas with varying lengths. The NA-771 is just one of several to consider.

Signal Stick by Signal Stuff

Another good antenna you can get is from a company called Signal Stuff and is a $20 antenna. These antennas 19" flexible steel whip antennas which can actually loop on themselves, so they are not sticking up. I have multiple of these myself and I really like them – They are extremely durable as well as being super flexible. Coiling the whip keeps the antenna from sticking up too far, and the coil of the antenna is almost like a trade-mark – Common for users of these antennas. (https://www.SignalStuff.com).

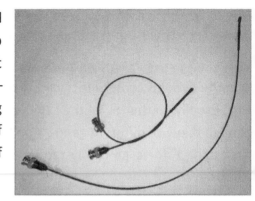

Signal Stick Antennas – SMA, BNC. Coiling is done to make the antenna more convenient on your radio when shorter is better.

Abbree Folding Whip

A third good antenna which started becoming popular in the past year or so is the Abbree which is a Military-style folding "Tactical" antenna. These are made of a metal ribbon, similar to a tape measure and are able to be folded. The antenna is insulated, and these come in lengths of up to 42.5 inches. Some YouTubers have performed range tests on the antennas to find they actually outperform many other popular antennas. I have one myself in my WinLink kit that I use a handheld radio for. These can be purchased on Amazon also and are under $15.00.

"Stubby" style Antennas

These little stubby antennas are marketed as good replacements for the stock antennas that come with many radios. I own a pair of these for my radios (Only one needed per radio) and I get surprising performance from it for receiving. These are more useful where you are not trying to push range but rather convenience of a short antenna. For better range I will always rely on one of my longer antennas.

Car-mounted and Mag Mount Antennas

Another type of antenna you can add to your resources is a simple car mounted or a magnet mount antenna. Used with your car, these antennas will allow you to get your transmitting signal outside of the car or truck for greater range. Likewise, you will have greater reception with one of these antennas if the metal of the car is removed as an obstacle from receptions. In fact – Once properly attached, the antenna will be free of the body of the car to get in the way, and the metal of the car will

act as a ground-plane for the antenna providing a better signal. The trick is though getting the signal to transmit out from within the car.

In addition to use in a car, you can also use one of these types of antennas elsewhere to enhance your transmission/reception capabilities of the radio. Some Hams will take a magnet mount antenna and attach it in the middle of a Pizza pan which then acts to radiate the antenna signal out. Or place one of these antennas to a pole or in a tree for additional height and you will greatly increase your radio's capabilities. (Best away from trees but the added height will help greatly).

For using the radio at home, you can greatly enhance your signal just by connecting an external antenna and getting the antenna outside and higher in the air.

Myself I have a 23' painter's extension pole from my last housing renovation project that I use. I will set it up outside with the antenna on it, and a length of coax cable running to my radio. I have instantly increased the range and quality of my signals in and out with a simple solution I can put up or take down as needed. Unfortunately, I am in a Homeowner's Association community that would have a fit with a big bright yellow painter's pole sticking up in the yard, but that is a discussion for another book.

Note – While this type of antenna works great for a VHF/UHF antenna, placing something unbalanced on it like a directional YAGI antenna will make the pole unbalanced needing guy lines to steady it.

Many folks who live in HOA controlled neighborhoods will place an antenna in the attic. This is usually by folks who are using base radios or even higher wattage mobile radios as a base station, but there is no reason you can't do this with your handheld radio also. In my own area I have no problems reaching the nearby repeaters with a home mobile radio that I use as a base and a mag mount antenna I use near a window in my office. The additional power and close proximity I have to most repeaters makes going to the trouble of an attic installation unnecessary. There is one repeater that I work with on a net weekly that this doesn't work for, but that is a 30-minute net once a week, so I simply work that net from my vehicle outside with my vehicle 50-watt mobile radio. My handheld would easily receive from that repeater, but my transmission would be scratchy and since I lead that net, I need to use a stronger radio than a handheld for a cleaner signal.

A Note about SWR
When attaching an external antenna, you should look at using an SWR meter to take a reading of the power out to the antenna. A properly matched antenna will enhance the radio while an antenna not matched properly will actually be a detriment. The SWR reading should be as low as possible. If you join in with a club, the club members are excellent resources to show you how to use one of these meters and can probably loan you one saving you the cost of purchasing one. In addition to the meter itself you will likely

need some connector adapters for your radio, so if you borrow or purchase make sure you have the right connections. In a later chapter we will take a look specifically at models of SWR meters and touch briefly on using an SWR Meter.

Interested in taking a stab at designing your own Antenna?

If you decide you would like to find out more about antenna design, or building your own antenna, check out the websites I have listed here:

- 2M/440 Dual Band Dipole:
  https://hamradioschool.com/wbotges-mighty-woof-2m440-mhz-dual-band-fan-dipole/

- Handheld directional antenna
  https://amsat-uk.org/projects/handitenna-440-beam-antenna/

- DX Zone Directory of user submitted antenna designs:
  https://www.dxzone.com/catalog/Antennas/

- 2M/70CM Vertical Pole Antenna
  http://www.hamuniverse.com/w7lpnvertdipole.html

7.5 - Coax Cable and Antenna Feed Lines – Using the "Right" Coax
The following I wrote as a part of a class on Ham Radio that focused on Antennas and setting up a proper feed line for minimizing loss based on frequency being operated on.

The purpose of the Antenna Feed line in Ham radio is to transmit the signal coming out of your radio to the Antenna. For HTs, this is done directly from the radio to the antenna on the radio. But if you want to use an external antenna as we will be doing later in this book, you will need to use a Coaxial feed line to connect the radio to the antenna.

In this section we are going to cover feed lines in a couple of categories:

1- Long distance feed lines which are usually 20' or longer
2- Short connection feed lines which connect to the antenna and allow a longer connection to be made.

The difference is just the length of cable and the connectors.

Long Distance Feed Lines
These are cables that will run usually from 18' (CB Radios) or to lengths of 100' or even longer. The lines we will be focusing on will be made of RG-58 Coaxial cable which is a 50-ohm low-loss cable that is most common for VHF/UHF Radio connections. Before we go deep in discussion, let's talk about the coax cable a bit first.

For Ham Radio, a common and popular cable type is 50-ohm RG-58 Coaxial cable. To purchase this cable in any long length, you will have to go either to an Electronics or Industrial supply/Electrical supply store, or you will need to go online such as to Amazon. Purchasing Coax cable in lengths of 50 feet to 100 feet can be very inexpensive. But if you need pre-made cables of 50 feet or 100 feet, you can often find these cables online for the same cost as the raw cable including dial PL259 connectors which are required by mobile and CB radios. These connectors also will connect to many antennas that have SO-239 connectors already on them. (PL-259 Connector screws onto and plugs into a SO-239 Connector). At home I usually keep at least two 50' RG-58 cables with dual PL-259 connectors already on them. Due to loss increases as the length of the cable increases as well as a 100' length of RG-8U cable which has a lower loss.

CABLE EFFICIENCY

The efficiency of a cable is determined by three factors:

- Cable selection
  Some cable types, such as LMR-400 is generally better for radio feed lines though much more expensive. For example purposes we are assume use of RG-58 Coaxial cable. It is inexpensive and for short lengths, say 25' or less has relatively low signal loss.

- Cable length
  The longer the cable, the more loss that will occur in the cable. To counter this increased loss, the best solution is often to move to another cable type. For instance, RG-58 cable at 100' in length will have significant signal loss – only 28% of your signal power will get through. With LMR-400 coax cable just over 70% of your signal power will get through.

- Frequencies being used
  As the transmitting frequency increases through the cable, both the dielectric and the resistive losses increase thus reducing the power transmission through the cable. Again using our RG-58 cable as an example, the signal loss through a 50' length of cable is 3.1 dB with an efficiency of only about 53% when transmitting at 146.52 MHz, where when using the same cable but transmitting at 446.0 MHz the dB loss increases to 5.5 dB with a lower efficiency of only 31.8%. Different cable types will have different specifications and efficiency ratings.

When running coax, RG-58 cable generally works well for cable runs up to 25 feet, depending on the radio, antenna and frequency you are using. Quality of your signal moving through the cable will vary based on the type of cable being used over various lengths. To connect a coax feed cable with dual PL-259 connectors on it to your Baofeng or other radio, you will need a SO-239 to SMA-Female connector on the cable. For radios such as the Baofeng Handheld which have an SMA or other type of antenna mount you will use an adapter to get the radio to a SO239 connector. My Yaesu FT-60R for instance uses a FEMALE SMA mount on it rather than a MALE SMA mount so I am required to use a different radio connector adapter on the radio itself. This will allow you to connect your handheld radio to the coax, then run the coax from your radio location out to the antenna. If you are going to be running an antenna feed line farther than 100' you should consider a lower loss cable that will work within the frequency range you will be operating in. Your other option of course is to have another connector on the cable itself that will match up with the radio. I have added BNC Connectors onto the coaxial cable sometimes to connect to a radio with an SMA-to-BNC adapter on it.

Selecting the appropriate cable and length

Whenever possible try to use the right cable and the best length for your connection. This week I have been doing some testing of my little Baofeng radio repeater connected to an antenna I have temporarily mounted into a tree. The radio I am using is a Baofeng BF-F8HP radio which is only putting out about 8-watts of power (Actually measuring just 6 watts from my SWR Meter). What I want is to get the best SWR on the radio out through the antenna, and to do so I need to look at the cables I have available to me. I Prefer not to have to cut a custom cable if I can avoid this so I am going to look at the cable lengths I already have. Here are my options:

Cable type	Length	dB loss	Efficiency	Power Out (Est)
RG-58 Coax Cable	20'	1.2	77.4%	4.6w
RG-58 Coax Cable	25'	1.6	72.4%	4.3w
RG-58 Coax Cable	50'	3.1	52.7%	3.2w
RG-8u Coax Cable	25'	.7	87.1%	5.2w
RG-8u Coax Cable	100'	2.7	57.5%	3.4w
LMR-400 Coax Cable	50'	.9	84.0%	5.0w
LMR-400 Coax Cable	25'	.4	91.6%	5.5w

The setup I have is the antenna run up a tree just outside of my den in the house. For length, the 20' and 25' lengths will be just a bit short, so I am going to use one of the 50' or longer lengths I do already have. If I use the RG-58/50' cable I will see extensive loss – almost 50% of my signal. Since I am using a 6-watt radio, this will affect my performance and range. My next choice is the LMR-400 coax cable as my next 50' cable. Here I will actually have 87.1% efficiency so 5.2 watts should get out. Pretty good. Lastly I have a 100' RG-8u cable which has a dB loss of 2.7 and an efficiency of 57.5%. That means only 3.4 watts of power getting – not good. So for my cable to use will be the 50' LMR Cable – It is a good length at over 25' (I need more than 25' to reach into the Den) and will provide a good power out level.

What about if I am going to operate the repeater from a mobile antenna just 20' off the ground while out camping? I have a weather-proof container for the repeater so I can actually leave it outside under the antenna tower, running off battery power. In this case – I can use one of my short cables. If I use the 20' RG-58 cable I will get 4.6-watts, and with the 25' RG-58 cable I will get 4.3 watts. If I use the 25' RG-8u cable I will get 5.2 watts. If I had (But I don't) a 25' LMR-400 cable I would get 5.5-watts out. So at these short lengths we can see there is less of a difference. In this case I will either use the 20' RG-58 cable at 4.6 watts or the 25' RG-8u cable at 5.2 watts – To get the most out of my range I will go with the RG-8u cable. (If I had a LMR-400 cable in 25', the additional .3 watts of power might not be worth the additional cost).

Cable Costs

With better performance comes higher cost. That is one reason the RG-58 cable is so much more popular, and why we are using RG-58 cable for our projects in this course. Once deciding on a cable type, you will also have to consider the connectors used on the cables. In some cases you may need different connectors. For the most part when I order cable I order RG-58 expecting to make shorter cables so I keep a good supply of RG-58 crimp connectors on hand as well. If I were cutting lengths of LMR or RG-8u cable I would need to take that into account and order crimping connectors specific to those cable types.

- A 100' spool of RG-58 online currently (Jan 2021) is running about $31.
- A 100' spool of RG-8u online is running about $70.
- A 100' spool of LMR-400 cable online is running about $120.

If you are running long runs of cable then absolutely look at a higher quality (though more expensive) cable. But if your lengths are relatively short – 25' or shorter, it really won't make as much difference.

Table 1: Coaxial Cable specifications for at 146.52 MHz at varying lengths, 10' to 100':

Coax Cable Type	Frequency	Length	Average Power	Normal Attenuation	Max Cable Assembly Insertion Loss	Cable Run Efficiency	Cable Run Time Delay
LMR-400	146.52 MHz	10	1500 Watts	1.5 dB/100 ft, 5.0 dB/100 m	.2 dB	96.6%	15.4 ns
LMR-400	146.52 MHz	25	1500 Watts	1.5 dB/100 ft, 5.0 dB/100 m	.4 dB	91.6%	38.5 ns
LMR-400	146.52 MHz	50	1500 Watts	1.5 dB/100 ft, 5.0 dB/100 m	.9 dB	84.0%	77.0 ns
LMR-400	146.52 MHz	100	1500 Watts	1.5 dB/100 ft, 5.0 dB/100 m	1.7 dB	70.5%	153.9 ns
RG-8	146.52 MHz	10	800 Watts	2.4 dB/100 ft, 7.9 dB/100 m	.3 dB	94.6%	15.4 ns
RG-8	146.52 MHz	25	800 Watts	2.4 dB/100 ft, 7.9 dB/100 m	.7 dB	87.1%	38.5 ns
RG-8	146.52 MHz	50	800 Watts	2.4 dB/100 ft, 7.9 dB/100 m	1.3 dB	75.8%	77.0 ns
RG-8	146.52 MHz	100	800 Watts	2.4 dB/100 ft, 7.9 dB/100 m	2.7 dB	57.5%	153.9 ns
RG-8/U	146.52 MHz	10	800 Watts	2.4 dB/100 ft, 7.9 dB/100 m	.3 dB	94.6%	15.4 ns
RG-8/U	146.52 MHz	25	800 Watts	2.4 dB/100 ft, 7.9 dB/100 m	.7 dB	87.1%	38.5 ns
RG-8/U	146.52 MHz	50	800 Watts	2.4 dB/100 ft, 7.9 dB/100 m	1.3 dB	75.8%	77.0 ns
RG-8/U	146.52 MHz	100	800 Watts	2.4 dB/100 ft, 7.9 dB/100 m	2.7 dB	57.5%	153.9 ns
RG-8X	146.52 MHz	10	200 Watts	4.5 dB/100 ft, 14.7 dB/100 m	.5 dB	90.2%	15.4 ns
RG-8X	146.52 MHz	25	200 Watts	4.5 dB/100 ft, 14.7 dB/100 m	1.3 dB	77.3%	38.5 ns
RG-8X	146.52 MHz	50	200 Watts	4.5 dB/100 ft, 14.7 dB/100 m	2.5 dB	59.7%	77.0 ns
RG-8X	146.52 MHz	100	200 Watts	4.5 dB/100 ft, 14.7 dB/100 m	5.0 dB	35.6%	153.9 ns
RG-58	146.52 MHz	10	200 Watts	5.6 dB/100 ft, 18.2 dB/100 m	.6 dB	88.0%	15.4 ns
RG-58	146.52 MHz	25	200 Watts	5.6 dB/100 ft, 18.2 dB/100 m	1.6 dB	72.6%	38.5 ns
RG-58	146.52 MHz	50	200 Watts	5.6 dB/100 ft, 18.2 dB/100 m	3.1 dB	52.7%	77.0 ns
RG-58	146.52 MHz	100	200 Watts	5.6 dB/100 ft, 18.2 dB/100 m	6.1 dB	27.8%	153.9 ns

Table 2: Coaxial Cable specifications for at 446.000 MHz at varying lengths, 10' to 100'

Coax Cable Type	Operating Frequency (MHz)	Cable Length (Feet)	Average Power	Normal Attenuation	Max Cable Assembly Insertion Loss	Cable Run Efficiency	Cable Run Time Delay
LMR-400	446.000	10	800 Watts	2.7 dB/100 ft, 8.9 dB/100 m	.3 dB	94.0%	15.4 ns
LMR-400	446.000	25	800 Watts	2.7 dB/100 ft, 8.9 dB/100 m	.8 dB	85.6%	38.5 ns
LMR-400	446.000	50	800 Watts	2.7 dB/100 ft, 8.9 dB/100 m	1.5 dB	73.3%	77.0 ns
LMR-400	446.000	100	800 Watts	2.7 dB/100 ft, 8.9 dB/100 m	3.0 dB	53.7%	153.9 ns
RG-8	446.000	10	500 Watts	4.4 dB/100 ft, 14.6 dB/100 m	.5 dB	90.3%	15.4 ns
RG-8	446.000	25	500 Watts	4.4 dB/100 ft, 14.6 dB/100 m	1.3 dB	77.5%	38.5 ns
RG-8	446.000	50	500 Watts	4.4 dB/100 ft, 14.6 dB/100 m	2.5 dB	60.0%	77.0 ns
RG-8	446.000	100	500 Watts	4.4 dB/100 ft, 14.6 dB/100 m	4.9 dB	36.0%	153.9 ns
RG-8/U	446.000	10	500 Watts	4.4 dB/100 ft, 14.6 dB/100 m	.5 dB	90.3%	15.4 ns
RG-8/U	446.000	25	500 Watts	4.4 dB/100 ft, 14.6 dB/100 m	1.3 dB	77.5%	38.5 ns
RG-8/U	446.000	50	500 Watts	4.4 dB/100 ft, 14.6 dB/100 m	2.5 dB	60.0%	77.0 ns
RG-8/U	446.000	100	500 Watts	4.4 dB/100 ft, 14.6 dB/100 m	4.9 dB	36.0%	153.9 ns
RG-8X	446.000	10	100 Watts	8.2 dB/100 ft, 26.9 dB/100 m	.9 dB	82.8%	15.4 ns
RG-8X	446.000	25	100 Watts	8.2 dB/100 ft, 26.9 dB/100 m	2.3 dB	62.4%	38.5 ns
RG-8X	446.000	50	100 Watts	8.2 dB/100 ft, 26.9 dB/100 m	4.5 dB	39.0%	77.0 ns
RG-8X	446.009	100	100 Watts	8.2 dB/100 ft, 26.9 dB/100 m	9.0 dB	15.2%	153.9 ns
RG-58	446.000	10	100 Watts	9.9 dB/100 ft, 32.6 dB/100 m	1.1 dB	79.5%	15.4 ns
RG-58	446.000	25	100 Watts	9.9 dB/100 ft, 32.6 dB/100 m	2.8 dB	56.4%	38.5 ns
RG-58	446.000	50	100 Watts	9.9 dB/100 ft, 32.6 dB/100 m	5.5 dB	31.8%	77.0 ns
RG-58	446.000	100	100 Watts	9.9 dB/100 ft, 32.6 dB/100 m	11.0 dB	10.1%	153.9 ns

Notice in these tables our dB loss and how those effect our efficiency
The greater the dB loss in our cable, the less our efficiency which results in the greater our signal loss. An RG-58 cable running 100' to an outdoor antenna will only have a 10.1% efficiency resulting in tremendous signal loss, whereas use of LMR-400 cable has an efficiency of 53.7%.

Also – The efficiencies at 146.52 MHz are better than at 400-MHz with less signal loss. When running HF frequencies the efficiencies will be much higher than in either of these telling us that the higher the frequency the greater the importance of running as short of cable runs as possible and as high of a quality of cable as possible.

7.6 - Anderson Power Connectors Intro – Why Hams standardize on Andersons

Anderson Power Connectors are a style of power connections that are highly popular among experienced ham radio

operators. They are particularly popular with operators who plan and work in emergency planning situations. These connectors are placed on radio equipment either as a replacement connector for the positive and negative power connections, or they are connected through power adapters allowing the radio's original power connectors to remain on but also allowing the connections for power to be established through sources using Anderson connectors.

The connectors are designed so they can be used independently, or they can lock as shown below here. The

connectors do require a special crimping tool to properly apply the metal connectors onto the wire. They an be connected to wire easily and quickly with simplicity after using them for a bit of time. Anderson power distribution panels are now available allowing power to be drawn from a single panels, some of which allow independent fusing for each device connected so that a short or high power draw that blows a fuse only effects that single device. The standard power pole plastic sleeve connectors accept metal crimp contacts that can be sized for 15, 30 and 45-amp sizes that crimp onto a variety of wire sizes.

Why Standardize?

As these standardized connectors are becoming more popular for several types of uses including some automotive uses more recently as connectors used for making solar panel and solar generator connections. The adapter cable here allows a solar panel or solar generator using an MC4 connector pair, which is popular for Solar panel uses, to connect to a device using an Anderson power pole.

For the purposes of this book my intention is to introduce you to what an Anderson Power connector is because of their popularity in the Ham operator world. For more information on these connectors, tools and their full scope of uses, check out PowerWerx website at https://www.PowerWerx.com.

7.7 – Beyond the Handheld – A Radio "Go" Kit

Most Soon-to-be Techs when starting to go through the process of getting their license will start off with a simple handheld. A great number of these students start off with the inexpensive Baofeng handheld radio which can be purchased for as little as $25. The Baofeng and similar handheld radios are great tools – But they are tools with limitations. After you have learned and mastered your new Handheld radio you may find the need for more "Kick" in the radio. I have mentioned earlier in the book that the best upgrade you can do for your radio between power and antenna will be to add a better antenna, or even better to attach an external antenna via Coax cable to the radio. Get your radio antenna as high as you can and with as clear of a line of site out as you can.

After the antenna, the next upgrade you can do is to increase your transmitting power. Most of the Baofeng radios will transmit out with between 4 and 8 watts, depending on the model and the band you are transmitting on. (The BF-F8HP 8-watt radio for instance will transmit out at 8-watts on VHF, 7-Watts on UHF though often you will get less than that).

Adding an Amplifier

The first thing you can do is to add an Amplifier t get up to 40-watts of output. The Amplifier will hook up to the SMA Antenna connection on your radio using that connection as an input feed into the amplifier, and then will amplify your signal out to an external antenna. The models sold by Baofeng Tech allow you to connect a Microphone to the unit though the amplifier for easier talking while driving. Channel selection still is made through the radio itself.

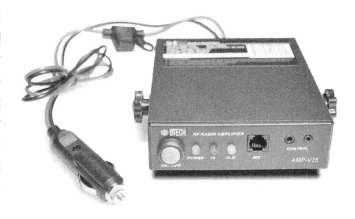

Radio Amplifiers will turn your handheld 5-watt or 8-watt radio into a full power 40-watt mobile radio.

The downside of the radio amplifier is that these devices are single band only. That means when you purchase one, you need to designate if you will be using it for 70-cm, 1.25-m, or 2-m operation. You will only be able to use it within the selected band for the model you purchase.

Moving to a Mobile Radio model

Your next option may be to move directly into a mobile radio. I have two 25-watt BTECH 25X4 radios that I have purchased for portable kits, installed into pelican-type cases for easy portable use. These radios are much more powerful than the handheld Baofeng radios are at 25-watts, however the power remains within the normal 10-amp limit of your vehicle's cigarette lighter/accessory plugs. The radio comes with a 12-v Cigarette lighter plug for easy power from your vehicle or can be plugged into a portable 12-volt power source such as a small battery pack or solar generator. I have two radio kits that I can use either during an emergency, as base camp radios, or even easily use in my vehicle in a non-mounted configuration.

A Sample Solution: BTech 25x4 mounted in a Harbor Freight Apache 1800 Case

Here I used double-sided tape to attach a short length of board to the bottom of an Apache 1800 case. I then mounted the radio to the board in the case leaving enough room to keep the microphone stored in with the radio. I did purchase a UHF PL-259 Male to UHF PL-259 Female L Shape Right Angle Coaxial Adapter Connector to add to the back of the radio prior to mounting to simplify attaching a coaxial cable to the radio. The radio uses a power cord with a cigarette lighter plug on it.

This radio is highly compact, and I can easily carry it and use it in my vehicle plugged into power and running an external mag-mount antenna to the radio. If I am using the radio at a campsite or from my camper, I will use a pole-mounted antenna. I have a 23' painter's pole that I can easily deploy with a light-weight antenna for better operation than from my handheld radio, and the additional power also helps with a better signal. If communicating to a repeater this configuration works much better than from my Baofeng handheld.

If using the radio from outside of my vehicle, I use either a solar generator, 12-volt battery, or other power source with a 12-volt cigarette lighter outlet. I have a plastic Ammo box that I have built out with a 12.8-volt/36-AH Lithium battery, a voltage meter for monitoring, a cigarette lighter outlet, a four-foot power cord with Anderson connectors, and a keyed power switch on it. (See section 9.2 on Battery boxes t see the particular batteries I built for remote use).

BTech 25x4 mounted in a Harbor Freight Apache 2800 Case

In this larger radio-in-a-box, I used the same BTECH 25-watt radio. But with the extra space in the box, I added a 12-volt/7-ah battery mounted in the kit and all power running to a pair of power-buses. I also here used a wood bord as the base that the radios, battery and power busses are mounted to.

Though small, the 7-ah battery provides enough power for short mobile use of the radio kit. Using the power busses, I have a power lead that can run, and either be plugged into a power source through a cigarette lighter outlet, or through an Anderson connector power lead that can plug to a larger battery or battery charger to keep the small lead-acid battery charged.

- Costs for the BTECH 25x4 radio is about $145.
- The Apache cases cost $13 for the smaller 1800 case, and $30 for the larger 2800 case.
- If you choose to add a battery you will be looking at about $30 for the battery – Look at Home Depot or Lowes for a small Alarm system battery.
- To connect all these together a set of "Terminal Strips" can be purchased from Amazon allowing you to centralize your power and ground connections.

As with the design of both of the battery boxes I designed, I am also using a short piece of 1x6 PVC board as you can see in the picture above that I have glued to the bottom of the pelican box. This gives be a good base that I can place screws into for holding mounting brackets for the radio, for the 10-ah battery I am using here, and for the terminal blocks like the one I am showing here to the right. All devices – Battery, Radio, and a power extension cord with Anderson power connectors on it all connect through the shared power strips. I use two of these power strips – one for the Positive power connections and the second for the negative here. The Anderson Connector power cable can be used to power the radio, or to connect to a battery charger for recharging the battery, or to the output side of a solar setup (PWM or MPPT Charge Controller) for recharging the battery through Solar power.

The 25-watt radio connects to a portable antenna that can be as simple as a magnetic-mount antenna, or through a longer coax feed line to a better outdoor antenna. If using a longer antenna, I prefer using either an RG-8, RG-8/U, or LMR-400 feed cable with a length of 50' or less to the antenna, but no more than 100' to minimize signal loss. Note that using an inexpensive RG-58 Coaxial cable is more than double the signal loss RG-8 and RG-8/u, and almost four times the loss as from LMR-400 cable.

Table: Coaxial Cable specifications for at 446.00 MHz at varying lengths, 50' to 100'

Coax Cable Type	Operating Frequency	Cable Length	Average Power	Normal Attenuation	Max Cable Assembly Insertion Loss	Cable Run Efficiency	Cable Run Time Delay
LMR-400	446.000 MHz	50	800 Watts	2.7 dB/100 ft, 8.9 dB/100 m	1.5 dB	73.3%	77.0 ns
LMR-400	446.000 MHz	100	800 Watts	2.7 dB/100 ft, 8.9 dB/100 m	3.0 dB	53.7%	153.9 ns
RG-8	446.000 MHz	50	500 Watts	4.4 dB/100 ft, 14.6 dB/100 m	2.5 dB	60.0%	77.0 ns
RG-8	446.000 MHz	100	500 Watts	4.4 dB/100 ft, 14.6 dB/100 m	4.9 dB	36.0%	153.9 ns
RG-8/U	446.000 MHz	50	500 Watts	4.4 dB/100 ft, 14.6 dB/100 m	2.5 dB	60.0%	77.0 ns
RG-8/U	446.000 MHz	100	500 Watts	4.4 dB/100 ft, 14.6 dB/100 m	4.9 dB	36.0%	153.9 ns
RG-8X	446.000 MHz	50	100 Watts	8.2 dB/100 ft, 26.9 dB/100 m	4.5 dB	39.0%	77.0 ns
RG-8X	446.000 MHz	100	100 Watts	8.2 dB/100 ft, 26.9 dB/100 m	9.0 dB	15.2%	153.9 ns
RG-58	446.000 MHz	50	100 Watts	9.9 dB/100 ft, 32.6 dB/100 m	5.5 dB	31.8%	77.0 ns
RG-58	446.000 MHz	100	100 Watts	9.9 dB/100 ft, 32.6 dB/100 m	11.0 dB	10.1%	153.9 ns

7.8 – Non-Ham Radio Planning

In this section we are going to touch briefly on Non-Ham radio communications

CB/Citizens Band Radio

Citizens Band Radio exploded into public back in the 70's before cellular telephones. It quickly became popular among truckers and drivers on the highways to communicate. It operates in the 27 MHz frequency range requiring much longer antennas than on other radio types making it less convenient for handheld use and more common for vehicles. Power limits are 4 watts for normal use and 12 watts for single-side-band use giving it a rough range, depending on antenna and conditions of between 2 and about 7 or 10 miles.

Antennas are generally several feet in length and external to the radio, usually mounted on a vehicle or outside. A full quarter-wave antenna for a hand-held radio would extend to over 9 feet in length which is why almost all hand-held versions of these radios use a less efficient shorter antenna. Due to antenna restrictions that come with the longer antenna lengths, radio communication distances will usually suffer when the antennas are less than optimal. One of the best performing antennas is the 102" whip antenna which you will sometimes see mounted to trucks. More commonly shorter wound antennas are used on vehicles which cuts into the radio's range. If being used as a base radio operated from an office location, it may be possible to run a 102" antenna outdoors mounted at a higher location.

No license is required for CB Radio, so you would be able to get operational immediately. CB Radios also operate in the HF frequency ranges of 27-kHz. As an HF Radio method, CB Radios do have the same characteristics of Ham HF radio allowing longer distances through radio propagation and signal bounce.

For much more information on CB Radio check out the YouTube channel "FarPoint Farms". The owner of the channel goes into deeper detail about various uses of CB Radio and from his location in the mountains of North Carolina he has established contacts hundreds of miles away, though these are not consistent contacts.

Notes about CB Radio:

- All modulation is AM (Amplitude) meaning a less clear signal than FM used by FRS, GMRS, and VHF/UHF Ham Radio. (Most HF Ham Radio uses AM Modulation)
- Standard power output is 4-watts. 12-watts can be used for SSB (Single Sideband). The FCC Limits legal radio operation to these power levels.
- Antenna lengths for CB Radio are LONG compared to other radio types. A full-wave antenna is 36' while a quarter wave is 9 feet. Better antennas will be over 102" or longer in length.
- Due to antenna length, handheld radio operation is not efficient though mobile and base CB radio still works well.
- The best antenna configurations will use a quality antenna mounted high (On a building). Mobile radios with mobile antennas will still work though not as well.
- CB Radio is HF Radio, meaning that signals can have the same characteristics as HF Radio systems do. A great YouTube channel talking about CB radio is Farpoint Farms. (https://www.youtube.com/c/FarpointFarms).
- CB Radio traffic is normally minimal. This mode of radio is no longer heavily used the way it was 30 years ago due in part to the advent of mobile phones, and GMRS Radio which performs better. However, during a crisis, most truckers still have CB Radios and when other communications are down, they will be back on the air and could help to relay a message if needed.
- If purchasing a CB Radio for emergency communications use, look for a radio that supports SSB (Single Sideband) which will offer better range. Available at online stores and at local truck stops.
- CB Radio is "Channelized" meaning you turn to a particular channel to work the radio
- Remember – CB Radio IS HF Radio – CB is in the 11-meter band and has the same characteristics as the Ham 10-Meter band (We will discuss in the next section). That means radio signals can and do skip through the atmosphere, though using the limited legal power of 4-watts for normal transmitting, 12-watts max for SSB transmitting.
- CB Radio is often considered as "Trash" radio due to the verbal language that can be heard in some areas. Be aware of this if you have minors.

GMRS Radio

GMRS is a step up from FRS with power levels up to 5 watts for hand-held radios and the ability to use external antennas as well as repeaters (External antennas are available only on dedicated GMRS Radios – Not combo radios). GMRS radio does require a license for legal use, but the license does not require a test.

The maximum range for GMRS with repeaters and an external antenna can easily extend to 10 miles or more depending on numerous factors, though the common FRS/GMRS Radios found in retailers will rarely get more than a mile or two depending on the area they are being used. These radios operate in the UHF radio bands in the 460 MHz range where the frequencies are "Line-of-site". Frequencies of this range are often blocked by obstacles and terrain which becomes their limiting factor and the reason an external antenna can be so beneficial to these. It is possible for two GMRS radio operators to communicate 20 miles or more with the right conditions.

Most common GMRS radios are have been packaged as "FRS/GMRS" combo radios. This combination packaging requires the antennas be permanently fixed to the radio though many of these radios will automatically switch power depending on if you are using an FRS or GMRS frequency. A GMRS radio license is required for use which costs $70 and lasts for 10 years, good for all members of the purchaser's family. As of this writing, the FCC is planning to discount the cost of the 10-year license to half – just $35 beginning April 2022.

What to look for in a GMRS Radio:

- GMRS is a LICENSED REQUIRED radio system – Costing $70 for a 10-year family license covering all immediate family members.
- A Handheld should be between 4- and 5-watts of power for best performance.
- Mobile radios can be up to 50-watts.
- Removable antenna – If the antenna is a permanent fixed antenna then the range will be limited.
- Look for a properly FCC Licensed GMRS Radio. Many Baofengs for instance can be programmed for GMRS Frequencies but are not legal for use on these frequencies. (Baofeng Tech does have a GMRS-V1 model which has been modified and is legal for GMRS Use).
- Battery type – Do you need to be able to swap out the battery when it goes dead? Some can only be recharged, while others support swappable batteries or AA batteries.
- GMRS is a "Channelized" Radio mode - You simply set the defined channel number and use the radio.
- Most common ranges will be between 1- and 3-miles radio to radio REGARDLESS of the manufacturer's claims. The long-distance ranges are possible in the best weather conditions where NO obstacles exist (Like talking from mountain top to mountain top, direct line of sight.

The biggest takeaway from GMRS Radios is – Do NOT believe the manufacturer's range claims, and GMRS is the ONLY radio system in this chapter that supports extended ranges through repeaters.

Zello VoIP for Emergency Planning

We are going to discuss one type of radio system that doesn't exactly fit our category for emergency radio and communications, and that is Zello VOIP.

Zello is a Voice-Over-IP (VOIP) communications application which can be installed onto your smart phone and allows access to hundreds of existing channels throughout the United States and the world on a wide variety of topics. Zello also allows the user the ability to create channels that can be shared with family members or friends that are private.

During an emergency event that leads to widespread power and communications loss, Zello will naturally be unavailable. It is dependent upon both Cellular carriers being up, but also dependent upon the data network being available through carriers. In some instances, you could find that cellular voice could be available, and internet data being down which also will knock out Zello. The Zello App is also a license-free communications tool – No license at all, paid for or test based, is necessary to communicate using Zello.

So why am I including Zello as part of an Emergency Communications plan when an event may make it unusable?

Pre-Planning is the reason. With a private Zello channel, you can establish a communications tool through which all family or participating members log in and can communicate in a one-to-many method. As you broadcast through Zello, all channel listeners will hear your message and can talk back in a group chat. Imagine this where you may have a dozen family members planning for a potential evacuation ahead of a storm. All members can coordinate together in group conversations with everyone listening knowing exactly what other family members are doing. This can include family members anywhere – those in the affected zone, or those outside of that zone hundreds or thousands of miles away. Members anywhere – at home preparing, shopping, or on the road traveling. As for planning groups - groups can participate together in a walkie-talkie style conversation hands free and free from texting through tools such as Signal, Messenger or group texts. If you are driving, you can even connect an external speaker/microphone allowing you to communicate as simply as picking up a handset and speaking.

If working with an emergency planning group or planning team, you can communicate to team members ahead of the event for planning. Team members may be licensed radio operators or not. Most often working with groups means working with members who are not ham radio operators so the inclusion of Zello in your radio plans can mean inclusion of more individuals.

Recently while picnicking with a group of friends, several of whom were ham radio operators, we had three of our younger kids who were supposed to be near us disappear for about 10 minutes. Even though we had a half dozen ham operators, only two of us had radios with us leaving the ten or so individuals splitting up to do so without a centralized comms system. As it turned out the kids simply went down the wrong boardwalk and came back shortly after we left to look for, however had we as a group had an established Zello channel then everyone out to look for the kids would have been able to talk together.

Zello is also, in addition to a planning tool, an educational tool. Groups meet on Zello channels and discuss topics such as Ham Radio, Gardening, Travel, Social topics, and have a wide range of various discussions. Groups that use Zello include PrepperNet which holds regular weekly discussions on Monday nights at 8 PM EST on varieties of topics. Other groups such as the Cajun Navy use Zello for post-event support planning for volunteers that are outside of the impacted areas to coordinate efforts, supplies, travel, and news for members. During Hurricane Michael while renovating a home for resale I listened for hours of efforts by the Cajun Navy to coordinate delivery and distribution of supplies and volunteers into the affected areas. Basically, as travelers were heading into the affected "Communications Dark Zone", they could get instruction via Zello until entering the affected area. Once in the dark communications zone, travelers had to rely on Ham or CB Radio while traveling, of barring either of those simply traveled into the areas based on traffic and road conditions they received over the car radio or instructions they received before losing cellular coverage.

By the way – If you happen to be interested in Ham Radio for the purposes of talking to other folks around the world – Zello may either be the answer to that or will at least be a great starting point needing only about 30 minutes of your time to get started. I have spoken to folks around the globe on Zello and there are some great worldwide groups. But – Word of warning – When I first started using Zello I would leave myself logged in when I went to bed with the phone charging on the nightstand. Then, at about 2am my time when morning came in England ad some of the folks started talking there, or folks from South Africa started talking, I heard voices in my bedroom as clear as if the individuals were standing in my room. Some Zello channels get busy at different times around the globe.

I am a strong believer in the use of Zello as a part of your plans and as a part of your family's emergency plans. While regular communications are up all members can participate and there are absolutely no license issues with getting established. Obtaining Zello is as simple as going to and Android Play store for Android devices, or the Apple App Store on IOS devices.

Once you get the application installed, you will need to search and add channels to communicate with others, or you can create channels on your own. When visiting the Zello website (http://www.Zello.com/) you will see that it is priced out for commercial use. Zello however does offer their product free of charge for personal use or for use by smaller groups. This is the use that we are referring to here, though if your business or organization does have interest in Zello for commercial use then it would be an excellent product for commercial use at an inexpensive cost of under $7.00 per user per month – less than most radio system costs for commercial use.

For information about Zello here are several good resources. In particular look over the later three of the list for specific information related to personal and small group use free of cost.

- Zello – VOIP Communications
  https://www.Zello.com/

- Zello Walkie Talkie Channels
  https://blog.zello.com/zello-radio-channels

- Zello Channels lists on Facebook
  https://www.facebook.com/ZelloMe/posts/here-is-the-complete-list-of-the-types-of-channels-that-zello-has-to-offer-and-s/1904385516328062/

- Handy Hints for Zello Users
  https://networkradios.weebly.com/zello-ptt.html

FRS & MURS for Short-range unlicensed Use

FRS is a low-power low-capability radio system designed for short distance license free communication. In May 2017, the FCC made a move to extend the power of FRS radio on some frequencies to 2 watts of power, but still mandates restrictions on antenna design which makes these radios good for short-distance use but not viable beyond and eighth to a quarter mile (You might get a half mile with no obstacles). New radios with the new power limits are yet to be available as of the time of this book in summer 2017 but should be hitting the market soon. Restrictions on the antenna requires the antenna to be permanently fixed to the radio which is the biggest limitation of these radios.

FRS/GMRS Combination radios were no longer being certified by the FCC in 2018 with newer models which no longer are mixed use FRS/GMRS radios will become available at some point.

Notes about FRS:

- FRS uses a subset of the GMRS channels, but with limited transmitting power of 2-watts on some channels, and ½-watt on other channels reducing the range.
- FRS has a fixed antenna. You cannot update the antenna, also limiting the range.
- FRS operates of UHF frequencies.
- FRS works well for short distances within a building
- No-License is needed – So you can distribute FRS radios to members of an emergency team without having to be concerned about FCC regulations.
- Because FRS and GMRS use some of the same frequencies, you can mix radios allowing those without a GMRS license to interact with those participants with GMRS licenses.

MURS is a 5-channel radio system that was carved out of the Business radio systems in 2000. The frequencies used are in the 151 and 154 MHz frequency ranges of VHF Radio and these radios work at 2 watts of power. The ability to utilize an externally connected antenna allows better communication signal but at 2 watts these still are more limited than a dedicated GMRS radio with an external antenna running at 5 watts. MURS radios are NOT allowed to use repeaters. Operation will be better however than an FRS radio even under the new FCC Limits of 2 watts for FRS due to the ability to use an externally attached antenna. In areas where businesses still hold older licenses for MURS frequency use those businesses do take precedence over public use on MURS channels.

MURS radios are not easily found. You would most likely need to order these through online vendors who specialize in a wide variety of radio systems. Baofeng Tech does sell a model of radio which is a MURS-V1 radio which has a swappable battery and a swappable antenna allowing use of a better-quality antenna or an antenna that can be mounted on your car or elevated up to 20' (FCC Limitation) outdoors.

Notes about MURS Radio Frequencies

- MURS is a License-FREE radio system
- MURS is a good alternative to FRS offering the same power (2-Watts) but better antenna options for better range capabilities
- Can be a more difficult type of radio to locate – Look to Amazon and online suppliers.
- MURS is channelized – Just set the channel and operate. (5 Channels).
- MURS Supports external antennas offering greater range over FRS radios.
- MURS operates in the VHF Frequency ranges between 151- and 154- MHz

7.9 – The Magic of 10-Meters

As a licensed ham operator, you will also have access to both the 6-Meter radio band and the 10-Meter radio band. The 6-Meter band is within the VHF range but with longer wavelengths (Around 50-Meters) it will have some range benefits over using the 2-Meter and 70-cm meter bands most common with technicians.

So why isn't the 50-Meter band as commonly used? The biggest reason is going to be around the design of most handheld radios. First, most HT Radios are best designed for shorter antennas which means shorter wavelengths. The ¼ wavelength antenna for a 70-cm band frequency is just under 7" in size. With the 2-Meter band wear are still at just 19" in length for ¼ wavelength – Not as convenient but still manageable. But – For the 6-Meter band (50-MHz) we are looking at an antenna length of 4.92 feet – almost 5' long! Not nearly as manageable. And – if we jump to 10-Meters, we are looking at an antenna length of over 8'.

Secondly, as a technician you are limited to operate within 28.000 MHz thru 28.500 MHz, only a portion of the band, and you are going to be limited to AM operation only. Most HT radios are actually FM radios – A difference in the modulation modes. You are not going to find a cheap AM Baofeng radio on the market supporting an 8' antenna.

So – Most of your radios that support both 6-Meters and 10-Meters will be mobile or base radios. These will use antennas externally mounted requiring planning for setup, but more reliable and effective. There are only a few mobile radios that will operate in these bands, but they do exist. More commonly you will be looking at radios that are both HF and VHF/UHF (All-band) radios for operating on these frequencies, with a limited number of exceptions.

Of the 6-Meter and the 10-Meter bands available to new Technicians, the 10-Meter band will most likely be the band you are going to be wanting to work with for being able to get distance. While most all-band radios are going to be priced well over $500, moving towards $1000 and higher even, there is a narrow set of 10-meter radios such as the Anytone 10-meter radios which can be purchased for under $100 (Mobile 15-watt) or the Stryker SR-94HPC 10-meter/45-watt radio for under $150. (The Stryker is a Non-SSB model radio, limited to under 10-watts in AM mode, 40+ watts in FM mode). More advanced 10-Meter radios can be found in the $200 to $300 range offering more options and more power.

So – What can we do with 10-Meters we cannot with 2-Meters and 70-CM?

I am glad you asked. This is where we start being able to work longer distances and really utilize skip and propagation with Ham bands. Remember before we also talked about CB radio being HF with these characteristics? Well with the Ham 10-Meter band we can legally add power – up to 200 watts of power over the 4/12-watts of CB Radio. Working with various designs of antennas, you will also be able to operate long distances, even into nearby countries, without repeaters. The key to this type of range will be using a radio that has Single-Sideband (SSB) capabilities in AM mode.

If you have a radio that operates in FM modes such as the QYT-9800 quad mode radio, you will still be able to operate longer distances than in 2-Meters or 70-cm, but operating in the FM portion of the 10-Meter band is going to be above your legal operating area – being up above 29.600-MHz. So, you are going to need an appropriate radio as a "Technician" for 10-meter operation.

Basically, as a Technician with the 10-meter band you have the following capabilities:

- 10-Meter band, 28.000 MHz thru 28.300 MHz – CW, RTTY/data, 200-Watts Max output PEP
- 10-Meter band, 28.300 MHz thru 28.500 MHz – CW, Phone (Voice), 200-Watts Max output PEP
- AM Modulation is only used in frequencies available for Technicians. (No FM Modulation – FM Modulation starts at 29.000 MHz and above which requires a GENERAL or EXTRA license.)
- Single Sideband (Preferred, necessary for AM Modulation)

Groundwave vs. Skywave

For groundwave distances on 10-Meters you will be able to get ranges of about 40-50 miles without using repeaters. This is in comparison to ranges of less than 10 miles (And often much less) with the popular 2-Meter and 70-cm frequencies. Already this places you at an advantage with 10-meters – but remember you still need to have an AM radio setup. For groundwave radio you will most likely be using a vertical mount antenna and the antenna should be mounted as high as you can manage it.

Skywave is propagation through the atmosphere of your radio signal and will be less predictable than groundwave transmissions. You may reach much greater distances with skywave transmissions but since your range will be dependent upon a number of factors including weather, sunspots, and atmospheric conditions, you may not be able to consistently reach the same contacts. But – In an emergency, any remote contact may be able to reliably relay a message for assistance. "Short Skip" propagation for 10-meters will be around 500-miles or less, while normal skip may reach thousands of miles.

https://www.hamuniverse.com/10meterinformation.html

7.A – Electrical Power Formulas in more Depth

I am adding this additional section to go more into depth on the two formulas that you will be using for calculating power. It is critical that you have a good understanding of these and how to get the variations of each formula. Once you learn the base formula format and how to extract the variations, it should be easy to take into the test with you my remembering the formulas. When you get to take the test, you will be allowed a pen/pencil and a scratch piece of paper, and a basic calculator (Not on your smart phone). I recommend if needed, write down the base formulas once you get to sit down for the test and extrapolate the variations.

There will only be 7 math-based questions, so probably only 2 or 3 based on these formulas. However – These are critical to remember for times if power goes out and you need to plan a backup power solution.

Formula 1: Power (P) calculated based on Current (I) and Voltage (E)

In this first formula we have our first power circle. The power circle is displayed as a circle with the top half represented with "P" and the lower half split and represented with "I" and "E". What this core version is meant to represent is P on top is equal to I x E, or P = I x E.

The first variation solves for Current, or "I". In the power circle we can see I and the other two factors are P "over" E or P/E, which works out as I=P/E.

The next variation of the formula solves for E, and just like the formula for current of "I=P/E", in the formula for voltage (E) the formula is E = P/I.

Remember with voltage, the meaning we are using is "Electrical Force" which is why the letter "E" is used. In other areas outside of Ham Radio, the abbreviation for voltage is commonly referred to as "V". But in Ham radio we use "E".

Formula 2: Calculating Voltage/Electrical Potential (V) with Current (I) and Resistance (R)

In this formula we are first calculating our Voltage based on the second two factors, Current (I) and resistance (R). In our circle to the right here, we can see that our voltage (E) can be calculated when we multiply our current (I) by our resistance (R) as follows: E = I x R.

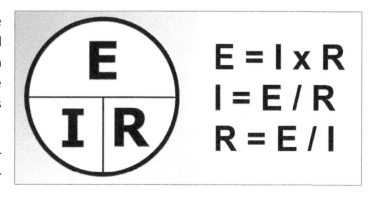

In our first variation we can solve for I by dividing our voltage (E) by our resistance value (R). Our formula for this therefore is I = E / R.

In our second variation we will solve for Resistance (R) by dividing voltage (E) by Current with the formula of R=E/I. This is also known as "Ohm's Law".

We covered the use of these formulas in our explanation section in chapter 5 for the various tests, and also in our Discussions chapter 6, so I am not going to go through examples. The primary purpose of this is to explain the variations formulas so you can use these when you sit down for your test. Memorize the two core formulas and understand their variations.

Chapter 8 - NEW Questions in the 2022-2026 Pool

This section is being included for those who may have already studied for your Ham examination using one of the books covering the 2018-2022 question pool and need a focus review of the 74 new questions. Similar to chapter 2 we are only providing the Questions and the correct answer for each question.

Section	Description of the Section	Question Groups	New Questions	Page
T1	COMMISSION'S RULES	6	5	8-2
T2	OPERATING PROCEDURES	3	10	8-2
T3	RADIO WAVE PROPAGATION	3	6	8-2
T4	AMATEUR RADIO PRACTICES	2	16	8-3
T5	ELECTRICAL PRINCIPLES	4	8	8-3
T6	ELECTRONIC AND ELECTRICAL COMPONENTS	4	8	8-4
T7	PRACTICAL CIRCUITS	4	5	8-4
T8	SIGNALS AND EMISSIONS	4	5	8-4
T9	ANTENNAS AND FEED LINES	2	4	8-5
T0	SAFETY	3	7	8-5

T1	B	01	Which of the following frequency ranges are available for phone operation by Technician licensees? ***28.300 MHz to 28.500 MHz***
T1	B	10	Where may SSB phone be used in amateur bands above 50 MHz? **In at least some segment of all these bands**
T1	C	04	What may happen if the FCC is unable to reach you by email? ***Revocation of the station license or suspension of the operator license***
T1	C	07	Which of the following can result in revocation of the station license or suspension of the operator license? ***Failure to provide and maintain a correct email address with the FCC***
T1	D	02	Under which of the following circumstances are one-way transmissions by an amateur station prohibited? ***Broadcasting***
T2	A	09	Which of the following indicates that a station is listening on a repeater and looking for a contact? ***The station's call sign followed by the word "monitoring"***
T2	B	03	Which of the following describes a linked repeater network? ***A network of repeaters in which signals received by one repeater are transmitted by all the repeaters in the network***
T2	B	09	Why are simplex channels designated in the VHF/UHF band plans? ***So stations within range of each other can communicate without tying up a repeater***
T2	B	12	What is the purpose of the color code used on DMR repeater systems? ***Establishes groups of users***
T2	B	13	What is the purpose of a squelch function? ***Mute the receiver audio when a signal is not present***
T2	C	02	Which of the following are typical duties of a Net Control Station? **Call the net to order and direct communications between stations checking in**
T2	C	03	What technique is used to ensure that voice messages containing unusual words are received correctly? ***Spell the words using a standard phonetic alphabet***
T2	C	04	What is RACES? ***An FCC part 97 amateur radio service for civil defense communications during national emergencies***
T2	C	06	What is the Amateur Radio Emergency Service (ARES)? ***A group of licensed amateurs who have voluntarily registered their qualifications and equipment for communications duty in the public service***
T2	C	07	Which of the following is standard practice when you participate in a net? ***Unless you are reporting an emergency, transmit only when directed by the net control station***
T3	A	01	Why do VHF signal strengths sometimes vary greatly when the antenna is moved only a few feet? ***Multipath propagation cancels or reinforces signals***
T3	A	02	What is the effect of vegetation on UHF and microwave signals? ***Absorption***
T3	A	06	What is the meaning of the term "picket fencing"? ***Rapid flutter on mobile signals due to multipath propagation***

T3	A	07	What weather condition might decrease range at microwave frequencies? ***Precipitation***
T3	B	01	What is the relationship between the electric and magnetic fields of an electromagnetic wave? ***They are at right angles***
T3	C	11	Why is the radio horizon for VHF and UHF signals more distant than the visual horizon? ***The atmosphere refracts radio waves slightly***
T4	A	01	Which of the following is an appropriate power supply rating for a typical 50-watt output mobile FM transceiver? ***13.8 volts at 12 amperes***
T4	A	02	Which of the following should be considered when selecting an accessory SWR meter? ***The frequency and power level at which the measurements will be made***
T4	A	03	Why are short, heavy-gauge wires used for a transceiver's DC power connection? ***To minimize voltage drop when transmitting***
T4	A	04	How are the transceiver audio input and output connected in a station configured to operate using FT8? ***To the audio input and output of a computer running WSJT-X software***
T4	A	05	Where should an RF power meter be installed? ***In the feed line, between the transmitter and antenna***
T4	A	06	What signals are used in a computer-radio interface for digital mode operation? ***Receive audio, transmit audio, and transmitter keying***
T4	A	07	Which of the following connections is made between a computer and a transceiver to use computer software when operating digital modes? ***Computer "line in" to transceiver speaker connector***
T4	A	09	How can you determine the length of time that equipment can be powered from a battery? ***Divide the battery ampere-hour rating by the average current draw of the equipment***
T4	A	10	What function is performed with a transceiver and a digital mode hot spot? ***Communication using digital voice or data systems via the internet***
T4	A	12	What is an electronic keyer? ***A device that assists in manual sending of Morse code***
T4	B	03	How is squelch adjusted so that a weak FM signal can be heard? ***Set the squelch threshold so that receiver output audio is on all the time***
T4	B	05	What does the scanning function of an FM transceiver do? ***Tunes through a range of frequencies to check for activity***
T4	B	07	What does a DMR "code plug" contain? ***Access information for repeaters and talkgroups***
T4	B	09	How is a specific group of stations selected on a digital voice transceiver? ***By entering the group's identification code***
T4	B	11	Which of the following must be programmed into a D-STAR digital transceiver before transmitting? ***Your call sign in CW for automatic identification***
T4	B	12	What is the result of tuning an FM receiver above or below a signal's frequency? ***Distortion of the signal's audio***
T5	A	04	What are the units of electrical resistance? ***Ohms***

T5	A	06	What is the unit of frequency? *Hertz*
T5	A	07	Why are metals generally good conductors of electricity? *They have many free electrons*
T5	A	09	Which of the following describes alternating current? *Current that alternates between positive and negative directions*
T5	A	11	What type of current flow is opposed by resistance? *All of these choices are correct*
T5	C	07	What is the abbreviation for megahertz? *MHz*
T5	D	13	In which type of circuit is DC current the same through all components? *Series*
T5	D	14	In which type of circuit is voltage the same across all components? *Parallel*
T6	A	08	What is the function of an SPDT switch? *A single circuit is switched between one of two other circuits*
T6	A	12	What type of switch is represented by component 3 in figure T-2? *Single-pole single-throw*
T6	B	01	Which is true about forward voltage drop in a diode? *It is lower in some diode types than in others*
T6	B	05	What type of transistor has a gate, drain, and source? *Field-effect*
T6	B	07	What causes a light-emitting diode (LED) to emit light? *Forward DC current*
T6	B	12	What are the names of the electrodes of a bipolar junction transistor? *Emitter, base, collector*
T6	C	12	Which of the following is accurately represented in electrical schematics? *Component connections*
T6	D	03	Which of the following is a reason to use shielded wire? *To prevent coupling of unwanted signals to or from the wire*
T7	B	04	Which of the following could you use to cure distorted audio caused by RF current on the shield of a microphone cable? *Ferrite choke*
T7	B	09	What should be the first step to resolve non-fiber optic cable TV interference caused by your amateur radio transmission? *Be sure all TV feed line coaxial connectors are installed properly*
T7	C	03	What does a dummy load consist of? *A non-inductive resistor mounted on a heat sink*
T7	D	08	Which of the following types of solder should not be used for radio and electronic applications? *Acid-core solder*
T7	D	10	What reading indicates that an ohmmeter is connected across a large, discharged capacitor? *Increasing resistance with time*
T8	A	12	Which of the following is a disadvantage of FM compared with single sideband? *Only one signal can be received at a time*

T8	C	09	Which of the following protocols enables an amateur station to transmit through a repeater without using a radio to initiate the transmission? ***EchoLink***
T8	C	10	What is required before using the EchoLink system? ***Register your call sign and provide proof of license***
T8	D	02	What is a "talkgroup" on a digital repeater? ***A way for groups of users to share a channel at different times without hearing other users on the channel***
T8	D	03	What kind of data can be transmitted by APRS? ***All these choices are correct***
T9	A	06	Which of the following types of antenna offers the greatest gain? ***Yagi***
T9	B	08	Which of the following is a source of loss in coaxial feed line? ***All these choices are correct***
T9	B	10	What is the electrical difference between RG-58 and RG-213 coaxial cable? ***RG-213 cable has less loss at a given frequency***
T9	B	12	What is standing wave ratio (SWR)? ***A measure of how well a load is matched to a transmission line***
T0	A	03	In the United States, what circuit does black wire insulation indicate in a three-wire 120 V cable? ***Hot***
T0	A	12	Which of the following precautions should be taken when measuring high voltages with a voltmeter? ***Ensure that the voltmeter and leads are rated for use at the voltages to be measured***
T0	B	01	Which of the following is good practice when installing ground wires on a tower for lightning protection? ***Ensure that connections are short and direct***
T0	B	02	What is required when climbing an antenna tower? ***All these choices are correct***
T0	B	05	What is the purpose of a safety wire through a turnbuckle used to tension guy lines? ***Prevent loosening of the turnbuckle from vibration***
T0	C	03	How does the allowable power density for RF safety change if duty cycle changes from 100 percent to 50 percent? ***It increases by a factor of 2***
T0	C	13	Who is responsible for ensuring that no person is exposed to RF energy above the FCC exposure limits? ***The station licensee***

Chapter 9 - More for Emergency Planning and Prepping

This book has been written to educated newcomers to Ham radio and to help guide you through the material you will need to understand to pass the ham radio test. If you are studying ham radio for either emergency radio operation or for emergency preparedness, there will be more that you will need to know and understand besides the operation of your ham radio.

Assuming you will be relying on your radio during an emergency when there is a power loss, there will be a number of items you need to have to be able to operate and power your radio equipment. Following is a list of items you should plan to have available in case you need to communicate without power.

- **Local area Frequencies of importance – Simplex**
  If you are in a community ad have others you plan on communicating with, establish what frequencies to use ahead of time. You should also use RepeaterBook (Website or Phone App), or an application such as CHIRP to get a list of local repeaters in your area or the areas you will be traveling in. This includes frequency, PL-Tone/CTCSS Tones, and any special frequency shifts.

  Emergency Radio Teams that are organized using ICS planning will utilize an ICS-205 form which they may publish for participants which lists the frequencies being used by the incident teams. This will not be publicly available, however if you are working a shelter or emergency function for a team then this will be the form that helps you to communicate with various teams or operators.

- **Spare Batteries for your Portables/handhelds**
  Carry 1-2 spare batteries for your portable radios and a way to charge them. Myself I like batteries that can be charged from a USB cable or USB port. Portables should be 2-Meter/70cm handhelds. Optionally – sets of FRS/GMRS radios could be used for localized communications. Remember FRS requires no license and at 2-watts have a decent range of ¼ to ½ mile allowing non-ham team members to talk nearby.

- **Ear phones will allow for private/quite operation, possibly needed for security purposes.**

- **ID Cards/Identification**
  If operating as part of a operations team, you should have your state ID, but also any team ID. Some operations groups will provide ID Cards or badges to show affiliation. Also carry your Ham Radio license.

- **Food/Water**
  Many times if operating as a volunteer operator you will be required to bring your own food and water with you. This will include cooking equipment, utensils, plates, etc. Assume you may be operating in an area with nothing. Take or have enough food for multiple days without the need to cook or refrigerate.

- **Portable Antenna and Coax, Antenna Pole (Maybe)**
  You may need to run an external antenna for better reach to repeaters or other operators. A Portable antenna could be as simple as a Mag-mount antenna, or you could run a more complex solution such as a directional YAGI antenna or an antenna pole to raise the antenna. Remember – The higher the better. And speaking of better – the longer you are going to run the coax, the better the quality of coax you should use. Consider an RG/8 or LMR-400 coax over an RG-58 for longer runs of 50' or greater. A good Yagi Gain antenna mounted high and pointing to a remote communication point will help pull in weak signals and extend your range.

- **Camping gear – Anything you would take on a Camping trip**
  This includes a variety of gear including Cots/Sleep matts, flashlights & batteries, shelter (Tent or camper), Toilet articles (Toilet Paper, Soap, Sanitary bags and garbage bags), cooking stove, propane, fire starting tools.

- **Tools (For radio use, camp use) including:**
  Screwdrivers, Pliers, Wire cutters, Wire strippers, Knife, Electrical tape, extra coax, connectors & Adapters.

- **Additional Clothing**
  Be sure to take weather appropriate clothing – Warm clothes, rain gear, extra shoes/socks, etc. Take enough clothing for multiple days. Remember you may be unable to wash or clean clothes. Also – Take a bathing suit/sandals for washing up in a semi-public area if needed as running water and privacy may be non-existent.

- **Power Systems and Fuel**
  You may be operating for days, a week, or weeks with limited or no power. You should plan for some type of generator operation for running power at night, and refrigeration and communications equipment. If using a fuel generator carry additional fuel and cans for getting fuel. If operating Solar power systems, make sure you have large enough of a system to provide power for your gear, and just as importantly if recharging from solar panels make sure you have enough panels to recharge. Consider at least 300-500 watts of panels (or more) – your power efficiency will be about 50% to 70%. 500-watts of panels will provide you 250-watts to 350-watts of actual power for charging. Include appropriately compatible lights – Low-power USB-based lighting can provide lights at a camp site powered from smaller battery solutions as well as from fuel-based generators.

- **Medical Supplies**
  First aid kit, prescriptions, Aspirin and pain relievers, bandages/wound dressings.

Organizations to get involved with

If interested in working with organizations for preparation of emergency volunteering, here are some good places to start:

ARES

The ARES organization is a group of emergency ham operators organized by the ARRL. These are local operators which work as teams in state or county levels and come together during disaster either locally, or at times available to travel to disaster sites.

http://www.arrl.org/ares   (ARES Organization Information)

http://www.arrl.org/sections   (ARES Local/Regional Section Directory)

RACES

RACES is a civil emergency radio organization created by FEMA and the FCC for emergency radio operation during disasters. Similar to ARES but operated and called up by government agencies.

https://www.usraces.org/

PrepperNet

This group is an organization of Preppers, or those who practice Preparedness. The PrepperNet group is a national group of individuals with many teaming up to offer training in a wide variety of readiness topics, including Radio, Self-defense, Food storage and growing, emergency sheltering, homesteading, and many other topics. Members are not affiliated with radio organizations or government agencies as ARES and RACES are. PrepperNet groups are also not called up during emergencies unless you organize that within your own private groups.

https://www.PrepperNet.com/

Community Emergency Response Team (CERT)

CERT Teams operate within Government but are made up of civilian volunteers in a wide variety of areas. CERT Team members are not required to be radio certified, and in natural disasters may actually operate license-free or non-testing licensed radios such as FRS or GMRS radio systems. These groups offer training in a variety of topics including emergency medical and emergency rescue operations.

https://www.ready.gov/cert

Local Clubs

Local ham radio clubs are an excellent place to get involved, and you will find many Ham clubs in your area. In the club are "Elmers" who are mentors and who enjoy speaking and working with new hams. Often these clubs participate with local ARES or RACES teams providing volunteers willing to help out during emergencies. For a list of local clubs check out this link here on the ARRL website:

http://www.arrl.org/find-a-club

Chapter 10 – Prepping for the Test

So – How do you prepare for the test? There are may ways to prepare, some of which work better for some while other methods work better for others. For myself, I spend a lot of time driving and I used both book preparation mixed in with audio studying and repetition to learn the material. As a graduate with an Associates degree in Electronics technology, much of the material was simple refresher for me. But you don't have to have a degree or past experience to pass the Technician's test. In all honesty – the level of depth for the content in electronics, math, and electrical knowledge is not deep. I have met many students who used repetition to memorize the answers – often not knowing or fulling understanding the concepts they were learning.

In addition to the use of this book and learning the materials through repetition such as used in chapters 2 and 3, or through discussions such as in chapter 6, here are some additional methods you may turn to.

- Online – Ham Radio Prep
  https://hamradioprep.com/free-ham-radio-practice-tests/

- Ham Exam (.org)
  https://hamexam.org/

- Ham Radio Prep
  https://hamradioprep.com/

- Ham Test Online
  https://www.hamradiolicenseexam.com/prices.htm
  Subscription tests - $24.95 and up. This website allows you to take practice tests and tracks your progress helping you to focus in on problem areas.

- Ham Test Prep App (iversoft.com) – Learn and Practice on your smart phone
  This is an Excellent application that you can load on your smart phone (Android or iPhone) and use to study while out and about.

- YouTube Videos on Test Prep – We will be releasing a series in June/July 2022 ourselves with a link that will be posted on our Website at http://www.BiddleBooks.com/

Methods of Learning

There are several styles of learning that work differently for different individuals. Self-study such as reading through this book and other types of reading materials. But is reading your best learning method? If so, you fall into the fourth category of learners we have listed here – Reading/Writing

1. **Visual Learners**

   Individuals who are visual learners are able to absorb best by seeing and observing content through presentations, hands-on learning, and observation. This works well with a classroom environment. You should consider use of YouTube videos, in-person classes, or any type of learning opportunities that include visual examples. Visual examples are going to help this type or learner the best with other learning resources being secondary.

2. **Auditory Learners**

   These types of learners will learn best from lectures, class discussions, group discussions, YouTube videos, and Zoom types of class opportunities.

3. **Kinesthetic Learners**

   Also known as Tactile learners, these types of students work best with hands-on learning when available. Some class opportunities for Ham Radio may offer the opportunity to see and touch some of the equipment we are studying about. From SWR meters to radios, antennas, and Feed lines, learning opportunities with these types of resources will make it easier for the Kinesthetic learner to absorb the materials and the concepts.

4. **Reading/Writing Learners**

   These types of learners are able to more easily self-learn through the use of books, written materials, and often self-study resources (Like this book). Besides reading, having the need to write about a topic offers an even higher level of learning and retention for students. This is why students are often required to write papers in High School and College about a topic. In my experience, my writing on the topics of Ham Radio, Emergency communications and Emergency Power planning my breadth of knowledge on these topics has grown much farther than studying for testing only would have accomplished.

Study Groups

You may find groups that are willing to study together either in person or online. Check on the PrepperNet (PrepperNet.com) website, or with local Prepper groups – there are often local individuals wanting to learn ham radio and willing to get together. I have taught radio classes via Zoom in the past this way. At the time of publishing for this book, recent world events have re-energized interest in Emergency and Ham radio in the prepper community. In many areas these groups will meet and work together for study of communications topics in general.

ARES groups also often are a good source for learning, and for groups to meet through Zoom meetings and in-person meetings. The ARES team that I work with in Florida holds monthly classes on a variety of topics including Ham Radio classes that are held quarterly (Fee based). I have held Zoom-based classes myself with students joining and dropping for study sessions until they get their tests.

Chapter 11 – Choosing your first Radio

When you have decided to jump into Ham radio, one of your first questions will be – what kind of ham radio should I start off with? This chapter is not intended to be a review of all radios. Rather – I am going to walk you through the features that many of the radios or similar radios that I have come with, why I chose them, and some suggestions of radios to look at.

Baofeng GT-5R

First – Your first radio. I recommend starting off with an inexpensive radio to begin with that has a simple setup. No need to spend a ton of money until you know that the Radio hobby will stick with you. Probably the cheapest and one of the most popular radios among preppers, new ham students, and even as a backup radio to many experienced emergency operators is the Baofeng handheld radio. These radios range from 5 watts to 8 watts in power and can be purchased for as little as about $25 on amazon. Now – These are not high-end radios, but they will give you all of the basics you need to have a starter radio. The newest versions of these radios sold in the United States are locked into only operate in the Ham frequencies for VHF and UHF in the 70-cm and 2-Meter bands. They will allow programming for receive-only operation for frequencies outside of these, such as MURS, GMRS/FRS, weather, and even many public service frequencies. (Many public service radios have moved to Digital modes such as P.25 which cannot be received by the analog Baofeng radios).

There are so many models of the Baofeng radio it can be confusing. Most have the same features though there are a few newer models emerging on the market which have more power and more channels for storing of your favorite frequencies and repeaters. My recommendation would be – to start – look at the GT-5R Radio for the following reasons:

- Backwards compatible with earlier versions
- 5-watts transmit power
- 128-programmable channels
- 2-Meter/70-CM Bands
- Supported by CHIRP which is a free software package for computer programming
- Supports external antennas
- Single Receiver/Dual-Monitor (Single receiver but splits between two frequencies for monitoring)
- Solves the historic "Spurious Emissions" problems Baofengs are known for
  (This is where the radio broadcasts on the set frequency, but on additional frequencies out of band also)
- Costs around $25 on Amazon
- Supports all accessories for the popular UV-5r/BF-F8HP model radios (Batteries, Microphones, Antennas, etc)

The Baofeng radios are considered "Throw-away" radios due to their low cost. If the radio fails even under warranty, the cost of shipping back to China for warranty repair/replacement exceeds the cost of the radio. If purchased through Amazon or a US source, usually a dead-on-arrival radio can still be replaced or even replaced within a short period but check the return/repair policy of the vendor you select from. One advantage that Baofengs have as a cheap radio is that a lot of folks have them. If you find yourself in need of a charger or replacement battery when with a group of other hams, you will have a better chance of finding someone else with a Baofeng.

If choosing the Baofeng GT-5R or one of the similar Baofeng radios, I recommend considering purchase, if needed, of my book "**So, You just bought a Baofeng Radio... Now what?**" which is available on Amazon. I designed this book to introduce the radio to the operator and to extend into depth additional topics beyond the radio including Repeater programming and use, programming with CHIRP, EchoLink and other topics of interest to the new Baofeng owner.

Yaesu FT-65R

If you are looking for a better-quality radio than the Baofeng from a company with a reputation for high-quality radios, then Yaesu is among the top along with Kenwood, Motorola and ICOM. The FT-65R Radio is one that I have not personally worked with but has been released by Yaesu to provide a low-cost option to compete with other manufacturers such as Baofeng that have been dominating the low-end/entry level market for years. At under $100 this radio has the same core features as the Baofeng above such as:

- 5-watts transmit power
- 2-Meter/70-CM Bands
- Single Receive/Dual Monitor (Fast scanning – faster than the Baofeng radio)
- Supported by CHIRP which is a free software package for computer programming
- Supports external antennas
- Costs around $100

Yaesu VX-6

This is one of my carry radios I own myself and is the most expensive of my handheld radios. It has a large number of features making it a better choice than any of my others but with a couple of drawbacks that keep it as my #3 carry radio. First – The Pros on this radio:

- Fully waterproof/submersible
- Very rugged casing – Metal not plastic
- Stores over 1000 frequencies in 1000 channels
- Triband (My only triband portable)
- Extremely wide band range – Though it only transmits on 70-cm/1.25-M/2-M, the radio will pick up on HF/SW Bands, 50-MHz, FM Radio band, Airband, VHF-TV Band, UHF-TV Band, and Information band. It can actually pick up frequencies from 0.5 MHz up to 998.990 MHz.
- Compatible with CHIRP – This makes it easy for me to keep channels synced up with my other radios.

Some of the Cons:

- Priced at $249 making it more expensive than a "Starter Radio"
- Single channel monitoring – Can only monitor one channel at a time which I consider the big limit on this radio.

I originally purchased this radio because I needed a very high-quality radio due to excessive noise that I was receiving from my Baofeng radios. I also needed a good waterproof radio for hiking as well as a radio I could charge from a USB port (This was before there were so many USB charging options for the Baofengs). After purchasing the radio I was happy with it – though I came to find out the noise problem I was receiving at times was due to an external source that was affecting all of my radios. The wide frequency reception capability has been great allowing me to pick up shortwave frequencies and CB Radio chatter while on the road – Yes, I can receive CB Channel 19. The biggest restriction I found was lack of dual-band monitoring. I have been in situations where I need to monitor more than one channel, and in a Prepping or Emergency operator situation you may as well. While the radio is great, this is a significant limitation for emergency use. But – if hiking – this is still probably my #1 radio thanks to the fully submersible waterproof level.

Baofeng Tech BTECH DMD-6X2/AnyTone AT-D878

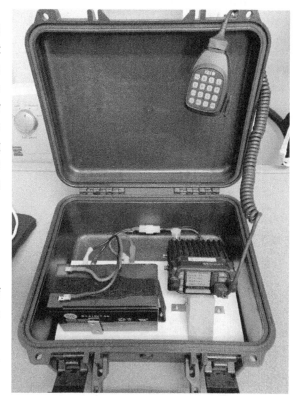

Upon deciding to venture into DMR Radio I chose the BTECH DMR-6x2 radio which is also Analog capable. This radio is built on the AnyTone AT-D878 platform with their own firmware. Though I do not use DMR regularly, this gave me a radio that I could play with it on as well as use for my everyday radio needs The radio supports up to 4000 channels that can be grouped together and has a "Turbo" mode allowing transmitting at 6-watts. Priced at over $200 this radio is priced above what I would consider to be a starter radio, however is still priced well for a DMR Starter radio.

You need a better antenna probably

For many of these radios your performance will be better if you install a better external antenna. If looking for an antenna to mount on the radio for portable use I suggest looking at:

- Abbree 18.5 inch or 42.5 inch antenna (Works great for VHF)
- Nagoya NA-24j or NA-771 Antenna (Works great for VHF)
- Nagoya NA-717 8.5" Super Whip antenna (UHF)
- Signalstick Whip Antenna

If you are looking for an external antenna that can be mounted on a car, filing cabinet, or used outside for temporary use you need to look for either a magnetic or an external vehicle mount antenna with adapters for your radio and additional coax. These types of antennas are covered more in section 7-4 in a prior chapter.

When you need to go beyond your Handheld

The radios we spoke about work well for handheld use and hitting repeaters. These though are all low-power radios and do have limitations. When you need more power and capabilities out of your radio it will be time to move up to a mobile radio, offering 25-watts to 50-watts of power in most cases. The radio can be mounted into your car, or can be set up similar to the BTECH 25-watt Mobile radio I have pictured here to the right. With this setup I installed a 7-Amp/hour battery into the case along with a 25-watt radio. When using the radio, I run an external antenna out and plug it into the back of the radio here. The 7-Amp/hour battery is enough to use the radio for a short period – it lasts longer when just receiving however will drain faster when transmitting.

For portable use in most cases I also connect the radio/kit into a larger 12-volt power source which can be one of many that I carry, from a smaller 36-ah 12.8v LiFePO4 battery kit to a larger 105-ah 12.8v LiFePO4 battery. These external batteries can recharge from either a solar panel kit during the day, or from a wall charger that is plugged into AC power if the grid is up, or a gasoline generator if power is out.

For my vehicle I use a TYT-9800TH 50-watt mobile radio mounted into my truck for mobile radio operation. This particular model is a 4-band radio supporting 70-cm, 2-Meter, 50-Meter and 10-Meter radio bands. This radio is FM only so you would not be able to take advantage of the HF Long-range capabilities than 10-Meter AM/SSB Radio modulation allows.

As we have talked about elsewhere in this book – if choosing between power and antenna quality, always upgrade and improve your antenna first. But – Moving from 5-watts to 25-watts or 50-watts does make a difference as well. For my own go kits I have (2) Baofeng Tech BTECH UB-25x4 radios mounted in pelican style cases.

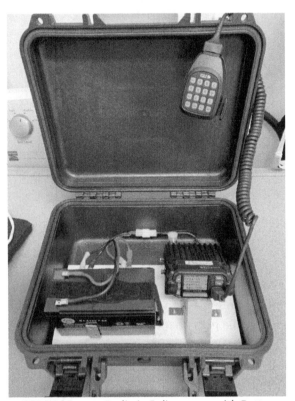

BTECH 25-watt Radio in Pelican case with Battery

BTECH 25-watt radio in small pelican case. This mount has no battery or antenna connection. Case protects the radio however which will connect to an external battery mounted in an Ammo case. The separate battery can be recharged from an AC charger plugged into the wall, plugged in to gas generator, or into solar panels if off-grid.

10-Meter and HF Radio Options

All the radios so far that we have talked about are focused on 70cm/2-Meter operation which will be by far the most common bands as a new Technician you will be using. But remember you do have access to part of the 10-Meter band for operation – specifically 28.000 thru 28.300 for CW/Morse code, and 28.300 to 28.500 MHz for voice over AM/SSM Mode. None of the radios we have seen so far are capable of working 10-Meter in SSB. In section 7.9 we talked about using 10-MHz and the capabilities for distance it could provide. To operate in the 10-MHz band you are going to need either a radio that does just 10-MHz, or you will need a full HF-band radio. I'm going to discuss a couple of options following for reference.

10-Meter Anytone AT-6666 10-Meter with AM, FM, SSB

This radio is a specialty radio that is specifically a 10-Meter radio available for about $240. The radio is a mobile radio designed for vehicle mounting. On AM-SSB the radio is capable of putting out 60-watts of transmitting power. This is a radio however that you will only use for 10-Meters, though it is much less in cost than the full-band HF Radios we will look at net.

ICOM IC-7100 Mobile Radio

This radio is the HF Radio I own myself. I like the mobile radios mostly because of their portability. I carry mine in a Pelican-style case however it is not permanently mounted in the case. The head of the radio is separate allowing it to be displayed more easily with the body of the radio better concealed. This is a full HF Band radio that can transmit up to 100-watts on HF bands, and a VHF/UHF Radio capable of transmitting at up to 50-watts on the higher frequency bands.

ICOM IC-7100

The radio includes a digital modem for digital communications and has two antenna ports – one for VHF/UHF and the second specific for HF communications. In addition to the radio which runs between $1000-$1100, you will need an antenna tuner for HF operations and a 12-volt power supply. All together with antenna and additional components you can expect to be investing around $1500 or more for this level of radio capabilities. The ICOM IC-7100 is unique in the portable radios available as it one of very few radios capable of full HF band modes as well as UHF/VHF in a single unit. In an actual emergency deployment, I would recommend the use of this radio in addition to a mobile radio to keep use of this radio focused on HF operation.

There are many good radios on the market with varying capabilities. By no means use the limited list of radios I have briefed about in this chapter as recommendations for purchase or your choice.

Chapter 12 – References

I truly hope that this book has been an enjoyable and useful resource for your journey to getting your Ham Radio license. I have been writing books on Ham Radio and Emergency Power planning now for the last 5 years and enjoy bringing a new project together. I have been an instructor for four years now and this book has been designed to not only cover the topics of Ham Radio but to also expand and introduce additional topics that ham radio students do not get introduced to during the class and course process.

If you have an interest in keeping up with updates to this and other books or have an interest in learning more about other books I have written please check out the website that I currently publish under which is located at http://www.BiddleBooks.com . All of my books can be found on Amazon.com with a couple even available for free for Amazon Kindle Unlimited members.

If you have more interest in Ham Radio and/or Emergency Power solutions, then please check out some of my other book titles below:

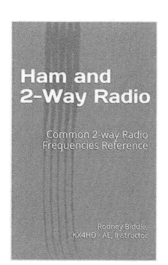

A Frequency Reference guide to new Hams - This book provides a list of common frequencies for Ham operators as well as Frequency information for FRS/GMRS, MURS, Citizens Band (CB), Popular Shortwave, and Public Radio frequencies. More importantly it serves as a guide with references to popular tools used by new Hams for plugging in. This book helps you to skip some of the confusion and answer many newcomer questions to help you decide what you need to get into the right radio technologies to meet specific needs. We also cover comparisons between radio technologies - CB, FRS/GMRS and MURS for instance, and help you decide what is the right communications methods for your needs. Antennas and basic Antenna theory is covered with an explanation why these are so important to your successful radio operation.

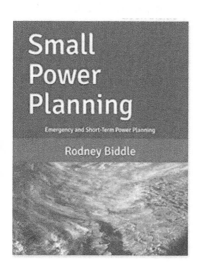

Are you ready to be without electricity for a few days? Or Weeks? Are you ready for possible Rolling blackouts? Small Power Planning is focused on helping the reader develop emergency and Short-term power solutions to help get through power loss. From unforeseen events from Hurricanes and Storms, Snowstorms, Rolling Blackouts, having an emergency plan for providing power for the conveniences to the necessities will help you have some level of protection. Electricity provides us comforts, necessities, and safety in our lives. This book helps the reader to understand sizing and planning for various alternative power sources, focusing on Generator and Solar power solutions. We cover selecting a generator based on your needs, solar generators, and solar solutions for the home and portable power. Our book also covers RV and Camper solutions for off-grid boondocking which are also covered by most of our Small Power Solutions we cover in the book.

This book is written as a Next-Steps guide for new Ham Radio Technician License holders. Covering topics that go beyond what was in the test - Finding clubs, locating, and using Repeaters, Antenna limits, Radio Limits, getting more range from your radio, and touching on topics including WinLink and Echolink.

Finding your way to your next steps with your Ham Radio license can be confusing – This is the book to help guide you through those next steps.

What do you do when the power goes out? Blackouts and Brownouts are becoming more common throughout the United States. Natural disasters can knock out your power for days or weeks. Lack of some form of backup power can become a security and safety issue, loss of modern conveniences such as refrigeration and cooling, communications, and other modern-day conveniences. In this book we cover a variety of topics from performing an energy audit to determine and plan how much power you need, to various forms of portable and home power backup solutions. We touch on whole home solar solutions and smaller battery and fuel-based backup solutions that can provide short term and partial power in your home for short-term and long-term use. We also look at several models of portable solar generators and characteristics to look for when planning a backup power solution.

New 2nd Edition - This is the book you NEED to go along with your BaoFeng Radio - We go into depth not just the controls of the radio, but also the "How-To's" and Real-Life Capabilities of the popular BaoFeng UV-5R/UV-82/BF-F8HP Radios. If you are an aspiring Ham operator, we will help you to better use your radio to extend your range. If you are a Prepper - We cover what you need to know about the radio BEFORE you set it aside in your "Just-In-Case" drawer so if you need it you are really ready to go... This is the book that every New Ham with a Baofeng UV-5R/UV-82/BF-F8HP Radio should have, and the book that every prepper using these radios should keep with their radio for the emergency use reference with the radio.

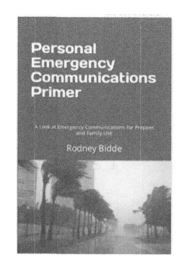

Are you ready for some form of alternative communications if the power or regular communications systems fail? Grid down, Cellular Towers down, and without a way to communicate after a storm or event that results in normal communications being down. What systems are available to the general public and what is the realistic range and use of these systems? We take a look at capabilities of various systems and more importantly limitations. Licensing requirements, touching on costs, and which systems work better than others as well as legal issues that surround each system.

In this book we look at FRS, GMRS, MURS, CB, Ham Radio, Zello, VHF Marine, Airband and Shortwave Radio systems for two-way and one-way communications. The book is designed to be a primer to guide you in the best direction for your needs and we look at systems ranging from 0-dollar cost to advanced radio systems.

The information we are providing in this book is intended for general public communications alternatives and does not cover military, government, or public service communications methods.

Are you running a Ham Radio Net? Are in interested in learning about a Ham Radio net? This book is an 80-page simple format logbook for tracking Net Check-ins and an introduction to being a Network Control Operator. We will provide you information on Net Messaging using the ARRL Radiogram, ICS-213, and planning a Script for your Net.

Watch also for our new book projects coming up in 2022 – "CB Radio for Emergency Operators", "Florida Boondocking for RV and Campers", and in late 2022/early 2023 our "Biddle's Ham Radio General Course for 2023-2027".

Made in the USA
Monee, IL
01 July 2022

98925972R00221